meXicana Roots and Routes

ARIZONA CROSSROADS

Series Editors
Anita Huízar-Hernández, Eric V. Meeks, Katherine G. Morrissey

Published in partnership with the Arizona Historical Society

meXicana Roots and Routes

Listening to People, Places, and Pasts

EDITED BY

Vanessa Fonseca-Chávez and Anita Huízar-Hernández

THE UNIVERSITY OF ARIZONA PRESS
TUCSON

The University of Arizona Press
www.uapress.arizona.edu

We respectfully acknowledge the University of Arizona is on the land and territories of Indigenous peoples. Today, Arizona is home to twenty-two federally recognized tribes, with Tucson being home to the O'odham and the Yaqui. Committed to diversity and inclusion, the University strives to build sustainable relationships with sovereign Native Nations and Indigenous communities through education offerings, partnerships, and community service.

ISBN-13: 978-0-8165-5514-7 (hardcover)
ISBN-13: 978-0-8165-5513-0 (paperback)
ISBN-13: 978-0-8165-5515-4 (ebook)

Cover design by Derek Thornton, Notch Design LLC
Typeset by Sara Thaxton in 10.5/14 Warnock Pro with Cassino WF, Goldenbook and Helvetica Neue LT Std

Library of Congress Control Number: 2024059207

Printed in the United States of America
♾ This paper meets the requirements of ANSI/NISO Z39.48-1992 (Permanence of Paper).

The co-editors would like to thank all those whose roots and routes have intersected with this volume. Thank you for allowing us to listen to and with you.

Contents

Foreword

ERIC V. MEEKS AND KATHERINE G. MORRISSEY

We are pleased to present *meXicana Roots and Routes: Listening to People, Places, and Pasts*, edited by Vanessa Fonseca-Chávez and Anita Huízar-Hernández, as the first book in the Arizona Crossroads series. Published by the University of Arizona Press in association with the Arizona Historical Society, and with series editors from the three state universities, the series clearly marks Arizona as its center. Yet, as its title signals, the series pays equal attention to routes and intersections beyond its borders. Throughout its history, Arizona has served as a crossroads for Native peoples, settler colonists, and immigrants from around the world. It has been a contested site among peoples, nations, and empires; it is also a place where events, decisions, and struggles have had far-reaching consequences beyond its shifting borders.

It seems appropriate as we kick off this series to share a few words about the project and its intents. Why did we name this series Arizona Crossroads, and what types of books and scholarship will it include? As its title suggests, this series seeks to deepen our understanding of Arizona as a diverse crossroads and meeting ground within broad national and transnational contexts, whether topical, thematic, or geographic (the region, the nation, the borderlands). As we foster this interdisciplinary conversation, we welcome scholarship that focuses on Arizona, but also scholarship that looks beyond state, national, and international borders; that situates issues within their historical contexts but also considers their contemporary resonances; and that brings together ideas and perspectives from different scholarly disciplines.

For millennia, the place we know as Arizona has been home to Indigenous groups of widely diverse origins who hunted and farmed, traded with one another, migrated, came into conflict, and interacted in ways that reshaped each other's cultures. In the sixteenth century, it became contested ground for newly arrived Spaniards who claimed the territory as their own and Indigenous peoples who outnumbered them and continued to dominate the region throughout the colonial period. By the early nineteenth century, after Mexico won its independence from Spain, migrants from the still-nascent United States moved to the territory in ever-increasing numbers until, by mid-century, the United States provoked a war that ended with its acquisition of half of Mexico's territory. Thereafter, growing numbers of migrants from around the world converged in Arizona, settling near and alongside one another in mining towns, farming communities, and emergent cities, influencing one another in countless ways. Over time, Anglo-Americans tried to impose their dominance through discriminatory policies, yet other ethnic groups resisted and asserted their agency in ways that fundamentally transformed the state. Though not always acknowledged, these shifts have shaped the Arizona we know today: a diverse and ever-growing Sunbelt state.

meXicana Roots and Routes joins a significant body of work published over the past two decades that has discussed Arizona as a crossroads by focusing on interethnic relationships, trade and migration, subaltern and working-class activism, transborder Indigenous peoples, the environment, and the political economy of the Sunbelt. The University of Arizona Press has been the publishing home for much of this scholarship.[1] Works by Phyllis Cancilla Martinelli and Sal Acosta explore cross-ethnic interactions by focusing, respectively, on the relationship between Italian immigrants and other immigrant groups in mining communities and on interethnic marriages in Tucson.[2] Andrae M. Marak and Laura Tuennerman's *At the Border of Empires* (2017) and Carlos G. Vélez-Ibáñez and Josiah Heyman's edited volume *The U.S.-Mexico Transborder Region* (2017) reveal the persistence of heterogeneous, interethnic, and binational spaces.[3] *Mexican Workers and the Making of Arizona*, edited by Luis F. B. Plascencia and Gloria H. Cuádraz (2019), and Linda C. Noel's *Debating American Identity: Southwestern Statehood and Mexican*

Immigration (2022) place contemporary immigration topics within the historical, cultural, and political contexts.[4] David H. DeJong's series about Pima Indians' historical struggles for Gila River resources and Thomas Sheridan's *Landscapes of Fraud* focus on environmental conflicts between O'odham peoples and settler colonists over water and land rights.[5] And Daniel D. Arreola's *Postcards from the Sonora Border* (2017) and Jennifer L. Jenkins's *Celluloid Pueblo* (2016, 2024) illuminate the contested role of Arizona in the cultural imaginary.[6]

This series also draws inspiration from works by historians, including those published by presses outside of Arizona over the past two decades. Among the influential volumes, Karl Jacoby's *Shadows at Dawn* (2008) demonstrates how the motives and agency of Indigenous and ethnic Mexican peoples shaped Arizona well after the United States took control of the region in 1848 and 1853, revealing a fascinating history not only of racism and violence, but of shifting alliances, negotiations, and contested memories.[7] Katherine Benton-Cohen's *Borderline Americans* (2008) examines the history of labor, capital, gender, and the racialization of people of Mexican and European descent, arguing that a complex racial patchwork was, by the 1920s, replaced by a stricter dichotomy between Anglos and others.[8] And in *Border Citizens* (2007, 2020), Eric V. Meeks discusses Arizona's economic and political incorporation into the U.S. nation-state and how race and ethnicity shaped labor markets, defined citizenship criteria, and inscribed national boundaries.[9] All three scholars emphasize how Mexicans, Indigenous peoples, and immigrants adapted and resisted in unanticipated, resilient, and sometimes defiant ways, altering the meaning of national belonging.

Recent scholarship focused on Arizona has enriched our understanding of how Native populations have maintained their autonomy and their cultural, kinship, and political ties across boundaries. Maurice Crandall's *These People Have Always Been a Republic* (2019) traces how Hopis, other Pueblos, Yaquis, and Tohono O'odham in Arizona, New Mexico, and Sonora struggled to assert sovereignty through four centuries of Spanish, Mexican, and U.S. colonialism. Rather than simply preserve traditional cultures and political systems, they "absorbed and adapted colonially imposed forms of electoral politics and exercised political sovereignty based on localized political, economic, and social needs."[10] And Brenden Rensink fruitfully compares the Yaquis of the U.S.-Mexico borderlands to the Chippewas and Crees of the U.S.-Canada borderlands, exploring how these groups were able to establish stable, autonomous communities, how they both contested and contributed to the construction of national borders, and why their historical trajectories differed so substantially.[11]

Others have stressed how individuals and communities have challenged the intensification of border enforcement over time. Samuel Truett's groundbreaking 2006 book *Fugitive Landscapes* examines the historical relationship between Arizona and Sonora from the mid-nineteenth to the early twentieth century, tracing "industrial crossroads . . . that extended deep into both nations" while emphasizing the agency of "Yaqui and Mexican villagers," "Chinese servants," "railroad builders," "ranchers and *mescaleros*," "polygamist Mormons," and various non-elite men and women.[12] Rachel St. John's 2011 book *Line in the Sand* traces the evolution of the western half of the international border from an intermittently marked boundary in the decades after the U.S.-Mexican War to a "meaningful marker of state power and national identities by the 1930s" while illuminating the continuously dynamic relationship between national policies and local arrangements that tempered federal authority.[13] And Geraldo Cadava's 2013 book *Standing on Common Ground* takes the discussion of the border into the "Sunbelt" era of the late twentieth century, demonstrating that connections and interdependency between Arizona and Sonora reemerged in the decades after World War II, thus "challenging narratives of a hardening border; illuminating transnational ties between the United States and Mexico; and demonstrating how Mexico continues to shape the modern Southwest."[14]

The historians Elizabeth Tandy Shermer and Andrew Needham have likewise focused on Arizona's rise as a Sunbelt state, turning their attention northward from Tucson and Sonora to Phoenix and its hinterlands. Shermer's *Sunbelt Capitalism* recasts Phoenix from a periphery of the northeastern core to a birthplace of political and economic transformations that changed the United States in the second half of the twentieth century. She argues that Phoenix's "region-specific, pragmatic, homegrown, developmental neoliberalism"—which left behind a largely segregated nonwhite working class—"eventually transformed the politics and market ethos of the entire country."[15] And Andrew Needham traces electrical power lines southward from the Colorado Plateau to Phoenix and across vast stretches of land and state lines to Los Angeles, Albuquerque, and elsewhere, to illuminate "the relationships between natural resources and metropolitan expansion; supplies of energy and demand for electricity; urban boosters, federal officials, and Navajo political leaders; and prosperity and underdevelopment" in the emergent Sunbelt region.[16]

Historians are not the only ones who have attended to Arizona's past. Writing as a literary and cultural studies scholar, Anita Huízar-Hernández unpacks the meanings of a nineteenth-century Arizona territorial land fraud case in *Forging Arizona: A History of the Peralta Land Grant and Racial Identity in the West* (2019), challenging myths about the nineteenth-century U.S. West by demonstrating how Arizona became the site of "counterfeit narratives and nostalgia."[17] And yet, as the co-editors of this volume note, while "the complexity that runs through the state's past has garnered notable attention among historians . . . Arizona remains persistently peripheral within the broader conversations happening in Chicanx and Latinx studies." Their attention is to how the rich scholarship examining Chicanx and Latinx communities often jumps over Arizona in its analyses. *meXicana Roots and Routes* is a volume intended to address this lacuna. The co-editors have brought together an exciting interdisciplinary group of scholars with expertise in history, literature, Spanish, sociology, education, Chicano and Latin American studies, and women's studies, to intervene in ongoing dialogues within Chicanx and Latinx studies.

As editors and authors, we are among a wonderful community of scholars who have produced enlightening stories about Arizona as a regional, national, and transnational crossroads, but many stories have yet to be told. Arizona continues to be a meeting ground and a contested space between diverse peoples and nations, and a place where ideas and meanings intersect. Consider the idiom "to be at a crossroads," which denotes reaching a critical juncture or a point of decision. To be at a crossroads is to be in a situation that requires that important choices be made. In the past and in the present, Arizona and the larger region within which it is situated have long been a crossroads in this sense as well. The Arizona Crossroads series intends to continue examining how peoples and cultures, events and struggles, ideas and practices, continue to impact the place we know today as Arizona. Open to any topic within any period of Arizona history, we invite you to join the conversation.

Notes

1. See also the essays in Katherine G. Morrissey, ed., "Exploring Arizona's Diverse Past," *Journal of Arizona History* 61 (Autumn/Winter 2020).
2. Phylis Cancilla Martinelli, *Undermining Race: Ethnic Identities in Arizona Copper Camps, 1880–1920* (University of Arizona Press, 2009), explores the history of racial and ethnic identity formation in Arizona by focusing on Italian immigrants' experiences in the copper mining camps. Sal Acosta, *Sanctioning Matrimony: Western Expansion and Interethnic Marriage in the Arizona Borderlands* (University of Arizona Press, 2016), uses careful quantitative research to demonstrate that despite Arizona's anti-miscegenation laws, passed in the late nineteenth and early twentieth centuries, marriages between ethnic Mexicans and white, Black, and Chinese spouses in Tucson increased between the mid-nineteenth century and the 1930s.
3. Andrae M. Marak and Laura Tuennerman, *At the Border of Empires: The Tohono O'odham, Gender, and Assimilation, 1880–1934* (University of Arizona Press, 2017); Carlos G. Vélez-Ibáñez and Josiah Heyman, eds., *The U.S.-Mexico Transborder Region: Cultural Dynamics and Historical Interactions* (University of Arizona Press, 2017).
4. Luis F. B. Plascencia and Gloria H. Cuádraz, eds., *Mexican Workers and the Making of Arizona* (University of Arizona Press, 2019); Linda C. Noel, *Debating American Identity: Southwestern Statehood and Mexican Immigration* (University of Arizona Press, 2022).
5. David H. DeJong, *Stealing the Gila: The Pima Agricultural Economy and Water Deprivation, 1848–1921* (University of Arizona Press, 2009); David H. DeJong, *Diverting the Gila: The Pima Indians and the Florence-Casa Grande Project, 1916–1928* (University of Arizona Press, 2023); David H. DeJong, *Damming the Gila: The Gila River Indian Community and the San Carlos Irrigation Project, 1900–1942* (University of Arizona Press, 2024); Thomas Sheridan, *Landscapes of Fraud: Mission Tumacácori, the Baca Float, and the Betrayal of the O'odham* (University of Arizona Press, 2006).
6. Daniel D. Arreola, *Postcards from the Sonora Border: Visualizing Place Through a Popular Lens, 1900s–1950s* (University of Arizona Press, 2017); Jennifer L. Jenkins, *Celluloid Pueblo: Western Ways Films and the Invention of the Postwar Southwest* (University of Arizona Press, 2016).
7. Karl Jacoby, *Shadows at Dawn: A Borderlands Massacre and the Violence of History* (Penguin Press, 2008).
8. Katherine Benton-Cohen, *Borderline Americans: Racial Division and Labor War in the Arizona Borderlands* (Harvard University Press, 2009).
9. Eric V. Meeks, *Border Citizens: The Making of Indians, Mexicans, and Anglos in Arizona*, rev. ed. (University of Texas Press, 2020), 4, 14.
10. Maurice Crandall, *These People Have Always Been a Republic: Indigenous Electorates in the U.S.-Mexico Borderlands, 1598–1912* (University of North Carolina Press, 2019), quote at 4.

11. Brenden W. Rensink, *Native but Foreign: Indigenous Immigrants and Refugees in the North American Borderlands* (Texas A&M University Press, 2018). See also Jeffrey M. Schulze, *Are We Not Foreigners Here? Indigenous Nationalism in the U.S.-Mexico Borderlands* (University of North Carolina Press, 2018), which focuses on Yaquis, Tohono O'odham, and Kickapoos who live on both sides of the U.S.-Mexico border. Other recent works that revise our understanding of Indigenous peoples in Arizona include Geraldo Cadava, "Borderlands of Modernity and Abandonment: The Lines Within Ambos Nogales and the Tohono O'odham Nation," *Journal of American History* 92, no. 2 (September 2011): 362–83; Katrina Jagodinsky, *Legal Codes and Talking Trees: Indigenous Women's Sovereignty in the Sonoran and Puget Sound Borderlands, 1854–1946* (Yale University Press, 2016); Meeks, *Border Citizens*; Colleen O'Neill, *Working the Navajo Way: Labor and Culture in the Twentieth Century* (University Press of Kansas, 2005); Marsha Weisiger, *Dreaming of Sheep in Navajo Country* (University of Washington Press, 2009); and Maurice Crandall, ed., "Indigenous Histories of Arizona," special issue, *Journal of Arizona History* 64, no. 2 (Summer 2023).
12. Samuel Truett, *Fugitive Landscapes: The Forgotten History of the U.S.-Mexico Borderlands* (Yale University Press, 2006), 4, 8, 9, 108, 182–84.
13. Rachel St. John, *Line in the Sand: A History of the Western U.S.-Mexico Border* (Princeton University Press, 2011), 11. For a book that can serve as an illuminating visual companion to St. John's discussion of border towns and border enforcement, see Arreola, *Postcards from the Sonora Border*.
14. Geraldo L. Cadava, *Standing on Common Ground: The Making of a Sunbelt Borderland* (Harvard University Press, 2013), 135, 199, 244–47. Some of this wording and the final quotation in this paragraph were originally published on H-Diplo, in Benjamin Johnson, Katherine Benton-Cohen, Flannery Burke, Eric V. Meeks, Andrew Needham, and Geraldo L. Cadava, "Roundtable Review of Geraldo Cadava's *Standing on Common Ground*," *H-Diplo Roundtable Reviews* 16, no. 19 (March 2, 2015), https://networks.h-net.org/node/28443/discussions/62841/h-diplo-roundable-review-vol-xvi-no-19-2015-standing-common-ground#_Toc412971526.
15. Elizabeth Tandy Shermer, *Sunbelt Capitalism: Phoenix and the Transformation of American Politics* (University of Pennsylvania Press, 2013), quote at 13.
16. Andrew Needham, *Power Lines: Phoenix and the Making of the Modern Southwest* (Princeton University Press: 2014), quote at 5. See also Michelle Nickerson and Darren Dochuk, eds., *Sunbelt Rising: The Politics of Space, Place, and Region* (University of Pennsylvania Press, 2011).
17. Anita Huizar-Hernández, *Forging Arizona: A History of the Peralta Land Grant and Racial Identity in the West* (Rutgers University Press, 2019).

meXicana Roots and Routes

Introduction

VANESSA FONSECA-CHÁVEZ AND ANITA HUÍZAR-HERNÁNDEZ, ARIZONA STATE UNIVERSITY

In fall 2017, the much-anticipated *Pacific Standard Time: LA/LA* (*PST: LA/LA*) premiered. The initiative, which was funded by the Getty Foundation, included over seventy linked exhibitions showcasing Latin American and Latinx art in museums across Los Angeles and Southern California.[1] As an assistant professor specializing in Chicanx/Latinx studies, I (Anita Huízar-Hernández) was eager to see the Latin(x) American takeover of Southern California's art scene. Together with my dear friend and colleague Dr. Kaitlin M. Murphy, I set off from where we both worked in Tucson, Arizona, to experience *PST: LA/LA* for myself.

When we arrived in Los Angeles, I was stunned to be surrounded by art that depicted my own roots and routes. Having grown up in Arizona, I was moved to witness so many representations of the borderlands people, places, and pasts I knew well. At the Hammer Museum's *Radical Women: Latin American Art, 1960–1985* exhibition, I literally saw myself in the art on display. Standing in front of Judith Baca's iconic *Las Tres Marías (The Three Marías)* triptych, I looked back at my own reflection in the mirrored center panel, flanked on one side by a 1940s pachuca and on the other by a 1970s chola. Sandwiched between these two figures, I recognized and understood myself as part of a continuum that linked us to one another across time and space.

My excitement was soon tempered, however, by a moment of misrecognition. At the Getty Museum, I found myself in front of a timeline of important events in Latin American and Latinx history. Having always been historically inclined, I read each detailed note with care, stopping suddenly when I came to 1846. In that year, the note explained, "the Mexican-American War begins. The conflict ceases in 1848 with the Treaty of Guadalupe Hidalgo. Half of Mexico's territory, **including the land now occupied by California, Nevada, New Mexico, and Texas,** is ceded to the United States" (emphasis mine). As I pictured a map of the southwestern United States in my mind, I found the gap between the land now occupied by California and Nevada on the one hand and by New Mexico and Texas on the other to be glaring. What had happened to Arizona? To be fair, the note never declared itself to be exhaustive and did not mention Utah, Colorado, or parts of Kansas, Wyoming, and Oklahoma, all of which were also formerly Mexican territory. Nevertheless, there was something particularly blatant about the big blank space along the U.S.-Mexico border that the unnamed Arizona occupied.

The juxtaposition of these two experiences—the misrecognition of the connection between meXicanidad and Arizona—is in many ways the impetus for this book, the inaugural publication of the University of Arizona Press's Arizona Crossroads series. We are delighted that this collection is the first to be published with the series, an ideal venue through which to explore the geographic, temporal, and thematic intersections that emerge within and around Arizona's histories and stories. The complexity that runs through the state's past has garnered notable attention among historians, though Arizona remains persistently peripheral within the broader conversations happening in Chicanx and Latinx studies.[2] As the Getty timeline so clearly demonstrates, neighboring Southwestern states dominate discussions of Chicanidad and Latinidad, all too often positioning Arizona as an afterthought. This volume intentionally flips that script, centering Arizona within broader comparative and cross-state dialogues. While not all the essays included here are about Arizona, Arizona is at the crossroads of the volume's five sections, all of which explore new dimensions within themes that are central to Chicanx/Latinx studies. Both structurally and thematically, this collection presents Arizona as a central node of borderlands roots and routes spanning from Los Angeles, California, to San Antonio, Texas.

The Roots and Routes of meXicanidad

Unlike Anita Huízar-Hernández, I (Vanessa Fonseca-Chávez) grew up in New Mexico, that "dirt patch to the east" of Arizona, as my husband affectionately called it when we first met. During my childhood, frequent trips to Nevada and California meant that traveling through Arizona was common. I can recall stopping to fuel up in Flagstaff and, just once, visiting Phoenix, where I have a memory of walking with my family around a city block to find a Catholic church. I eventually came to call Arizona home, first during my doctoral studies, and again in 2016 when I joined the faculty at Arizona State University (ASU).

As I began teaching Spanish at ASU as part of my graduate program, I quickly realized the perceptions that people had of New Mexico and, for the first time, found myself interrogating my roots. Much like what is described in Huízar-Hernández's chapter that closes this volume, I felt a sense of dislocation in Arizona—not as an Arizonan, but as a New Mexican who admittedly knew very little about our neighbor to the west. Only later would I learn that these Southwestern-rooted neighbors had a much more connected history than I was previously aware of.[3] Of course, we know New Mexico and Arizona became territories together, grappled with statehood together (in distinct fashions), and officially joined the union together on January 6 and February 14, 1912, respectively.[4] I was less aware, however, that my own family roots were strong in Arizona. My maternal grandfather, Lázaro Ponce, and great-grandfather, Francisco Ponce, were copper miners, much like many Hispanos/Mexicanos in nineteenth-century Arizona. As Gloria Holguín Cuádraz's chapter in this volume (as well as her larger body of scholarship) demonstrates, the copper economy is an essential one in the state, and many Mexicanos have been part of that economic past.[5] Economic migrations occurred in copper mining throughout the southeastern part of Arizona, and industries like sheepherding thrived in the late nineteenth and early twentieth centuries in places like Apache County. We, indeed, are connected through our roots and routes. Rather than perceiving New Mexico as merely a dirt landscape and Arizona as a place I only traveled through, I have appreciated and embraced the opportunity to build bridges, to listen to the stories of their residents, and to connect to others whose experiences in both states are multifaceted and multigenerational.

The roots of this collection appropriately go back to the sixty-second annual Arizona History Convention, when I presented alongside Arizonans Christine "Chris" Marin and Andrea Tovar on Latinx collective subjectivities in Arizona. Following the panel, Lora Key, then managing editor of the *Journal of Arizona History*, reached out to further discuss a journal article that might highlight Latinx community and collaboration—a theme that has historically enjoyed less representation in the journal than other topics. After a series of enriching discussions and collaborative efforts, we decided that a special issue of the *Journal of Arizona History* dedicated to Latinx voices in the Southwest was the best way to highlight the established and emerging scholars taking up themes of community building, oral histories, and collective memory in the region. However, the newly launched Arizona Crossroads book series, a collaboration between the University of Arizona Press and the Arizona Historical Society, presented an enticing opportunity to rethink the dissemination of this scholarship in the form of the current volume.

The following chapters collectively explore the diverse roots and routes of meXicanidad. Here we follow Rosa-Linda Fregoso, who in her book *meXicana Encounters: The Making of Social Identities on the Borderlands* defines the term *meXicana* in this way:

> As the interface between Mexicana and Chicana, "meXicana" draws attention to the historical, material, and discursive effects of contact zones and exchanges among various communities on the Mexico-U.S. border, living in the shadows of more than 150 years of conflict, interactions, and tensions. "meXicana" references processes of transculturation, hybridity, and cultural exchanges—the social and economic interdependency and power relations structuring the lives of inhabitants on the borderlands.[6]

The chapters in this volume extend Fregoso's framing beyond the gender-specific *meXicana* to examine a broad cross-section of meXicanidad across time and space.[7] In other words, although all contributors identify as Mexicana or Chicana and are rooted in their experiences growing up in the U.S.-Mexico borderlands, their scholarship focuses on a range of subjects from bracero workers to bilingual educators, examining "the historical, material, and discursive effects of contact zones and exchanges" on specific borderlands communities in Arizona and beyond. We have chosen to maintain the feminine *meXicana* in the title of this collection to underscore the positionality of the contributors, as our collective roots and routes traverse the spectrum of the meXicana experience.

Viewing meXicanidad through the lens of roots and routes highlights the tension between deep connections and displacement, a seeming contradiction that is nonetheless central to placemaking and belonging in the borderlands. As the chapters within this collection demonstrate, there is no monolithic story of how communities negotiate spaces or identities. The strategies they employ are often fraught, informed by centuries of colonialism and its epistemological, geographical, and cultural aftershocks. As the authors follow the roots and routes that traverse their essays, they foreground the diverse political, economic, and cultural stakes that shape their paths.

Listening to People, Places, and Pasts

Despite an array of interdisciplinary approaches to people, places, and pasts, the chapters gathered here are united in their focus on listening. Listening has deep roots within Chicana feminist praxis, which itself takes cues from Latin American testimonio.[8] Listening bridges the diverse methodologies and materialities of all the chapters here, which employ ethnography, autoethnography, archival research, and literary analysis to analyze expressive culture, oral histories, and archival materials.

The opening section, "Mujeres, Memory, and Place," listens to mujeres who have created and cultivated intentional spaces of dialogue to impart and assert their knowledge through memory. The authors in this section set the tone for the volume by focusing on the corporeal aspects of self and the wisdom that comes from a deep connection to and rootedness in the land and in place. At the same time, they consider the changing dynamics of their respective communities in New Mexico, Colorado, and Arizona. They rely on spaces of dialogue to uncover memories, sites, and movidas in their collective work and join a litany of memory makers in Chicana studies.[9]

In "Embodiment and Place: Chicanas as Sites of Knowledge," Karen R. Roybal takes us to Colorado and New Mexico to discuss women who are land grant heirs. She draws upon the work of Indigenous, Chicana, and

Black scholars to emphasize the importance of memory in asserting a sense of self and the process of embodied knowledge related to place. Roybal affirms that women function as "sites of knowledge" and that their telling and retelling of memories is an active process of recuperation and bridging of past and present. Through this process, women are affirmed not as secondary players in the larger history of land grant movements, but as central figures who draw from Indigenous and meXicana epistemologies to mine the complex layering of multiple settler-colonial displacements in the region. While Roybal's own family is situated in New Mexico, her position at Colorado College has opened new routes of inquiry and new possibilities of community building. She discusses these openings in her essay and, in doing so, emphasizes the importance of relationships formed via Sendejo's conceptualization of "*mujerista* ethnography." She writes about intergenerational sharing and takes us on the road with her as she listens to women from New Mexico and Colorado who recount their experiences advocating for their respective land grants. Interviewees Andrea, Rita, Esther, and Shirley demonstrate that their corporeal knowledge of the land and their activism uproot popular notions of land grant movements being led solely by men.

In "Digital Reminiscing: Telles Mujeres on 'Arizona Roots y Reuniones' in the Time of COVID-19," Andrea Tovar listens to the memories and stories of her Telles family, whose connection to Arizona dates back more than 150 years. She asserts that there remain significant gaps in our understanding of Arizona's Hispanic families, particularly those who contributed to the growth of the region during the territorial period, as well as of those histories that predate colonization. Tovar draws from archival research, oral histories, testimonios, and family materials to bring twelve female participants together in a digital multimedia space. Through digital storytelling, the women mark their presence and their history on the landscape of Arizona, New Mexico, Texas, and the larger U.S.-Mexico borderlands. Tovar demonstrates their close ties to and rootedness in the U.S. Southwest as a function and expression of their querencia, their love of place. The reunion-style format of the essay offers the reader snippets of history and memories, in a conversational environment that contributes to ongoing efforts to ensure that women's stories are valued as an integral part of the narrative of southern Arizona. Tovar frames these familial stories through the lenses of other scholars in the collection, including Karen R. Roybal's work on herederas, Anita Huízar-Hernández's work on territorial Arizona, and Vanessa Fonseca-Chávez's work on querencia. Of course, one cannot forget (and Tovar does not) the foundational work of Patricia Preciado Martin and her long-standing commitment to Hispanic women's stories in southern Arizona.

The second section, "Language, Education, and Resilience," listens to individuals whose contributions to education in Arizona resonate within and beyond the state. From Arizona's territorial period through today, schooling processes and language choices have remained contentious topics. The essays that make up this section encompass two approaches to teaching Spanish speakers. While Christine Marin's essay focuses on the needs of Spanish speakers in eastern and central Arizona during the early twentieth century regarding English-language education and, later, access to Spanish-language curriculum, Lillian Gorman's essay focuses on the recuperation of the Spanish language for heritage language speakers in the southern part of the state in the twenty-first century. Ultimately, these authors demonstrate the charged politics of language over time and the ways in which local communities have responded to the changing linguistic demographics of their respective areas.

In "Grácia Liliana Fernández: Arizona Territory Professor, Educator, Librarian, 1900–1912," Christine Marin listens to the story of a schoolteacher hailing from the University of Maine. Grácia Liliana Fernández arrived in St. Johns, Arizona, in 1900, during Arizona's territorial period. Her bilingual and bicultural heritage was pivotal to addressing the local needs of teaching English to Spanish-speaking children whose families moved from the New Mexico Territory to Arizona in the second half of the nineteenth century. The children were able to learn from Fernández because she understood their background and heritage. Of additional benefit was that Apache County schools fulfilled their demand for bilingual teachers. This strategy, however, was part of an overall Americanization process as Arizona vied for statehood alongside its eastern neighbor, New Mexico. Fernández would later find herself at the Tempe Normal School as a Spanish professor and librarian, two historic firsts for a woman of Hispanic descent in Arizona.

Marin's essay elucidates the conversations around language and linguistic accommodations during Arizona's territorial period. While Fernández initially was brought to Arizona to teach English to Spanish-speaking children, she eventually went on to create a Spanish language curriculum for the territory while employed at the Tempe Normal School. As the Tempe Normal School became Arizona State University, Spanish language classes continued to be an integral part of the university's educational curriculum.

Lillian Gorman's essay, "Uncovering Southern Arizona's Tradition of Critical Language Pedagogies: Recovery, Reclamation, and Adalberto Guerrero's Early Spanish Heritage Language Classes," confronts the cultural and linguistic terrorism that has characterized the state through anti-immigrant and anti-Spanish legislation. She notes that Arizona is the only state in the United States with an English-only law and that generations of students have effectively grown up without access to bilingual education programs, despite the large Spanish-speaking communities throughout the state. She listens to Adalberto "Beto" Guerrero, a trailblazing teacher who developed the first Spanish as a heritage language (SHL) courses at Pueblo High School in Tucson, the same city that was at the center of Arizona House Bill 2281, also known as the ethnic studies ban, in 2011. Guerrero created SHL courses in 1959 before the advent of the Chicano Movement, and they were the first classes of their kind in the United States. SHL curriculum has incorporated resilience strategies to combat the linguistic and cultural terrorism that Spanish-speaking students have faced since the onset of Americanization programs that sought to erase the Spanish language from public spaces.

Guerrero's contributions to heritage language and bilingual education, as Gorman writes, were revolutionary for their time. His awareness of "culturally sustaining pedagogies," in a career spanning more than sixty years, is revealed in this essay through the creation of intergenerational pláticas that Gorman engaged in with Guerrero, Latinx students, and community members. This approach considers not only Guerrero's legacy, but also the lessons that continue to bridge generations.

The third section, "Labor, Migration, and Community," listens to laboring communities through their own oral histories. This section provides a nuanced understanding of the ways in which labor frames a community ethos and how oral histories can aid in our comprehension of stories that often are erased by more dominant narratives. Both authors emphasize what can be revealed when we look more attentively and intentionally into dynamics of community mobilization related to national and regional labor formations.

Alina R. Méndez's essay, "'We Never Separated': Bracero Family Migration to the California/Arizona-Mexico Borderlands," explores the well-known Bracero Program, a guest worker program that ran for twenty-two years (1942–64) as part of a binational agreement between the United States and Mexico. Méndez focuses her analysis on aspects of family separation and reunification in the California/Arizona borderlands and expounds upon the strategies of networking and the interpersonal relationships that allowed families and communities to mediate immigration regimes. While men were the primary workers and laborers in the Bracero Program, Méndez explores the labor that women, children, and networks of kin performed to ensure that they stayed together through various relocations. She highlights the importance of the community connections that bridged familial roots to the migration routes of the program, which extended far beyond the places where the men worked. Méndez listens to oral histories conducted as part of the Smithsonian's Bracero History Archive to highlight ten bracero families whose lives were changed by the Bracero Program. Méndez draws from their stories, foregrounding the lens of family separation and reunification in the borderlands.

In her essay "'All of Us Had Our Jobs': Mexican Women's Work in a Cotton Company Town," Gloria Holguín Cuádraz also draws from oral history interviews to discuss Mexican women workers in Litchfield Park, a company town built around cotton fields in central Arizona, just west of Phoenix. Cuádraz examines the roles women played in the company town through producing and reproducing labor in public and private spaces. She listens to oral history interviews and archival records to demonstrate the presence of Mexican women in Litchfield during two pivotal times in the town's history, "the boom and bust period from 1917 to 1921" and the period from 1929 to 1986. While the examination of the former period relies more heavily on archival records, the latter is informed by oral histories conducted as a part of the Mexican Americans of Litchfield Park Oral History Project. Through her analysis of these primary sources, Cuádraz argues that the formation of the cotton company town was vital to the state, as cotton was one of five major historic sectors within Arizona's early economy, collectively known as the five C's (cotton, citrus, climate, copper, and cattle). The cotton produced in Litchfield Park was largely used in the automotive industry, and Cuádraz argues that women were "central to the capitalistic development of the area." She explores the work that Mexican women engaged in, their connections to one another, their memories of living in the camps and the company town, and the contributions they made to a place they claimed as their own.

The fourth section, "Sounds and Silences," focuses on soundscapes, or the ways in which we experience sound as part of the landscape. These authors not only focus on sounds produced via music and radio programming, but also uncover the attendant silences that result from these soundscapes. These essays elaborate on what is produced and for whom, as well as what is excluded from those productions. They also continue the conversation from previous sections, foregrounding the themes of labor, memory, and place.

In "Turning On the Journey: Silences, Music, and the Politics of Listening in the Bracero Program," Liliana Toledo-Guzmán listens to musical sources that contest the oral history narratives produced as the official accounts of worker experiences during the Bracero Program. She argues that workers who contributed to the Bracero History Archive elided discussing the negative or unfavorable aspects of the guest worker program. In so doing, they participated in reproducing an official narrative that uplifted the program and they self-silenced the full range of their lived experiences. Toledo-Guzmán looks to the radio and to music to offer an alternative reading of those silences.

Toledo-Guzmán analyzes three corridos through the lens of the "politics of listening" to offer a more nuanced understanding of the bracero experience. These corridos, produced and recorded/published in 1953, 1959, and 1975, respectively, are important soundscapes that, according to Toledo-Guzmán, help address the silences in oral histories and offer an "aural repertoire" from which new conclusions can be drawn. These corridos address workplace injuries, border crossings, family separation, and a life mired in an unending cycle of generational labor, among other topics. Toledo-Guzmán emphasizes the importance of the radio and song to disrupt censoring practices that were intended to silence braceros.

In "Remembering the Rancho: Nineteenth-Century Discourses and Creating Stories of Mexican California, 1920–1945," Yvette J. Saavedra listens to a twentieth-century radio program titled *The Romance of the Ranchos*, which was produced to transport listeners to an earlier time in California's history that functioned according to the imagined constructs of race and gender that defined Euro-American and Californio/Mexican men during the early U.S. colonial period. As a scholar of nineteenth-century California history, Saavedra is attentive to the strategies used by the radio show to portray American men as saviors who embody an ideal masculinity. In contrast, Mexican/Californio men are portrayed as deficient and morally inept, and women need to be saved by American white men. In this way, Saavedra builds on Toledo-Guzmán's discussion of the aural repertoire of the Bracero Program, especially how the imaginary of the hacienda mentality mapped onto the rancho in the popular song, and film of the same name, "Allá en el rancho grande."

As Saavedra argues, *The Romance of the Ranchos* effectively extends a nineteenth-century imagination and maps it onto a twentieth-century California landscape as a "project of settler-colonial emplotment." The radio show debuted during the World War II period, when Mexican Americans in California were opposing war efforts and engaging in resistance strategies to defy conformity and assimilation. The radio show utilized aural cues to reinforce racism and stereotypes ascribed to California's Mexican population. It conveniently elided the racial politics of the 1940s and instead employed strategic soundscapes to explicitly justify white supremacy in the past and implicitly condone it in the present.

The final section, "Representation and Belonging," begins with Valerie Martínez's essay "The Benito Juárez Squadron: The Recruitment of Tejana Servicewomen and Their Reclamation of Cultural Citizenship During World War II." In her essay, Martínez listens to Mexican American women service members who participated in the Escuadrón Benito Juárez in the mid-1900s. Martínez writes that the strategic decision to call Mexican American women to serve through marketing campaigns in the United States and Mexico was intentional, and symbolic of the imagined hemispheric unity that was part of the 1933 Good Neighbor Policy in the United States. To bolster its transnational aspect, the campaign utilized the iconic imagery of Benito Juárez, the first Indigenous president of Mexico, in a move that was supported by Mexican president Manuel Ávila Camacho. Martínez further elaborates on the different strategies that were utilized to encourage Mexican American women to serve. This process, as Martínez writes, had a significant impact on the lived experiences of Mexican American women at the time, many of whom had to navigate the imposed societal and familial expectations of their communities. Martínez utilizes oral histories from women who served to demonstrate the challenges Mexican American women faced in asserting their rights to citizenship and bodily autonomy, and in openly defying the expected norms of their gender and generation. Martínez ultimately demonstrates that this effort to create a space for women to belong in the military did not consider the structural ways in which women have been excluded from those spaces.

The final chapter of this volume, Anita Huízar-Hernández's "Between Place and Plot: Reimagining the Story of Arizona," listens to the dissonant tellings and retellings of Arizona's story. This essay was first published in the *Journal of Arizona History*'s special issue "Imagining Arizona" and appears here in an updated version.[10] Huízar-Hernández specifically listens to three narrative strands that have come to define Arizona's story: its metropolises, its border(s), and its politics. She demonstrates that a wide chasm often separates the perceived story of Arizona from the daily reality of those living in the state. She argues for a broader listening practice to better grasp the diversity of stories that together contribute to the state's past, present, and future.

As the authors of this volume grapple with the roots and routes of meXicanidad, they consider what it means to listen to their own positionality and sense of querencia—that is, their sense of place and belonging—while practicing what María Lugones refers to as world traveling. Lugones writes that women of color can participate in generative practices of "learning to travel to each other's 'worlds.'"[11] This volume proposes listening as key to world traveling, suggesting that its practice opens new roots and routes of recognition and reciprocity. As such, the chapters are not fixated solely on roots as genealogy and routes as physical movement, though both come into view. Rather, the essays that follow explore the roots and routes of social movements, political ideals, individual and communal identities, and time as a nonlinear entity. These explorations, then, allow for a fuller expression of the roots and routes of each scholar's commitment to the communities they are from and the communities, or worlds, they have cultivated with one another.

In so doing, this volume does not shy away from investigating the internal fissures that run through borderlands communities, challenging us to consider the precarity with which coalitions are built and sustained. Ultimately, the authors collectively propose listening as an essential practice not only for world traveling, but also for worldmaking. We invite you to listen alongside them.

Notes

1. Maximilíano Durón, "Galleries Partner to Present Latin American and Latinx Artists as Part of Pacific Standard Time: LA/LA," *ARTnews*, July 11, 2017, https://www.artnews.com/art-news/market/galleries-partner-to-present-latin-american-and-latinx-artists-as-part-of-pacific-standard-time-lala-8673/.
2. For an overview of historical inquiry regarding Arizona, see Katherine G. Morrissey, "Introduction: What's Arizona Got to Do with It?," *Journal of Arizona History* 61, nos. 3 and 4 (2020): 341–45.
3. See Flannery Burke, *A Land Apart: The Southwest and the Nation in the Twentieth Century* (University of Arizona Press, 2017).
4. See Linda C. Noel, *Debating American Identity: Southwestern Statehood and Mexican Immigration* (University of Arizona Press, 2014).
5. See Luis F. B. Plascencia and Gloria H. Cuádraz, eds., *Mexican Workers and the Making of Arizona* (University of Arizona Press, 2019).
6. Rosa Linda Fregoso, *meXicana Encounters: The Making of Social Identities on the Borderlands* (University of California Press, 2003), xiv.
7. In their edited collection, Aída Hurtado and Norma E. Cantú also utilize "meXicana" to refer to Chicana and other Latin American expressions of identity. See Aída Hurtado and Norma E. Cantú, eds., *meXicana Fashions: Politics, Self-Adornment, and Identity Construction* (University of Texas Press, 2020).
8. See, for example, Cherríe Moraga and Gloria Anzaldúa, eds., *This Bridge Called My Back: Writings by Radical Women of Color* (State University of New York Press, 1981); and Latina Feminist Group, *Telling to Live: Latina Feminist Testimonios* (Duke University Press, 2001).
9. See Dionne Espinoza, María Eugenia Cotera, and Maylei Blackwell, eds., *Chicana Movidas: New Narratives of Activism and Feminism in the Movement Era* (University of Texas Press, 2018), for a discussion about movidas.
10. For the original article, see Anita Huízar-Hernández, "Between Place and Plot: Reimagining the Story of Arizona," *Journal of Arizona History* 63, no. 3 (2022): 263–79.
11. María Lugones, "Playfulness, 'World'-Travelling, and Loving Perception," *Hypatia* 2, no. 2 (1987): 4.

Bibliography

Burke, Flannery. *A Land Apart: The Southwest and the Nation in the Twentieth Century*. University of Arizona Press, 2017.

Espinoza, Dionne, María Eugenia Cotera, and Maylei Blackwell, eds. *Chicana Movidas: New Narratives of Activism and Feminism in the Movement Era*. University of Texas Press, 2018.

Fregoso, Rosa Linda. *meXicana Encounters: The Making of Social Identities on the Borderlands*. University of California Press, 2003.

Huízar-Hernández, Anita. "Between Place and Plot: Reimagining the Story of Arizona." *Journal of Arizona History* 63, no. 3 (2022): 263–79.

Hurtado, Aída, and Norma E. Cantú. *meXicana Fashions: Politics, Self-Adornment, and Identity Construction*. University of Texas Press, 2020.

Latina Feminist Group. *Telling to Live: Latina Feminist Testimonios*. Duke University Press, 2001.

Lugones, María. "Playfulness, 'World'-Travelling, and Loving Perception." *Hypatia* 2, no. 2 (1987): 3–19.

Moraga, Cherríe, and Gloria Anzaldúa, eds. *This Bridge Called My Back: Writings by Radical Women of Color*. State University of New York Press, 1981.

Morrissey, Katherine G. "Introduction: What's Arizona Got to Do with It?" *Journal of Arizona History* 61, nos. 3 and 4 (2020): 341–45.

Noel, Linda C. *Debating American Identity: Southwestern Statehood and Mexican Immigration*. University of Arizona Press, 2014.

Plascencia, Luis F. B., and Gloria H. Cuádraz, eds. *Mexican Workers and the Making of Arizona*. University of Arizona Press, 2019.

PART I

Mujeres, Memory, and Place

CHAPTER 1

Embodiment and Place

Chicanas as Sites of Knowledge

KAREN R. ROYBAL

> *You need to protect the land that you have. You need to harvest it. You need to work the land. [. . .] The land and the water is what's really going to bring you life and it is our existence. And he [my grandfather] used to make that very clear to us, that without the water and without that land, we don't exist.*
>
> —ESTHER GARCÍA, QUOTING HER GRANDFATHER, JUNE 2018

During the summer of 2018, I left Colorado Springs, Colorado, with my four-year-old daughter in tow, to conduct interviews with a select group of Chicanas in New Mexico and southern Colorado who were part of the contemporary land-grant movement.[1] I had met three of the women roughly ten years earlier, when I was a graduate student at the University of New Mexico (UNM). At that time, I was a research assistant with the Land Grant Studies Program, founded and directed in 2008 by Dr. Manuel García y Griego, a land grant heir and professor of history at UNM. The program provided an internship, graduate fellowships, and a community outreach program through which university students connected to New Mexico's active community land grants. I kept in touch with the Chicanas I met during my assistantship because it was their lived experiences and family histories that provided me with such a robust understanding of the topic on which I would eventually focus my dissertation and, later, my first book.[2] The women I met in New Mexico and southern Colorado documented their own families' histories in ways similar to those of the female authors discussed in my book. I knew that although the Chicana land-grant heirs' experiences closed the book, I would return to their stories to provide a more complete narrative about women and land in New Mexico and southern Colorado.

The interviews with women involved in the contemporary movement offer new insights as part of a new archival repository that honors Chicanas and their significant roles as holders of historical and cultural knowledge about land, community, and family in the historically significant region of the U.S. Southwest. I build on the work of women-of-color feminist scholars bell hooks, Brenda Sendejo, and Mishuana Goeman (Tonawanda Band of Seneca) in my analysis of the interviews with women of the land grant movement in New Mexico and southern Colorado. Chicanas' corporeal knowledge of land grant history is a form of embodiment through which the women themselves can be read as "place[s] of memory," as bell hooks asserts, and their shared experiences as land grant heirs can be valued as "sites of knowledge."[3]

The Chicanas interviewed come from families that were part of the tumultuous history of dispossession and land reclamation that defines the U.S. Southwest. I draw from Goeman's Native feminist spatial practice in considering the complexity of Chicanas' embodiment of this history.[4] Goeman builds on feminist geographer Doreen Massey's writings on space, which decenter Spanish colonizers as the "history and mapmakers" and instead ask us to "reimagine space" and "think of it as a 'meeting-up of histories.'"[5] Goeman's feminist spatial practice specifically centers Native women's writings that draw attention to "gendered sets of spatial practices" as a form of "spatial intervention."[6] The Chicanas whose stories I focus on in this chapter embody complex identities as descendants of both the colonizer and colonized. I engage Goeman's spatial intervention in my reading of these women as places of memory who literally embody the meeting of histories to which Massey refers. These Chicanas "reorient" our understanding of place and space through their distinct gendered spatial practices, maintaining community through active processes of listening, recording through memory, and (re)telling the experiences of past and present generations of the land grant community.[7] Men have generally been the face of the history of land struggle and the land grant movement, and of history more broadly. These women's embodied experiences help us reimagine the significant tie between women and land. Their stories reveal how they engage in practices of communal preservation *and* self-preservation that counter heteropatriarchal claims about space and knowledge, and they provide a way in which we might reckon with one layer of the violent history of settler colonialism, by reorienting ourselves and focusing on gender and land.

In *Belonging: A Culture of Place,* bell hooks explains that our sense of self rests in a place of memory guided and maintained by rituals that call us to recognize this place's value as a site of recollection that preserves memories and protects them from disappearing or being forgotten.[8] Understanding Chicanas' positions as holders of these memories offers insights about women's roles in the past, present, and future of the land movement in the Southwest and challenges the tired trope of the history of land being a story by and about men. Brenda Sendejo's Chicana feminist and ethnographic methodologies also inform my research, especially her concept of "*mujerista* ethnography"—a methodological practice through which she views "the relationship between researcher and study participants as sites of knowledge." She continues, "*Mujerista* ethnographies examine the lived experiences and histories of Latinas/Chicanas/indigenous women and their communities. They draw on autoethnography, oral history, *testimonio,* feminist research methods, and indigenous methodologies."[9] Sendejo explains that this methodology involves "reconstructing experiences from the past and understanding how they bear on cultural practices and social life in the present."[10]

I draw from these women-of-color feminists in my centering of four Chicana land-grant heirs' lived experiences to provide a more holistic interpretation of both land and women *as* places that hold memory and are active sites of knowledge production. In so doing, I do not suggest that the material realities of these contemporary Chicana land-grant heirs mirror the experiences of Native/Indigenous women. Rather, through my invocation of Native, Black, and Chicana feminist scholarship, I attempt to make visible how these women's stories provide insights about how to reorient our understanding of place as solely a thing; instead, they remind us that place is "meaningful [and] lived."[11] As the epigraph with which I began this essay affirms, women like Esther García are an embodiment of the land and thus hold the responsibility to care for and preserve it both literally and through the memories that ensure it will not disappear or be forgotten.

Blurring Borders

When I moved to southern Colorado in 2016, on my many trips home to visit family and friends in New Mexico I was reminded of the blurred and false border that divided my beloved home in New Mexico from southern Colorado and other Southwestern regions. On the 2018 trip to interview land grant heirs, my daughter and I drove south on Interstate 25 toward New Mexico. We made a stop in Pecos, the small rural village where I grew up, to visit my parents, and then I drove to Tomé to interview Rita Padilla-Gutiérrez and her sister, Andrea Padilla. I first met Rita at the same time I met Esther García and Shirley Romero Otero, during the first land grant meeting I attended in 2009 in Questa, New Mexico, when I was a graduate student. I attended the meetings to serve as a liaison between UNM and the local land-grant communities, and to interview land grant activists and learn more about activities organized by them as they continued efforts toward land reclamation. Land grants stem from a history that is both violent and racist, as the king of Spain and then American and Mexican politicians deemed Native/Indigenous peoples inferior and often enacted brutality against them. Contemporary land-grant communities recognize the need to eradicate this type of ideology for Native/Indigenous tribes and Hispano land-grant communities, to resist power structures built in the service of white supremacy, and to avoid repeating the past. The New Mexico Land Grant Council, established in 2009, makes clear their respect for Native/Indigenous rights and acknowledges that the politics of property law must be scrutinized as part of the healing process that responds to histories of dispossession.[12]

This chapter focuses on women involved in the land movement, who provide insight about gendered land-based identities. When I first encountered the women I interviewed for this project when I was a graduate student, I witnessed how they established their agency within male-dominated spaces. Those encounters consistently reminded me that my role was also to write about women and their relationship to land. By the time 2018 came, and since I had last seen Esther, Shirley, and Rita, I had had my daughter, Summer Luna. Now four years old, Summer was serving as my research assistant because I did not have childcare that summer. This process and the life changes that influenced my interactions and relationships with these women are elements of the type Sendejo describes as central to mujerista ethnography, which

> attends to the importance of the research participants to the research and recognizes the value of our relationships to them. My approach insists upon honoring those connections between researcher and informant from the moment we enter them. This involves acknowledging that these unions we establish as people—intellectually, spiritually, and physically—are key to conducting socially responsible, ethical and compassionate research.[13]

As I reflect on that experience now, I recognize the intergenerational knowledge sharing that also is significant to this type of feminist methodological practice. Three of the women I interviewed had children and grandchildren of their own; they explained how Summer's presence was a welcome addition because they knew what it was like being working mothers. In fact, on the day I interviewed her, Rita was taking care of her young grandson, so he also was exposed to the stories his grandmother and great-aunt shared with me. In my follow-up interview with her, Rita explained, "We [women] run households, we send kids to school, we wash their clothes, we feed the husbands, we . . . I mean multitasking at the highest level."[14] Importantly, Esther and Shirley also asked Summer questions about her experiences on the road with Mom; they knew I was trying to navigate the interview and my child simultaneously, and they insisted she sit in because even if she did not grasp all that was being shared, she would carry with her the memory of being there. Summer may not have realized it then at four years old, but she was receiving one of her first lessons in the significance of preserving Chicana voices in the historical record; she was witnessing the bonds created with the women whom I had known for many years and whom I was now interviewing as part of my research, and she was hearing firsthand from women who had and continued to hold memory and place within them.

Intersections of Power and Land

The history of land grants extends across the Spanish colonial period, the Mexican period, and the years 1846–48, when the Mexican-American

War occurred. The signing of the 1848 Treaty of Guadalupe Hidalgo, which ended the war, was intended to protect land grants issued by the Spanish and then Mexican governments. This history is connected not only to what we today identify as New Mexico, but also to the areas then considered part of the New Mexico Territory: Arizona and parts of Colorado and Nevada. The story also connects to the histories of Texas and California.[15]

The period just after the signing of the treaty left New Mexico and Arizona in a precarious position that relegated the areas to the status of territories for sixty-four years. The reason for this liminality stemmed from what federal lawmakers deemed an unfit citizenry, because of the large Mexican and Indigenous populations in these areas. Literary scholar Anita Huízar-Hernández asserts that "Arizona's territorial leaders elaborated [a] counterfeit narrative" through which they "quantitatively and qualitatively minimized the state's non-Anglo, primarily Mexican and Native American population, arguing that they were too insignificant to pose a threat to the racialized borders of U.S. national identity."[16] In New Mexico, Hispano territorial leaders similarly generated a "counterfeit narrative" when they attempted to lay claim to whiteness to defend New Mexicans' "fitness" as U.S. citizens. These rhetorical moves were political ones that worked in favor of territorial leaders who sought social, political, and cultural power over and control of these significant regions. Though citizenship rights were extended to multiethnic populations in both New Mexico and Arizona, in many cases those rights were de jure, not de facto. Historian David G. Gutiérrez explains that Mexican Americans' U.S. citizenship was not immediate, as Mexican officials had been told, but in fact it took them time to gain legal status under the treaty.[17] The false sense of belonging extended to the treaty's stipulations guaranteeing property rights that had been established via land grants given by the Spanish and then Mexican governments. For example, in cases where families had been granted land by the Mexican government and those property rights were supposed to be protected once the U.S. legal system was established in former Mexican territories, Mexican landholders were ordered to provide their property deeds, surveys, and grant paperwork. Even when they did, and presented these documents in court, often their grants were not honored and land was taken from them.[18] Historian Jacobo Baca explains, "In the late seventeenth and early eighteenth century, land grants were made to the colonial elite who participated in the reconquest and requested the lands of abandoned pueblos or those adjacent to existing ones," or they were made to establish settlements that would essentially ward off raids by local Native tribes.[19] Historian María E. Montoya describes how during the Mexican period, in November 1828, the Regulations for the Colonization of the Territories

> gave territorial governors the power to distribute three types of land grants to either foreigners or citizens: community, individual, and empresario grants. In New Mexico, which at this time still included Arizona, governors usually bestowed community grants to Hispano villages or Indian pueblos that wished to gain legal security for customary lands or to go out onto the frontier and establish a satellite community.[20]

These grants were supposed to be protected under the stipulations of the 1848 Treaty of Guadalupe Hidalgo. However, rather than honoring the grants, U.S. government officials, in tandem with a cadre of dubious white male lawyers and land-hungry settlers who were convinced that the land was their God-given right, worked to dispossess Native/Indigenous peoples and then Mexicanos of these lands.

After the Treaty of Guadalupe Hidalgo, land remained important. The 1853 Gadsden Purchase influenced the separation of Arizona from the New Mexico Territory. This second purchase was negotiated not only to transfer land, but also to settle lingering tensions concerning agreed-upon financial compensation to Mexico as well as the United States' responsibility to protect Mexicans against attacks from neighboring Native tribes. Really, the Gadsden Purchase was about capitalism, as it was intended to enable the United States to develop a southern transcontinental railroad (though the railroad would ultimately be built farther north), as well as to free the country from any additional financial obligations to Mexico, and the U.S. army from the obligation delineated in Article 11 of the treaty to protect northern Mexico from Comanche and Apache raids.[21] Through the Gadsden Purchase / Treaty of La Mesilla, signed between the United States and Mexican president Antonio López de Santa Anna, the United States acquired what had been deemed hostile and desolate Sonoran desert lands, which became part of the Territory of New Mexico. Historian Brian DeLay claims that "the United States bought its way out of Article 11 in 1854 as part of the Gadsden Purchase."[22] The Treaty of Guadalupe Hidalgo and the Gadsden Purchase are important for understanding the malleability of borders in the nineteenth century and the long-standing issues caused by the U.S. government's unwillingness to uphold its agreed-upon obligations with respect to land, which continue to impact communities in the U.S. Southwest today.

Some one-hundred-plus years after the signing of the Treaty of Guadalupe Hidalgo and the Gadsden Purchase, in the 1960s, the land grant movement in New Mexico gained national attention when Pentecostal preacher Reies López Tijerina founded the Alianza Federal de Mercedes (Federal Alliance of Land Grants), a group dedicated to land reclamation. La Alianza brought national attention to the historic losses of land that had occurred because legal articles from the treaty designed to protect land grants were not honored as intended. The Alianza's actions against this injustice resulted in the infamous 1967 Tierra Amarilla courthouse raid, when some of its male members stormed the county courthouse and placed district attorney Alfonso Sánchez under citizen's arrest. This raid and the longer history of land grants in what is now the southwest United States give the impression that this was exclusively a male struggle, told by men, but the interviews shared here reveal that women have always played a significant role in the movement and in relation to land.[23]

The ways the history of land grants have been told reflect a Western framing of property that centers capitalism. Reading this history through a different lens, where women are centered as sites of knowledge and as place, compels a new reading that honors Native/Indigenous epistemologies and women-of-color feminist methodologies. This reframing allows us to understand this history by "seeing with two eyes," as Potawatomi botanist Robin Wall Kimmerer posits. Kimmerer uses this phrase to describe how she understands our society's need to think more holistically about the relationship between Western science and Native/Indigenous lived experiences and epistemologies.[24] I apply her practice of "seeing with two eyes" to read how Chicanas embody place. This reading of Chicana embodiment of place exemplifies "what decolonization wants," as explained by Eve Tuck and K. Wayne Yang, because it emphasizes the material reality of women as land and makes it clear that "decolonization is not a metaphor."[25]

I apply Kimmerer's concept of seeing with two eyes and Chicanas' embodiment of place alongside Southwestern tribes' heterogeneous relationships to land/Mother Earth. Native American studies scholar Gregory Cajete (Santa Clara Pueblo) understands Pueblo life and land as intimately interconnected: "their [Natives'] landscapes are seen as metaphoric extensions of their bodies."[26] Similarly, but not identically, the Diné concept of *hózhó* connotes a holistic way of being and of understanding the "sense of goodness" that derives from "happiness, healthiness, beauty, goodness, prosperity, balance, and harmony interconnected as an underlying unity in the context of Diné locality."[27] Pueblo lifeways and other Native epistemologies from the Diné, Ute, Apache, and other neighboring tribes interconnect with the ways of land-based Hispanos/Chicanos because these groups have lived, worked, intermixed, and communed together for centuries. These relationships have not always been easy, and they were historically complex and continue to be so; yet they serve as a reminder of intercultural exchanges of knowledge, history, and traditions that persist today. I acknowledge the violence of these histories, as well as the processes of forced acculturation and accommodation that developed as a result. These relationships and processes relate directly to the women whose interviews are included in this study, as members of land-based peoples, and serve as a reminder of what Goeman describes as "the complexities of spatial subjectivities and geographic histories."[28]

Colonial Power and the Impacts of Dispossession

In her study of Native American cultural production, Goeman explains that "place continues to hold these fragile, complex, and important relationships."[29] This description aligns directly with the lived experiences told here. The Chicanas whose stories I share come from families that were part of the violent history of dispossession and land reclamation that defines what is today the U.S. Southwest. Part of this history centers on the Spanish colonial period, during which, in the sixteenth century, the Crown sent colonizers to the New World to augment the Spanish state and church. We have accounts written by colonizers and the Franciscan friars who accompanied them that document the violent acts driving these colonization efforts: genocide, slavery, and attempted conversion of Native/Indigenous peoples to Christianity. The Pueblos, Apaches, Comanches, and Diné in New Mexico resisted colonization efforts, and they defended their people, their land, their religious and spiritual beliefs, and their provisions. In southern Colorado's San Luis Valley, the ancestral homelands of several Native tribes, bands, and clans, including the Jicarilla Apache, the Diné, the Southern Ute, the Ute Mountain Ute, and several Upper Rio Grande and Western Pueblo tribes, these peoples similarly resisted Spanish colonization efforts.

This chapter's focus on the significance of cultural and historical memory makes it imperative here to recognize that these Native tribes suffered the loss of cultural memory—a direct result of forced removal from their ancestral homelands, forced acculturation, and language loss. Here I do not provide a full account of colonization in what is today the western and southwestern United States; there are many books, archives, and exhibits dedicated to recording that history.[30] In this chapter, I acknowledge that history, albeit briefly, to emphasize how it has impacted Chicanas' embodiment of the land. Goeman asserts, "Stories create the relationships that have made communities strong even through numerous atrocities and injustices."[31] As descendants of both the colonizer and the colonized, the Chicana land-grant heirs whose stories are analyzed here provide insight into the liminality and the land-based character of Chicano identity. Their stories are but one way in which we might begin to reckon with the multilayered processes of dispossession that have occurred because of colonialism and settler colonization. New Mexico Land Grant Council program manager Arturo Archuleta provides important insight about how we categorize land grants, noting that "the terms 'Spanish and Mexican land grants' denote who the governmental regime was at the time [read: who held the power]; that label should not be used to identify who the people were because it does not address the diverse identities and life experiences of the peoples of the region."[32] Additionally, communities like those highlighted in this chapter may have been land rich, but they were economically poor and working class; they relied on communal lands to sustain their families' food sources and connections to the land/environment.

Acts of Remembrance in Tomé, New Mexico

Located just south of Albuquerque, Tomé was founded in 1739 and is one of the oldest villages in New Mexico. The village is situated along El Camino Real de Tierra Adentro, the Royal Road traveled by Spanish colonizers Juan de Oñate and Diego de Vargas. Today, Tomé is a land-grant community, but we know it was first home to the Pueblo peoples, and one of the largest of New Mexico's nineteen pueblos, Tsugwevaga (Isleta Pueblo), which surrounds Tomé farther south. Tomé was also a genízaro community, a group that "occupied an ethnic, identifiable space between Spanish, Pueblo Natives, and mestizos."[33] According to the Town of Tomé Land Grant website:

> On April 5, 1871, a patent was issued to the Town of Tomé Land Grant. The original boundaries were described as follows: the west boundary being the Rio del Norte (the Rio Grande River). On the south by the stopping place commonly called the three cottonwoods; on the east at the point of sunrise within the sierra madre called Sandia, and on the north by the punta de las esteras del llano called Thome Dominguez.[34]

As happened with many land grant communities in the nineteenth century, the original 300,000-acre grant was divided in two, with almost half of that acreage given to another village, Casa Colorada. Following that split, in 1906, land was taken by the federal government when President Theodore Roosevelt issued a proclamation in which he gave the U.S. Forest Service approximately 50,000 acres of the Town of Tomé Land Grant.[35] Additionally, almost 75,000 acres of the grant were lost a year later due to unpaid taxes, and then in 1968, 47,000 acres were sold off to private owners not tied to the original grant.

Sisters Rita Padilla-Gutiérrez and Andrea Padilla are heirs to the Town of Tomé Land Grant. Their family has deep ties to the land on which the grant sits. During my interview with her, Andrea, current president of the Town of Tomé Land Grant, shared that their family has been there since the early 1700s: "Tomé was established in 1739, and you see the Padilla name shortly after that in this area. So we have a long history here. And on my mom's side with the Baca side, again, there's a long history. So we have a long history in this area in this valley."[36] When I followed up by asking how long her family has been connected to the Town of Tomé Land Grant, she stated: "For all our life. We learned from my father the love for the land. My mom as well. So, we go back, you know, five hundred years."[37]

Andrea explained, "Most land grants are genízaros," and in Tomé, Hispanos, Pueblos, Comanches, and Apaches frequently intermarried.[38] Her sister Rita further articulated, "I think literally for centuries we have coexisted with our Native American communities. The genízaro connection is so strong."[39] Both sisters made clear that both Hispanos and the Native tribes of the region are land-based peoples, and they acknowledged the complicated and violent histories of the region, especially as they pertain to land. During our discussion, not only did Andrea share the long line of family members attached to the land, but she described how the land was part of her: "It's kind of just in our blood. So we love the land, we love protecting it."[40] Her sister Rita reaffirmed this deep connection between them and the land: "It was our playing field, it was a food source, it was an identity. I mean, it was so many things [. . .]. I mean, we were a land-based people [. . .]. You know, it was a life source."[41] Padilla and Padilla-Gutiérrez's descriptions of their connection to the land reflect Kimmerer's assertion that land is a "source of belongings" in providing not only physical sustenance for the survival of the Padilla family and community, but also sustenance for the women's corporeal presence, knowledge, and attachments to the land.[42] The land is also their relative, which holds memory.

The sisters' descriptions of the various ways their families were tied to the land demonstrate their understanding of reciprocity. For example, Padilla-Gutiérrez explains: "My father and many others [. . .] use[d] the land, the common lands, for pasturing and grazing and taking out some of the mineralites [*sic*] like sand and gravel. So we've grown up with it, knowing that the land gave you these things."[43] Communal land grants were designed to provide families with equal access to water, space for agriculture, a plaza for gathering, and "commons for hunting, gathering, and grazing."[44] In Padilla-Gutiérrez's description, her father's and other land grant members' uses of the land were communal; they were not extractive, they were reciprocal. Padilla acknowledged, "I learned you do for your community, you do for your church, the land grant, you do for your people [. . .] you do for each other. That's how you keep yourself going. [. . .] That's what we watched my mom and dad do. And that's what we learned and that's what we continued."[45] Padilla-Gutiérrez similarly made clear that their land grant is focused on ensuring that the original intention of communal land is central to the work they do: "the pendulum has swung back to the word *communal, community*."[46] Understanding the land, place, and the history surrounding these areas is important to her identity, as well as the identities of her family and community members: "So it goes back a long way in terms of knowing from whence we came, you know."[47]

This type of understanding of the land and its value is distinct from Western imperial conceptions of land as a tool to be exploited for financial gain; it is emblematic instead of a "regenerative economy" built on reciprocity.[48] This association with the land extends beyond state-imposed borders. Regina Lopez-Whiteskunk (Weminuche/Ute Mountain Ute) explains, "You never take more than you need. You always keep in mind that someone or something is going to come behind you."[49] The Padilla sisters' ethos similarly understands and respects the fact that what they do with the land impacts future generations. They are currently working to acquire land that can be leased to the younger generation so that they can farm and build homes on it—an important step that they hope will keep youth in the community instead of seeing them forced out by the current situation, in which developers are buying large swaths of land and turning it into overpriced subdivisions.

Padilla and Padilla-Gutiérrez hope to encourage youth to develop their own connection to the land. The sisters' embodied experiences shared through their stories ensure that we "remember important connections to land and community," which is integral to our survival as land-based people.[50] In addition to passing down this love for the land through the practices of land stewardship, they are also intent on passing that knowledge down through the Tomé Domínguez Community Center, a space where this history is documented and available to the public, as well as through a scholarship program developed by Padilla that provides monies to heirs and all community members who want to get an education and remain in, or return to, their community in Tomé.[51]

Settler-colonial practices and the development of a capitalist economy pushed communities toward individualism and attempted to disrupt and destroy their communal practices centered on reciprocity. Padilla-Gutiérrez remembers how, in the 1970s, when she and some of her siblings left Tomé to attend New Mexico Highlands University in Las Vegas, parts of the Town of Tomé Land Grant were sold. These sales had devastating impacts on Padilla-Gutiérrez. She explained, "And then when we came back [to Tomé] after the sale was done, then we had to deal with that horrific sadness, really, and the part of people who lost it, you know? Lost their tie to the land, their ancestral kinship to the land."[52] Padilla-Gutiérrez's memory of the impact of this land loss provides insight beyond the abstract notion of dispossession, as she describes the embodied connection and relationship to land, as well as the visceral reaction she and others had when they learned the news. She and her sister are intent on helping to better prepare the youth of the community so that they understand their history as land-based people and so that they acquire skills and credentials through trade schools or universities that will allow them to continue advocating for the people and lands of Tomé.

Despite the detrimental impacts associated with selling the land, for the Padilla sisters, their family, and the Tomé community, the Town of Tomé Land Grant was and remains a sacred space where they are safe from the dominant culture. In her writings, bell hooks describes it in this way: "There [on the land, in nature] dominator culture (the system of imperialist white supremacist capitalist patriarchy) could not wield absolute power. For in that world, nature was more powerful. Nothing and no one could completely control nature."[53] The Padilla sisters at once demonstrate the agency of nature and their own agency, through which they share memories and lived experiences associated with the Town of Tomé Land Grant that produce a new way of understanding the significance of this land to their lived realities and to their identities.[54] Their stories are a way to "restore any imbalance" caused by land loss or historical erasure, and to create a path toward healing for all land-based peoples.[55] Padilla recognizes that healing must happen not only for the land grant communities, but also for their Native/Indigenous relatives and neighbors. She says, "I'd like to see more women involved": she believes the women can "sit down and talk" with the surrounding tribes, because "we have something to give, and as women, we can move both of our cultures forward, both of our communities forward."[56] This type of solidarity of land-based peoples ensures restoration.[57]

Caring for the Land so It Remains in Us and in Our Memories

After interviewing the Padilla sisters, Summer and I drove to northern New Mexico, up the high road to Taos and into the small village of Questa. That June afternoon, I met with then-mayor Esther García, at the Village of Questa office. This visit remains especially meaningful. Little did I know that this was one of the last times I would get to spend time with and speak to Esther, who passed away shortly after our visit, in January of 2020.

When we walked into the Village of Questa office, Esther greeted Summer and asked her how she was enjoying our trip, what she had learned, and whether she would be helping her mama with the interview, which Summer pretended to do when she put her headphones on and "recorded" on her tablet. I reflect on this exchange often because I documented the moment with photographs of Esther sitting at her desk and Summer sitting at the desk opposite her, both prepared to engage in the interview. This type of exchange emulated the oral storytelling tradition common in Native and Chicano communities, especially as these stories are often intended to inform and/or teach lessons to younger generations. For Esther, this intergenerational exchange was especially important considering that her relationship to land had been highly influenced by her grandfather, who shared insights with her in the same way she was doing with Summer and me that day. As we began our conversation, Esther shared with me the words that I used as an epigraph to begin this chapter, making clear that her grandfather had instilled in her a deep appreciation for the land that would become a significant part of her. She said, "At the time, I didn't quite understand what he was trying to tell me, but as I grew older I knew what he was telling me and what he wanted me to do, and that was to make sure we protected our land and water," because, as Esther understood, they "are our survival."[58] With this statement, Esther not only revealed her personal attachment to the land but also connected it to her family's and her community's survival as a whole, which became especially evident when she explained how she emphasized to her own immediate family: "It's your heritage. It's part of your culture."[59]

When Esther and the other women I interviewed discussed the land grants of which they are a part, they did not focus on the grants as pieces of private property. German philosopher and political theorist Karl Marx conceived of private property as closely connected to new class structures and new forms of oppression.[60] When the U.S. government established new property laws, those laws were firmly rooted in Western individualism, not the spirit of communal land as was practiced in much of the Southwest, and in New Mexico and Colorado in particular. This different conception of land and property ushered in new ways for the government to assume power and control over what had been shared lands. In addition to the push against common lands in favor of private property, Esther discussed how the establishment of national monuments in the name of preservation was another way the government recorded the significance of land. However, the act of creating a national monument enabled a form of exclusion, particularly for the peoples indigenous to the lands which the monument includes. Esther provided the example of the 2013 designation of the Rio Grande del Norte National Monument in Embudo, New Mexico, located just miles from Questa.[61] This designation was proposed in the name of "conservation," she explained. She knew this because she was part of the group that fought for that designation. However, the land grant of which she was an heir, the Cañón del Río Colorado Land Grant, was not honored in the same way.

Esther explained how she acted by calling the office of then–U.S. senator Jeff Bingaman and speaking with one of his staff members, Jorge Silva Benavides. She said to Benavides:

> Well, you're proposing a conservation area. I said, "Do you know that there is a land grant that is right in the middle of this conservation area you're proposing?" [. . .] What I was told is they didn't much care. And I said, "Well, I think you better care because this is our land and we're going to voice a strong opposition to some of the things you're proposing in this conservation area." So within like three days, they had people from D.C. coming out. And so I called the Land Grant Board, and I said, "They're coming and I think we need to sit down with them and we need to be very firm about what it is that we want and we don't want them taking over and just telling us this is what's going to happen to our land."[62]

This act by Esther resulted in S.667, the Rio Grande del Norte National Conservation Area Establishment Act.[63] The bill was designed to "protec[t] our water, our land. And we had a seat at the table when management decisions were going to be made. And because we said this is part of our history, part of our culture, and it's our heritage."[64] Importantly, as Esther reiterated throughout the interview, the land was part of the community identity, and her own identity in particular; it was an herencia symbolizing a "gendered . . . spatial practice" that demonstrated her understanding of the "land as an ancestral responsibility."[65]

Esther and the other women included in this chapter recognized the grants in a way that was quite the opposite of Western framings of land as property. The land is something that must be nurtured; a reciprocal relationship with it must be embraced, for, as her grandfather reminded her, "if you don't take care of your land and protect it, it will become the land of tomorrow [. . .] and we'll become nothing."[66] In this statement and at many points in our conversation, Esther reiterated this inherent embodiment of the land. She went on to say, "I know that my existence is because of this land and the hard work my ancestors, my grandfather, and his father did for us to have this land."[67] Her statements emphasized her recognition that the land provided for her, her family, and her community, and that it was their job to devote themselves to the land. Specifically, Esther's lifelong work centered on "advocat[ing] for restoration of [the] San Antonio del Río Colorado Land Grant, so that heirs could freely practice cultural traditions on common lands like wood-cutting, fishing, herb and piñon gathering, hunting and horseback riding."[68] Her conception of preservation was in the service of the community of land-based peoples.

When Esther traveled to Washington, D.C., to testify before Congress regarding the national monument designation, she recalled being questioned by a senator who could not conceive of the reasons why Esther wanted the land grant included in the designation: "He was questioning me and I said, 'Well, I think you don't quite understand.' I said, 'I think you have to come to northern New Mexico to understand.' But I said, 'You see, the trees in the forest and my roots are as deep as those trees in the forest in my community. That's how deep my roots are.' And it's so important for us. It really is important to us."[69] The sentiments expressed by Esther are reminiscent of the ways bell hooks describes Native/Indigenous and African peoples' relation to land, as they share "a respect for the life-giving forces of nature, of the earth," and "cultivate a spirit of wonder and reverence for life."[70]

At the time I interviewed Esther in 2018, my questions focused on women's relationships with the land and her family history; I did not focus on her, her family, or her community's understanding of the longer history of dispossession associated with the process through which Hispano families like hers acquired their land. In the absence of an opportunity for a follow-up interview, I turn to others from her community for insight. Founder of the digital repository Native Bound/Unbound, Dr. Estevan Rael-Gálvez, who like Esther is from Questa, reminds us, "Early on, this region did not only sit on the edges of indigenous pueblo communities but opened up into a fertile valley that was *home* to Mouache and Capote bands of Ute Indians and used as a hunting ground for other nomadic tribes, including Kiowas, Apaches, Comanches, Cheyenne and Navajos."[71] I have no doubt that Esther, too, knew this history. In his recollection of Esther, New Mexico Wild board member Ernie Atencio said, "She was a trailblazer in many ways and left behind an impressive legacy of care and protection for the land, her community, and the age-old Indo-Hispano traditions of acequias and land grants."[72] Mark Allison, executive director of New Mexico Wild, shared, "I saw Esther as a peacemaker and a bridge builder, who helped bring together acequia parciantes, land grant heirs, pueblos, local governments, businesses, hunters and anglers, communities of faith, and conservation groups around shared values and a love of the land. When Esther was in the room, there was an implied expectation that everyone would listen to one another and treat everyone with dignity and respect. And when Esther spoke, people listened."[73] Based on my own interactions with her and understanding of her character, combined with the reflections of others about her, I can only speculate that Esther would have recognized what Rael-Gálvez describes as "the stories of *población*, or the peopling of this area," while at the same time she likely understood that "it is also important to recognize that *población* often comes hand in hand with *despoblación*, the dis-peopling of an area."[74] Her commitment was always to land-based peoples.

These processes of dispossession are layered, complex, and violent. As we reckon with this history, as I attempt to do in this chapter, we are reminded about how white supremacist structures and systems of oppression created through state power have consciously "order[ed] our reactions and relations to those around us."[75] The examples shared here reveal, in part, what happens when our communities are forced away from our land or it is disrespected through extraction and dispossession of the peoples who tend to it; these acts cause great harm that works in the service of white supremacy intended to separate Black and Brown communities from their sacred land.[76] This separation causes "profound epistemic, ontological, cosmological violence."[77] The women interviewed in this study reiterate the multiple types of violence that continue to impact the land on which they and their communities rely for their survival. More importantly, they remind us also of the significance of reciprocity with the land because it is a part of us.

"The Land Gives Us Our Complete Identity"

San Luis, Colorado, has historically been a contested space, especially in the nineteenth century, when Anglo settlers and military leaders sought to claim it from the Ute, Diné, Apache, Comanche, Pueblo, and then Mexicano peoples who called it home for hundreds of years prior to their arrival. San Luis was the first town founded in Colorado in 1851, and it remained part of the New Mexico Territory until 1861, when Colorado became its own territory. As a graduate student, I had been to San Luis many times to visit Shirley Romero Otero. She had always been generous with her time and knowledge, and she has served as my unofficial mentor for many years. As Summer and I sat in her flower-filled yard in the center of San Luis on a beautiful summer morning, Shirley shared with me that for "those of us who have deep roots here in San Luis and the other Rio Culebra villages [. . .] the relationship to the land gives us our complete identity."[78] Like Esther, Rita, and Andrea, Shirley identifies closely with the land on which she resides, and she embodies it; it is a direct extension of her. That connection, she says, has given her and her ancestors their complete identity "for many, many generations."[79] Shirley makes clear that Indigenous tribes inhabited the lands on which the Sangre de Cristo land grant in San Luis sits. She recognizes her responsibility as an heir, saying, "As a Chicana land grant activist, I realize and acknowledge that multiple Indigenous groups were here before my community was established in the 1800s."[80] Intermixing of Hispanos and Native peoples was inevitable because multiple groups were in this place at the same time. Shirley also made clear that these groups were and are land-based peoples subject to forced removal and forced to adhere to settler-colonial laws and customs. She understands her responsibility as an heir to serve as a steward of that land in order to heal from these historical traumas. The sentiments and lived reality shared by Shirley evoke what bell hooks describes with respect to her own experiences and her ancestors' connections to the land: the way through which "collective black self-recovery takes place" by "renew[ing] our relationship to the earth, when we remember the way of our ancestors."[81]

As a Chicana, Shirley is mixed-race, but she does not claim a tribal affiliation. She affirms: "I am the descendant of some of the first Mexicano settlers that came into the Sangre de Cristo Land Grant here in San Luis. Currently I am living back home after being gone for about thirty years of a teaching career at Grand Junction."[82] The Sangre de Cristo grant was first conferred by the Mexican governor of New Mexico, Manuel Armijo, to Narciso Beaubien and Stephen Luis Lee in 1844. Historian María E. Montoya explains that this granting of land was "suspect" because "Lee was an American—not a Mexican citizen," while "Narciso Beaubien was only a young boy and had no stature or ability to lure citizens to the frontier to create new settlements," as was promised in the initial request for land.[83] The intention of this grant is obvious now, as it was eventually acquired by Carlos Beaubien in 1848 when his son Narciso was killed in the Taos uprising. The grant has changed hands over the past 175 years, including being owned by former Colorado territorial governor William Gilpin. In the 1960s, a North Carolina investor named Jack Taylor purchased a significant amount of the communal land within the Sangre de Cristo Land Grant, which led to a decades-long legal fight between Taylor and grant heirs.[84] Shirley is one of the co-founders of the Land Rights Council, established in 1978.[85] She has worked tirelessly for over forty years as an heir to the Sangre de Cristo Land Grant in a class-action lawsuit originally filed in 1981, which has exposed the violence of the U.S. legal system, as heirs have endured a hard-won fight to gain access to la sierra, the surrounding mountain range, so that families in the area have access to grazing, firewood, and water. Like many of the grants in northern New Mexico and southern Colorado, this fight began because much of the communal land grant was purchased by a white settler and has been bought and sold by private landowners who either do not understand or do not care about the deep connection residents of San Luis have to their land. By closing the common lands, Taylor denied locals the ability to maintain their traditional land use. Residents resisted this denial of access. Shirley asserts that the "diligence of this community to continue to go through the highs and lows and all of the other violence that has been perpetuated on this community" shows their resilience. "We continue to fight," she says, and "that's a victory in and of itself."[86]

Shirley has been a lifelong organizer; she was active in the Chicano Movement and thus recognizes that "justice comes very slow, but we keep moving forward."[87] Her motivation to continue her fight for the Sangre de Cristo Land Grant centers on the fact that the land sustains her community—as a land-based people, Chicanos in the San Luis Valley have relied on the land for sustenance and survival. But further, Shirley states that her connection to the land "continues to increase. It's sacred. My connection to the land is sacred."[88] Shirley's understanding of the land as sacred illustrates a philosophy like that of Kimmerer, who explains that "as people remember what's good for the land is also good for the people," they participate in "acts of restoration" that "honor . . . the way we live" as land-based peoples.[89] This connection restores what the late anthropologist Alfonso Ortiz (Owe'neh Bupingeh / Ohkay Owingeh Pueblo) calls the "imbalance" that disrupts the "harmony of life."[90] Private property owners like Taylor disrupted this restoration and honoring of land; Taylor's actions "threaten[ed] both their [community members'] use of the land as a commons and the stability of the watershed," and, more importantly, he "threaten[ed] the distinct nature of the San Luis community."[91] However, thanks to their dedication to ensuring the legal battle over access to the commons would be won, the community has maintained the intention of communal land by continuing practices like gathering firewood for heating their homes in winter, accessing timber for building, and allowing those who have cattle access to grazing space.

Additionally, Shirley is president of the Move Mountains Project, a program dedicated to developing youth leaders in San Luis by encouraging the next generation to learn about root causes of systemic oppression that have impacted their own Indigenous and Latino/Chicano populations in the San Luis Valley. Students in the program have established a community garden, and they work with local farmers, grazers, and ranchers to address significant land and water issues in the area.[92] These intergenerational practices ensure the continuance of the land-based philosophies that guide land stewards in the San Luis Valley. Unlike residents of the valley, private owners who do not live on, or have deep connections to, this land purchase it without understanding its sacredness and merely equate it with capital value. This conception of land runs counter to the lived realities of the spiritual and personal value of the land expressed by the women in this study. Of the private owners, Shirley says, "They don't get it. But we do."[93] For her, the land "is a foundation from which people in this community for multi-generations at least for over two hundred years have been here and definitely identify with the land."[94] Shirley goes on to say that it "is a sacred piece of land to us that has allowed us to subsist in this community and still be what we are today."[95] Shirley also honors her gendered association with the land, saying, "We [women] have a different connection to the land as mothers that bear the children that are going to inherit the land."[96] For Shirley, the inheritance runs much deeper than passing down property; it means offering a piece of oneself as part of the land because one embodies it.

The process of reciprocity for Chicanas also includes claiming their agency through what Brenda Sendejo describes as a process of "self-making," in which women undo "some of the gender conditioning in their earlier lives."[97] For women involved in the land grant movement in southern Colorado and New Mexico, undoing the conditioning means "changing the patriarchal system" so that women not only are seen as capable of "manag[ing] land"—and thus their bodies, because the land is an inherent part of them—but also can "share that with the rest of the family" and assert their agency.[98] When it comes to acknowledging women's central roles, this process of change does not always come easily.

Women like the mothers and grandmothers of Rita, Andrea, Esther, and Shirley were previously understood by men involved in the land grant movement as background characters despite their significant roles in preparing meals and tending to their families, and as holders of records and significant cultural memories. But Shirley, as a member of the next generation of Chicanas in the movement, "met more resistance because I would push more, I would question more."[99] Driving Shirley was the fact that she "knew that personally it [the land] was part of gaining my cultural identity as a woman, as a Chicana, and someone who was involved in the movement and saw changes coming about."[100] In many ways, Shirley inherited this agency from her paternal grandmother,

Benina Romero, whom "the godfather of the land grant movement," Apolinar Rael, described to Shirley by saying, "I remember in the early '60s when we were organizing and we were meeting and after a meeting on a cold night she was wearing a dress and an apron and those socks they would roll up in their black shoes, and she would say, 'Okay, we've met plenty. There's a plan now.'"[101] Rael's recollections of Shirley's grandmother confirmed for her that "there was female involvement in my family prior to me coming to the scene and that we were all links of this chain of the land grant movement that we continue today."[102] Padilla similarly reaffirmed the actions of women in the current movement, saying, "And the women say, vámonos, let's go, let's get it done, and then we start bringing different people to come in, and kids, and it gets done. It just brings that community back together."[103] Sendejo's study of Tejanas as agents of their own spiritual practices within the Catholic Church offers great insight into the ways women function within and beyond patriarchal institutions like the church and, in this case, the land grant movement. Sendejo explains that the women do not simply "function within a structure of domination" because "*they* control the degree to which they engage patriarchal structures. That is, while the institution itself may be structured as a patriarchal institution, at various times women are shifting in and out of the shadow of such dominance through subverting it."[104] As Shirley describes, women of her grandmother's generation reveal "the oppression within our culture that women should be seen and not heard."[105] Chicanas in the land grant movement challenge the tired trope of women as background characters and enact their agency through their embodiment of the land and the memories it holds.

Renewal in a Place of Memory

This chapter interprets Chicanas as "place[s] of memory" based on their corporeal knowledge of land-based history in southern Colorado and northern New Mexico. By placing value on the women as "sites of knowledge," we can more fully honor how, as land grant heirs, their embodiment of communal preservation and self-preservation elucidates familial and regional histories related to the tumultuous experiences associated with dispossession and land reclamation in the U.S. Southwest, countering heteropatriarchal claiming of space and knowledge. The interviews with Andrea, Rita, Esther, and Shirley center women in discussions about land, honor the significant role these women play in our memory, and "reorient" our understanding of the sacredness of land.[106] Their experiences, shared through their oral stories, are one way we can move toward the "elsewhere" of decolonization that values the relationship between embodiment, reciprocity, and land.[107] Their stories also provide an entry point through which we can begin to reckon with the complex histories of dispossession and gender that define the U.S. Southwest.

Notes

1. I conducted follow-up interviews in July 2024 with three of the women: Shirley Romero Otero, Rita Padilla-Gutiérrez, and Andrea Padilla.
2. The book, *Archives of Dispossession: Recovering the Testimonios of Mexican American Herederas, 1848–1960* (University of North Carolina Press, 2017), examines what I call "archives of dispossession" recorded by Mexican American women in the nineteenth and twentieth centuries who held ties to land via grants in what are now the states of California, Texas, and New Mexico.
3. bell hooks, *Belonging: A Culture of Place* (Routledge, 2009), 5. Brenda Sendejo, "'The Face of God Has Changed': Tejana Cultural Production and the Politics of Spirituality in the Borderlands" (PhD diss., University of Texas at Austin, 2010), 41.
4. Mishuana Goeman, *Mark My Words: Native Women Mapping Our Nations* (University of Minnesota Press, 2013), 5.
5. Goeman, *Mark My Words*, 5; Doreen Massey, *For Space* (Sage Publications, 2005), 6–7.
6. Mishuana R Goeman, "Notes Toward a Native Feminism's Spatial Practice," *Wicazo Sa Review* 24, no. 2 (2009): 178; Goeman, *Mark My Words*, 3.
7. In *For Space*, Massey asks readers to imagine what it would "mean to reorient this imagination [of space], to question that habit of thinking of space as surface" (7).
8. hooks, *Belonging*, 5. Goeman similarly regards place as intimately connected to belonging and "more than just a point on a graph or local, but that which carries with it a 'way of being-in-the-world.'" Goeman, *Mark My Words*, 9. Goeman is quoting Martin Heidegger, *Being and Time* (Blackwell, 1962).
9. Sendejo, "Face of God," 1.
10. Sendejo, "Face of God," 2. Sendejo coins "*mujerista* ethnography" in this same dissertation.
11. Massey, *For Space*, 11.
12. Arturo Archuleta, phone interview with Karen Roybal, July 2024.
13. Sendejo, "Face of God," 83.

14. Rita Padilla-Gutiérrez, interview with Karen Roybal, Tomé, N.Mex., July 2024. In personal interviews quoted in this chapter, ellipses set within brackets indicate omission, while unbracketed ellipses indicate pauses or similar features of the discourse itself.
15. Roybal, *Archives of Dispossession.*
16. Anita Huízar-Hernández, *Forging Arizona: A History of the Peralta Land Grant and Racial Identity in the West* (Rutgers University Press, 2019), 11.
17. David G. Gutiérrez, *Walls and Mirrors: Mexican Americans, Mexican Immigrants, and the Politics of Ethnicity* (University of California Press, 1995), 13–38.
18. For additional information, see Huízar-Hernández, *Forging Arizona*; and Roybal, *Archives of Dispossession.*
19. Jacobo Baca, "Somos Indígena: Ethnic Politics and Land Tenure in New Mexico, 1694–1965" (PhD diss., University of New Mexico, 2015), 5. Geographer David Correia further explains that these grants were used to "guard valuable mining regions south of Santa Fe from powerful Indian nations." David Correia, *Properties of Violence: Law and Land Grant Struggle in Northern New Mexico* (University of Georgia Press, 2013), 1.
20. María E. Montoya, *Translating Property: The Maxwell Land Grant and the Conflict over Land in the American West, 1840–1900* (University of Kansas Press, 2005), 163.
21. See Brian DeLay, *War of a Thousand Deserts: Indian Raids and the U.S.-Mexican War* (Yale University Press, 2008), for a detailed discussion of the impacts of modifications to Article 11 of the Treaty of Guadalupe Hidalgo on U.S.-Mexican relations.
22. Brian DeLay, "Forgotten Foes," *Berkeley Review of Latin American Studies*, Fall 2010, 19.
23. See Correia, *Properties of Violence*, for a full discussion of Tijerina and the Tierra Amarilla courthouse raid.
24. Robin Wall Kimmerer, "The Honorable Harvest: Indigenous Knowledge for Sustainability," Timothy C. Linnemann Memorial Lecture on the Environment, Colorado College, Colorado Springs, Colo., November 30, 2022; Robin Wall Kimmerer, *Braiding Sweetgrass: Indigenous Wisdom, Scientific Knowledge, and the Teachings of Plants* (Milkweed Editions, 2013).
25. Eve Tuck and K. Wayne Yang, "Decolonization Is Not a Metaphor," *Decolonization: Indigeneity, Education and Society* 1, no. 1 (2012): 3.
26. Gregory Cajete, *Native Science: Natural Laws of Interdependence* (Clear Light Publishers, 2000), 185. Anthropologist Alfonso Ortiz describes the sacredness of the land, specifically the four mountains "understood by the Tewa to be endowed with sacredness in several ways. First, a lake or pond is associated with each, and within this body of water live the 'Dry Food Who Never Did Become,' of the appropriate directional color." Alfonso Ortiz, *The Tewa World: Space, Time, Being and Becoming in a Pueblo Society* (University of Chicago Press,

1969), 19. The significance of land and water intimately connects land-based peoples culturally and epistemologically.

27. Brian Burkhart, *Indigenizing Philosophy Through the Land: A Trickster Methodology for Decolonizing Environmental Ethics and Indigenous Futures* (Michigan State University Press, 2019), 191.
28. Goeman, *Mark My Words*, 11.
29. Goeman, 12.
30. For in-depth historical studies about colonization in New Mexico and Colorado, see James Brooks, *Captives and Cousins: Slavery, Kinship, and Community in the Southwest Borderlands* (University of North Carolina Press, 2002); Jared M. Beeton, Charles Nicholas Saenz, and Benjamin James Waddell, eds., *The Geology, Ecology, and Human History of the San Luis Valley* (University of Colorado Press, 2020); Laura E. Gómez, *Manifest Destinies: The Making of the Mexican American Race* (New York University Press, 2007); Virginia Sánchez, *Pleas and Petitions: Hispano Culture and Legislative Conflict in Territorial Colorado* (University of Colorado Press, 2020); Moises Gonzales and Enrique R. Lamadrid, eds., *Nación Genízara: Ethnogenesis, Place, and Identity in New Mexico* (University of New Mexico Press, 2019); Baca, "Somos Indígena"; the digital archive project Native Bound, Unbound: Archive of Indigenous Slavery, founded by Dr. Estevan Rael-Gálvez, https://nativeboundunbound.org/; and the Fort Garland Museum and Cultural Center's myriad well-thought exhibits focused on the complex history of the region.
31. Goeman, *Mark My Words*, 28.
32. Archuleta, phone interview (see note 12).
33. Gonzales and Lamadrid, *Nación Genízara*, 2. Estevan Rael-Gálvez explains that the word *genízaro* "originated in the fourteenth century as a marker given to captives, evolving over time into a distinct identity," and that in New Mexico it was used "as a euphemism for slavery." Estevan Rael-Gálvez, "*Recordando el Futuro* / Remembering the Future: Mal-criados, Memory, and Memorials," in Gonzales and Lamadrid, *Nación Genízara*, xvi and xvii. Lamadrid and Gonzales state, "The term *Genízaro*, 'janissary,' emerged as an ethnonym designating a sizable sector of the indigenous population, whose descendants are still present in the region," and, "Genízaros were an ethnic assemblage of individuals and communities of Native peoples of mixed origins, mostly Apache, Navajo, Ute, Paiute, Kiowa, Comanche, and Pawnee." Gonzales and Lamadrid, *Nación Genízara*, 1.
34. "History of Tomé Land Grant," Town of Tomé Land Grant (website), accessed July 2, 2018, https://www.townoftomelandgrant.com/history.
35. "History of Tomé Land Grant."
36. Andrea Padilla, interview with Karen Roybal, Tomé, N.Mex., June 2018.
37. Padilla, interview, June 2018.
38. Andrea Padilla, interview with Karen Roybal, Tomé, N.Mex., July 2024.
39. Rita Padilla-Gutiérrez, interview with Karen Roybal, Tomé, N.Mex., July 2024.

40. Padilla, interview, June 2018.
41. Rita Padilla-Gutiérrez, interview with Karen Roybal, Tomé, N.Mex., June 2018.
42. Kimmerer, "Honorable Harvest."
43. Padilla-Gutiérrez, interview, June 2018.
44. Montoya, *Translating Property*, 37.
45. Padilla, interview, July 2024.
46. Padilla-Gutiérrez, interview, July 2024.
47. Padilla-Gutiérrez, interview, June 2018.
48. Kimmerer, "Honorable Harvest."
49. Regina Lopez-Whiteskunk, "Ute Ethnobotany and Land Stewardship," talk at the Ute Indian Museum, Montrose, Colo., July 10, 2022, video, 53:20, posted on August 29, 2022, by Colorado History, https://www.youtube.com/watch?v=t5DD9rXgyy4. Lopez-Whiteskunk is a Southern Ute activist and cross-culture program manager at Montezuma Land Conservancy.
50. Goeman, *Mark My Words*, 29.
51. For more information on the community center, see https://www.townoftomelandgrant.com/. Padilla, interview, July 2024.
52. Padilla-Gutiérrez, interview, June 2018.
53. hooks, *Belonging*, 8.
54. Sendejo, "Face of God," 19.
55. Alfonso Ortiz, "The Pueblo Restoration of 1680," in *Po'pay: Leader of the First American Revolution*, ed. Joe S. Sando and Herman Agoyo (Clear Light Publishing, 2005), 3.
56. Padilla, interview, July 2024.
57. Ortiz, "Pueblo Restoration."
58. Esther García, interview with Karen Roybal, Questa, N.Mex., June 2018.
59. García, interview, June 2018.
60. Karl Marx, *Capital: A Critique of Political Economy*, vol. 1, bk. 1, *The Process of Production of Capital* (1867; repr., Progress Publishers, 1887), 419, 437, 511, 513, 539.
61. President Barack Obama proclaimed this land a national monument on March 25, 2013, under the provisions of the Antiquities Act.
62. García, interview, June 2018.
63. "S.667–112th Congress (2011–2012): Río Grande del Norte National Conservation Area Establishment Act," Congress.gov, January 13, 2012, https://www.congress.gov/bill/112th-congress/senate-bill/667. For more information on the bill and national monument designation, see the press release by Senator Martin Heinrich, "Signed! Río Grande del Norte Now a National Monument," Martin Heinrich: U.S. Senator for New Mexico (website), March 25, 2013, https://www.heinrich.senate.gov/newsroom/press-releases/signed-rio-grande-del-norte-now-a-national-monument. See also: *Current Public Lands and Forests Bills: Hearing Before the Subcommittee on Public Lands and Forests of the Committee on Energy and Natural Resources, United States Senate*, 112th

Cong. 22 (May 18, 2011); and *Rio Grande del Norte National Conservation Area Establishment Act*, 22. S.Hrg. 112–39 (May 18, 2011).

64. García, interview, June 2018.
65. Goeman, *Mark My Words*, 5; Kimmerer, "Honorable Harvest."
66. García, interview, June 2018.
67. García, interview, June 2018.
68. Carrie Leven, "Esther García, Mayor of Questa," Remarkable Women of Taos, Profiles: Business, Taos.org, January 2012, https://womenoftaos.org/women/profiles-businesswomen?/item/97/Esther-Garcia-Mayor-of-Questa.
69. García, interview, June 2018.
70. hooks, *Belonging*, 35–36.
71. Estevan Rael-Gálvez, "Independence Day—Imagining the Nation, in Questa, New Mexico," Creative Strategies 360 (website), July 4, 2018, https://www.creativestrategies360.com/post/independence-day-imagining-the-nation-in-questa-new-mexico.
72. Ernie Atencio, "New Mexico Wild Presents the Inaugural Esther Garcia Conservation Champion Award to John Olivas," New Mexico Wild (website), June 24, 2023, https://www.nmwild.org/2023/06/24/new-mexico-wild-presents-the-inaugural-esther-garcia-conservation-champion-award-to-john-olivas/. Atencio also stated during a phone interview that Esther "understood the dynamics, she, 'You know you want the local community to support this stuff? You need to acknowledge our history and the kinds of conservation that we care about.'" Ernie Atencio, phone interview with Karen Roybal, August 20, 2024.
73. Mark Allison, as quoted in Atencio, "New Mexico Wild Presents."
74. Rael-Gálvez, "Independence Day."
75. Goeman, *Mark My Words*, 33.
76. hooks, *Belonging*, 38–39.
77. Tuck and Yang, "Decolonization," 5.
78. Shirley Romero Otero, interview with Karen Roybal, San Luis, Colo., June 2018.
79. Romero Otero, interview, June 2018.
80. Shirley Romero Otero, phone interview with Karen Roybal, July 2024.
81. hooks, *Belonging*, 40.
82. Romero Otero, interview, June 2018.
83. Montoya, *Translating Property*, 212.
84. The original case is *Espinoza v. Taylor*. See Ricardo Simmonds, "Sangre de Cristo Land Grant," *Colorado Encyclopedia*, last modified October 18, 2022, https://coloradoencyclopedia.org/article/sangre-de-cristo-land-grant; and Montoya, *Translating Property*, 209–16.
85. "The Land Rights Council is a non-profit organization located in San Luis, Colorado, dedicated to preserve the rights of the area's citizens to have access to La Sierra. The council is also striving to improve the relationship between the citizens and the owners of the mountain. The organization works hard to

protect, honor, and expand the rights to include other activities." "About," Land Rights Council (website), 2023, https://www.lrcsanluis.org/about.

86. Romero Otero, interview, June 2018.
87. Romero Otero, interview, June 2018.
88. Romero Otero, interview, June 2018.
89. Kimmerer, *Braiding Sweetgrass*, 195.
90. Ortiz, "Pueblo Restoration," 2.
91. Montoya, *Translating Property*, 209.
92. For more information on the Move Mountains Project, see http://www.movemountainsprojects.org/.
93. Romero Otero, interview, June 2018.
94. Romero Otero, interview, June 2018.
95. Romero Otero, interview, June 2018.
96. Romero Otero, interview, June 2018.
97. Sendejo, "Face of God," 250.
98. Romero Otero, interview, June 2018.
99. Romero Otero, interview, June 2018.
100. Romero Otero, interview, June 2018.
101. Romero Otero, interview, June 2018.
102. Romero Otero, interview, June 2018.
103. Padilla, interview, July 2024.
104. Sendejo, "Face of God," 251–52; italics in original.
105. Romero Otero, interview, June 2018.
106. Goeman, *Mark My Words*.
107. Tuck and Yang, "Decolonization," 36.

Bibliography

Archuleta, Arturo. Phone interview with Karen Roybal. July 2024.

Atencio, Ernie. Phone interview with Karen Roybal. August 20, 2024.

Baca, Jacobo. "Somos Indígena: Ethnic Politics and Land Tenure in New Mexico, 1694–1965." PhD dissertation, University of New Mexico, 2015.

Beeton, Jared M., Charles Nicholas Saenz, and Benjamin James Waddell, eds. *The Geology, Ecology, and Human History of the San Luis Valley*. University of Colorado Press, 2020.

Brooks, James. *Captives and Cousins: Slavery, Kinship, and Community in the Southwest Borderlands*. University of North Carolina Press, 2002.

Burkhart, Brian. *Indigenizing Philosophy Through the Land: A Trickster Methodology for Decolonizing Environmental Ethics and Indigenous Futures*. Michigan State University Press, 2019.

Cajete, Gregory. *Native Science: Natural Laws of Interdependence*. Clear Light Publishers, 2000.

Correia, David. *Properties of Violence: Law and Land Grant Struggle in Northern New Mexico*. University of Georgia Press, 2013.

DeLay, Brian. "Forgotten Foes." *Berkeley Review of Latin American Studies*, Fall 2010, 14–19.

DeLay, Brian. *War of a Thousand Deserts: Indian Raids and the U.S.-Mexican War*. Yale University Press, 2008.

García, Esther. Interview with Karen Roybal. Questa, N.Mex., June 2018.

Goeman, Mishuana R. *Mark My Words: Native Women Mapping Our Nations*. University of Minnesota Press, 2013.

Goeman, Mishuana R. "Notes Toward a Native Feminism's Spatial Practice." *Wicazo Sa Review* 24, no. 2 (2009): 169–87.

Gómez, Laura E. *Manifest Destinies: The Making of the Mexican American Race*. New York University Press, 2007.

Gonzales, Moises, and Enrique R. Lamadrid, eds. *Nación Genízara: Ethnogenesis, Place, and Identity in New Mexico*. University of New Mexico Press, 2019.

Gutiérrez, David G. *Walls and Mirrors: Mexican Americans, Mexican Immigrants, and the Politics of Ethnicity*. University of California Press, 1995.

hooks, bell. *Belonging: A Culture of Place*. Routledge, 2009.

Huízar-Hernández, Anita. *Forging Arizona: A History of the Peralta Land Grant and Racial Identity in the West*. Rutgers University Press, 2019.

Kimmerer, Robin Wall. *Braiding Sweetgrass: Indigenous Wisdom, Scientific Knowledge, and the Teachings of Plants*. Milkweed Editions, 2013.

Kimmerer, Robin Wall. "The Honorable Harvest: Indigenous Knowledge for Sustainability." Timothy C. Linnemann Memorial Lecture on the Environment, Colorado College, Colorado Springs, Colo., November 30, 2022.

Lopez-Whiteskunk, Regina. "Ute Ethnobotany and Land Stewardship." Talk at the Ute Indian Museum, Montrose, Colo., July 10, 2022. Video, 53:20. Posted on August 29, 2022, by Colorado History. https://www.youtube.com/watch?v=t5DD9rXgyy4.

Marx, Karl. *Capital: A Critique of Political Economy*. Vol. 1, book 1, *The Process of Production of Capital*. Progress Publishers, 1909. Originally published in 1887.

Massey, Doreen. *For Space*. Sage Publications, 2005.

Montoya, María E. *Translating Property: The Maxwell Land Grant and the Conflict over Land in the American West, 1840–1900*. University of Kansas Press, 2005.

Ortiz, Alfonso. "The Pueblo Restoration of 1680." In *Po'pay: Leader of the First American Revolution*, edited by Joe S. Sando and Herman Agoyo, 2–4. Clear Light Publishing, 2005.

Ortiz, Alfonso. *The Tewa World: Space, Time, Being and Becoming in a Pueblo Society*. University of Chicago Press, 1969.

Padilla, Andrea. Interview with Karen Roybal. Tomé, N.Mex., June 2018.

Padilla, Andrea. Interview with Karen Roybal. Tomé, N.Mex., July 2024.

Padilla-Gutiérrez, Rita. Interview with Karen Roybal. Tomé, N.Mex., June 2018.

Padilla-Gutiérrez, Rita. Interview with Karen Roybal. Tomé, N.Mex., July 2024.

Rael-Gálvez, Estevan. "*Recordando el Futuro* / Remembering the Future: Mal-criados, Memory, and Memorials." In Gonzales and Lamadrid, *Nación Genízara*, xv–xxiii.

Romero Otero, Shirley. Interview with Karen Roybal. San Luis, Colo., June 2018.

Romero Otero, Shirley. Phone interview with Karen Roybal. July 2024.

Roybal, Karen. *Archives of Dispossession: Recovering the Testimonios of Mexican American Herederas, 1848–1960*. University of North Carolina Press, 2017.

Sánchez, Virginia. *Pleas and Petitions: Hispano Culture and Legislative Conflict in Territorial Colorado*. University of Colorado Press, 2020.

Sendejo, Brenda. "'The Face of God Has Changed': Tejana Cultural Production and the Politics of Spirituality in the Borderlands." PhD dissertation, University of Texas at Austin, 2010.

Tuck, Eve, and K. Wayne Yang. "Decolonization Is Not a Metaphor." *Decolonization: Indigeneity, Education and Society* 1, no. 1 (2012): 1–40.

CHAPTER 2

Digital Reminiscing

Telles Mujeres on "Arizona Roots y Reuniones" in the Time of COVID-19

ANDREA TOVAR

> *Our reunions always started with a prayer. In the early days, my granny would ask a Catholic priest to lead the prayer at the family shrine. As the years went by, family members took over this reunion responsibility.*
>
> —SHIRLEY GASTELUM CREW, REMINISCING ABOUT HER NANA JUANA TELLES, MARCH 5, 2021

Soy de una familia grande. I situate myself as an Arizona Chicana, drawing from my father's herencia in South Texas and my mother's Arizonan and Nuevomexicana heritage. For as long as I can remember, we've shared stories. Oral historian and ethnographer Patricia Preciado Martin implores us to remember our stories. She reminds us that "the story of our beautiful and resilient heritage will never be silenced . . . as long as we remember to run our fingers through the nourishing and nurturing soil of our history and sing the names and stories of our *antepasados*, ancestors, to the generation to come as if they were a litany."[1] The initial years of COVID-19 highlighted the need for story, awakening the familiar spirit of kinship and arousing for my own family, the Telles family, our understanding of our rooted past. To that end, we planned a much-anticipated family reunion. Conocimiento and evocations of "coming home" ensued as many of the mujeres in our family found their way onto social media as a means to maintain communication across borders and generations while sharing their memorias about their common frontera kinship.[2] This chapter examines our family's freighting, mining, stagecoaching, and ranching story through the presentation of digital testimonios, oral

FIGURE 2.1 Telles family reunion, Elgin, Arizona, ca. 1928. Olivia Telles Flores collection.

history, family photos, newspaper clippings, and historic state and territorial documents that reveal the hushed and the hidden.[3] According to Cindy O. Fierros and Dolores Delgado Bernal, "There is an understanding that *pláticas* as methodology have the potential to get what is missing, passed over, or sometimes avoided." Additionally, pláticas "draw on life experiences and provide a potential space for healing."[4] Informal pláticas and testimonios are valuable in their telling and retelling as they refresh our memories and our hope.

Significant gaps exist in the telling of Arizona's history from late territorial days to the present (1872–today) with regard to acknowledging the socioeconomic presence and the enduring and exceptional cultural contributions of the Southwest's Indo-Hispano/a population. An interdisciplinary sampling of scholars influenced this chapter's analysis of the Telles family pláticas and testimonios gathered through digital means and intended as healing herstory/history to aid in filling those historical gaps. Querencia for the beloved land, as described by Martin and further conceptualized by scholars Vanessa Fonseca-Chávez, Levi Romero, and Spencer R. Herrera in their edited volume of the same name, is an ofrenda to the landscape and the languages of the frontera.[5]

We understand literary scholar Karen R. Roybal when she proclaims, "The lack of recordings [archives] of women's voices is indicative of . . . the absence of women's *influence on* and *stories about* patriarchy, patrimony, property, and gender."[6] Scholar Emma Pérez declares that "women have been relegated to silences. . . . The gendered history that many women of color contemplated, however, claimed that one could not study women of color without reflecting upon the intersections of race and class with gender." She reminds us that a gendered history "[has] negated half its population."[7] Additionally, Alessandro Portelli's words resonate when we engage in interpreting women's acts in the world: "to tell a story is to take arms against the threat of time, to resist time, or

FIGURE 2.2 Juana Hughes Telles with daughter Maria Lydia (Lila) in her arms, and her other daughters Rufina (Ruth) on the left, Anita in front of Ruth, Margaret at center in the chair, and Dora to the right. Tombstone, Arizona, ca. 1916. Olivia Telles Flores collection.

to harness time."[8] In other words, a veiled presence must find her way into (hi)stories and backstories, thereby centering the feminine while challenging hegemonic representation. This is what the Telles mujeres have done as they've mapped their genealogies, their herencia, across centuries in what is now the U.S. Southwest. What was initially presented in the initial phase of COVID-19 as an Adobe Spark Glideshow photo-essay of forty-plus digital photographs evolved into the testimonios and intergenerational pláticas shared with me by—and co-constructed by me with—ten of the Telles women who met or were reintroduced in our family Facebook group.

Roybal, much like Emma Pérez, further implores us to recover and (en)gender the archives. Roybal describes testimonio as "historical narratives," or memories rooted in "collective suffering, politicized struggle, in communal survival."[9] These testimonios of recovery and resilience are valuable in their telling and retelling, refreshing the mujeres' memories and their hope for all human beings, thus shifting their sense of longing to belonging. Historian Erika Pérez holds mujeres to be "intermediaries and transmitters of cultural knowledge to their children, offering continuity and comfort in moments of dislocation."[10] As community conduits, they create stability and a sense of individual security. In line with these concepts, Indo-Hispana women have confronted hegemonic masculine representation in the transmission of cultura.[11]

The effort to recover Arizona's stories and tell its untold narratives is among the relevant themes that Anita Huízar-Hernández addresses in her work; she affirms that "the people who share their stories also bear witness to a linguistic and cultural resilience that defies characterization of the Arizona-Sonora border as an impenetrable line of separation."[12] Multiethnic populations flowed freely back and forth across the U.S.-Mexican border in the years following the Treaty of Guadalupe Hidalgo of 1848. The acquisition of Arizona and New Mexico's southern lands through the Gadsden Purchase in 1853 furthered the cross-border economic trade and international familial relationships that existed during the initial expansion of the United States into México's northern region. The ancestors of the Telles family would migrate south from the New Mexico Territory into northern México, and re-cross/immigrate back into the United States in 1875, in what had by then become the highly racialized and contested Arizona Territory.

Digital Spaces of Storytelling

The Facebook page that gave voice to Telles family members during COVID-19 was designed initially to plan the next face-to-face Telles family reunion in southeastern Arizona in real time. The social media platform proved to be a safe place for family members to check in to engage in an intergenerational online community. For some, the (re)living of generational family trauma and the more recent loss of family members to COVID-19 while in lockdown amplified their grief, yet the connections via Facebook allowed others to rally familial support and unity. I have chosen to focus on the oral communications, digital testimonios and pláticas, digital photos, and family news articles and artifacts shared via social media, texting, and email by las mujeres, las meras meras, of the familia.[13] Roni Sabala, a great-granddaughter of Epifanio Telles I's oldest daughter, Aurelia Telles, announced via a Facebook post in the spring of 2020: "Our families are everything, so we need to keep everyone safe. The reunion is rescheduled for 2021."[14] COVID-19, however, would force the Telles reunion to be rescheduled for the fall of 2023.

Comunidad was maintained across generational and physical borders using socio-tech tools to strengthen familial ties. The eldest family member who participated in phase one of this archival project was ninety-six-year-old Olivia Telles Flores, a granddaughter of Epifanio Telles I and daughter of Pablo Telles. She expressed pride in her parents' responsible voting habits. By phone, Olivia stated that her parents, Pablo and Guadalupe Telles, "were proud Americans whose only son fought in World War II." Olivia, too, had served in the female civilian ranks. She repeatedly circled back to her father's emphasis on voting and why it was important for women to participate in civic rights.[15] Olivia's sixty-seven-year-old daughter Roseanna Telles Flores Acero, a retired state-level business analyst, recalled that her mother remembered how excited Pablo (Roseanna's grandfather) would be on election day: "My grandparents [Guadalupe Telles] and [Pablo Telles] would always make sure to go out and vote."[16] Pablo registered as a voter on August 3, 1906, in Carr Canyon in the Arizona Territory. Pablo Telles also proudly participated in his first election in the state of Arizona in 1914.[17]

The Telleses were partial to political participation. Pablo's father, Epifanio Telles I, was listed as having registered to vote on May 25, 1876.[18]

Epifanio Telles I was of Indo-Hispano/Mexican/Nuevomexicano descent. He was documented as both a rancher and a wood hauler, a naturalized citizen of Mexican descent born in San Antonio, Texas. Epifanio Telles I's father, Juan Agaton Telles, a registered business trader and freighter, owned a home in Fort Quitman, Texas, in the 1860s and a home in Silver City, New Mexico Territory, in the 1880s.[19] The Telles family had roots in the previous century in Santa Fe and Albuquerque, with relatives in El Paso, Texas, and in Mesilla, México, prior to its 1853 status as part of New Mexico Territory.

Nonetheless, the context for Arizona Territory citizens of Indo-Hispana/o-Mexican descent participating in local and territorial politics was complex and interconnected with race, status, labor, language, and gender.[20] Historian Howard R. Lamar quoted Governor Conrad Meyer Zulick as stating in 1887 that the Arizona Territory was being "peopled by a sturdy, liberal, and progressive body of citizens" who were "making social as well as industrial progress."[21] Those people included diverse familias like the Telleses, among others.

The legacy of Indo-Hispana women's contributions in Arizona Territory's move into statehood has largely been neglected. I draw upon the oral history work of Mary Rothschild and Pamela Hronek; when they speak of "the range of women's activities in Arizona, not just famous women . . . but the everyday work that 'ordinary' women did to create today's Arizona," it rings true.[22] These women survived the imperial transition from Spanish colonialism to Mexican independence, and then the early years of U.S. colonialism. The work of historian Vicki L. Ruiz sets the stage for border journeys and the gendered roles of Indo-Hispana/Mexicana women across several centuries in the U.S. Southwest as wives to soldiers, freighters, traders, ranchers, mineros, zanjeros, and farmers.[23] Oral historian Patricia Preciado Martin has shared the stories of many Hispanic southeastern Arizona families across several of her Arizona publications, some of them including Telles ancestry.[24] The Telles roots can be traced to a variety of ethnic and racial identities. Subjectively and collectively, the Telleses recognize their diverse heritage and celebrate their ancestral Indigenous and European bloodlines. Nine Telles mujeres shared their conocimiento, their understandings, as well as their facultad, their truths, with me through various digital and social-media means. These mujeres shared reunion stories, and their researched and (re)claimed genealogy, to tell of our family's commitments and covenants, adversities overcome, tragedies (re)told, patriotism (re)kindled, and faith and love restored.

Telles (Digital) Pláticas and Testimonios of Querencia

In a phone plática, Mercy Telles Baker, a retired nurse and small business owner, and the great-granddaughter of Epifanio Telles I and granddaughter of Pablo Telles, said, "Our proud mestizaje is represented in every color of gente under the Arizona sun at those juntas [gatherings]. I feel a sense of heartfelt homecoming every time I attend a family reunion in southeastern Arizona."[25] Mercy, like many in the Telles familia, has an intimate sense of place—of querencia—based in her ancestral roots. Mercy recalled the barbacoas and dozens of ways pasta salads and potato salads were prepared. She stated: "I confess, I favored my mother's potato salad with boiled eggs, tomatoes, celery, chunky onions, creamy mayonesa, a hint of ground German mustard, and lots of salty, black olivas, or olives. ¡Qué rico! My mother Isabel [Telles Bracamonte] told me that my abuelito Pablo's mother [Rufina Lange Chávez Telles] made a variation of this potato salad for her familia when he was young." Mercy also remembers photo albums shared with love and joy at each reunion. Mercy explained that "packing and showcasing your familia albums was a tradition [at the reunions]." She recalled that some of the reuniones she attended were in Tucson and others in the grasslands of Elgin, Arizona.

Mercy also remembered her mother Isabel's early childhood reunion memories in the sierras que corrieron siempre (hills that ran forever) in Patagonia, Arizona. Describing that time, Mercy said, "Those were the years that the reunions were held along the Patagonia-Sonoita Creek in the late 1910s." Isabel Telles Bracamonte had explained to Mercy, in her youth and in years to come, that the reunions were organized with querencia around the Catholic feast day of San Juan.[26] "My mother, who was the oldest of Pablo Telles's children, would drive her parents from downtown Phoenix, Arizona, to the reunions down south as early as her late teens. She looked forward to the weeks spent with her primas and primos in the Sonoran tierra and in time with other Telleses." Isabel's father,

Pablo Telles—who was the eldest of Epifanio Telles I's children—began to lose his eyesight in late childhood because of the chemicals he was exposed to while working as a water carrier and wood hauler in the copper mines in Bisbee. He labored alongside his father so that his siblings could go to school. The mining chemicals Pablo was exposed to caused him to go blind in young adulthood. His sacrifice would be recognized by his extended family for generations to follow.[27] According to historian Katherine Benton-Cohen, "Bisbee was one of the territory's largest cities. By 1910, with Bisbee's help, Arizona had surpassed Michigan and Montana in copper production, a status it has never relinquished."[28]

Mercy recounted: "Tía Carolina was the youngest of Abuelito Epifanio I's children. Epifanio's wife, Abuelita Rufina Lange Chávez Telles, was born in the New Mexico Territory. Sadly, Abuelita Rufina had contracted a respiratory infection and unexpectedly passed away shortly after giving birth to Carolina." The family resided in Bisbee, Arizona, at the time.[29] In 1902, tragically, Epifanio Telles I was shot to death over a homestead claim and water spring dispute just east of Douglas, Arizona.[30] Although he was defending his then-motherless children as well as his homestead claim, Epifanio Telles I would lose his life that day and leave his Telles children orphaned. This loss would be felt across generations of Telleses to follow and would create what historian Gloria Anzaldúa referred to as "*una herida abierta*," a spiritual and historic trauma, an open wound.[31] Tragedies and transgressions were common along the borderlands. University president, public health researcher, and economist Adela de la Torre states, "*Pláticas* are powerful spiritual and, by extension, physical healing processes because they provide the empathetic balm that heals new and old wounds."[32]

According to Mercy, "Most family members are familiar with these Telles Arizona Territory experiencias—many family members don't realize that there is a Telles Street in Tucson that was also named after a distant family relative who was among Tucson's early presidio soldiers. We have Telles descendants represented at our juntas from the earliest of [New] Spain's colonial days in what is now Arizona, New Mexico, and Tejas [Texas]. More than three hundred members attended reunions in the 1980s and in the 1990s. . . . There were a lot of family members from out of state in attendance in those years."[33]

At the spry age of ninety-six, doña Olivia Telles Flores, daughter of Pablo and Guadalupe Telles, great-granddaughter of Epifanio Telles I, and the only surviving sister of Isabel Telles Bracamonte, is the matriarch of the family. By phone, she shared memorias from the 1920s that included "horseback riding and cattle scenes." She would liken those experiencias to her favorite John Wayne movies; perhaps it was because many of John Wayne's Hollywood western movies were filmed in Elgin and Patagonia, Arizona. Olivia shared, "You know I have cousins and tías and tíos that were real cowboys and real rancheros and rancheras. You know that, don't you?"[34]

Olivia is conscious of her own generational experience. She recounted: "I grew up in the city, in downtown Phoenix. My life was different than my primas y primos en el rancho. [Yet] I always felt at home when I visited my cousins. Somos de aquí y allá [We are from here and there]. . . . My mom and oldest sister [Isabel] drove my dad everywhere when I was a little girl. He was blind so my oldest sister had to go drop out of elementary school and go work at a young age to help my parents. You know that, don't you?" Olivia was also quick to remind me that her husband served in World War II and that she was the first Telles female in civilian service in the family. She served at the McChord Field Air Force base in the state of Washington while her husband was briefly stationed with the army in Washington prior to his service in World War II. Olivia took pride in her first employment, as an early twentysomething, in one of downtown Phoenix's first department stores. She would tell many family members over the years that she was one of the first mujeres hired to serve as a sales representative as well as a Spanish-to-English translator for Spanish-speaking customers.

Olivia also expressed orgullo (pride) in her ancestry and recognized her mother, Guadalupe Telles, as a pura mestiza. Olivia reminded me that her mama "was a brave and strong woman. . . . You know that she was the oldest in her family, too, don't you?" Olivia's mother, my great-grandmother, came to America as a young child. She would listen to the news on the radio as a young woman, attuned to the happenings in both México and America. Abuelita would also sharecrop with my great-grandfather in Phoenix's West Valley and would be among the first mujeres spotted driving in downtown Phoenix. Abuelita Guadalupe was

FIGURE 2.3 Pablo and Guadalupe Telles, wedding picture. Bisbee, Arizona, 1913. Olivia Telles Flores collection.

a devout Catholic and was also among Phoenix's first Guadalupanas, devoted to the Virgen de Guadalupe and the Sacred Heart of Jesucristo at the church across from her first Phoenix home, Saint Anthony's Catholic Church in downtown Phoenix.

Extended summer reunion days for the Telles families centered around Día de San Juan. After the gatherings, Olivia distinctly remembers her tío Juan loading her dad's Chevy truck with bags of flour and beans, lard, canned goods, sugar, and iced steaks for a return to Phoenix from the Sonoita Plains, the high desert grasslands. Her tío Juan and tía Juana's generosity in her family's times of need are memorias that increased Olivia's commitment to giving to the poor in her adulthood as a lived expression of generosity. Olivia's three daughters, Roseanna, Linda, and

Olivia Henrietta, would discover their mother's querencia when learning about the treasure of family photographs she had cared for. There was also the treasure of meeting new and familiar relatives at family gatherings en el rancho. Roseanna Telles Flores Acero, Olivia Telles Flores's youngest daughter, stated by phone: "My sisters and I enjoy looking at our mother's collection of pictures because they hold a lot of our family's history. They helped us learn about who we are and to learn more about Arizona history."[35] Roseanna's conocimiento was reflected in our pláticas, our Facebook posts, and our email correspondence. She posted fotos de la familia con amor y cariño, further displaying her querencia digitally. She recognized that our online family space had evolved into a place of reclamation of our New Mexican and Arizonan heritage for younger and older Telles familia members alike.

If there were cottonwood, oak, mesquite, and mulberry trees nearby, you can bet there were Telles family members to be found enjoying a moment of respite from their work as cattlemen (and cattlewomen) in the sombra (shade) of these mammoth árboles. Juan and Juana Telles's homestead in Elgin, Arizona—an adobe house and a cattle and mule ranch—was in such a dreamy location that Anglo-American newcomers to the Southwest and to southeastern Arizona came along and offered a reasonable price to buy it.[36]

A Place of Patriotism and a Space of Worship

"She [Juana Hughes Telles] vowed that if her sons would return safely from the war, she would build a shrine to the Sacred Heart. They did, so [Juana] kept her promise."[37] At Juana's request, Juan Telles, the second-oldest son of Epifanio Telles I, began the task of building the family shrine. It was built not on his homestead but on a mountainside between Nogales and Patagonia, Arizona, on the shoulder of Highway 82. The location was chosen for its ease of access for weary roadside travelers in need of inspiration and a descanso. This historical monument was built with converging spiritual and patriotic emotions.[38] The religious monument based on the World War II deployment of Ralph Telles would be officially recognized as a state historical site by the Pimería Alta Historical Society in 1998 on San Juan's Day.[39]

The work of building the shrine was backbreaking, but Juan Telles was up to the labor-intensive task, which would require eight years of breaking stone and creating a small cave/grotto in honor of the Sacred Heart of Jesus. Juan Estevan Arellano described his own ways of expressing querencia as being with "both words and with pick and shovel, with poetry, and by planting trees."[40] Juan Telles's querencia, strengthened by personal sacrifice, and his reverence and respect for his familia and their history, translated into public religious and patriotic commitment. The safe return home of military men and women from World War II was at the center of Juan and Juana's vow to almighty God. As if cattle ranching, raising a large family of nine children, and community activities with his wife Juana were not enough, one of Juan's last actions would be building the shrine.[41] Juan and Juana Telles's son Ralph Telles would return from army service in Germany to marry Ethelyn Houston, the daughter of a retired elementary-school principal and fellow rancher near Elgin, Arizona. Their son, Richard Telles, would return years later from U.S. Army service in the Korean War. Military service as an act of duty and patriotism was an expectation of the Telles familia, as it was for other Mexican American families of southeastern Arizona.[42]

Telles family reunions always revolved around prayer, a spirit of gratitude, and food. During an extensive phone call, Shirley Gastelum Crew recalled: "Our [reunion] potlucks always had beef, cowboy beans, and arroz rojo with tomatoes as main staples. I loved making deviled eggs with paprika sprinkled on top. They were a popular choice for summer potlucks and picnics. Prima Alice Etchart made the hottest salsa in the familia in the 2000s and 2010s."[43] My plática with Shirley and her testimonio demonstrate what Roybal envisions in her contribution to this volume when she remarks on the New Mexican mujeres she interviewed about their herencia, who "continued to hold memory and place within them."[44] This would translate into courageous women who carry the past forward into the present, further enacting their agency to preserve the sacred found in sites and in the memory of mujeres.

Facebook, a Ferris Wheel, and Faith

A phone call ensued with Arizona-born Martha Stevenson Telles in spring 2021 after one of her timely Facebook reunion posts: "Mija, I'm in the middle of praying the rosary, can you call me later tonight?" she requested. So began my pláticas and memoria-building with my eighty-six-year-old prima. One of our pláticas would be via Zoom with her husband, Richard, and her daughter, Teresa Telles Farmer. Martha Stevenson Telles's mother, Petra Figueroa, was of Mexican American heritage, born in Benson, Arizona, in 1897. Petra attended grammar school through the eighth grade in Benson. Martha's father, an Anglo carpenter from Illinois, was working for the Southern Pacific Railroad Company in Arizona when he met and fell in love with Petra at her sister's Mexican home restaurant based in her casita's kitchen. Her sister operated this small restaurant for miners and railroad workers in Benson, and Petra assisted with waitressing and food preparation. Unbeknownst to Martha, two of her own sons would later work in and retire from the railroad industry.[45]

Martha continued our conversation by describing the victory garden her mother planted during World War II in support of the war effort, along with a collection of war bond stamps she would trade in decades later. She went to work in a civilian capacity at both Fort Huachuca Army Base in Sierra Vista and Davis-Monthan Air Force Base in Tucson, Arizona. She sweetly recalled, "I fell in love with Richard Telles on the top of a Ferris wheel at the annual Tombstone [Arizona] 'Helldorado' event."[46] Richard had recently come back from service in the United States Marines and returned to St. David to help his father (Epifanio Telles II, the youngest of Epifanio Telles I's three orphaned sons) purchase equipment for his ranchito. Unlike his brothers Juan and Pablo Telles, Epifanio Telles II was a company man at the Apache Powder Company for over twenty years in St. David, Arizona. "Many of the familias had family members employed in the mines or at the Apache Powder Company. When things went *BOOM!* at the Powder Company, wives showed up with buckets."[47]

Richard Telles would go on to become a city council member and then mayor of the city of Needles, California, in the 1970s. Martha and Richard Telles would jointly own and operate a gas station and a hardware store for decades in Needles. Martha actively raised a family of five and was involved in church activities while dutifully performing her co-business responsibilities. She fondly remembers Telles family reunions in Tucson and in Elgin, Arizona, with classic home-cooked dishes like frijoles de la olla, nopalitos, y sopa de fideo. Hayrides in the picturesque Sonoita Mountains during the Elgin reunions created the backdrop to the festivities. Martha added, "I wrote a poem about the Telles familia that has been read and shared at the reunions for over three decades." A feeling of querencia coalesced in Martha's story-share. Martha's daughter, Teresa Telles Farmer, recalled taking her parents to Telles reunions and finding joy in meeting up with cousins she had not seen since her teen years: "We always planned trips to Tucson, Tombstone, or Benson to visit family and see the old historical sites [during Telles reunion weekends]. We have a lot of old Arizona family in the area. Remind me to send you some of the pictures from Benson."[48] Martha and Teresa expressed their querencia in lively pláticas with me.

Homesteads, Herencia, and Hope

Eighty-seven-year-old Stella Telles Ohnersorgen—a retired state-level administrator, granddaughter of Epifanio Telles I and daughter of Epifanio Telles II—and her daughter Teresa Telles Ohnersorgen Golojuch, a banking operations analyst, recalled several family reunions they helped to plan. They fondly remember the years when colored Team Telles T-shirts represented each of Rufina and Epifanio Telles I's children's familias in attendance. The 1988 reunion in Tucson, Arizona, was a celebration at which many of the Telles family members met their great-aunt Carolina Griego, who, coincidentally, was eighty-eight that year. Carolina Telles Griego was born in 1900 and, as the youngest of Rufina and Epifanio Telles I's orphaned children, was taken from Bisbee, Arizona, and raised by extended familia in New Mexico. Stella recalls: "That was a special reunion for us. It truly was a heartfelt homecoming for Tía Carolina. She had so many stories to share with us."[49] One of Carolina's New Mexican descendants would be one of America's first Chicana PhDs in electrical and computer engineering.

Stella's querencia entwines her memories of land, the past, and her family. Teresa, Stella's daughter, stated by phone: "I have learned so much about both my Telles and Ohnersorgen heritage through the reunions, pictures that have been shared on our Facebook page about both my Telles and Ohnersorgen family history. I remember one year [of the reunions] when my son was the youngest person in attendance and my Uncle Ed [Telles], living in Costa Rica but he flew in for the reunion, he won a prize [as the oldest Telles in attendance that year]. We always have fun with the family—family feels like home."[50] Patriotism and service to America were never far away in family conversations. Stella sweetly remembered:

> Rudy [Bernal Ohnersorgen] proposed to me by mail. I was surprised to receive an engagement ring from Rudy while he was still at Tri-State College in Indiana. He had served in Korea in the Navy. Tri-State prepared him for his lifelong career at Northrop Corporation in California. As for me, I earned my undergraduate and graduate degrees in California after my children were born. I was my high school's Girl State representative [in the 1950s]. Not very many of the familia know that about me. Love of country and the importance of education are some things I carry close to my heart, and, of course, my familia.[51]

Stella's husband Rudy Bernal Ohnersorgen's great-great-grandfather, Carl Wilhelm (William/Billy) Ohnesorgen, was a German immigrant who arrived in America in 1853 from Hanover, Germany.[52] His parents lived briefly in San Antonio, Texas, then moved to Mesilla, Nuevo México. Wilhelm then traveled and moved, with an uncle and a cousin, to the Arizona Territory. According to Benson family historian Dora K. Ohnesorgen, Carl Wilhelm would marry a widow from El Pitiquito, Sonora, México, named Mrs. María Jesús Ruiz. They would have eight children of their own and raise a stepdaughter. Young William would build the first Catholic church in Benson, Arizona. His family would raise sheep and cattle in Tres Alamos alongside other distant Telles relatives in the Rincon Valley.[53] He would venture into business as well. The Ohnesorgen and [Howard C.] Walker stagecoach line ran from Tombstone to Tucson, Arizona Territory, in the 1870s, with a station located on the San Pedro River just outside of what would become Benson, Arizona. When the Southern Pacific Railroad Company displaced the stagecoach lines, William/Billy Ohnesorgen would own a livery stable, a saloon, and a bathhouse in Benson, Arizona, as alternate business ventures. He would also serve as Benson's first justice of the peace as well as a member of the Ninth Territorial Legislature in 1877.[54]

Telles roots run deep in southeastern Arizona. It was and remains a common practice among the Telles family to bring genealogical herencia to family reunions. Pages and pages of family trees and pedigree charts

FIGURE 2.4 George Benjamin (Bennie) Lowe and Maria Lydia (Lila) Telles Lowe, wedding picture, Sacred Heart Catholic Church, Nogales, Arizona, 1936. Shirley Gastelum Crew collection.

are posted on walls or posterboard and displayed for new and old reunion members alike so that they can ask clarifying questions about their ancestors. It's not a reunion—digital or otherwise—without sharing family his/herstory. Shirley Gastelum Crew, a retired U.S. customs supervisor, a previous family reunion coordinator, and one of the many Telles genealogists, recalled her antepasados con querencia:

> We have a lot of familia in Tubac [Arizona], including the Lowes. My tía Lila [María Lydia] Telles married my tío Bennie [George Benjamin Lowe] in 1935. Tío Bennie's father was one of the founding fathers of modern-day Tubac, William H. Lowe. Tía Lila and Tío Bennie would go to the Telles reunions. Their children and grandchildren have also attended Telles familia reunions. Tía Dora Telles married Reynaldo Salcido of Tubac. The Salcido adobe ranch house still stands today.[55]

According to Tubac historian Nancy Valentine, Anna Burruel, from an established Tubac familia dating back to the 1750s, married William H.

Lowe in 1902. Lowe would become Tubac's postmaster and run a mercantile company from their family home across from the historic Tubac Presidio. The presidio dates to 1752, in Spanish colonial times. The presidio is considered the oldest European settlement in the state of Arizona. A portion of the Lowe family ranch house is officially within the presidio's original boundaries, and the Lowe House continues to have historic status.[56]

Shirley recalled games and water fun during the reunions of her childhood. Shirley would become one of the primary Telles reunion coordinators during most of her adult life, an act of love for her family and her family's homeland (querencia). These traditions of herstory-building were passed on from Shirley's mother, Anita Telles Gastelum, daughter of Juana and Juan Telles, and her tía Elvira Telles Rivera, aka Boots. Shirley is among the Telleristas: the ones who pass down Telles familia his/herstory and querencia. Shirley lovingly remembered reunions from the 1960s and 1970s and the special sentiment of the gatherings in the 2000s when her cousin Carl Telles Etchart, a University of Arizona engineering graduate and by then retired electrical engineer, moved back to Elgin, to his small ranch, CJEtchart, to enjoy ranching and carpentry.

CJEtchart Ranch was not far from his grandfather Juan Telles's 1919 ranch homestead and his grandfather's second Elgin ranch. Carl and his brother Alfred "Buddy" Etchart, both retired to a life of small ranching, would host reunions in Elgin which began with the Telles familia gathering at the Telles Family Shrine/Grotto in Patagonia, Arizona. The weekend's homecoming and gathering would always begin with prayers and an opening address by a family member. Shirley recounts, "In the late 40s and into the 50s, Granny Juana [Hughes Telles] would have a Catholic priest come out to the shrine and give a blessing for the reunion to commence. There was a strong sense of belonging amongst us . . . and longing as we parted from our celebrations."

Shirley, much like her tío Luis Acuña Gastelum, would express her querencia, her love of the beloved land of her ancestors, through her active engagement in comunidad as well as her commitment to relatives in planning and organizing family reunions. Shirley remains one of the most knowledgeable in the Telles family about our his/herstory in the American Southwest, in territorial Arizona, and in Arizona's early days as a state. In her tío Luis Acuña Gastelum's *Journal of Arizona History* article titled "Memories of My Youth in Tubac: From the Old Homestead to Adulthood," he dedicated these special words to her: "To Niece Shirley, so that you will have a documented record of your paternal roots, Love, Uncle Luis."[57] To a family whose ancestors were orphaned and struggled for survival, roots, records, and reunions speak of security and belonging. Shirley's keen intellect plays out in Telles family reunions and in her pláticas de la familia. Shirley remembered her granddad Santiago Gastelum and his strong cowboy spirit: "Granddad roped, raced, and trained horses his whole life." She shared:

> He was 81 years old and still ropin'. He would team up with my dad [Jim] and my Tío Al in rodeo competitions. . . . He was in his boots asleep the night he passed. Granddad was planning on participating in a rodeo competition that morning. He was a cowboy, rancher, and a member of the [Professional] Rodeo Cowboys Association. It was called something else at the time but that's what it's called now.

Santiago would serve as a deputy sheriff under Santa Cruz County sheriff Jay Lowe. He was also inducted into the Santa Cruz Cowboy Hall of Fame.[58] Her uncle Steven Gastelum would continue their family tradition of researching their Southwestern heritage in Tubac as the director of the Rio Rico Historical Society.[59] "The single *l* vs double *ll* in Gastelum is another story in itself," said Shirley.

The conocimiento of memorias del pasado serves as a reminder of who we are and where we have been.[60] By phone, Heather Telles Everson, a former Arizona rodeo queen and public education teacher, fondly recalled how her cousin Shirley would ask for her school pictures to add to the family's photo albums for forthcoming reunions. Heather explained: "It was a joy to see my pictures in her albums at reunions. Our history and service both in Arizona and outside of the state is something to take pride in: our military service, national park service, national security, engineers, JDs, PhDs [and one EdD], educators, coaches, and medical, educational, and civic administrators along with a grant writer across city, state, and national public services as well as small business owners, nurses, a pharmacist, a physical therapist, clergymen, lawyers, and two medical doctors—all doing great things." Heather also recollected, "Seeing the [online/digital] pictures of our family and at our [reunion] potlucks reminded me of how diverse we are and how our family has grown over time."[61] Unbeknownst to Heather, she is being groomed as a next-generation reunion assistant coordinator, and eventually a reunion coordinator.

Heather's grandfather Alfred Telles, of the Rex Allen Museum and Willcox Cowboy Hall of Fame, married Carolyn Stearns in 1944. Carolyn was the niece of a prominent Sonoita rancher originally from London, England. Alfred was a cattleman on the Stearns Rose Tree Ranch when he met and fell in love with Carolyn. Alfred and Carolyn would later own the VJ Ranch, the Double U Ranch, the Box Bar Ranch, the Bayo Ranch, and the X Triangle Ranch.[62] Heather added: "Granddad Alfred was also a rodeo cowboy in his youth. I recently learned this through our Facebook reunion page. I also learned that Great-Uncle Octavio 'Willy' Telles Celaya was a bronc and bull rider after he returned from his service in the Navy." Heather's herencia and querencia are conocimientos that she saddles with an understanding of the complexities and celebrations of her borderland knowings. Heather centered her heritage and her knowings as "reclamation sites" through intergenerational pláticas, as described by interdisciplinary scholar Lillian Gorman.[63] Gorman's most recent research on the recovery of "reclamation sites," although situated in an Arizona university setting, ought to be an archival priority of Chicana/o/x/e, Latina/o/x/e, and Hispanic his/herstoriography and his/herstory development.

Conclusion

Memories can inform, inspire, and heal—if we engage them. "Without stories, we would not know when it is time to plant or harvest, how to bring life into this world, or even how to fall in love, fall out of love, and then forgive and make up. Stories provide us a means for how to relate our experiences and share our memories. . . . [We do this because] we know that many times, our stories are not told in the history books or in the classroom."[64] The Telles women spoke about common herencia, their beloved querencia, and the spicy power of kicky reunion potlucks. Although not one of these mujeres currently lives on their ancestral tierra sagrada, they carry it in their cherished words and in memorias that cannot be silenced. They tell the untold borderlands narrative of southeastern Arizona. Their mestiza voices carry their conocimiento, their knowledge of who they are and how they have been able to further educate and empower generaciones to follow.

Notes

1. Patricia Preciado Martin, *Beloved Land: An Oral History of Mexican Americans in Southern Arizona*, photographs by José Galvez (University of Arizona, 2004), xxiii.
2. Conocimiento is a seven-stage spiritual journey toward healing life and generational wounds. Anzaldúa's epistemology is based on reflective self-knowledge and practices of acknowledging and affirming her mestiza heritage and its borderlands knowledge. Conocimiento is key to understanding her auto-historia-teoría. See Gloria Anzaldúa and AnaLouise Keating, eds., *This Bridge We Call Home: Radical Visions for Transformation* (Routledge, 2002).
3. Dolores Delgado Bernal, Rebecca Burciaga, and Judith Flores Carmona acknowledge that testimonios can be utilized both in and out of educational settings to heal the mind, body, and spirit. Testimonios take many forms: written, oral, and digital, to name a few. As both product and process, testimonios connect generations and lived experiences, and are a methodological "data" tool. Furthermore, they are used to expose truth/facultad and inequities while eliciting positive social change through the conocimiento that emerges. See Dolores Delgado Bernal, Rebecca Burciaga, and Judith Flores Carmona, "Chicana/Latina Testimonios: Mapping the Methodological, Pedagogical, and Political," *Equity and Excellence in Education* 45, no. 3 (2012): 363–72.
4. Cindy O. Fierros and Dolores Delgado Bernal, "Vamos a Platicar: Contours of Pláticas as Chicana/Latina Feminist Methodology," *Chicana/Latina Studies* 15, no. 2 (Spring 2016): 115.
5. Martin, introduction to *Beloved Land*, xx–xxiii; Patricia Preciado Martin, *Images and Conversations: Mexican Americans Recall a Southwestern Past*, rev. ed., photographs by Louis Carlos Bernal (University of Arizona Press, 1996); Vanessa Fonseca-Chávez, Levi Romero, and Spencer R. Herrera, eds., *Querencia: Reflections on the New Mexico Homeland* (University of New Mexico Press, 2020); and Juan Estevan Arellano, *Enduring Acequias: Wisdom of the Land, Knowledge of the Water* (University of New Mexico Press, 2014), 5–6.
6. Karen R. Roybal, *Archives of Dispossession: Recovering the Testimonios of Mexican American Herederas, 1848–1960* (University of North Carolina Press, 2017), 3.
7. Emma Pérez, *The Decolonial Imaginary: Writing Chicanas into History* (Indiana University Press, 1999), 22.
8. Alessandro Portelli, *The Death of Luigi Trastulli and Other Stories: Form and Meaning in Oral History* (State University of New York Press, 1991), 59.

9. Roybal, *Archives of Dispossession*, 36.
10. Erika Pérez, *Colonial Intimacies: Interethnic Kinship, Sexuality and Marriage in Southern California, 1769–1885* (University of Oklahoma Press, 2018), 8, Kindle.
11. Sarah Deutsch, *No Separate Refuge: Culture, Class, and Gender on an Anglo-Hispanic Frontier in the American Southwest, 1880–1940* (Oxford University Press, 1987), 9–11.
12. Anita Huízar-Hernández, "Between Place and Plot: Reimagining the Story of Arizona," *Journal of Arizona History* 63, no. 3 (Autumn 2022): 274.
13. Christine Marin, "Oral History Guide" (unpublished document used for classroom workshops, 2012), with modifications due to COVID-19, was used to inform the protocol for informal pláticas with the Telles mujeres.
14. Roni Sabala, "Reunion Re-scheduled," Facebook, April 27, 2020.
15. Olivia Telles Flores, phone interview by Andrea Tovar, February 18, 2021.
16. Roseanna Telles Flores Acero, phone interview by Andrea Tovar, March 6, 2021.
17. Ancestry.com, *Arizona, U.S., Voter Registrations, 1866–1955*, Carr Canyon, Cochise County, Arizona Territory, Precinct No. 1, p. 247. Carr Canyon is located between Sierra Vista and Hereford, Arizona.
18. Ancestry.com, *Arizona, U.S., Voter Registrations, 1866–1955*, Pima County, Arizona Territory, Precinct No. 9, p. 171.
19. For a description of freighters as business traders during the early to middle territorial days, see Thomas E. Sheridan, "The Freighters and the Railroads," in *Arizona: A History*, rev. ed. (University of Arizona Press, 2012), 111–13. Although this analysis is specific to the southeastern Arizona Territory, its history parallels that of its Southwestern sister, the New Mexico Territory.
20. For elaboration on the intersectionality of race, status, labor, language, and gender, see Flannery A. Burke, *A Land Apart: The Southwest and the Nation in the Twentieth Century* (University of Arizona Press, 2017), 34–43; Howard Roberts Lamar, "Arizona: Politics and Progress, 1877–1900," in *The Far Southwest, 1846–1912: A Territorial History*, rev. ed. (University of New Mexico Press, 2000), 399–418; and Katherine Benton-Cohen, "Common Purposes, Worlds Apart: Mexican-American, Mormon, and Midwestern Women Homesteaders in Cochise County, Arizona," *Western Historical Quarterly* 36 (Winter 2005): 428–52, esp. 435–38.
21. Lamar, *Far Southwest*, 418.
22. Mary Logan Rothschild and Pamela Claire Hronek, introduction to *Doing What the Day Brought: An Oral History of Arizona Women* (University of Arizona Press, 1992), xxvii.
23. Vicki L. Ruiz, *From Out of the Shadows: Mexican Women in Twentieth-Century America*, 10th anniversary ed. (Oxford University Press, 2008), 4. See also Katherine Benton-Cohen, "A Shared World in Tres Alamos," in *Borderline Americans: Racial Division and Labor War in the Arizona Borderlands* (Harvard University Press), 18–47, esp. 35–41.

24. Martin, author of *Beloved Land, Images and Conversations*, and *Songs My Mother Sang to Me*, documented the oral histories of many Hispanic southeastern Arizona families across several of her University of Arizona Press publications. The Telles women were married into the following families who feature in Martin's oral history analysis: the Acuñas, Bernals, Bracamontes, Burruels, Bustamontes, Carillos, Celayas, Casanegas, Cotas, Felixes, Figueroas, Flores, Gallegos, Gastel(l)ums, Griegos, Lujans, Madrids, Martinezes, Ochoas, Ortizes, Oteros, Sabalas, Riveras, Robleses, Ruízes, Salazars, Salcidos, Sabalas, and Verdugos.
25. Mercy Telles Bracamonte Baker, phone interview by Andrea Tovar, February 12, 2021. All material and quotes attributed to Mercy in the following four paragraphs come from this same interview. In all personal interviews and pláticas in this chapter, ellipses indicate omission.
26. For more on the Catholic feast day of Día de San Juan, see Johanna Eubank, "El Día de San Juan Fiesta," Tucson.com, June 24, 2022, video, https://tucson.com/news/local/watch-now-el-d-a-de-san-juan-fiesta/video_94fd3f35-9831-5a32-bcbf-274ea8e09926.html.
27. Baker, phone interview.
28. Benton-Cohen, *Borderline Americans*, 12.
29. U.S. Census Bureau, *Twelfth Census of the United States* (1900), Bisbee, Cochise County, Arizona Territory, Enumeration District 7 T623, 1854, roll 78 (Ehaine Delles [Epifanio Telles]).
30. "American Shoots a Mexican in a Dispute over a Spring," *Arizona Republican*, May 19, 1902, p. 8, https://www.newspapers.com/image/119196649/?terms=epifanio%20telles&match=1. Epifanio Telles's six children would be instantly orphaned, and five of them would be sent to live with their uncle Román Telles on his farm in Hereford, Arizona. The homestead's value rested in its potential farmland and proximity to mining opportunities. Epifanio's land claim had been filed in Tucson, Arizona, a month before his death.
31. Gloria Anzaldúa, *Borderlands / La Frontera: The New Mestiza*, 4th ed., 25th anniversary ed. (Aunt Lute Books, 2012), 3.
32. Adela de la Torre, "Countering the Pain That Never Heals: Pláticas That Mend the Soul," in *Speaking from the Body: Latinas on Health and Culture*, ed. Angie Chabram-Dernersesian and Adela de la Torre (University of Arizona Press, 2008), 44–45, Kindle.
33. For more early Hispanic and U.S. colonial history that mentions the Telles family, see James E. Officer, "Myth and Reality in the Upper Pimería," in *Hispanic Arizona, 1536–1856* (University of Arizona Press, 1987), 1–24 (esp. 14–15); Douglas J. Preston and José Antonio Esquibel, *The Royal Road: El Camino Real from Mexico City to Santa Fe*, photographs by Cristine Preston (University of New Mexico Press, 1998), 147–50; "Historic Landmarks," Downtown Tucson Partnership (website), accessed January 21, 2023, https://downtowntucson.org/explore/historic-landmarks; and Tucson Presidio Museum (website), accessed January 21, 2023, https://tucsonpresidio.com/.

34. Olivia Telles Flores, phone interview by Andrea Tovar, February 18, 2021. All material and quotes attributed to Olivia in the next three paragraphs come from this same interview. Three Hollywood movies starring John Wayne (Marion Robert Morrison) were filmed in Elgin, Arizona, in the 1930s and 1940s. Mark Nothaft, "Here's Why John Wayne Loved Arizona and Adopted It as His Own," *Arizona Republic* (Phoenix), updated November 8, 2017, https://www.azcentral.com/story/news/local/arizona-history/2017/11/01/heres-why-john-wayne-loved-arizona-and-adopted-his-own/808273001/.
35. Roseanna Telles Flores Acero, phone interview by Andrea Tovar, March 6, 2021.
36. The circa-1919 property is currently in the care of the Appleton-Whittell Research Ranch sanctuary, managed by the Audubon Society. Carl E. Bock and Jane H. Bock, *The View from Bald Hill: Thirty Years in an Arizona Grassland* (University of California Press, 2000), 6. For more about the Appleton-Whittell Ranch and the Telles Tank natural water source, see WestLand Resources, *Ecological Overview: Appleton Ranch Parcel, Santa Cruz County, Arizona* (report prepared for Resolution Copper Company, 2004), https://www.resolutionmineeis.us/sites/default/files/technical-reports/westland-ecological-overview-appleton-parcel-20040526.pdf.
37. Joe Salkowski, "Thankful Mother's Shrine Noted as Historical Site," *Arizona Daily Star*, June 24, 1989, p. 6, https://www.newspapers.com/image/166790934/?terms=telles%20thankful%20mother%27s%20shrine%20the%20daily%20star&match=1.
38. Jennifer K. Ladino, *Memorials Matter: Emotion, Environment, and Public Memory at American Historical Sites* (University of Nevada Press, 2019), 45.
39. For more on San Juan's Day, see the Pimería Alta Museum website, https://pimeriaaltamuseum.org/ (accessed January 21, 2022).
40. Arellano, *Enduring Acequias*, 6.
41. Betty Barr, "Gunfight with Tellez a Battle He Didn't Want," *The Nogales International*, July 4, 2005, https://www.nogalesinternational.com/the_bulletin/news/gunfight-with-tellez-a-battle-he-didnt-want/article_f7cb8a4e-7ff6-5e04-ab63-f0bb01da7c2a.html5e04-ab63-f0bb01da7c2a.html.
42. Lora M. Key, "The Right to Represent: Mexican Americans and the World War II Draft Board in Tucson, Arizona," *Journal of Arizona History* 60, no. 2 (Summer 2019): 159–82.
43. Shirley Gastelum Crew, phone interview by Andrea Tovar, March 5, 2021.
44. See chapter 1 in this volume.
45. Martha Stevenson Telles, phone interview by Andrea Tovar, February 16, 2021. All material and quotes attributed to Martha in the next two paragraphs are from this same interview.
46. For more about the annual "Helldorado" event celebrated in Tombstone, Arizona, since 1923, see "Tombstone Helldorado, Inc.," Tombstone Chamber of Commerce (website), accessed January 21, 2022, https://tombstonechamber.com/directory/tombstone-helldorado-inc/.

47. Martha Stevenson Telles, phone interview (see note 45). Worker wage incongruencies existed throughout the mining industry in the Arizona Territory and in the state of Arizona through the 1960s. See Christine Marin and Luis F. B. Plascencia, "Mexicano Miners, Dual Wage, and the Pursuit of Wage Equality in Miami, Arizona," in *Mexican Workers and the Making of Arizona*, ed. Luis F. B. Plascencia and Gloria H. Cuádraz (University of Arizona Press, 2018), 203–25, esp. 203–4.
48. Teresa Telles Farmer, phone interview by Andrea Tovar, February 16, 2021.
49. Stella Telles Ohnersorgen, phone interview by Andrea Tovar, February 14, 2021.
50. Teresa Telles Ohnersorgen Golojuch, phone interview by Andrea Tovar, February 14, 2021.
51. S. Ohnersorgen, phone interview.
52. My family added an additional *r* to the name decades later, explaining the difference in spelling.
53. See Dora Katherine Ohnesorgen, *William (Billy) Ohnesorgen* (published by author, 2006); Gerhard Grytz, "'Triple Identity': The Evolution of a German Jewish Arizonan Ethnic Identity in Arizona Territory," *Journal of American Ethnic History* 26 (Fall 2006): 20–49, esp. 25; and Benton-Cohen, *Borderline Americans*, 34–37.
54. See D. Ohnesorgen, *William (Billy) Ohnesorgen*, for more about the Ohne(r)sorgen family of the Arizona Territory and Benson, Arizona.
55. Shirley Gastelum Crew, phone interview with Andrea Tovar, March 5, 2021. Material and quotes attributed to Shirley in the next five paragraphs come from this same interview. See Nancy Valentine, *300 Years of Tubac Times: Writings, Illustrations, and Recollections of Those Who Lived in Tubac from 1601 to 2002* (published by the author, 2002), 121. William and Anna Lowe would also own Las Cienegas Ranch south of Tubac. William H. Lowe would go on to serve as the justice of the peace, Democrat precinct committeeman and commissioner, and highway commissioner, as well as on the county board of supervisors and the local school board. He was also thought of fondly by the Tubaqueños for his support of landowning Mexican Americans who continued to rightly lobby for their land claims specific to Baca Float No. 3 for decades.
56. Valentine, *300 Years*, 138–39; and Nancy Valentine, The Historic Lowe House (website), accessed January 22, 2022, https://lowehouseproject.com/tubac-history/. The Lowe House is on the National Register of Historic Places.
57. See Luis A. Gastelum, "Memories of My Youth at Tubac: From the Old Homestead to Adulthood," *Journal of Arizona History* 36 (Spring 1995): 1–32.
58. Martin, *Beloved Land*, 128–29.
59. For the Rio Rico Historical Society's website, see https://www.rioricohistoricalsociety.org/ (accessed January 22, 2023).
60. Anzaldúa and Keating, *This Bridge We Call Home*.
61. Heather Telles Everson, phone interview by Andrea Tovar, March 21, 2021. Quotes attributed to Heather in this and the next paragraph come from this same interview.

62. Rex Allen "Arizona Cowboy" Museum and Willcox Cowboy Hall of Fame (website), accessed January 21, 2023, https://www.rexallenmuseum.org/.
63. See Lillian Gorman's chapter in this volume for more on reclamation sites.
64. Fonseca-Chávez, Romero, and Herrera, *Querencia*, 271.

Bibliography

Acero, Roseanna Telles Flores. Phone interview by Andrea Tovar. March 6, 2021.

Anzaldúa, Gloria E. *Borderlands / La Frontera: The New Mestiza*. 4th ed., 25th anniversary ed. Aunt Lute Books, 2012.

Anzaldúa, Gloria E., and AnaLouise Keating, eds. *This Bridge We Call Home: Radical Visions for Transformation*. Routledge, 2002.

Arellano, Juan Estevan. *Enduring Acequias: Wisdom of the Land, Knowledge of the Water*. University of New Mexico Press, 2014.

Baker, Mercy Telles Bracamonte. Phone interview by Andrea Tovar. February 12, 2021.

Benton-Cohen, Katherine. *Borderline Americans: Racial Division and Labor War in the Arizona Borderlands*. Harvard University Press, 2011.

Benton-Cohen, Katherine. "Common Purposes, Worlds Apart: Mexican-American, Mormon, and Midwestern Women Homesteaders in Cochise County, Arizona." *Western Historical Quarterly* 36 (Winter 2005): 428–52.

Bernal, Dolores Delgado, Rebecca Burciaga, and Judith Flores Carmona. "Chicana/Latina Testimonios: Mapping the Methodological, Pedagogical, and Political." *Equity and Excellence in Education* 45, no. 3 (2012): 363–72. https://doi.org/10.1080/10665684.2012.698149.

Bock, Carl E., and Jane H. Bock. *The View from Bald Hill: Thirty Years in an Arizona Grassland*. University of California Press, 2000.

Burke, Flannery A. *A Land Apart: The Southwest and the Nation in the Twentieth Century*. University of Arizona Press, 2017.

Crew, Shirley Gastelum. Phone interview by Andrea Tovar. March 5, 2021.

de la Torre, Adela. "Countering the Pain That Never Heals: Pláticas That Mend the Soul." In *Speaking from the Body: Latinas on Health and Culture*, edited by Angie Chabram-Dernersesian and Adela de la Torre, 44–56. University of Arizona Press, 2008. Kindle.

Deutsch, Sarah. *No Separate Refuge: Culture, Class, and Gender on an Anglo-Hispanic Frontier in the American Southwest, 1880–1940*. Oxford University Press, 1987.

Everson, Heather Telles. Phone interview by Andrea Tovar. March 21, 2021.

Farmer, Teresa Telles. Phone interview by Andrea Tovar. February 16, 2021.

Fierros, Cindy O., and Dolores Delgado Bernal. "Vamos a Platicar: The Contours of Pláticas as Chicana/Latina Feminist Methodology." *Chicana/Latina Studies* 15, no. 2 (Spring 2016): 98–121.

Flores, Olivia Telles. Phone interview by Andrea Tovar. February 18, 2021.

Fonseca-Chávez, Vanessa, Levi Romero, and Spencer R. Herrera, eds. *Querencia: Reflections on the New Mexico Homeland*. University of New Mexico Press, 2020.

Gastelum, Luis A. "Memories of My Youth at Tubac: From the Old Homestead to Adulthood." *Journal of Arizona History* 36 (Spring 1995): 1–32.

Golojuch, Teresa Telles Ohnersorgen. Phone interview by Andrea Tovar. February 14, 2021.

Grytz, Gerhard. "'Triple Identity': The Evolution of a German Jewish Arizonan Ethnic Identity in Arizona Territory." *Journal of American Ethnic History* 26 (Fall 2006): 20–49.

Huízar-Hernández, Anita. "Between Place and Plot: Reimagining the Story of Arizona." *Journal of Arizona History* 63, no. 3 (Autumn 2022): 263–79.

Key, Lora M. "The Right to Represent: Mexican Americans and the World War II Draft Board in Tucson, Arizona." *Journal of Arizona History* 60, no. 2 (Summer 2019): 159–82.

Ladino, Jennifer K. *Memorials Matter: Emotion, Environment, and Public Memory at American Historical Sites*. University of Nevada Press, 2019.

Lamar, Howard Roberts. *The Far Southwest, 1846–1912: A Territorial History*. Rev. ed. University of New Mexico Press, 2000.

Marin, Christine, and Luis F. B. Plascencia. "Mexicano Miners, Dual Wage, and the Pursuit of Wage Equality in Miami, Arizona." In *Mexican Workers and the Making of Arizona*, edited by Luis F. B. Plascencia and Gloria H. Cuádraz, 203–25. University of Arizona Press, 2018.

Martin, Patricia Preciado. *Beloved Land: An Oral History of Mexican Americans in Southern Arizona*. Photographs by José Galvez. University of Arizona Press, 2004.

Martin, Patricia Preciado. *Images and Conversations: Mexican Americans Recall a Southwestern Past*. Rev. ed. Photographs by Louis Carlos Bernal. University of Arizona Press, 1996.

Officer, James E. *Hispanic Arizona, 1536–1856*. University of Arizona Press, 1987.

Ohnersorgen, Stella Telles. Phone interview by Andrea Tovar. February 14, 2021.

Ohnesorgen, Dora. *William (Billy) Ohnesorgen*. Published by the author, 2006.

Pérez, Emma. *The Decolonial Imaginary: Writing Chicanas into History*. Indiana University Press, 1999.

Pérez, Erika. *Colonial Intimacies: Interethnic Kinship, Sexuality and Marriage in Southern California, 1769–1885*. University of Oklahoma Press, 2018. Kindle.

Portelli, Alessandro. *The Death of Luigi Trastulli and Other Stories: Form and Meaning in Oral History*. State University of New York Press, 1991.

Preston, Douglas J., and José Antonio Esquibel. *The Royal Road: El Camino Real from Mexico City to Santa Fe*. Photographs by Cristine Preston. University of New Mexico Press, 1998.

Rothschild, Mary Logan, and Pamela Claire Hronek. *Doing What the Day Brought: An Oral History of Arizona Women*. University of Arizona Press, 1992.

Roybal, Karen R. *Archives of Dispossession: Recovering the Testimonios of Mexican American Herederas, 1848–1960*. University of North Carolina Press, 2017.

Ruiz, Vicki L. *From Out of the Shadows: Mexican Women in Twentieth-Century America*. 10th anniversary ed. Oxford University Press, 2008.

Sheridan, Thomas E. *Arizona: A History*. Rev. ed. University of Arizona Press, 2012.

Telles, Martha Stevenson. Phone interview by Andrea Tovar. February 16, 2021.

Trujillo, Patricia Marina, Corrine Kaa Pedi Povi Sanchez, and Scott Davis. "The Revolution Begins at the Cocina!" In Fonseca-Chávez, Romero, and Herrera, *Querencia*, 287–307.

Valentine, Nancy. *300 Years of Tubac Times: Writings, Illustrations, and Recollections of Those Who Lived in Tubac from 1601 to 2002*. Published by the author, 2002.

PART II

Language, Education, and Resilience

CHAPTER 3

Grácia Liliana Fernández

Arizona Territory Professor, Educator, Librarian, 1900–1912

CHRISTINE MARIN

By 1890, Apache County in the Arizona Territory was dominated in areas by a growing population that was Spanish-speaking and Mexican. Nevertheless, children were taught by Anglo-American teachers who did not speak or understand the Spanish language. The Anglo-American teachers' pupils did not advance in their education, and school districts grappled with a growing and continuous demand for Spanish-speaking teachers. As a result, school superintendents and administrators in Apache County began the early groundwork to bring Spanish-speaking bilingual teachers to the schools to enable Spanish-speaking children to succeed and do well.

Though this chapter focuses on the history of bilingual teachers, it does not present the history of bilingual education in the Arizona Territory before Arizona statehood in 1912. The practice called bilingual education today was not named and recognized as such in that period. Instead, I focus on the educational pathways for Spanish-speaking pupils during Arizona's territorial period by recovering the biography of bilingual educator Grácia Liliana Fernández, who taught in Apache County, Arizona Territory, from 1900 to 1906, and at the Tempe Normal School (today Arizona State University) from 1907 to 1912. I argue that she used her bilingualism as an educational gift to bolster success in the elementary schools in Apache County and as a tool of empowerment in higher education in Tempe. Fernández was Tempe Normal School's first professor of Spanish and the first full-time librarian of the Tempe Normal School library, and she brought, for the first time, bilingual library services to the educational environment in the Arizona Territory. Fernández implemented the new Spanish curriculum at the Tempe Normal School, initiated in 1907 by school president Arthur John Matthews, and she enabled and prepared students to enroll in her beginning and advanced courses in Spanish. Those students were also bilingual teachers who met the demand for Spanish speakers within higher education in the Arizona Territory. In essence, Fernández legitimized and introduced Spanish as a course of study and contextualized its regional importance in eastern and central Arizona.

Fernández's educational biography as a bilingual teacher from 1900 to 1912 is an important forerunner to the broader history of bilingual education within and beyond Arizona. In the following chapter in this volume, Lillian Gorman, a scholar of Hispanic studies and director of the Spanish as a Heritage Language Program at the University of Arizona, discusses more recent developments within bilingual education in the state. Gorman highlights a different educator, Adalberto Guerrero, and important events related to "Tucson's role in bilingual education and Spanish heritage language education" in Arizona today. In this chapter, I offer historical contextualization for Gorman's work by presenting the educational biography of Grácia Liliana Fernández. In the conclusion, I offer some brief comments on Gorman's history of bilingual education in Pima County.

From Maine to Puerto Rico to Apache County, Arizona Territory

Mexicans and New Mexicans are the earliest non-Indigenous residents of the St. Johns, Concho, and San Antonio regions of Apache County, Arizona. They came as ranchers, farmers, and sheepherders primarily via New Mexico in 1865.[1] Juan Candelaria's flock of sheep followed the trail from Cubero, New Mexico Territory, to St. Johns. His sheep were the descendants of seventy head of sheep that his maternal grandmother and her family led from Veracruz, México, to Cubero in the early nineteenth century. The trail from Cubero to St. Johns crossed the Zuni-held region and continued southward, approximately 155 miles, to where St. Johns lay near the Little Colorado River.[2] The Spanish-speaking New Mexicans and Mexicans wanted schools built for their children where they would learn English. The families taught reading, writing, and spelling to children in the Spanish language in their homes. Residents became school trustees and property owners; they formed at least twenty-two school districts, such as St. Johns, No. 1; San José del Tule, or Tule, No. 5; Concho, No. 6; and San Antonio, No. 9. Spanish was the dominant language spoken in and outside the home, including in these schools. The length of school terms did not exceed five months due to limited funds from county taxes, school closures, and extremely harsh winters in the region, which made traveling distances difficult.

In his 1905–6 biennial report on the instruction of children in the territory of Apache County, where the Spanish language dominated in the schools, John T. Hogue, county superintendent of public instruction, called out the need for bilingual teachers in the schools and laid the groundwork to create schools for Spanish-speaking children. His report reflected on the decrease in daily attendance of Spanish-speaking pupils in classrooms where there was no Spanish-speaking teacher. Additionally, he observed that pupils did not advance satisfactorily when the teacher did not speak Spanish. His recommendations advocated for the addition of Spanish-speaking teachers, as well as English-speaking teachers, in Apache County schools.[3]

How and when Grácia Liliana Fernández learned of the need for bilingual teachers in Apache County, leading her to apply for a teaching position in the county in 1900, is unclear. Historian Laura Muñoz suggests that as early as the 1880s, Mexican and Mexican American school trustees in Apache County "solicited teachers through employment bureaus, word-of-mouth, and newspaper advertisements."[4] Superintendent Hogue may have been the one who recruited Fernández, a twenty-four-year-old bilingual high-school and elementary-school teacher of Spanish and English from Dexter, Maine, and an 1898 graduate with a bachelor of liberal arts degree from the University of Maine, to come to Apache County and St. Johns on October 17, 1900. She was hired to teach English for the 1900–1901 school term at two schools: the San Antonio school, in District 9, located about twenty miles north of St. Johns, and the San

José de Tule, or Tule, school (the word *tule* in Spanish means "cattail"), in District 5, about fifteen miles south of St. Johns. She was paid $60 per month, and from 1902 to 1904 she was assigned to teach in the St. Johns school, in District 1, at a salary of $85 per month. In an article in *The St. Johns Herald,* her bilingual skills were noted as "an accomplishment which few teachers of our county can claim," and it was said that "she will prove a very valuable addition to Apache County's corps of teachers."[5]

It's important to note here that Fernández possessed strong, useful, and considerable teaching experience prior to her arrival in St. Johns in 1900, which served her well in Apache County schools. After her Dexter High School graduation in Maine in May of 1892, she taught English at the Gilman school in Sangerville, Maine, where she lived with her parents: her farm-owner father Fernando Fernández, a naturalized American citizen born in Spain who taught his daughter at a young age how to speak Castilian Spanish, and her mother, Francine Gilman Fernández, a weaver of wool at the mill in Dexter who learned Castilian Spanish from her husband. The people who worked at the mill and lived in the surrounding area spoke English and Castilian Spanish, and Francine spoke both languages with them in her supervisory role. Grácia Liliana Fernández taught English at Dexter High School until the summer of 1895, and enrolled as a freshman at Maine State College in Orono. After graduating from the University of Maine in 1898, she registered with the Boston Bureau of Education, a teacher placement agency, hoping to gain a teaching position in Maine's public schools.[6] Instead, she accepted a position as an education specialist at a teachers' institute in San Juan, Puerto Rico.[7]

Her responsibilities in the twenty-three months she lived and worked in Puerto Rico, from August 1898 to July 1900, included her bilingual assistance in the formation, organization, and implementation of the newly funded 1898 "Americanization program." The concept of American colonization rose quickly in Puerto Rico after the United States' acquisition of the island in the Spanish-American War of 1898. Teaching English to Puerto Rican children in the public schools became a priority for the U.S. government. The program required Fernández to recruit American schoolteachers to come to Puerto Rico and its schools to teach English, United States history, and American civics at all grade levels. Puerto Rican teachers continued to teach mathematics, science, and Spanish, which were solid courses already incorporated into the curriculum.

Fernández's bilingualism in English and Spanish and her expertise in translating, reading, and writing both languages enabled her to recruit American teachers, convincing them to come to Puerto Rico and teach in the classrooms and urban schools. However, a strong new anti-American nationalist movement emerged in Puerto Rico, and American assimilation waned.[8] Over two years' time, Fernández and her American teacher friends and colleagues became aware of anti-American attitudes and opinions held by the Puerto Ricans. They resented the strong American presence on the island after the nine-month Spanish-American War of 1898 ended. Fernández felt uneasy and began to dislike hearing the anti-American comments expressed within her working environment.

A few American teachers and friends returned to the United States rather than remain in Puerto Rico. Fernández began to develop scathingly critical opinions of the character and lifestyles of Puerto Ricans, which she expressed in the letters she wrote to her brother, Orman Fernández. He shared one of them as a point of political interest with Marcellus Emery, the publisher and editor of the *Bangor Commercial* newspaper in Bangor. Emery published Fernández's opinions in the July 25, 1900, issue of the *Bangor Commercial*, and another editor reprinted them in the *Portland Daily Press* on July 31, 1900:

> The people . . . are far from being appreciative of what the U.S. has done or is doing for them [and they have] a great dislike for Americans [and] as a rule are lazy and improvident and it may be said that nearly all the suffering and starvation that has occurred in the past year has been directly traceable to this trait in their character. . . . Illiteracy is found among a very great percent of the people and there seems little disposition to grow out of it. . . . The streets [of San Juan] are of a most vile character, and all the refuse is thrown from the buildings to the streets, which are lined with a mass of decaying matter of every character describable and giving off such an offensive odor that few have stomachs strong enough to stand it, especially if they are Americans. . . . The homes of the upper [class] to a great extent are without books or papers. The walls are without pictures, the floors are never carpeted, and the floors are never washed.[9]

Fernández grew angry and disenchanted with the Puerto Ricans and her surroundings, and she saw a growing dislike for Americans, due to the political nature of the Spanish-American War and the threats presented by U.S. military posts in San Juan. She grew depressed and fearful, became ill, and notified her employer that she no longer wanted to remain in her administrative position in San Juan. She sought permission to return home to Maine. Her request was granted, and Fernández left Puerto Rico, returning to her parents' home in Maine in July. In October 1900, she arrived in St. Johns, Arizona Territory, as a bilingual teacher ready to teach English to the Spanish-speaking children in the schools of Apache County.

Fernández began her work in the San Antonio School, District 9, and in the San José de Tule school, District 5, in October 1900. Thirty-seven students between the ages of six and twenty-one lived in District 9. However, the average attendance of pupils at the school remained at only twenty pupils per day in the years 1900–1902.[10] She became principal and the only teacher at the St. Johns school for the 1903–4 school year, and it became clear that Fernández needed help with the daily instruction of English to approximately seventy-three pupils. School officials brought in Clara Barth—the bilingual daughter of Refugio Landavazo Barth, born in Cubero, New Mexico, in 1855, and Solomon Barth, former member of the 1881 and 1899 Arizona Territorial Legislature—to assist Fernández in teaching the younger Spanish-speaking children the alphabet. It is likely that Refugio Landavazo Barth taught Clara the Spanish language, which she herself had learned from her father, Francisco Landavazo y Ortega, born in Spain and elected in 1857 to the New Mexico Territorial Senate.[11] In an article for *The Albuquerque Daily Citizen* on January 27, 1902, a newspaper writer praised Carlota "Lottie" Barth Taylor, Clara's sister, for her language skills in English and in Spanish, noting, "She is a very accomplished lady and is thoroughly educated in both English and Spanish," another indication that Refugio Landavazo Barth had probably taught her daughter Clara the Spanish language.[12] In November 1903 it was reported that "the school is in good running order and the pupils are advancing rapidly under their able instructors."[13]

How did the Spanish-speaking children learn English from Miss Grácia Liliana Fernández and Miss Clara Barth? To try and understand how, I reviewed a blog post containing sections of *McGuffey's Eclectic Primer*, used in St. Johns in 1900 to teach children how to read in English. The word method taught children to recognize words as a whole, especially single words that were similar: for example, *rat, cat, a cat, a rat.* After whole words were taught, children were told the names of the letters, and they learned how to pronounce the letters and spell the words. In the phonic method, the pupil was then taught to combine the sounds into words.[14] The problem here for Fernández's Spanish-speaking children was that they already knew the sounds of the words they heard when spoken to in Spanish and may have already known how to spell in Spanish. Spanish-speaking parents in Apache County taught reading, writing, and spelling to their children in the Spanish language in their homes. Unfortunately, my research failed to locate Fernández's classroom notes or the books she used to teach English to her Spanish-speaking pupils in the years she taught in Apache County's schools. Consequently, it is not clear how Fernández's students learned English. Schoolbooks and school supplies likely became available throughout the school term for use in the classroom. The St. Johns Drug Company, for example, touted the sale of all schoolbooks used in Apache County in its advertisement in the November 18, 1899, issue of the *St. Johns Herald* newspaper. Teachers, parents, school administrators, and individuals purchased pens, stationery, ink, pencil boxes, and notebooks, as well as crayons and slates for children.

By contrast, Sylvia Gonzales Jiménez Almeyda explained in an interview with me in 2017 how she was taught to speak, write, and understand English as a kindergarten pupil in her segregated "Mexican school"—the Bullion Plaza Elementary School in the copper mining town of Miami, Arizona—in 1923. Her teacher, Miss Nan L. Hamilton, used a string of colored beads made of wood. The colors signified words, letters of the alphabet, or numbers. Miss Hamilton played the piano and the children learned to memorize the words of the songs she played. By rote memorization, word repetition, and color coding, Sylvia did well learning English, as did the other Spanish-speaking children.[15]

Fernández's teaching methods encountered challenges too. When the Territorial Legislature passed Title 19 of the educational code in 1899, Arizona's schools were mandated to teach in the English language. This requirement became a justification for establishing separate schools for Spanish-speaking children. Fernández taught at three of these in the early 1900s as a bilingual teacher: the St. Johns, San Antonio, and El Tule schools in Apache County. The editor of *The St. Johns Herald,* in his article about her on October 3, 1903, described the St. Johns school as "the Mexican school."[16] Her knowledge of English and Spanish was beneficial to students in that they could speak Spanish easily and comfortably with Fernández in the classroom, and she could work with students toward the new educational code of teaching in the English language.

Her liking for Apache County is clear in her letter to a friend in Bangor, Maine, of which a portion was published in the March 23, 1901, issue of *The St. John's Herald*:

> The most favorable feature of Apache County is the delightful climate. . . . While the public school system prevails, schools are maintained only about five months in the year often due to harsh winters, and to shortage of funds to keep schools open longer. . . . I made the stage trip from Tule to St. Johns with a Mexican family on route to Winslow and liked the company. We spoke freely.

A few months later, *The St. Johns Herald* praised her ease within the town and recognized her participation and notable strong presence at the annual Apache County Teachers' Institute of 1901, noting that she "read a good paper in rhetoric."[17] Eighteen teachers from fourteen county schools attended the institute and discussed the current trends in education and the concerns teachers faced, such as salaries, new teaching methods, and student success rates or failures in the county. Apache County school superintendent John T. Hogue (1899–1906) presided over the meeting and gave a speech entitled "Supervision, the relation of the different parties concerned or interested in public schools." Fernández's "speech of appreciation" lauded the work of Superintendent Hogue and thanked him for his dedication to education in Apache County.[18]

These newspaper articles, as well as Fernández's limited personal writings and notes, do not express how she felt about her teaching experiences at these "Mexican schools." Her archives are not housed in the Apache County Historical Society Museum in St. Johns, nor at the Arizona State Library Archives and Public Records in Phoenix. They are not housed at the Fogler Library Special Collections and Archives at the University of Maine. Nevertheless, what is clear about her students is this: the fact that they did not speak English did not mean a lack of intelligence. Mexican parents understood the value of children learning English. Fernández's key to successful Spanish-speaking student outcomes was her bilingualism in the classroom. White teachers in schools in Apache County neither spoke nor understood the Spanish language, and this presented a barrier to Mexican children's success in school. The issue became a major and growing concern for Superintendent John T. Hogue.

In 1903 Fernández experienced a successful teaching year in the segregated "Mexican school," the St. Johns school. Nevertheless, Apache County school superintendents continued to grapple with more daunting county school problems—specifically, the growth of the Mexican student population and its link to disturbing dropout and truancy rates in the county, as well as the lack of bilingual teachers to help Spanish-speaking students progress in their education and stay in school. Alfred Ruiz, Apache County superintendent, expressed his opinion to the Arizona Territorial Board of Education: territorial normal schools must better prepare bilingual teachers by offering courses in Spanish. An article in *Snips & The St. Johns Herald,* dated August 20, 1904, touted a two-year Spanish course offering at the Northern Arizona Normal School. Alongside four years of Latin, students could take "two [years] of Spanish, which enables those who take the Spanish to speak it well."[19]

In his biennial report for 1907–8 as Coconino County's superintendent of public instruction, J. E. Jones made no reference to the success or failure of the two-year academic course in Spanish being taught at the Northern Arizona Normal School in Flagstaff, sometimes called the Flagstaff Normal School, since 1904.[20] Instead, his report praised the teachers in Coconino County schools for their diligence and efficiency in regulating the financial difficulties faced by the schools. Did the normal school in Flagstaff prepare bilingual teachers to help Spanish-speaking pupils learn English and become successful students in the Coconino County public schools, as Apache County superintendent Alfred Ruiz suggested? My review of the weekly *Coconino Sun* of Flagstaff from 1904 to 1908 found no published articles that indicated this. I did not find information about bilingual issues or difficulties faced by graduates of the Northern Arizona Normal School who went on to teach English to Spanish-speaking children in the Coconino public school system.

The year 1907 signaled the presence in St. Johns of the important and influential Alianza Hispano-Americana (AHA, the Hispanic-American Alliance), a mutual aid society founded by ethnic Mexicans along Masonic lines in Tucson in 1894 that provided life, death, and burial insurance to its members.[21] In January of 1907, Samuel Brown of Tempe, Arizona, AHA Supreme President since 1898 and organizer of Tempe's AHA Lodge No. 5 in 1897, who had been elected president of the Tempe Public School Board in 1905, and his good friend, the Tempe surgeon and physician Dr. Charles H. Jones, the secretary of Lodge No. 5, came to St. Johns together. Nathan Oakes Murphy, Arizona territorial governor, appointed Jones to serve as secretary of the Tempe Normal School Board for the term from 1902 to 1904. Brown and Jones came to meet with their good friend Alfred Ruiz, to discuss the recruitment of AHA members in St. Johns and to form a lodge.[22] I speculate that Alfred Ruiz engaged his friends in a conversation about the need for Spanish-speaking teachers in Apache and Maricopa Counties. Perhaps Ruiz suggested that a course in Spanish be taught at the Tempe Normal School, and by a bilingual teacher of English and Spanish in St. Johns that he had heard much about in his own work as the Apache County school superintendent—Grácia Liliana Fernández. After all, Brown and Jones shared valued educational experiences as important links to the success of the Tempe Normal School, and their opinions about the management of the school mattered. It is my conjecture that Brown and Jones shared Ruiz's opinion about Fernández with President Arthur John Matthews of the Tempe Normal School.

After their meeting with Ruiz regarding AHA business, Jones and Brown met with Reamer Ling, editor of the *St. Johns Herald and Apache News*. They requested that an item in the newspaper be printed about the formation of a new lodge of the AHA in St. Johns. As a result, the editorial of January 31, 1907, acknowledged the presence of "La Gran Sociedad Alianza Hispana Americana" in St. Johns, with congratulatory greetings to the Alianza.[23] In the same issue, Ling announced to the subscribers of *St. Johns Herald and Apache News* a new two-page Spanish supplement. This supplement was edited and managed by Lázaro Acosta, a St. Johns resident and Samuel Brown's friend. Acosta translated the articles in the newspaper from English to Spanish. The bilingual section appeared for approximately five months, after which Ling returned to publishing the newspaper in English only. Two months later, Ling hinted in his editorial of July 18, 1907, that Grácia Liliana Fernández would no longer remain in St. Johns in her role as principal or teacher in the local elementary schools. His single sentence identified Miss Katherine Rudd as the new principal at the St. Johns school; no mention was made about Fernández moving to Tempe.[24] The editor of the *Daily Kennebec Journal*, published in Augusta, Maine, reported on September 16, 1907, that Fernández earned an annual salary of $1,100 as "instructor in Spanish at the Tempe Normal School."[25] In addition, a September 26, 1907, article in the *St. Johns Herald and Apache News* states, "Miss Fernandez, who was principal of school in Dist No. 1 the past year, is now instructor in Spanish and librarian of the Tempe Normal School."[26] Fernández continued teaching in Apache County until she joined the Tempe Normal School faculty in the fall term that began on September 9, 1907.[27]

The Tempe Normal School

The official records of Tempe Normal School president Arthur John Matthews document his hiring of Grácia Liliana Fernández and her dual appointment as a faculty member teaching Spanish and the first full-time librarian. Laura Dobbs, President Matthews's secretary, previously held the position of librarian.[28] Fernández was the first professor of Spanish for the Tempe Normal School and the first librarian offering bilingual library services in English and Spanish for the Tempe Normal School library and to the faculty, staff, and students at the Tempe Normal School. The description of Tempe Normal School's first offering of the new course, Spanish, appears in the school's 1907–8 annual catalogue. The course is described as an addition to Latin as a foreign language requirement and "to equip our graduates for better work as teachers in our Territorial schools."[29] I interpret the words "better work" to mean meeting the demand for bilingual teachers to teach English to Spanish-speaking students and make a difference in their progress as successful students in the classroom. An added description of the Spanish course includes the note that "facility in easy conversation in Castilian Spanish will occupy a prominent place in the work."[30] Fernández's description of her course reflects Tempe Normal School's unique place in the early history of the promotion of using the English and Spanish languages together in the classroom to teach Spanish in the Arizona Territory.

As librarian, Fernández wasted no time in acquiring current bilingual publications for the library on a variety of subjects such as history,

FIGURE 3.1 Miss Fernández. El Picadillo, 1911. Tempe Normal School Yearbook, page 10.

politics, and American literature. She collected books and journals that reflected new thinking in the physical and life sciences. Textbooks about philosophy, engineering, physics, and geology soon occupied spaces on the library shelves in the reading room. In preparation for teaching classes in the Spanish language, Fernández ordered books in Spanish about the history and culture of México and Latin America and made them available for use in the library and for the students enrolled in her Spanish classes. These books included Spanish novels and texts on Spanish grammar, comprehension, and linguistics. She relied on her own teaching background and her academic training in liberal arts acquired from her alma mater, the University of Maine, to know what to order for the library.[31] The reference books section in the reading room represented interdisciplinary themes in the social sciences, architecture, and education. Her selections of Spanish literature and Spanish-language dictionaries became popular reference tools among her students. The progressive-minded educational reformist President Matthews noticed her accomplishments. He took pride in linking the holdings in the library to the Tempe Normal School's success in the training of teachers. Within a short time, the Tempe Normal School Library held six thousand volumes and had subscriptions to numerous leisure magazines, scholarly journals, and newspapers from throughout the United States.

When President Matthews added Spanish to the Tempe Normal School curriculum via his hiring of Grácia Liliana Fernández in 1907, he knew of the Arizona Territory's growing demand for bilingual teachers and understood early on that he bore the responsibility for making sure the Tempe Normal School filled the need to help Spanish-speaking pupils become successful students. Her course descriptions for two of her classes, Elementary Spanish and Advanced Spanish, appeared under her name as "Miss Fernández," and the name of her department, Spanish, in the *Tempe Normal School of Arizona at Tempe, Arizona: Annual Catalogue, 1911–1912.*[32] The description of the course Elementary Spanish is direct and informative: "This elementary course includes a careful drill in Castilian and Spanish-American pronunciation. Much importance is attached to the conjugation of the Spanish verb." Her second course, Advanced Spanish, promises to be challenging: "During this year, all class work is conducted in Spanish. A thorough knowledge of syntax is demanded. Frequent dictations and sight readings from Spanish newspapers afford ample opportunity for the development of idiomatic expression."[33] Tempe Normal School students who enrolled in the Spanish courses taught by Miss Fernández were expected to meet her rigid and demanding expectations and come away with new skills in reading, speaking, and writing the Spanish language. They would be better bilingual teachers for the grammar-school students in the territory who needed them, and teachers with these language skills easily found employment. Their work among the Spanish-speaking pupils in other regions of the Arizona Territory enabled children to make progress in the classroom and to advance in their education. Fernández's bilingual students became the new generation of teachers who personified the living language of Spanish, becoming just what their professor of Spanish trained them to become: Teachers. Good teachers. Teachers of Spanish. Bilingual teachers.

Fernández left her faculty position as professor of Spanish and librarian at the Tempe Normal School by 1912 to return to Maine, her home state. Her twelve-year career as a bilingual teacher, professor, and librarian in the Arizona Territory from 1900 to 1912 is exemplary. The legacy of her academic and educational leadership is evident in the Spanish-language major and courses at Arizona State University. The program inspires bilingual teachers, as well as up-and-coming professors, to work with students to acquire language skills in Spanish. It is a legacy that benefits Arizona and its schools, students, families, and libraries. Spanish remains the living language that Tempe Normal School professor Grácia Liliana Fernández knew it to be.

Nevertheless, despite Fernández's success as a bilingual teacher in Apache County schools and as a professor of Spanish and librarian in higher education at the Tempe Normal School in the Arizona Territory prior to Arizona's statehood in 1912, what is known today about the benefits of a bilingual education remains controversial. The subject is examined by Gorman in the chapter that follows this one. She notes that Arizona's English-only law, also known as Proposition 203 (passed in 2000), requires public-school students to be taught in classrooms where only English is spoken. As a result, Latino students have experienced the loss of a connection to their culture, heritage, and identities, and of the ability to speak Spanish and retain their bilingualism. Fernández's experiences from 1900 to 1912 were different. As a bilingual teacher, she celebrated the language skills of the Spanish-speaking children she taught in Apache County. Her pupils succeeded in learning English, made progress in their education, and retained their culture. In fact, bilingualism became a positive example of educational empowerment and success when she taught Spanish at the Tempe Normal School. Gorman's chapter provides an important history of bilingual education in Pima County that begins in 1959, when Pueblo High School in Tucson became the first high school in the nation to offer Spanish for Spanish Speakers. Her examination of the contemporary history of bilingual education in Arizona is rich in detail and significance.

Notes

1. E. M. DeGlane, *Concho, the Enchanted Pearl: A History of Concho, Arizona* (Quality Printing Company, 1981), 5; Will C. Barnes, *Arizona Place Names*, University of Arizona Bulletin vol. 6, no. 1 (University of Arizona Press, 1935), 107.
2. Bert Haskett, "History of the Sheep Industry in Arizona," *Arizona Historical Review* 7 (July 1936): 19.
3. John T. Hogue, "Reports of County School Superintendents, Apache County," in *Biennial Report of the Superintendent of Public Instruction of the Territory of Arizona for the Years Ending June 30, 1905 and June 30, 1906*, by R. L. Long (H. H. McNeill Company, 1906), 12–14.

4. Laura K. Muñoz, "Desert Dreams: Mexican American Education in Arizona, 1870–1930" (PhD diss., Arizona State University, 2006), 38. Muñoz reports that Fernández was among the seventy-seven Latinx teachers who joined the teaching ranks in Apache County in the Arizona Territory and early Arizona state between 1888 and 1930. The author thanks Laura K. Muñoz, professor of history at University of Nebraska, Lincoln, for bringing Grácia Liliana Fernández to her attention.
5. "Local News of the Week," *St. Johns Herald*, October 20, 1900, p. 3.
6. Rick Whitney, communication mailed to the author, August 10, 2021.
7. Whitney, August 10, 2021 (see previous note).
8. See Solsiree del Moral, "Colonial Lessons: The Politics of Education in Puerto Rico, 1898–1930," *The American Historian* 42 (May 2018): 41; Arturo Morales Carrión, *Puerto Rico: A Political and Cultural History* (W. W. Norton, 1983); and Solsiree del Moral, *Negotiating Empire: The Cultural Politics of Schools in Puerto Rico, 1898–1952* (University of Wisconsin Press, 2013).
9. "From Porto Rico: Experiences of a Maine Resident in the Island; Miss Grácia Fernandez of Sangerville Tells an Interesting Story," *Bangor Commercial* (Bangor, Maine), July 25, 1900. The article is reprinted on July 31, 1900, in the *Portland Daily Press* in Portland, Maine.
10. N. G. Layton, *Report of the Superintendent of Public Instruction for the Biennial Period Ending June 30, 1902* (The Gazette Print, 1902), 22.
11. For more about the Barth family, see Steve Goldstein, "Women of the West: Refugio Barth Landavazo," radio broadcast, *KJZZ* (Phoenix), April 1, 2020, https://www.kjzz.org/2020-04-01/content-1512121-women-west-refugio-barth-landavazo.
12. "Married at Safford," *The Albuquerque Daily Citizen*, January 27, 1902, p. 5.
13. "Local and Personal News," *Snips & The St. Johns Herald*, November 21, 1903, p. 2.
14. Stephen Parker, "A Brief History of Reading Instruction," Stephen Parker: Teacher, Author, Dad (website), updated December 23, 2021, https://www.parkerphonics.com/post/a-brief-history-of-reading-instruction.
15. Sylvia Gonzales Jiménez Almeyda, interview with the author, Miami, Ariz., August 23, 2000. After graduation from Miami (Arizona) High School in 1935, Sylvia worked as a nurse's aide at the Miami Inspiration Company Hospital and in 1943 entered St. Mary's School of Nursing in Tucson, Arizona, for two years of training in the United States Cadet Nurses Corps. She continued her nursing career at St. Mary's Hospital in Phoenix, Arizona, and at a hospital in California. Sylvia Gonzales Jiménez Almeyda passed away in Miami, Arizona, on December 15, 2011, at the age of ninety-three.
16. "Local News," *Snips & The St. Johns Herald*, October 3, 1903, p. 2.
17. "County Teachers Institute," *The St. Johns Herald*, December 21, 1901, p. 1.
18. Dolly Patterson, "John T. Hogue, Apache County Superintendent of Students, 1899–1906," Adventures at the Museum (blog), Apache County Historical So-

ciety Museum, November 13, 2016, https://apachecountyhistoricalsociety.blogspot.com/2016/11/john-t-hogue-apache-county.html.

19. "Northern Arizona Normal School," *Snips & The St. Johns Herald*, August 20, 1904, p. 2.
20. J. E. Jones, "Coconino County," in *Report of the Superintendent of Public Instruction Territory of Arizona for the Period Ending June 30, 1908*, by Robert L. Long (H. H. McNeil Company, 1908), 14–15.
21. Matt S. Meier and Feliciano Rivera, *Dictionary of Mexican American History* (Greenwood Press, 1981), 12. The Alianza promoted acculturation and civic virtues and provided low-cost sickness, death, and burial benefits as well as social and political activities for its members.
22. "Samuel Brown, for instance, whose father was from Maine, had a Mexican-born mother, and was born in California. He and his adolescent brother, Alfred, came to Tempe in the 1870s, and there Samuel married Bertha González." Jaime R. Aguila and F. Arturo Rosales, "Lost Land and México Lindo: Origins of Mexicans in Arizona's Salt River Valley, 1865–1910," in *Mexican Workers and the Making of Arizona*, ed. Luis F. B. Plascencia and Gloria H. Cuádraz (University of Arizona Press, 2018), 81. For more about Samuel Brown, see "La Segunda Convencíon de la Alianza Hispano Americana," *El Observador Mexicano*, October 22, 1898; Thomas Sheridan, *Los Tucsonenses: The Mexican Community in Tucson, 1854–1941* (University of Arizona Press, 1986); and Pete Dimas, curator, "Palimpsests of Arizona History Exhibit," Braun Sacred Heart Center and School of Human Evolution and Social Change, Arizona State University, September 9–December 3, 2021.
23. "¡Ojalá y los señores de St. Johns penetrados de las grandísimas ventajas de dicha sociedad, no vacilaran y vencieran en cuantos obstáculos se les presentaran á fin de fundar en su pueblo la logia aludida que les traería inmensos beneficios á sus familias." "La Gran Sociedad Alianza Hispano Americana," *St. Johns Herald and Apache News*, January 31, 1907, p. 4.
24. *St. Johns Herald and Apache News*, July 18, 1907, p. 4.
25. "Educational Matters," *Daily Kennebeck Journal*, September 16, 1907, p. 10.
26. "Local News," *St. Johns Herald and Apache News*, September 26, 1907, p. 2. No announcements or notices about Grácia teaching Spanish at Tempe Normal School and becoming the librarian of the Tempe Normal School library in the fall of 1907 appeared in the newspapers near Tempe, such as the *Arizona Republic* and the Tempe Normal School newspaper, *The Normal*.
27. *The Tempe Normal School of Arizona at Tempe: Annual Catalogue, 1907–1908* (Tempe Normal School, 1908).
28. Ernest J. Hopkins and Alfred Thomas Jr., *The Arizona State University Story* (Southwest Publishing Co., 1966), 146–47.
29. *Annual Catalogue, 1907–1908*, 37.
30. *Annual Catalogue, 1907–1908*, 37.

31. "Library Acquisitions, 1901–1914," vol. 33, series III, Tempe Normal School Records, 1885–1930, MSS-149, University Archives, Arizona State University, Tempe, Ariz.
32. *The Tempe Normal School of Arizona at Tempe, Arizona: Annual Catalogue, 1911–1912* (Tempe Normal School, 1912), 52.
33. *Annual Catalogue, 1911–1912*, 52.

Bibliography

Aguila, Jaime R., and F. Arturo Rosales. "Lost Land and México Lindo: Origins of Mexicans in Arizona's Salt River Valley, 1865–1910." In *Mexican Workers and the Making of Arizona*, edited by Luis F. B. Plascencia and Gloria H. Cuádraz, 60–89. University of Arizona Press, 2018.

Barnes, Will C. *Arizona Place Names*. University of Arizona Bulletin, vol. 6, no. 1. University of Arizona, 1935.

DeGlane, E. M. *Concho, the Enchanted Pearl: A History of Concho, Arizona*. Quality Printing Company, 1981.

del Moral, Solsiree. "Colonial Lessons: The Politics of Education in Puerto Rico, 1898–1930." *The American Historian* 42 (May 2018): 40–44.

del Moral, Solsiree. *Negotiating Empire: The Cultural Politics of Schools in Puerto Rico, 1898–1952*. University of Wisconsin Press, 2013.

Gonzales Jiménez Almeyda, Sylvia. Interview by the author. Miami, Ariz., August 23, 2000.

Haskett, Bert. "History of the Sheep Industry in Arizona." *Arizona Historical Review* 7 (July 1936): 3–49.

Hogue, John T. "Reports of the County Superintendents, Apache County." In *Report of the Superintendent of Public Instruction of Arizona Territory for the Biennial Period Ending June 30, 1906*, by R. L. Long, 12–14. H. H. McNeil Company, 1906.

Hopkins, Ernest J., and Alfred Thomas Jr. *The Arizona State University Story*. Southwest Publishing Co., 1960.

Layton, N. G. *Arizona Report of the Superintendent of Public Instruction for the Biennial Period Ending June 30, 1902*. The Gazette Print, 1902.

Long, Robert L. *Biennial Report of the Superintendent of Public Instruction of the Territory of Arizona for the Years Ending June 30, 1905 and June 30, 1906*. H. H. McNeil Company, 1906.

Long, Robert L. *Biennial Report of the Superintendent of Public Instruction of the Territory of Arizona for the Years Ending June 30, 1907 and June 30, 1908*. H. H. McNeil Company, 1908.

Meier, Matt S., and Feliciano Rivera. *Dictionary of Mexican American History*. Greenwood Press, 1981.

Morales Carrión, Arturo. *Puerto Rico: A Political and Cultural History*. W. W. Norton, 1983.

Muñoz, Laura K. "Desert Dreams: Mexican American Education in Arizona, 1870–1930." PhD dissertation, Arizona State University, 2006.

Sheridan, Thomas. *Los Tucsonenses: The Mexican Community in Tucson, 1854–1941.* University of Arizona Press, 1986.

Tempe Normal School. Records, 1885–1930. MSS-149. University Archives, Arizona State University, Tempe, Ariz.

The Tempe Normal School of Arizona at Tempe: Annual Catalogue, 1907–1908. Tempe Normal School, 1908.

The Tempe Normal School of Arizona at Tempe, Arizona: Annual Catalogue, 1911–1912. Tempe Normal School, 1912.

CHAPTER 4

Uncovering Southern Arizona's Tradition of Critical Language Pedagogies

Recovery, Reclamation, and Adalberto Guerrero's Early Spanish Heritage Language Classes

LILLIAN GORMAN

> *I come from a Mexican household, but my mom is the only generation in her family that does not speak Spanish just because of the culture that my grandma grew up in in a small town in Arizona. Lots of discrimination, lots of suppression of culture and language, so she didn't want her children . . . to kind of protect them, she didn't teach them the language.*
>
> —NATALIA SLOAN, UNDERGRADUATE STUDENT AT UNIVERSITY OF ARIZONA

Arizona is the only state in the United States with an active, restrictive English-only law. With the passage of Proposition 203 in 2000, an entire generation of Arizona students, like Natalia, have grown up without access to bilingual education. On November 28, 2017, Arizona Public Media (AZPM) published a story entitled "English Only: Millennials Reflect on Growing Up Latino in Arizona Schools." The story highlighted the experiences of a generation of young Latinxs whose schooling was dominated by the state's English-only policy, and addressed the sense of loss that many students felt when bilingual education ended due to the implementation of Proposition 203. One student felt "like English-only classes denied her a chance to connect with her culture." Another student explained to AZPM that "even when she was a young kid, she wanted to learn Spanish. So, she really liked her bilingual classes. They allowed her to connect with her Mexican culture in a more intimate way. . . . When her bilingual education ended, though, she lost most of her Spanish. And not being able to speak the language of her people caused and still causes her to question her identity as a Latina."[1] The state's 2010 anti-immigrant law SB 1070 and its HB 2281 (better known as the bill banning ethnic studies), along with Proposition 203, have contributed to a contemporary image of Arizona as a proponent of cultural and linguistic terrorism.[2]

Yet southern Arizona also has a radical history of defending language and cultural rights. The demonstrated excellence of the Tucson Unified School District's Mexican American Studies Program and an almost sixty-year history of developing cutting-edge Spanish as a heritage language (SHL) courses at the high-school and university levels contribute to southern Arizona's legacy as a space of cultural and linguistic activism.[3] In fact, in 1959 under the direction of Adalberto "Beto" Guerrero, Tucson's Pueblo High School was the first in the nation to offer Spanish for Spanish Speakers classes (now referred to as "Spanish as a heritage language" courses) at the high-school level.[4] Indeed, Tucson was at the forefront of implementing pedagogical approaches that are consistent with today's frameworks of critical language awareness and culturally sustaining pedagogies.[5] Tucson was a leader in Spanish heritage language education and bilingual education before these designations existed.[6]

This chapter serves to recover Latinx community voices around this understudied linguistic legacy. Specifically, I turn to the construction and recovery of the archive around Adalberto "Beto" Guerrero's impact on Latinx language experiences in Tucson. In her work on recovering Latina voices of the nineteenth-century Southwest, Karen R. Roybal explains, "I employ the parentheses around the prefix (re) to indicate that we must return to the past to gain a new understanding of the history of dispossession and to redefine our interpretation of the archive."[7] Roybal suggests a method for understanding the future based on the past. Similarly, I conceptualize the archive of Guerrero's work not only as a past achievement, but also as a present-day living archive that creates a space of abuelito/elder epistemologies that continues to transform Latinx language experiences.[8] My attempt to recover Guerrero's archive first reviews central concepts in critical pedagogies and then outlines key points in Arizona's Spanish-language history. I then highlight central events related to Tucson's role in bilingual education and Spanish heritage language education. I emphasize the lack of documentation of these events in academic literature and draw on Guerrero's Spanish-language memoir to fill in the blanks. Then I turn to the process of co-creating what I term "reclamation spaces," in which Guerrero shares his own accounts through a series of intergenerational pláticas with me, current Latinx students, and community members. It is in these spaces that I document key aspects of Guerrero's pedagogies and contextualize them in relation to current notions of critical pedagogies.

Critical Pedagogies

The beginnings of critical pedagogies are generally attributed to Paulo Freire's call for "critical consciousness" as a rejection of traditional models of education that framed students as passive recipients of knowledge.[9] Tucson's Mexican American studies program was undoubtedly rooted in critical pedagogies.[10] As scholars Janet Fuller and Jennifer Leeman explain, critical approaches to the study of language and society generally share "the underlying goals of examining phenomena within their sociohistorical context, investigating the relationships between social and political structures and exposing inequalities in society."[11] These approaches encompass a range of critical pedagogical and research frameworks. Among them, critical language awareness (CLA) was established in the United Kingdom in the 1990s and centered discussions of power in language instruction. CLA rejects the goal of students assimilating their language varieties to prestige varieties.[12] More recently, Loza and Beaudrie describe the increased dialogues around CLA in Spanish heritage language education as a "critical turn" in the field. They explain that "CLA is a theoretical and pedagogical framework with the potential to correct the social injustices that SHL scholars have long observed and contested at the macro-, meso-, and micro-levels of US society. . . . The notion of critical is understood as an explicit positionality against ideological and institutional discrimination."[13] Just as UK scholars encouraged an approach that goes beyond simple language awareness, the call for CLA in the field of SHL demands classroom practices that interrogate power structures and go beyond sociolinguistic awareness.[14] Yet critical language awareness was in practice in Tucson many years before the "critical turn." The educational practices under the larger rubric of what are termed "culturally sustaining pedagogies" also have a historical presence in Spanish heritage language classes in Tucson. According to Paris, "The term *culturally sustaining* requires that our pedagogies be more than responsive of or relevant to the cultural experiences and practices of young people—it requires that they support young people in sustaining the cultural and linguistic competence of their communities while simultaneously offering access to dominant cultural competence."[15] Culturally sustaining pedagogies and critical language awareness are not often discussed together within the same study, yet they both are clearly at play in Guerrero's track record of heritage language instruction.

Past and Present Arizona Language Policies

The state of Arizona passed "English for the Children," or Proposition 203, in 2000. The law first took effect in the 2001–2 school year. Cammarota and Aguilera explain, "Essentially, 'English for the Children' banned bi-lingual education from Arizona public schools and thus the most effective means for teaching ELL students."[16] The Tucson Unified School District and the Sunnyside School District (both located in Tucson) were able to maintain some bilingual education during the first year of the law's implementation through a waiver process. However, in 2002, the newly elected state superintendent of public instruction promised to ban bilingual education from all districts and rewrote the waiver process to make it nearly impossible for any bilingual education programs to remain in existence.[17] Indeed, Proposition 203 reflects an ideology of normative monolingualism that has been part of Arizona's history since the time of U.S. annexation in 1848. After joining the United States as part of the New Mexico Territory, Arizona split from New Mexico in 1863. In terms of Spanish language acceptance in the newly formed territory of Arizona, Rosina Lozano explains: "Despite the continued presence of Spanish speakers, the Arizona territorial government demonstrated little enthusiasm or support for translations. The few calls for translations that did occur came from Yuma and Pima counties, both located along the border with Mexico."[18] Laura Muñoz's monograph provides detailed accounts of the struggles of Arizonenses (Arizona Mexicans) for educational access and the ways in which they confronted anti-Mexican educational politics during the territorial and early statehood periods.[19] Muñoz highlights widespread Arizonense support for bilingual schooling and Spanish language maintenance, particularly in Tucson in the late nineteenth century.[20] In the chapter that preceeds mine in this volume, Christine Marin highlights the contributions of bilingual educator and Spanish professor Grácia Liliana Ferńandez in the early twentieth century as part of Arizona's historical legacy of bilingual education. Yet it is important to note that bilingual education in the case of Fernández is viewed as a pathway to English acquisition rather than Spanish language maintenance. This differs from the struggles documented by Muñoz among Tucson families. Similarly, Fernández's Spanish instruction at Tempe Normal School centered on educating English-dominant non-Mexican educators in Spanish. These uncritical pedagogical approaches contribute to Arizona's Spanish language situation standing in stark contrast to neighboring New Mexico's Spanish-dominated political and legislative system.[21]

Ethnic Mexican treaty citizens of Arizona were rapidly outnumbered by Anglo settlers. Yet, despite the dominance of both Anglo settlers and the English language in Arizona, Pima County demonstrates a record of making oppositional moves in this context. As mentioned above, Pima was one of two counties to call for Spanish translations in the territorial period, as well as one of the only counties to elect Spanish-surnamed representatives.[22] Also, as previously mentioned, two of the school districts that attempted to maintain bilingual education during the implementation of Proposition 203 were also in Pima County. In the 1960s, when national-level discussions around bilingual education were in their infancy, Pima County was a leader in hosting regional and national conversations around best educational practices for Spanish-speaking students. It is this history that I would like to bring to the forefront.

Much scholarship around bilingual and heritage language education cites the Coral Way Elementary School in Miami, Dade County, Florida, as the first post–World War II bilingual program in the United States.[23] Yet the National Education Association's *Invisible Minority* report of 1966 highlights established classes and course sequences in Southwestern states that were in place before 1963. The report documents the results of the NEA-Tucson Survey on the Teaching of Spanish to the Spanish-Speaking.

The survey committee visited fifty-eight schools in Arizona, New Mexico, Texas, Colorado, and California. Unlike Coral Way Elementary School, these programs were not the recipients of large grants providing financial support for their bilingual approaches. Yet the language pedagogies utilized in these Southwest schools were contributing to the overall academic success of Mexican American students in these communities. Because of key educators in Tucson, including María Urquides and Adalberto Guerrero, bilingual education practices in the Mexican American context were gaining national attention, and Tucson educators were laying the groundwork for congressional support for federal funding that later would be available through the Bilingual Education Act.

Tucson and Adalberto Guerrero's Place in Spanish Heritage Language Education

Despite Tucson's key role in sustaining regional and national conversations around bilingual education, very little previous research has documented this activism. Crawford makes a brief mention of the *Invisible Minority* report in his work on the politics of bilingual education in the United States.[24] Also, Moore discusses in more detail the Tucson-NEA survey and the resulting symposium as "prequels to bilingual education."[25] In the *Encyclopedia of Bilingual Education,* entries by Mary Carol Combs on Adalberto Guerrero and María Urquides and an entry on the NEA-Tucson symposium written by Josué González provide more detailed accounts of Tucson's part in the early years of bilingual education.[26] Additionally, De La Trinidad's dissertation provides a detailed chapter about bilingual education in Tucson with a special focus on Adalberto Guerrero.[27]

However, it is in the epilogue to Adalberto Guerrero's 2020 Spanish-language memoir *Cuando mis hijos sean grandes: Memorias* that one can access a firsthand account of these important events.[28] From the epilogue we learn that in 1965 Tucson's Pueblo High School garnered national attention for its Spanish for Spanish Speakers classes, receiving the National Education Association (NEA) and *Parade* magazine's Pacemaker Award. The award recognized the efforts that Guerrero initiated in 1959 by establishing the first Spanish for Spanish Speakers course in the nation.[29] In only four years, the single course progressed into a four-course honors sequence of Spanish for Spanish Speakers classes. Local Tucson educator María Urquides was the regional director for the NEA at the time and utilized the attention from the Pacemaker Award to petition the NEA to support a survey of programs serving Spanish-speaking students in the Southwest. Urquides received the NEA funding and was appointed the chair of the NEA-Tucson Survey on the Teaching of Spanish to the Spanish-Speaking. Soon thereafter she designated Guerrero as secretary.

The NEA-Tucson Survey on the Teaching of Spanish to the Spanish-Speaking committee visited schools throughout Arizona, New Mexico, Texas, Colorado, and California, and shortly after publishing its report, the NEA sponsored a first-of-its-kind symposium in Tucson to discuss the survey's findings. The NEA-Tucson Survey committee organized the symposium under the name "Las Voces Nuevas del Sudoeste (New Voices of the Southwest) Symposium: The Spanish-Speaking Child in the Schools of the Southwest." The symposium was held for two days in downtown Tucson and featured successful strategies for serving Spanish-speaking students observed by the committee. It also created space for discussions around future steps. Along with professors and K–12 educators from across the region, key officials from the NEA and members of Congress were also in attendance. Interestingly, neither the College of Education nor the College of Liberal Arts and Sciences of the University of Arizona were interested in hosting the conference.[30] Not only was the symposium "a watershed moment" for neighboring states like New Mexico,[31] it was also the impetus for widespread support of the Bilingual Education Act in 1967, and it led to the eventual formation of the National Association for Bilingual Education (NABE).

Guerrero's work was not only a prelude to contemporary notions of bilingual education,[32] but also a prelude to the field of Spanish as a heritage language (SHL). Even though Guerrero started the first Spanish for Spanish Speakers classes in 1959 at the high-school level and the first university-level classes at the University of Arizona in 1965,[33] these efforts are absent from the SHL literature. Beaudrie et al.'s text *Heritage Language Teaching: Research and Practice* references "the growing presence of educational programs designed for heritage learners of many different languages" and states that "to date there has not been a national survey of the presence of heritage language programs at different course levels and in different languages."[34] There is no mention of the NEA-Tucson

Survey on the Teaching of Spanish to the Spanish-Speaking, whose goal was precisely to document the presence of programs teaching Spanish to the Spanish-speaking in K–12 schools. Despite the discussions that occurred more than fifty years earlier at the Tucson symposium, Fairclough and Beaudrie's comprehensive volume *Innovative Strategies for Heritage Language Teaching: A Practical Guide for the Classroom* states that "it was not until the turn of the twenty-first century that the field of HL education gained the attention of a wide group of researchers, policy makers, administrators, and practitioners."[35] One explanation for this omission is the perspective that the events in Tucson are part of bilingual education's trajectory, rather than the field of Spanish as a heritage language. Yet in the 1960s these categories and concepts were in their infancy. The NEA-Tucson Survey's main concern was documenting the existence of courses serving Mexican American students, regardless of whether these programs would fall under certain future categories. Guerrero himself recognizes that in the early 1960s "ni siquiera el término conocíamos de 'educación bilingüe'" (we didn't even know the term "bilingual education").[36] More recent work questions these artificial divisions between the fields of Spanish heritage language and bilingual education.[37] The term "bilingual education" may not have been in circulation in the early 1960s, but Guerrero's collaborative work with the department head of Spanish, Renato Rosaldo, around creating a bilingual teachers' institute in Mexico took on an explicit mission to serve teachers who worked in high-Latinx-population schools, following the model of the Spanish for Spanish Speakers classes at Pueblo High School. The NDEA (National Defense Education Act) Institute's location alternated between Guadalajara (1962–64, 1967–68) and Tucson (1965 and 1969). This was most likely the first heritage-language pedagogical institute serving primarily heritage and native speaker teachers. That a largely Latinx bilingual teachers' institute designed around effective pedagogies for teaching Latinx Spanish-speaking students existed in the 1960s is astounding and progressive to say the least. Few of these programs have been documented in recent years, much less fifty years ago.[38]

In my work I have cited some of the earliest pedagogical recommendations for the Spanish heritage classroom as hailing from those whom I term "the madrinas of Spanish as a heritage language" in the 1970s and early 1980s.[39] Yet after I came to know about Guerrero's legacy, it became clear that the *Invisible Minority* report should also be positioned as a cornerstone of SHL history and as a work that provides some of the earliest SHL pedagogical recommendations. For example, the report

> strongly recommends that Spanish teachers for native speakers of Spanish be themselves native speakers of Spanish. As much as is possible, these persons should have a background similar to that of the students whom they are to teach.
>
> Special training for the teacher should include work in anthropology and sociology which will further his knowledge and understanding of the intercultural problems to be encountered. Practical field studies should afford him intimate acquaintance with special neighborhood projects such as the "Head Start" programs now part of the "War on Poverty" and others having particular promise which may be developed.[40]

Additionally, the report calls for instructors to be trained in the history of the Spanish language, multiple areas of linguistics, "Mexican and Southwestern U.S. dialects," and various areas of literature and cultural studies. The recommendations for teacher preparation are rigorous and culturally relevant. In fact, not only are these recommendations applicable to today's SHL classroom, they also demonstrate how SHL pedagogical research has been slow to recognize, document, and respond to the implementation of some of these key suggestions from nearly sixty years ago. Specifically, the importance of native speakers/heritage learners teaching native speakers/heritage learners has not been addressed. Aside from the work of Briceño et al., Bustamente and Novella, Alvarez, and Gorman, there is little to no documentation of this scenario.[41] Additionally, the report calls for interdisciplinary training of instructors. Beaudrie observes that the most successful Spanish heritage language programs require heritage pedagogy training.[42] Yet there is no mention of interdisciplinarity within this training. The report also suggests that instructors be engaged with the local community of their students. Potowski and Carreira's study argues for the incorporation of certain National Council on the Teaching of English standards such as "the importance of recognizing the impact of poverty, ethnic and cultural discrimination, family illiteracy and sociopolitical disenfranchisement on learning."[43] This recommendation is in line with the *Invisible Minority* report's emphasis on neighborhood programs and socioeconomic challenges. Beyond this reference from nearly forty years after the report's publication, these elements are not highlighted as critical for instructor profiles.

Intergenerational Pláticas and Creating Reclamation Spaces

In the same way that research has made clear the importance of ethnic studies to allow students to see themselves reflected in curricula and to understand our often-erased Chicanx/Latinx histories, I assert that it is equally important to understand these legacies within the academic literature. As a Chicana scholar of Latinx language experiences and heritage pedagogy, it is important for me (and other Latinx scholars in this field) to see that there is a tradition of Chicanx heritage language / bilingual education practitioners focused on the same issues that are of concern to us today. In many ways, the recommendations and the pedagogical approach Guerrero practiced were more progressive than the methods that followed in subsequent decades. It is critical to understand both the written/academic archive and the living community voices around these practices to provide a counternarrative to the narrative of Arizona's anti-Spanish and anti-Latinx standing.

Creating this space for reclamation and recovery is not separate from my process of conocimiento around Guerrero's living archive. Anzaldúa characterizes "conocimiento" as a "deep awareness" and as "the aspect of consciousness urging you to act on knowledge gained."[44] Therefore, it is not enough to simply become aware of Guerrero's contributions to bilingual education and Spanish as a heritage language; it is also necessary to act. Chicana feminist epistemologies provide me with the tools to move forward. Delgado Bernal's notion of "cultural intuition" allows me to put my viewpoint as a Chicana, my personal experience, and the collective experiences of my community into dialogue with my professional experience and the existing research.[45] Pláticas serve as another tool and as a "disruptive methodology" that "in turn produces different posibilidades for understanding or seeing a particular nuanced experience that may not be captured through other methods."[46] Indeed, it is through the co-construction of conversations and the opportunity for participants (including myself) "to assess or theorize about their own lived experiences" that the recovery process takes place.[47]

My path to conocimiento in this context began in 2015 when I started my role as SHL director at the University of Arizona and quickly familiarized myself with the Latinx student center. The center's name was the Adalberto and Ana Guerrero Student Center, and a picture of the couple hung prominently on the wall. Most referred to the center as the Guerrero Center. Over the next few years, I held multiple events in this Latinx space for the Spanish as a Heritage Language Program. Yet it was not until the thirty-eighth graduation convocation for the Adalberto and Ana Guerrero Center in 2021 that I came to know of Adalberto Guerrero's connection to the program I was directing and our shared commitment to instilling cultural and linguistic pride in our Chicanx/Latinx students. I was serving as one of the name readers for the graduation ceremony, and Guerrero was receiving an honorary doctoral degree. As we both sat on the stage, I listened while one of my colleagues read his introduction and outlined Guerrero's amazing achievements in the field of bilingual education. She underscored his role at Pueblo High School in developing Spanish for Spanish Speakers classes and his leadership as the first Chicano assistant dean of students at University of Arizona. As director of the SHL program, a scholar of heritage language pedagogy and Chicanx/Latinx studies, and former faculty in an institute for K–12 bilingual teachers, I was stunned that this was the first time I was hearing about these important contributions. In the months following the ceremony, I began a recovery process, guided by my cultural intuition, and came to know that it was Guerrero who not only started Spanish heritage courses in Tucson at the high-school level but also began these same courses at the university level. The program that I now direct was effectively started by Adalberto Guerrero. Why did I not know this? Why was there no mention of this on the department's website or in our college? His contributions to the Department of Spanish and Portuguese were completely absent.

The historic erasure of U.S. Latinxs and U.S. Latinx language practices from Spanish departments is not new.[48] Aparicio consistently critiques the continued disconnect in Spanish departments from local Chicana/o/x and Latina/o/x literatures and cultural studies in favor of Latin American and peninsular literatures.[49] Valdés et al. and García make similar critiques.[50] García states: "Spanish is promoted as a global language of authority outside the United States, and at the same time, it distances itself from the practices of bilingual subaltern subjects. The result . . . is the failure of Spanish language education in the United States for all."[51] Given this legacy of erasure, the invisibility of Guerrero's role in the Spanish department is not surprising. Yet as a Chicana, a heritage learner, and the director of the Spanish as a Heritage Language Program, it was more than clear to me that I needed to recover and honor his legacy for our current generation of Proposition 203 Arizona students.

In a welcome and surprising occurrence, Guerrero reached out to my college's dean after the SHL program was featured in a College of Humanities newsletter. The email was forwarded to me, and I immediately wrote to Guerrero. I expressed my gratitude for his message and my desire to meet with him in person and potentially set up an event with the students in the program. From this email exchange came a series of breakfast and lunchtime pláticas, community gatherings, and a student event in Guerrero's honor. From the moment we met at Blue Willow Café in Tucson, I felt a different type of conocimiento, a familiarity with this ninety-two-year-old *profesor*. When I told him I was from New Mexico, he called me "manita," and it was clear he knew my querencia (love of home, love of place).[52] Rudolfo Anaya explains that "querencia means vecinos."[53] In fact, I felt a form of linguistic querencia (a connection of linguistic practices to place or home) platicando with Guerrero.[54] Our conversations took place primarily in Spanish, and I felt as if I was talking with my grandpa. Even though I am a Spanish professor, I am still a Spanish heritage learner; linguistic insecurities are always present. As with my grandpa, Guerrero felt like familia, and there was a sense of linguistic home or querencia. In all, we met eight times over six months and our conversations lasted two to three hours. The pláticas truly reflected and "honored the rich cultural tradition of communicating and transferring cultural knowledge, wisdom and consejos (advice) in our familias."[55] This space for intergenerational Latinx knowledge sharing recalls Gonzales's concept of "abuelita epistemologies." These epistemologies emphasize "a critical examination of the centralized role grandmothers have in cultural and linguistic maintenance and survival [and] the techniques used to teach grandchildren about their heritage."[56] I extend this notion to grandfathers and acknowledge that "academic grandfathers" exist. In what follows, I highlight several instances of recovery embodied in these intergenerational reclamation spaces.

On a Saturday morning at an event at Pima County Library in December 2022, community members and scholars gathered to honor Guerrero and the publication of his memoir. One of Guerrero's former students and the former director of the Adalberto and Ana Guerrero Student Center contributed to the discussion from the audience: "Nomás quiero comentar que como estudiante en la universidad y en la Pueblo—I'm going to get emotional, Profesor—cuando estaba usted ahí, nos acercábamos como si fuera nuestro padre [crying]" (I just want to say that as a student at the university and at Pueblo—I'm going to get emotional, Profesor—when you were there, we came to you as if you were our father). Indeed, Guerrero's presence in the university and high-school settings provided a sense of familia and an academic father or grandfather. Not only is it important to underscore this role he played in the past, it is also important to acknowledge the "reclamation space" being created during that very moment at the public library. After the former student's words, Guerrero responded: "Son a los estudiantes a los que debo cualquier tipo de éxito que haya tenido. Entonces yo les agradezco siempre siempre." (It's to the students that I owe any success that I have had. So I am always grateful to them.) This exchange brings the memory of his mentorship into the present, while also actively creating a space for intergenerational knowledge sharing that points to a framework of mentoring for the future. The conversation continued from the audience after Guerrero responded. A current Chicano professor at the University of Arizona shared:

> Quiero expresar mi agradecimiento personal al Profesor Guerrero porque . . . ahora hablamos de HSIs, Hispanic-serving institutions, pero él era HSI en la Universidad de Arizona por muchos años. Y fue la persona que a la cual acudimos . . . y en su oficina encontrábamos no solamente consejos, refugio, café, dulces, pero un apoyo que no lo había en aquel tiempo. Entonces, yo como exalumno del departamento agradezco mucho porque si no fuera por él, yo no hubiera llegado hasta donde estoy ahora, ¿no? Y es algo que hay que reconocerle al Profesor Guerrero. Generaciones de estudiantes pasaron por ese quinto piso de Modern Languages en esa oficina y teníamos ese apoyo, ese saludo, ese gesto de que sí se puede las cosas. No, entonces quiero agradecer al Profesor Guerrero mucho esto,

> porque a veces vemos ahora un edificio con su nombre, pero eso es precisamente el símbolo de la comunidad usted ha traído a la universidad y sigue estando ahí.
>
> (I want to express my personal gratitude to Profesor Guerrero because . . . now we talk about HSIs, Hispanic-serving institutions, but he was HSI at the University of Arizona for many years. He was the person whom we could go to . . . and in his office we found not only advice, refuge, coffee, sweets, but support that wasn't there at that time. So, as a former student of the department I want to express how grateful I am, because if it wasn't for him, I would not have achieved all that I have today, right? And it's something that we have to recognize about Profesor Guerrero. Generations of students who passed through that fifth floor of Modern Languages had that support, that assurance that we could do this. So then I want to thank Profesor Guerrero very much for this, because sometimes we see a building with his name on it, but it is precisely the symbol of community that you brought to the university that continues to be there.)[57]

Guerrero's role is contextualized in current discussions of "servingness" within the university's designation as a Hispanic-Serving Institution.[58] This space of sharing allows for a reclamation of the "serving" in Hispanic-Serving Institution as a practice directly related to Guerrero's pedagogies inside and outside of the classroom. Guerrero refers to himself as an "extraoficial advisor para la mayor parte de los alumnos de habla hispana" (an unofficial advisor for most Spanish-speaking students).[59] Bringing this tradition of servingness to life recovers the concept as a community-based Chicanx practice, rather than simply a recent (and often empty) government designation.

Beyond the mentorship role, it is important to note the counterspaces to linguistic terrorism and language discrimination that Guerrero sustained and continues to sustain.[60] A close friend, scholar, and pioneer in bilingual education in Arizona, Dr. Macario Saldate, joined every plática with Guerrero. Saldate recalls:

> Well, what I remember about Profesor Guerrero is I never had him for a class. But my sister, my younger sister had him, and she was always talking about him and a lot of people were talking. And I wonder who this fellow

> was because everybody, "El profesor Guerrero y el Sr. Guerrero," y éste y que el otro, and I never had a class with him or anything like that. But I do remember that at Pueblo High School [. . .] here comes a professor with a little mustache. And for the first time that I have ever heard Spanish in an institution, he comes by saying, "Buenos días, muchachos. ¿Cómo les ha ido? ¿Qué pasó?" And we just literally, our mouth stayed open like this and everybody said, What's going on? And what is going on? It was the first time we ever saw this.[61]

Saldate and his classmates in the early 1960s were reacting to Guerrero's efforts to normalize Spanish in a public space. At a time when the effects of linguistic discrimination and dispossession stemming from the Americanization efforts of the 1930s were still present in the collective memories of Tucson Mexican Americans,[62] Guerrero reclaimed a space for Spanish that existed with pride rather than shame. Additionally, the fact that in every one of our pláticas, whether at the Guerrero Center, the library, Guillermo's restaurant, or Café Santa Rosa in South Tucson, Guerrero maintained our conversations almost entirely in Spanish. In this way, he continuously reinserts Spanish into the public sphere in present-day Tucson.

Saldate adds that Guerrero's impact extended beyond the linguistic pride he inspired. He continues, "So from there on, I think Beto has influenced a great deal of what we wanted to be. Because in many instances, it wasn't just the fact that he spoke Spanish well and he was our ideal model for that. But culturally he was the same way."[63] Similarly, Guerrero added, "Una de las cosas que más me gustó fue el hecho de que yo me veía en mis estudiantes, yo me identificaba con ellos. Tal vez ellos no hayan sido de familias tan humildes como la mía, pero yo me identificaba con ellos. Y así es que, es que éramos todos iguales." (One of the things that I liked the most was the fact that I saw myself in my students, I identified with them. Maybe they weren't from families as poor as mine, but I identified with them.)[64] It is important to mention that during our very first plática, Guerrero began by mentioning the importance and the rarity of having a Mexican Spanish professor at the University of Arizona. He described his experience with Renato Rosaldo and made clear the ways in which this experience impacted his trajectory as an undergraduate student.[65] Guerrero embodies the previously mentioned recommendation of the

NEA-Tucson Survey report. There is a long-lasting positive impact created when the professor is of the same cultural and linguistic background as the students. Guerrero leveraged this common profile to achieve student success. Saldate underscores this point: "Y lo curioso y lo más bonito de todo eso es que comenzó a quebrar estereotipos, porque esos mismos alumnos no tan solo les iba bien en las clases de español, por eso les comenzó a ir bien en otras clases también" (And the most amazing and special thing about all this is that it started to break down stereotypes, because these same students were not only doing well in their Spanish classes, but also they started to do well in their other classes as well).[66] In effect, Guerrero reclaims the pedagogical role of the Spanish teacher: instead of one that rejects Mexican Americans and Mexican American language practices, it becomes one of affirmation.

This affirmation is consistently present in Guerrero's descriptions of his teaching philosophy and embodies a critical language awareness that has not been documented from this time. At a special community event entitled "Nuestras Raíces: Una Conversación con Adalberto Guerrero," the Spanish heritage language students at the University of Arizona were invited to share space with Guerrero on a Wednesday evening at the Guerrero Center. Close to fifty students, instructors, and community members attended. Guerrero began his extended plática with the following words:

> Las caras de ustedes son como los alumnos que tuvimos en aquel entonces. Alumnos muy sobresalientes como ustedes y que normalmente ellos sabían mucho más que yo. Lo que yo sabía era el vocabulario que se requería en las universidades para analizar la gramática o para analizar el idioma que estaban estudiando los estudiantes. Los estudiantes ya conocían, ya conocían el idioma. Ya conocían la gramática. Lo que no conocían ellos era sencillamente ese vocabulario. Pero más importante que eso, ellos querían saber un poquito más acerca de su idioma, porque muchos de ellos eran de aquí y estaban acostumbrados a que los profesores que mal hablaban el español aquí en la universidad, profesores que creían que el único español que tenía mérito era el español peninsular y continuamente les decían, "You people don't even know your own language. Why don't you learn Iberian Spanish, Castilian Spanish?" Pero es que es verdad que el español de nosotros, no que acostumbramos aquí los académicos, sino

que el español del pueblo, es un español muy correcto y era una de las cosas nuestras, el hacer comprender a nuestros estudiantes que en efecto no tenían por qué avergonzarse, sino que tenían que estar orgullosos del español, del cual ya tenían ellos dominio . . . Y entonces, esto es lo que nosotros queríamos aprender. Un español no que fuera más correcto, sino que fuera más universal, que se aceptara en cualquier lugar donde fuera uno donde se hablara español.

(All of your faces are like the faces of all of the students that we had back then. Outstanding students who usually knew more than me. What I knew was the vocabulary that was used in the university to analyze the grammar or to analyze the language that they were studying. The students already knew, they already knew the language. They already knew the grammar. What they didn't know was simply the vocabulary. But more importantly, they wanted to know a little bit more about their language because many of them, they were from here and they were used to professors who didn't speak Spanish well, telling them that the only Spanish that had merit was Peninsular Spanish, and they continuously told them, "You people don't even know your own language. Why don't you learn Iberian Spanish, Castilian Spanish?" But it is true that our Spanish, not the Spanish of the academics, but our Spanish of the people, is a very correct Spanish, and it was one of our goals to make sure that our students knew that they had no reason to be ashamed but should be proud of the Spanish that they had mastery over . . . So that is what we wanted to learn. A Spanish that wasn't more correct, but was more universal and would be accepted in any Spanish-speaking place.)[67]

Guerrero made several key discursive moves in this conversation. First, he established the students as experts in their own language and lived experiences. Second, he called attention to the linguistic discrimination present among Spanish professors in the department. The elevation of a "correct" Peninsular Spanish is made to look absurd. Third, he questioned the notion of correctness and validated "el español del pueblo." Lastly, in Guerrero's use of "universal" he referenced the democratization of education by means of providing students with tools for access, but not with the intention of eradicating or replacing their existing linguistic tools. Guerrero's account of his teaching practices is a clear representation of key elements within CLA. Referencing Beaudrie et al., Beaudrie and Loza summarize several key goals for CLA instruction. First, they state, "students will be able to see language variation as natural and recognize the intrinsic value of their own variety and all others."[68] Not only did Guerrero emphasize the value of "el español del pueblo," but he also challenged linguistic hierarchies around Peninsular Spanish and the language ideologies perpetuated by Spanish professors. On another occasion Guerrero elaborated,

> Por ejemplo, en los grupos nuestros ya tenemos nosotros dominio de poder comunicarnos con nuestros padres, con nuestros amigos, etcétera, pero a veces estamos limitados si vamos a estar en otro ambiente, en un ambiente que sea más académico, un ambiente profesional. Entonces lo que buscamos nosotros es tener esos conocimientos, no importa en qué situación estemos, si se nos antoja, si nos da la real gana poder hacerlo nosotros.
>
> (For example, in our communities we are already able to communicate with our parents, our friends, etc., but sometimes we are limited if we are going to be in other environments, in an environment that is more academic or professional. So what we are looking for is to have this knowledge, so that no matter the situation, if we feel like it, we can communicate.)[69]

In this instance, Guerrero spoke of student agency in being able to choose when and how to speak without limitations caused by a lack of linguistic tools. Again, Guerrero's philosophy aligns with principles of CLA for the SHL classroom. Beaudrie and Loza highlight another goal in CLA instruction: "Students will be empowered to exercise agency in making their own decisions about language use and bilingualism."[70] Guerrero's approach clearly falls within a CLA framework and is consistent with early notions of CLA in the Spanish heritage language field around classroom-based dialect awareness.[71] Guerrero's words are almost a precursor to Martínez's now-famous declaration:

> If the students walk into the classroom saying *haiga* and walk out saying *haya*, there has been, in my estimation, no value added. However, if they walk in saying *haiga* and walk out saying either *haya* or *haiga* **and** having

> the ability to defend their use of *haiga*, if and when **they** see fit, then there has been value added.[72]

Additionally, Guerrero recognizes the need to challenge students' internalized language ideologies. When recounting that his students wanted to "aprender a hablar bien el español," Guerrero countered this intention. He explained,

> Les dije, "Miren, ¿por qué no somos claros? Ustedes tienen un dominio completo ya del español. Ustedes lo dominan ya. ¿Qué es lo que queremos? ¿Por qué no hacemos esto? ¿Por qué no hablamos acerca de, no un español más correcto, sino que un español más universal, para que ustedes tengan la habilidad de comunicarse con el grupo que sea?"
>
> (I told them, "Look, why don't we be clear? You all have complete mastery of Spanish. You all have mastered it. What do we want? Why don't we talk, not about a more correct Spanish, but instead a more universal Spanish, so that you all can communicate with whoever you want?")[73]

Similarly, in a scenario that occurred with his former students, which he recounted to the current heritage language students, Guerrero further challenged the standard language ideology.[74] He remembered asking his former students if the following phrase was correct: "Órale, préstame las llaves para la ranfla, porque quiero llevar a mi chava al mono" (Hey, lend me the keys to your car so I can take my girlfriend to the movies). He continued, "Los alumnos decían, 'No es correcto,' y dije, 'Sí es correcto . . . el español que hablamos es correcto dentro de tal o cual situación.'" (The students would say, "That's not correct," and I would say, "Yes, it is correct . . . the Spanish we speak is correct depending on the situation.")[75] Here he discussed linguistic registers, challenged ideologies of correctness, and recalled the lexical choices based in Caló that were part of his 1960s linguistic repertoire. Incidentally, this move toward linguistic validation of Caló also contributed to my feeling of linguistic querencia because my paternal grandfather often spoke using these phrases.

Guerrero also communicated classroom strategies that would be equated with today's notion of culturally sustaining pedagogies. In an innovative move toward co-constructing curriculum, Guerrero described his practices during the first days of class. He recounted his words to his students: "Quiero que entre todos nosotros indiquemos qué es lo que queremos que sea esta clase. Es una clase para ustedes y yo tengo la obligación de tratar de ver de qué manera puedo cumplir con los deseos de ustedes." (I want all of us to decide what we want this class to be. It's your class and I have the obligation to determine how I will implement your wishes.)[76] The students would reiterate their desire to learn "good Spanish," but they would also discuss their interests in Mexican history, literature, and culture. Guerrero would encourage students to get to know their own family histories. He explained, "En nuestras clases, una de las primeras tareas que yo les ponía a mis estudiantes era el de que fueran a sus casas y que preguntaran, 'Oye, Papá, ¿cómo fue que llegamos aquí a Tucson? [. . .] ¿Quiénes fueron mis abuelos maternos? ¿Quiénes eran ellos? ¿Cuántos apellidos hay?'" (In our classes, one of the first assignments that I would give was to have the students ask their parents, "Hey, Dad, how did our family arrive to Tucson? [. . .] Who were my maternal grandparents? Who were they? How many last names do we have?")[77] Aparicio's discussion of the importance of the autobiografía lingüística as a key pedagogical tool in the Spanish heritage classroom aligns with Guerrero's call to use the students' lives as a living text within the classroom.[78] The students were encouraged to create their own cultural and linguistic archive. Not only are culturally sustaining pedagogies at play in this situation in the sense that Guerrero supports "young people in sustaining the cultural and linguistic competence of their communities,"[79] but we also see an additional dimension to his critical language awareness approach. Leeman reminds us that this critical approach "attempts to make heritage speakers' own linguistic experience a more central part of the classroom,"[80] and Guerrero's teaching philosophy seems to center on this point. Furthermore, Guerrero extends the invitation to students' families to also form part of the living text of the classroom at the university. Guerrero explained,

> Queríamos siempre ver de qué manera podíamos atraer a otras gentes de habla hispana, a nuestros parientes aquí . . . Los jueves teníamos nosotros dedicados a invitados a la clase. Les decía yo, "Miren, en sus casas les han de preguntar, '¿Cómo son tus clases en la universidad? ¿Qué es lo que hacen durante un día en la universidad?'" Les decía, "Tráiganselos el jueves."

> [. . .] Llegaban los padres de los alumnos, los primos, amistades. Llegaba tanta gente a las clases y aprendían ellos.
>
> (We always wanted to see how we could attract other Spanish-speaking family members to the classroom . . . On Thursdays we dedicated the class session to special invited guests. I would tell them, "Look, in your homes they must wonder, 'What are your classes like at the university? What is it you do at the university?'" I told them, "Bring them on Thursdays!" [. . .] Parents, cousins, friends all came to class. So many people would come to the class, and they would learn too.)[81]

In this case, Guerrero creates a space for intergenerational knowledge production within the very space of the Spanish heritage language classroom while also exposing hundreds of first-generation college students' families to an academic space that was not generally welcoming to local Mexican American communities. De los Ríos, López, and Morrell argue, "One of the key reasons that young people are often not interested in school is not because they do not care about education, rather they do not see education as connected to their lives."[82] Guerrero intentionally connected the students' Spanish-language education to their local realities and to their families, effectively creating a linguistic home within the university setting.

Guerrero, again, accomplished this same type of intergenerational Latinx knowledge production at the Guerrero Center gathering many years later. When he concluded his conversation with the students and community, one Latina bilingual educator in attendance stated, "Solo quería aplaudirle el trabajo que hace, que ha hecho. Nosotras somos maestras bilingües y graduadas del Pueblo. Entonces me siento muy honrada de estar aquí en su presencia por todo el trabajo que ha hecho. Nomás quería agradecer." (I just wanted to applaud the work that you do and have done. We are bilingual teachers who are graduates from Pueblo. So I feel very honored to be here in your presence because of all the work you have done. I just wanted to thank you.) Immediately following these comments, an older woman who was attending the event with her daughter, a Spanish heritage language learner at the university, exclaimed, "Yo tengo una cosa que decir. Él era, yo iba a la Pueblo High School. En 1962 yo me gradué y aquí traigo el yearbook y él está en este con el bigotito negro. [. . .] Pero quiero decir que sí fue un maestro excelente." (I have something I would like to say. He was, I went to Pueblo High School. I graduated in 1962 and here I have the yearbook and he is here with the little black mustache. [. . .] But I just want to say that he was an excellent teacher.) At this moment, the entire room erupted in applause. The intergenerational connections were simultaneously remembered and activated with the current students. The event contributed to the living archive of Adalberto Guerrero.

Conclusion

Returning to the morning of December 3 at the Pima County Library in South Tucson and the panel discussing Guerrero's memoir, I would like to focus on Guerrero's opening words after the panelists had spoken about him. Guerrero recalled his students telling him, "¿Sabe qué, profesor? A nosotros no nos incluyen en las historias de Estados Unidos. Es como si no hubiéramos existido nunca." (You know what, Professor? We are not included in U.S. history. It's as if we never existed.) Guerrero described his response: "Entonces, yo les decía, 'Bueno, si es que quieren que nosotros aparezcamos nosotros en la historia, nosotros tenemos que escribir esa historia'" (So I would tell them, "Well, if we want to be included and appear in history, we have to write that history"). Not only has Guerrero written his own story through his memoir, but it is my hope that this chapter contributes to Latinx language scholars writing about our foundational figures, our academic abuelitos/as/xs. Particularly in Arizona, where an entire generation has grown up under discriminatory and oppressive language policies, it is our responsibility as engaged scholars to create these reclamation spaces and highlight community voices as acts of recovery. Just as Flores highlights community work in his profile of the Young Lords' historical role in bilingual education,[83] the archive of early Latinx/Chicanx activist work in both the K–12 and university settings must be uncovered and recovered before we no longer have these community and academic elders with whom to dialogue. In this volume, Roybal centers both land and Chicanas as "places that hold memory and are active sites of knowledge production," and I assert that Guerrero's reclamation spaces also function as active sites of knowledge production. By finding these spaces and hidden stories, we can insert early Latinx/Chicanx scholars and critical practitioners into departmental and academic histories that have historically been spaces of displacement and exclusion. Guerrero's living archive confronts the painful histories of linguistic terrorism and rewrites Arizona's history of language dispossession as one of transformation and reclamation. It is my hope that the Spanish as a Heritage Language Program at the University of Arizona honors Guerrero's legacy and provides a model for intergenerational knowledge production and language recovery.

Notes

1. Brenna Bailey, "English Only: Millennials Reflect on Growing Up Latino in Arizona Schools," *Arizona Public Media*, November 28, 2017, https://www.azpm.org/s/52424-english-only-millennials-reflect-on-growing-up-latina-in-arizona-schools/.
2. See Julio Cammarota and Michelle Aguilera, "'By the Time I Get to Arizona': Race, Language, and Education in America's Racist State," *Race Ethnicity and Education* 15, no. 4 (2012): 485–500; and Gloria Anzaldúa, *Borderlands / La Frontera: The New Mestiza* (Aunt Lute Books, 1987).
3. Nolan L. Cabrera, Jeffrey F. Milem, Ozan Jaquette, and Ronald W. Marx, "Missing the (Student Achievement) Forest for All the (Political) Trees: Empiricism and the Mexican American Studies Controversy in Tucson," *American Educational Research Journal* 51, no. 6 (2014): 1084–1118.
4. Adalberto Guerrero, *Cuando mis hijos sean grandes: Memorias* (Ali Abroad Academic Language Institute, 2020).
5. Sergio Loza and Sara M. Beaudrie, eds., *Heritage Language Teaching: Critical Language Awareness Perspectives for Research and Pedagogy* (Routledge, 2021). Django Paris and H. Samy Alim, "What Are We Seeking to Sustain Through Culturally Sustaining Pedagogy? A Loving Critique Forward," *Harvard Educational Review* 84, no. 1 (2014): 85–100.
6. Mary Carol Combs, "Adalberto Guerrero," in *Encyclopedia of Bilingual Education*, ed. Josué M. González (Sage Publications, 2008).
7. Karen R. Roybal, *Archives of Dispossession: Recovering the Testimonios of Mexican American Herederas, 1848–1960* (University of North Carolina Press, 2017), 14–15.
8. Sandra M. Gonzales, "Abuelita Epistemologies: Counteracting Subtractive Schools in American Education," *Journal of Latinos and Education* 14, no. 1 (2015): 40–54.
9. Paulo Freire, *Pedagogy of the Oppressed* (Continuum Publishing Company, 1970).
10. Curtis Acosta, "Developing Critical Consciousness: Resistance Literature in a Chicano Literature Class," *English Journal* 97, no. 2 (2007): 36–42.

11. Janet Fuller and Jennifer Leeman, *Speaking Spanish in the US: The Sociopolitics of Language* (Multilingual Matters, 2020), 5.
12. Romy Clark, Norman Fairclough, Roz Ivanič, and Marilyn Martin-Jones, "Critical Language Awareness Part I: A Critical Review of Three Current Approaches to Language Awareness," *Language and Education* 4, no. 4 (1990): 249.
13. Loza and Beaudrie, *Heritage Language Teaching*, 2.
14. See Glenn A. Martínez, "Classroom Based Dialect Awareness in Heritage Language Instruction: A Critical Applied Linguistic Approach," *Heritage Language Journal* 1, no. 1 (2003): 44–57; Jennifer Leeman, "Engaging Critical Pedagogy: Spanish for Native Speakers," *Foreign Language Annals* 38 (2005): 35–45; Jennifer Leeman and Ellen Serafini, "Sociolinguistics and Heritage Language Education: A Model for Promoting Critical Translingual Competence," in *Spanish as a Heritage Language in the United States: The State of the Field*, ed. Martha Fairclough and Sara M. Beaudrie (Georgetown University Press, 2016); Jennifer Leeman, "Critical Language Awareness in SHL: Challenging the Linguistic Subordination of US Latinxs," in *Handbook of Spanish as a Minority/Heritage Language*, ed. Kim Potowski (Routledge, 2018); and Loza and Beaudrie, *Heritage Language Teaching*.
15. Django Paris, "Culturally Sustaining Pedagogy: A Needed Change in Stance, Terminology, and Practice," *Educational Researcher* 41, no. 3 (2012): 95.
16. Cammarota and Aguilera, "By the Time I Get to Arizona," 488.
17. Wayne Wright, "The Political Spectacle of Arizona's Proposition 203," *Educational Policy* 19 (2005): 680.
18. Rosina Lozano, *An American Language: The History of Spanish in the United States* (University of California Press, 2019), 61.
19. Laura K. Muñoz, *Desert Dreams: Mexican Arizona and the Politics of Educational Equality* (University of Pennsylvania Press, 2024).
20. Muñoz, *Desert Dreams*, 35.
21. Lozano, *American Language*, 100.
22. Lozano, 100.
23. See Ofelia García, *Bilingual Education in the 21st Century: A Global Perspective* (Wiley Blackwell, 2009), 168; and Sarah C. K. Moore, *A History of Bilingual Education in the US: Examining the Politics of Language Policymaking* (Multilingual Matters, 2021).
24. James Crawford, "Language Politics in the USA: The Paradox of Bilingual Education," *Social Justice* 25, no. 3 (73) (1998): 54.
25. Moore, *History of Bilingual Education*.
26. Combs, "Adalberto Guerrero"; Mary Carol Combs, "María Urquides," in González, *Encyclopedia of Bilingual Education*; Josué González, "NEA Tucson Symposium," in González, *Encyclopedia of Bilingual Education*.
27. Maritza De La Trinidad, "Collective Outrage: Mexican American Activism and the Quest for Educational Equality and Reform, 1950–1990" (PhD diss., University of Arizona, 2008).

28. Guerrero, *Cuando mis hijos sean grandes*, 245–57.
29. Guerrero, 247.
30. Guerrero, 252.
31. Rebecca Blum-Martínez, "Initial Policies, Legislation, and Decisions," in *The Shoulders We Stand On: A History of Bilingual Education in New Mexico*, ed. Rebecca Blum-Martínez and Mary Jean Habermann López (University of New Mexico Press, 2020), 122.
32. See Moore, *History of Bilingual Education*.
33. Guerrero, *Cuando mis hijos sean grandes*, 249.
34. Sara M. Beaudrie, Cynthia Ducar, and Kim Potowski, *Heritage Language Teaching: Research and Practice* (McGraw-Hill Education, 2014), 8.
35. Martha Fairclough and Sara Beaudrie, *Innovative Strategies for Heritage Language Teaching: A Practical Guide for the Classroom* (Georgetown University Press, 2016), 1.
36. Adalberto Guerrero, interview with Cindy Trejo and Lillian Gorman, Tucson, Ariz., January 25, 2023. All translations from Spanish to English in this chapter are mine.
37. Nancy Dominguez-Fret, "Sowing Seeds of Resistance: Heritage Spanish Teachers Engaging in Testimonio and Critical Action Research" (PhD diss., University of Illinois at Chicago, 2023).
38. See Robert Luis Carrasco and Florencia Riegelhaupt, "META: A Model for the Continued Acquisition of Spanish by Spanish/English Bilinguals in the United States," in *Mi Lengua: Spanish as a Heritage Language in the United States*, ed. Ana Roca and M. Cecilia Colombi (Georgetown University Press, 2003); and Rebecca Pozzi, Chelsea Escalante, and Tracy Quan, eds., *Heritage Speakers of Spanish and Study Abroad* (Routledge, 2021), for some key examples of programs.
39. Lillian Gorman, "Reflections on the Legacy of Frances R. Aparicio's Politics of Language," *Latino Studies* 18, no. 2 (2020): 266. For the work by the "madrinas" referenced here, see: Guadalupe Valdés-Fallis, "A Comprehensive Approach to the Teaching of Spanish to Bilingual Spanish-Speaking Students," *Modern Language Journal* 62 (1978): 102–10; Erlinda Gonzales-Berry, "From Shame to Language Maintenance: Some Suggestions for a Beginning SNA Class," *System* 7 (1979): 201–4; and Frances R. Aparicio, "Teaching Spanish to the Native Speaker at the College Level," *Hispania* 66, no. 2 (1983): 232–39.
40. NEA-Tucson Survey on the Teaching of Spanish to the Spanish-Speaking, *The Invisible Minority: Report of the NEA-Tucson Survey on the Teaching of Spanish to the Spanish-Speaking* (Dept. of Rural Education, National Education Association, 1966), 32.
41. See Allison Briceño, Claudia Rodriguez-Mojica, and Eduardo Muñoz-Muñoz, "From English Learner to Spanish Learner: Raciolinguistic Beliefs That Influence Heritage Spanish Speaking Teacher Candidates," *Language and Education* 32, no. 3 (2018): 212–26; Carolina Bustamante and Miguel Á. Novella G.,

"When a Heritage Speaker Wants to Be a Spanish Teacher: Educational Experiences and Challenges," *Foreign Language Annals* 52, no. 1 (2019): 184–98; Stephanie M. Alvarez, "Evaluating the Role of the Spanish Department in the Education of US Latin@ Students: Un Testimonio," *Journal of Latinos and Education* 12, no. 2 (2013): 131–51; and Lillian Gorman, "Intergenerational Transmission of Heritage Language Identities: Spanish Heritage Learners as Spanish Heritage Language Instructors," conference presentation, Seventh National Symposium on Spanish as a Heritage Language, Albuquerque, N.Mex., February 27, 2020.

42. Sara Beaudrie, "Key Issues in Spanish Heritage Language Program Design and Administration," in *The Routledge Handbook of Spanish as a Heritage Language*, 1st ed., ed. Kim Potowski (Routledge, 2018), 375–88.
43. Kim Potowski and María Carreira, "Towards Teacher Development and National Standards for Spanish as a Heritage Language," *Foreign Language Annals* 37, no. 3 (2004): 433.
44. Gloria Anzaldúa, "(Un)natural Bridges, (Un)safe Spaces," in *This Bridge We Call Home: Radical Visions for Transformation*, ed. Gloria Anzaldúa and AnaLouise Keating (Routledge, 2013), 5; Gloria Anzaldúa, "Now Let Us Shift . . . the Path of Conocimiento . . . Inner Work, Public Acts," in Anzaldúa and Keating, *This Bridge We Call Home*, 577.
45. Dolores Delgado Bernal, "Using a Chicana Feminist Epistemology in Educational Research," *Harvard Educational Review* 68, no. 4 (1998): 555–82.
46. Cynthia M. Saavedra and J. Joy Esquierdo, "Pláticas on Disrupting Language Ideologies in the Borderlands," in *Disrupting and Countering Deficits in Early Childhood Education*, ed. Fikile Nxumalo and Christopher P. Brown (Routledge, 2019), 39.
47. Cindy O. Fierros and Dolores Delgado Bernal, "Vamos a Platicar: The Contours of Pláticas as Chicana/Latina Feminist Methodology," *Chicana/Latina Studies* 15, no. 2 (Spring 2016): 109.
48. Jennifer Leeman and Manel Lacorte, "Critical Approaches to Teaching Spanish as a Local/Foreign Language," in *The Routledge Handbook of Hispanic Applied Linguistics*, ed. Manel Lacorte (Routledge, 2014), 275–92.
49. Frances R. Aparicio, "La enseñanza del español para hispanohablantes y la pedagogía multicultural: Praxis y teoría," in *La enseñanza del español a hispanohablantes: Praxis y teoría*, ed. María C. Colombí and Francisco X. Alarcón (Houghton Mifflin, 1997); Frances R. Aparicio, "Of Spanish Dispossessed," in *Language Ideologies: Critical Perspectives on the Official English Movement*, vol. 1, ed. Roseann Dueñas Gonzalez and I. Melis (Lawrence Erlbaum Associates, 2000); and Frances R. Aparicio, "Insisting on Race, Ethnicity, and Gender: Reflections of a Latina Scholar (Who Is Also a Professor of Spanish)," *Profession* 8 (2013), https://profession.mla.org/insisting-on-race-ethnicity-and-gender-reflections-of-a-latina-scholar-who-is-also-a-professor-of-spanish/.

50. Guadalupe Valdés, Sonia V. González, Diana L. García, and Patricio Márquez, "Language Ideology: The Case of Spanish in Departments of Foreign Languages," *Anthropology & Education Quarterly* 34, no. 1 (2003): 3–26; and Ofelia García, "US Spanish and Education: Global and Local Intersections," *Review of Research in Education* 38, no. 1 (2014): 58–80.
51. O. García, "US Spanish and Education," 60.
52. See Rudolfo Anaya, "Foreword," in *Querencia: Reflections on the New Mexico Homeland*, ed. Vanessa Fonseca-Chávez, Levi Romero, and Spencer Herrera (University of New Mexico Press, 2020), vi.
53. Anaya, "Foreword," xv.
54. See Lillian Gorman, *Zones of Encuentro: Language and Identities in Northern New Mexico* (Ohio State University Press, 2024), 187.
55. Saavedra and Esquierdo, "Pláticas on Disrupting Language Ideologies," 39.
56. Gonzales, "Abuelita Epistemologies," 81.
57. In quotes from oral interviews and conversations in this chapter, bracketed ellipses indicate omission, while unbracketed ellipses indicate pauses or similar features of the speaker's discourse itself.
58. Gina Ann Garcia, *Becoming Hispanic-Serving Institutions: Opportunities for Colleges and Universities* (Johns Hopkins University Press, 2019).
59. Guerrero, interview, January 25, 2023.
60. "Linguistic terrorism" is a key concept in Anzaldúa, *Borderlands.*
61. Guerrero, interview, January 25, 2023.
62. See Patricia MacGregor-Mendoza, "Aquí no se habla español: Stories of Linguistic Repression in Southwest Schools," *Bilingual Research Journal* 24, no. 4 (2000): 355–67; and Aparicio, "Of Spanish Dispossessed."
63. Macario Saldate, interview with Cindy Trejo and Lillian Gorman, Tucson, Ariz., January 25, 2023.
64. Guerrero, interview, January 25, 2023.
65. Adalberto Guerrero, interview with Lillian Gorman, Tucson, Ariz., November 17, 2022.
66. Macario Saldate, conversation with Spanish as a Heritage Language Program students, instructors, and Lillian Gorman, Tucson, Ariz., February 23, 2023.
67. Adalberto Guerrero, conversation with Spanish as a Heritage Language Program students, instructors, and Lillian Gorman, Tucson, Ariz., February 23, 2023.
68. Sara M. Beaudrie and Sergio Loza, "The Central Role of Critical Language Awareness in Spanish Heritage Language Education in the United States: An Introduction," in Loza and Beaudrie, *Heritage Language Teaching*, 9.
69. Guerrero, interview, January 25, 2023.
70. Beaudrie and Loza, "Central Role of Critical Language Awareness," 9.
71. Martínez, "Classroom Based Dialect Awareness."
72. Martínez, "Classroom Based Dialect Awareness," 10.

73. Adalberto Guerrero, interview with Lillian Gorman, Tucson, Ariz., November 30, 2022.
74. See Rosina Lippi-Green, *English with an Accent: Language, Ideology, and Discrimination in the United States* (Routledge, 1997).
75. Guerrero, conversation, February 23, 2023.
76. Guerrero, conversation, February 23, 2023.
77. Guerrero, conversation, February 23, 2023.
78. Aparicio, "La enseñanza del español."
79. Paris, "Culturally Sustaining Pedagogy," 95.
80. Leeman, "Engaging Critical Pedagogy," 37.
81. Guerrero, conversation, February 23, 2023.
82. Cati V. de los Ríos, Jorge López, and Ernest Morrell, "Toward a Critical Pedagogy of Race: Ethnic Studies and Literacies of Power in High School Classrooms," *Race and Social Problems* 7 (2015): 93.
83. Nelson Flores, "A Tale of Two Visions: Hegemonic Whiteness and Bilingual Education," *Educational Policy* 30, no. 1 (2016): 13–38.

Bibliography

Acosta, Curtis. "Developing Critical Consciousness: Resistance Literature in a Chicano Literature Class." *English Journal* 97, no. 2 (2007): 36–42.

Alvarez, Stephanie M. "Evaluating the Role of the Spanish Department in the Education of US Latin@ Students: Un Testimonio." *Journal of Latinos and Education* 12, no. 2 (2013): 131–51.

Anaya, Rudolfo. "Foreword." In *Querencia: Reflections on the New Mexico Homeland*, edited by Vanessa Fonseca-Chávez, Levi Romero, and Spencer Herrera, xiii–xxii. University of New Mexico Press, 2020.

Anzaldúa, Gloria. *Borderlands / La Frontera: The New Mestiza.* Aunt Lute Books, 1987.

Anzaldúa, Gloria. "Now Let Us Shift . . . the Path of Conocimiento . . . Inner Work, Public Acts." In *This Bridge We Call Home: Radical Visions for Transformation*, edited by Gloria Anzaldúa and AnaLouise Keating, 540–78. Routledge, 2013.

Anzaldúa, Gloria. "(Un)natural Bridges, (Un)safe Spaces." In *This Bridge We Call Home: Radical Visions for Transformation*, edited by Gloria Anzaldúa and AnaLouise Keating, 1–5. Routledge, 2013.

Aparicio, Frances R. "Insisting on Race, Ethnicity, and Gender: Reflections of a Latina Scholar (Who Is Also a Professor of Spanish)." *Profession* 8 (2013). https://profession.mla.org/insisting-on-race-ethnicity-and-gender-reflections-of-a-latina-scholar-who-is-also-a-professor-of-spanish/.

Aparicio, Frances R. "La enseñanza del español para hispanohablantes y la pedagogía multicultural: Praxis y teoría." In *La enseñanza del español a hispanohablantes: Praxis y teoría*, edited by María C. Colombí and Francisco X. Alarcón, 222–32. Houghton Mifflin, 1997.

Aparicio, Frances R. "Of Spanish Dispossessed." In *Language Ideologies: Critical Perspectives On the Official English Movement*, vol. 1, edited by Roseann Dueñas Gonzalez and I. Melis, 248–75. Lawrence Erlbaum Associates, 2000.

Aparicio, Frances R. "Teaching Spanish to the Native Speaker at the College Level." *Hispania* 66, no. 2 (1983): 232–39.

Beaudrie, Sara M. "Key Issues in Spanish Heritage Language Program Design and Administration." In *The Routledge Handbook of Spanish as a Heritage Language*, 1st ed., edited by Kim Potowski, 375–88. Routledge, 2018.

Beaudrie, Sara M., Cynthia Ducar, and Kim Potowski. *Heritage Language Teaching: Research and Practice*. McGraw-Hill Education, 2014.

Beaudrie, Sara M., and Sergio Loza. "The Central Role of Critical Language Awareness in Spanish Heritage Language Education in the United States: An Introduction." In Loza and Beaudrie, *Heritage Language Teaching*, 1–19.

Blum-Martínez, Rebecca. "Initial Policies, Legislation, and Decisions." In *The Shoulders We Stand On: A History of Bilingual Education in New Mexico*, edited by Rebecca Blum-Martínez and Mary Jean Habermann López, 122–37. University of New Mexico Press, 2020.

Briceño, Allison, Claudia Rodriguez-Mojica, and Eduardo Muñoz-Muñoz. "From English Learner to Spanish Learner: Raciolinguistic Beliefs That Influence Heritage Spanish Speaking Teacher Candidates." *Language and Education* 32, no. 3 (2018): 212–26.

Bustamante, Carolina, and Miguel Á. Novella G. "When a Heritage Speaker Wants to Be a Spanish Teacher: Educational Experiences and Challenges." *Foreign Language Annals* 52, no. 1 (2019): 184–98.

Cabrera, Nolan L., Jeffrey F. Milem, Ozan Jaquette, and Ronald W. Marx. "Missing the (Student Achievement) Forest for All the (Political) Trees: Empiricism and the Mexican American Studies Controversy in Tucson." *American Educational Research Journal* 51, no. 6 (2014): 1084–1118.

Cammarota, Julio, and Michelle Aguilera. "'By the Time I Get to Arizona': Race, Language, and Education in America's Racist State." *Race Ethnicity and Education* 15, no. 4 (2012): 485–500.

Carrasco, Robert Luis, and Florencia Riegelhaupt. "META: A Model for the Continued Acquisition of Spanish by Spanish/English Bilinguals in the United States." In *Mi Lengua: Spanish as a Heritage Language in the United States*, edited by Ana Roca and M. Cecilia Colombi, 170–97. Georgetown University Press, 2003.

Clark, Romy, Norman Fairclough, Roz Ivanič, and Marilyn Martin-Jones. "Critical Language Awareness Part I: A Critical Review of Three Current Approaches to Language Awareness." *Language and Education* 4, no. 4 (1990): 249–60.

Combs, Mary Carol. "Adalberto Guerrero." In *Encyclopedia of Bilingual Education*, edited by Josué M. González, 333–36. Sage Publications, 2008.

Combs, Mary Carol. "María Urquides." In *Encyclopedia of Bilingual Education*, edited by Josué M. González, 870–71. Sage Publications, 2008.

Crawford, James. "Language Politics in the USA: The Paradox of Bilingual Education." *Social Justice* 25, no. 3 (73) (1998): 50–69.

De La Trinidad, Maritza. "Collective Outrage: Mexican American Activism and the Quest for Educational Equality and Reform, 1950–1990." PhD dissertation, University of Arizona, 2008.

Delgado Bernal, Dolores. "Using a Chicana Feminist Epistemology in Educational Research." *Harvard Educational Review* 68, no. 4 (1998): 555–82.

de los Ríos, Cati V., Jorge López, and Ernest Morrell. "Toward a Critical Pedagogy of Race: Ethnic Studies and Literacies of Power in High School Classrooms." *Race and Social Problems* 7 (2015): 84–96.

Domínguez-Fret, Nancy. "Sowing Seeds of Resistance: Heritage Spanish Teachers Engaging in Testimonio and Critical Action Research." PhD dissertation, University of Illinois at Chicago, 2023.

Fairclough, Martha, and Sara Beaudrie. *Innovative Strategies for Heritage Language Teaching: A Practical Guide for the Classroom*. Georgetown University Press, 2016.

Fierros, Cindy O., and Dolores Delgado-Bernal. "Vamos a Platicar: The Contours of Pláticas as Chicana/Latina Feminist Methodology." *Chicana/Latina Studies* 15, no. 2 (Spring 2016): 98–121.

Flores, Nelson. "A Tale of Two Visions: Hegemonic Whiteness and Bilingual Education." *Educational Policy* 30, no. 1 (2016): 13–38.

Freire, Paulo. *Pedagogy of the Oppressed*. Continuum Publishing Company, 1970.

Fuller, Janet, and Jennifer Leeman. *Speaking Spanish in the US: The Sociopolitics of Language*. Multilingual Matters, 2020.

Garcia, Gina Ann. *Becoming Hispanic-Serving Institutions: Opportunities for Colleges and Universities*. Johns Hopkins University Press, 2019.

García, Ofelia. *Bilingual Education in the 21st Century: A Global Perspective*. Wiley Blackwell, 2009.

García, Ofelia. "US Spanish and Education: Global and Local Intersections." *Review of Research in Education* 38, no. 1 (2014): 58–80.

Gonzales, Sandra M. "Abuelita Epistemologies: Counteracting Subtractive Schools in American Education." *Journal of Latinos and Education* 14, no. 1 (2015): 40–54.

Gonzales-Berry, Erlinda. "From Shame to Language Maintenance: Some Suggestions for a Beginning SNA Class." *System* 7 (1979): 201–4.

González, Josué M. "NEA Tucson Symposium." In *Encyclopedia of Bilingual Education*, edited by Josué M. González. Sage Publications, 2008.

Gorman, Lillian. "Intergenerational Transmission of Heritage Language Identities: Spanish Heritage Learners as Spanish Heritage Language Instructors." Conference presentation, Seventh National Symposium on Spanish as a Heritage Language, Albuquerque, N.Mex., February 27, 2020.

Gorman, Lillian. "Reflections on the Legacy of Frances R. Aparicio's Politics of Language." *Latino Studies* 18, no. 2 (2020): 262–68.

Gorman, Lillian. *Zones of Encuentro: Language and Identities in Northern New Mexico*. Ohio State University Press, 2024.

Guerrero, Adalberto. Conversation with Spanish as a Heritage Language Program students, instructors, and Lillian Gorman. Tucson, Ariz., February 23, 2023.

Guerrero, Adalberto. *Cuando mis hijos sean grandes: Memorias.* Ali Abroad Academic Language Institute, 2020.

Guerrero, Adalberto. Interview with Lillian Gorman. Tucson, Ariz., November 17, 2022.

Guerrero, Adalberto. Interview with Lillian Gorman. Tucson, Ariz., November 30, 2022.

Guerrero, Adalberto. Interview with Cindy Trejo and Lillian Gorman. Tucson, Ariz., January 25, 2023.

Leeman, Jennifer. "Critical Language Awareness in SHL: Challenging the Linguistic Subordination of US Latinxs." In *Handbook of Spanish as a Heritage Language*, edited by Kim Potowski, 345–59. Routledge, 2018.

Leeman, Jennifer. "Engaging Critical Pedagogy: Spanish for Native Speakers." *Foreign Language Annals* 38 (2005): 35–45.

Leeman, Jennifer, and Manel Lacorte. "Critical Approaches to Teaching Spanish as a Local/Foreign Language." In *The Routledge Handbook of Hispanic Applied Linguistics*, edited by Manel Lacorte, 275–92. Routledge, 2014.

Leeman, Jennifer, and Ellen Serafini. "Sociolinguistics and Heritage Language Education: A Model for Promoting Critical Translingual Competence." In *Innovative Strategies for Heritage Language Teaching: A Practical Guide for the Classroom*, edited by Martha Fairclough and Sara M. Beaudrie, 56–79. Georgetown University Press, 2016.

Lippi-Green, Rosina. *English with an Accent: Language, Ideology, and Discrimination in the United States.* Routledge, 1997.

Loza, Sergio, and Sara M. Beaudrie, eds. *Heritage Language Teaching: Critical Language Awareness Perspectives for Research and Pedagogy.* Routledge, 2021.

Lozano, Rosina. *An American Language: The History of Spanish in the United States.* University of California Press, 2019.

MacGregor-Mendoza, Patricia. "Aquí no se habla español: Stories of Linguistic Repression in Southwest Schools." *Bilingual Research Journal* 24, no. 4 (2000): 355–67.

Martínez, Glenn A. "Classroom Based Dialect Awareness in Heritage Language Instruction: A Critical Applied Linguistic Approach." *Heritage Language Journal* 1, no. 1 (2003): 44–57.

Moore, Sarah C. K. *A History of Bilingual Education in the US: Examining the Politics of Language Policymaking.* Multilingual Matters, 2021.

Muñoz, Laura K. *Desert Dreams: Mexican Arizona and the Politics of Educational Equality.* University of Pennsylvania Press, 2024.

NEA-Tucson Survey on the Teaching of Spanish to the Spanish-Speaking. *The Invisible Minority: Report of the NEA-Tucson Survey on the Teaching of Spanish to the Spanish-Speaking.* Dept. of Rural Education, National Education Association, 1966.

Paris, Django. "Culturally Sustaining Pedagogy: A Needed Change in Stance, Terminology, and Practice." *Educational Researcher* 41, no. 3 (2012): 93–97.

Paris, Django, and H. Samy Alim. "What Are We Seeking to Sustain Through Culturally Sustaining Pedagogy? A Loving Critique Forward." *Harvard Educational Review* 84, no. 1 (2014): 85–100.

Potowski, Kim, and María Carreira. "Towards Teacher Development and National Standards for Spanish as a Heritage Language." *Foreign Language Annals* 37, no. 3 (2004): 427–37.

Pozzi, Rebecca, Chelsea Escalante, and Tracy Quan, eds. *Heritage Speakers of Spanish and Study Abroad*. Routledge, 2021.

Roybal, Karen R. *Archives of Dispossession: Recovering the Testimonios of Mexican American Herederas, 1848–1960*. University of North Carolina Press, 2017.

Saavedra, Cynthia M., and J. Joy Esquierdo. "Pláticas on Disrupting Language Ideologies in the Borderlands." In *Disrupting and Countering Deficits in Early Childhood Education*, edited by Fikile Nxumalo and Christopher P. Brown, 37–52. Routledge, 2019.

Saldate, Macario. Conversation with Spanish as a Heritage Language Program students, instructors, and Lillian Gorman. Tucson, Ariz., February 23, 2023.

Saldate, Macario. Interview with Cindy Trejo and Lillian Gorman. Tucson, Ariz., January 25, 2023.

Valdés, Guadalupe, Sonia V. González, Diana L. García, and Patricio Márquez. "Language Ideology: The Case of Spanish in Departments of Foreign Languages." *Anthropology & Education Quarterly* 34, no. 1 (2003): 3–26.

Valdés-Fallis, Guadalupe. "A Comprehensive Approach to the Teaching of Spanish to Bilingual Spanish-Speaking Students." *Modern Language Journal* 62 (1978): 102–10.

Wright, Wayne. "The Political Spectacle of Arizona's Proposition 203." *Educational Policy* 19 (2005): 662–97.

PART III

Labor, Migration, and Community

CHAPTER 5

"We Never Separated"

Bracero Family Migration to the California/Arizona-Mexico Borderlands

ALINA R. MÉNDEZ

By the time Cirilo Díaz Bojórquez was sixteen, he not only was an independent young man living on his own but also worked in Yuma, Arizona, as an undocumented migrant. Díaz Bojórquez was six in 1944 when his mother passed away, leaving him in the care of his godparents, who subsequently left Jalisco in central Mexico to resettle in Baja California, taking Díaz Bojórquez with them. It was in Baja California that Díaz Bojórquez first worked for Chinese farmers cutting radishes and bunching cilantro, after leaving his godparents' house when he was fourteen. Díaz Bojórquez's first stint as a guest worker in the United States came in 1953 when he managed to obtain a special permit that authorized him to participate in the Bracero Program despite being only seventeen years old.[1] The Mexican men like Díaz Bojórquez who labored in U.S. agriculture under the Bracero Program were commonly referred to as braceros because they worked with their brazos (arms) and hands.[2] In 1953, when Díaz Bojórquez obtained his first bracero contract, the guest worker program had been in operation for over a decade, and it would continue until 1964.[3]

Employed under a three-month bracero contract, Díaz Bojórquez went to work in Fullerton, California, picking oranges. His time in California was short because he joined a few other braceros in protesting the poor quality of the food they received at the labor camp where they lived, and later took an unauthorized leave to return to Mexicali, Baja California, for a few days. Denied a new contract, Díaz Bojórquez was forced to return to Baja California, where he picked cotton for the next three years. Díaz Bojórquez's next opportunity to work in the United States came in 1956, when he was a married man. According to Díaz Bojórquez, a friend went looking for him at the ranch where he lived with his wife (most likely in the Mexicali Valley) and asked him if he was interested in going to work in the United States. Incredulous at this offer, Díaz Bojórquez assented. All that Díaz Bojórquez needed to obtain a new bracero contract, his friend assured him, was the identification card that he had received from the U.S. Immigration and Naturalization Service when he had first worked as a bracero. With that card in hand, his friend explained, Díaz Bojórquez would enter the United States as a "special" bracero. Díaz Bojórquez reentered the United States under a six-month contract, which his new employer—a labor contractor who operated a labor camp in Winterhaven, California—was happy to renew several times. Situated across the Colorado River from Yuma, Arizona, Winterhaven is approximately thirty miles north of San Luis Río Colorado, Sonora, Mexico. After working for the same labor contractor for a couple of years, Díaz Bojórquez then went to work for another employer who operated a ranch in the irrigated desert outside of Yuma.

Living and working in the Yuma area, Díaz Bojórquez was relatively close to his wife and children, who remained in Mexico. In 1958, when Díaz Bojórquez went to work for a new employer in Somerton, Arizona (located southwest of Yuma and only fifteen miles from San Luis Río Colorado), he welcomed his employer's offer to live in Mexico and commute to Somerton every day. This employer gave contract workers the option of living in Mexico if they had family there.[4] Given the opportunity to live alongside his family, Díaz Bojórquez relocated them from the ranch where they had been living to San Luis Río Colorado. Díaz Bojórquez's employer picked him and others up every morning in San Luis, Arizona, and drove them in a tarp-covered truck to the Somerton fields. At the end of each workday, the grower promptly returned the workers to the border, where they each crossed the port of entry into San Luis Río Colorado on foot. Besides allowing Díaz Bojórquez to live in Mexico with his family, this Somerton grower also granted him a letter supporting his application for legal permanent residence in the United States. Díaz

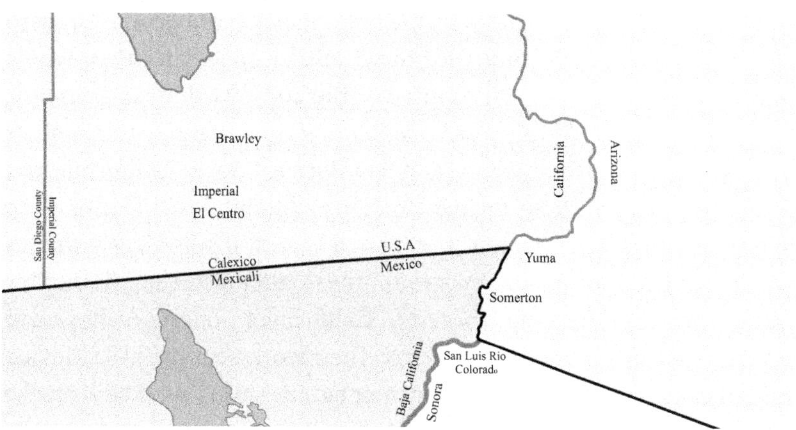

FIGURE 5.1 Map of the California/Arizona-Mexico borderlands. Map by Francisco J. Ayala Herrera.

Bojórquez obtained his green card in 1960, later found employment as an irrigator, and ultimately obtained legal permanent residence for his eight children and wife. When the Institute of Oral History of the University of Texas at El Paso interviewed Díaz Bojórquez for the Bracero Oral History Project in May 2006, he proudly noted that none of his children worked in the fields. His participation in the Bracero Program, Díaz Bojórquez concluded, had been akin to a "trampoline" that allowed him to become a legal permanent resident and later a U.S. citizen.

Family reunification in the California/Arizona-Mexico borderlands is remarkable when we consider the devastating consequences of family separation under the Bracero Program. One historian has described the program as an "assault on family life" that occurred just a decade after the massive repatriation of ethnic Mexicans in the 1930s, producing an extended "state of emergency" for transnational Mexican families.[5] In Mexico, women faced emotional and economic hardship when letters and remittances were infrequent or insufficient. Braceros' children struggled in the absence of their fathers, especially when they were forced to take on the adult responsibilities that their bracero fathers left unattended. In the United States, braceros often lived in isolated labor camps, which increased their longing for their homes and families or for the personal and intimate relationships that they would have built had they not left Mexico.

Like Díaz Bojórquez, many former braceros described the Bracero Program as a great opportunity for them, and ultimately for their whole families, when asked for their opinion of the guest worker program. Interviewed across the Southwest, in small towns and large cities such as Blythe, Coachella, Heber, Perris, and San Bernardino, in California, and Tucson, in Arizona, these former braceros explained that if they were living their retirement years in the United States, it was largely thanks to their participation in the program. These men also shared another thing in common: they had labored in California's Imperial Valley or in the Yuma, Arizona, region as braceros. Their work near the U.S.-Mexico border had allowed these men to see their families every weekend, or, like Díaz Bojórquez, to live with them in Mexico and commute daily to jobs in the United States. These experiences, though common in the California/Arizona-Mexico borderlands region, were a local and rather remarkable adaptation of the Bracero Program. After all, the Bracero Program was a guest worker program, designed with the idea that the workers would spend several months in the United States and then return to their country of origin (in this case Mexico) upon completion of their contracts. Program rules in fact required growers to provide housing to braceros. Nevertheless, as Díaz Bojórquez explained in his oral history interview, his employer justified shuttling workers to and from the border as a matter of family reunification.

This chapter examines the experiences of ten bracero families who lived in the California/Arizona-Mexico borderlands and who enjoyed a physical proximity uncommon for most bracero families. Situated across the international border from California and Arizona respectively, Baja California and Sonora provided braceros a unique opportunity for family reunification. Although women and children were unofficially excluded from the Bracero Program, thousands of families left their homes in the Mexican interior and settled in border towns like Mexicali and San Luis Río Colorado to live in proximity to husbands, fathers, or sons. By the mid-1950s, many braceros lived with their families in these two Mexican border towns and commuted daily across the border to jobs in California and Arizona. Others who did not have the chance to live in Mexico, or who perhaps resided farther north of the border, utilized their free weekends to visit their families.

Internal migration to the Mexican north enabled some families to circumvent the Bracero Program's gendered restrictions, which separated most bracero families. Weary of program participants' permanent migration to the United States, the Mexican government agreed to launch the binational labor agreement in 1942 with the condition that only men would participate. As Gloria Holguín Cuádraz explains in the following chapter in this volume on the women of Litchfield Park, Arizona, growers considered Mexican families the "unit of production" and relied on ethnic Mexican women's productive and reproductive labor to reap enormous profits. Leaving women and children behind, the assumption thus went, Mexican men would be forced to return to their families after completing their labor contracts in the United States. This assumption reflected the gendered ideology dominant in mid-twentieth-century Mexico, which cast men as breadwinning patriarchs.[6] Whether as sons or husbands, men's gendered roles required them to financially support their families while also rewarding them with patriarchal authority over the women in their households.[7]

When bracero families moved to Mexicali and San Luis Río Colorado, migrating outside of the defined parameters of the binational labor agreement, their internal migration resembled what sociologist Néstor Rodríguez calls "autonomous migration." Rodríguez uses the term to theorize Mexicans' international migration to the United States as "independent of state authorization and regulation."[8] Although the families who moved to Baja California and Sonora moved within Mexico, they did so independently of the official state policies aimed at keeping bracero families in their places of origin, thus challenging the Mexican state's efforts to circumscribe their mobility. Migrants relied on extensive social networks to find labor and settle in the border region. Besides family reunification, residence in Mexicali or San Luis Río Colorado provided braceros increased opportunities to obtain a green card and greater employment security in the California/Arizona-Mexico borderlands. Interpersonal relations with foremen, contractors, and small growers enabled these contract workers to secure employment not only for themselves, but also for their friends and kin. Similarly, the first families who relocated to border towns from central Mexico aided those from the same villages and towns who migrated in later years. The histories of these families illustrate the importance of family reunification under immigration regimes that separate workers from their loved ones, and they underscore the importance of humane immigration laws that account for migrants' full lives, not just their work lives or economic capacities.

Former braceros' oral history interviews help us understand how the bracero families who resettled in border regions navigated and minimized the separation that the Bracero Program imposed on millions of Mexican families in the mid-twentieth century. The oral history interviews that I examine in this chapter are part of the Bracero Oral History Project.[9] These interviews were conducted between 2005 and 2008, when the University of Texas at El Paso collaborated with the Smithsonian National Museum of American History and several other institutions to produce an online archive focused on the history of the Bracero Program. Oral history interviews, especially those recounting events that occurred decades earlier, are, as Monica Perales reminds us, "filtered, altered, and selective."[10] In her chapter in this volume, for instance, Liliana Toledo-Guzmán rightly argues that many of the oral history interviews collected in the Bracero Oral History Project skew toward a positive assessment of the Bracero Program. Interviewed in their senior years, former braceros who permanently settled in the United States and went on to see their adult children become successful professionals, for example, could proudly conclude that their participation in the Bracero Program had been a key opportunity to build new lives for themselves and their families in the United States. These positive recollections contrast sharply with the testimonies that scholar Henry P. Anderson collected among hundreds of braceros in the mid-twentieth century. Risking potential retaliation and blacklisting, braceros shared with Anderson haunting experiences of inhumane living conditions and gross exploitation by employers determined to reap record profits off the backs of America's newest source of cheap labor.[11]

These limitations notwithstanding, oral history interviews are an invaluable source that allows historical actors to tell their own stories in their own words.[12] In Spanish or English, the interviewers with the Bracero Oral History Project utilized a standard question guide that included the following sections: (1) family background, childhood, education, early employment; (2) the hiring process; (3) job experiences; (4) daily routine and living conditions; (5) salary; (6) problems on the job; (7) recreation;

(8) life after bracero work; and (9) final reflections. The use of a standard guide made these oral history interviews in some ways uniform. As former braceros and their families skipped over some questions or focused more on others, of course, they made each interview unique. Interviewers also made each interview different by adding their own clarifying or follow-up questions. In some instances, the reader is left wondering about the name of the interviewee's spouse or a particular detail that the interviewer did not try to clarify or skipped over. When wives or daughters accompanied former braceros to their interviews, they made these oral histories infinitely richer by providing their own accounts and details related to what the men were recollecting. Small quibbles aside, this online archive is an invaluable resource that documents the experiences of braceros and their families as the interviewees remembered and reflected on them in the early 2000s.

One of the families that reunited in the U.S.-Mexico borderlands was Leonardo Chavira Carrillo's. Like Cirilo Díaz Bojórquez, Chavira Carrillo worked in the United States as an undocumented worker before he obtained employment as a bracero. In his oral history interview, Chavira Carrillo explained that when he first worked in the United States as a young bachelor in the late 1940s, he sent money orders of $200 to $500 to his mother in Jalisco, Mexico. However, he decided to stop sending these remittances after an aunt told him that his mother was squandering his hard-earned dollars. At this point, Chavira Carrillo decided to return to Jalisco to find a wife. In his narration of the story behind his decision to find a marriage partner, Chavira Carrillo implied the gendered expectations that structured his relationships with his mother and with his future wife. Viewing himself as a provider for his family, Chavira Carrillo set out to find a wife who, unlike his mother, would act as a responsible recipient of his remittances.

Marriage did not spell the end of Chavira Carrillo's circular migration to the United States. After the birth of his first son in 1953, he left his family in Jalisco and obtained a bracero contract by bribing Mexican authorities in the contracting center in Empalme, Sonora. Although Chavira Carrillo returned to Jalisco every year to "plant a child" (as he euphemistically put it in his oral history interview), he continued seeking work in the United States under the Bracero Program. After several years of long-distance separation, the Chavira family relocated to Mexicali, where Leonardo visited them every weekend while he worked in Thermal, California. Chavira Carrillo owned a car during these years and was thus able to navigate the eighty miles between Mexicali and Thermal with more ease than those who depended on rides or public transportation. If he was able to purchase his own vehicle and live within driving distance of his family, this was largely because he had developed a strong relationship with his employer. Once he became a bracero, he requested to work for the same employer in Thermal with every new contract. This employer provided him the support letter he needed to become a legal permanent resident in 1959. That same year, the Chavira family moved to Mexicali, which demonstrates the importance of his new legal status in the family's decision to resettle in the Mexican north. When his wife and five children also obtained green cards several years later, it was again thanks to Chavira Carrillo's longtime employer.[13]

The migration experience of the López family illustrates the importance of social networks in the resettlement of bracero families to Mexicali. Margarita and Higinio López were both from the state of Aguascalientes. Higinio had first worked as an unauthorized worker in the Imperial Valley, having been encouraged by relatives who migrated seasonally to the United States. The couple married in 1950 during one of Higinio's trips back to Aguascalientes. In 1956, when Higinio was laboring as a bracero in the Imperial Valley, Margarita and their two children migrated to Mexicali to be closer to him. During their first years in Mexicali, the López family did not rent a house or room, but instead lived in homes made of cachanilla (a plant native to the region that locals mixed with dirt to use as building material). Higinio's bracero wages were generally sufficient to support the family, except for the times when his contract ended and he became unemployed. It was during these periods that the family's larger social networks became crucial. While Higinio traveled to the Mexican interior to obtain a new bracero contract, often spending more than a month away from his family, Margarita worked washing and ironing clothes for neighbors and received help from a brother and sister who had also migrated to Mexicali. As difficult as these times were, Margarita appreciated the fact that Higinio was beside her during all her pregnancies, for the couple went on to have nine more children in Mexicali. With Higinio coming and going across the border, Margarita asserted in her oral history interview, the family "never separated." The couple, moreover, was able to purchase land and began building their own house three years after moving to Mexicali.[14]

Migrants like Margarita and Higinio were key to the demographic growth that Mexicali experienced in the mid-twentieth century, not only because they established new households, but also because they expanded the translocal social fields that connected their towns in the Mexican interior with the U.S.-Mexico borderlands.[15] With Margarita and Higinio well established in the region, the López home also became a space for family gatherings and a place away from the isolating labor camps. When Higinio's brothers and a second cousin worked in the Imperial Valley, for instance, they took advantage of their proximity to Mexicali to visit the family every weekend. It was Higinio, moreover, who transported the men across the border in his own car.[16] This pattern replayed itself in countless families: when employment became scarce in the Imperial Valley, or while workers awaited their next contract, the homes of relatives or close friends offered shelter. Guadalupe García González, originally from the northern Mexican state of Sinaloa, lived with an aunt in Mexicali for eight months while he waited for a bracero contract. Because García González worked in the afternoons, he was able to stand outside the contracting center each morning and wait to hear his name called. This arrangement proved effective, and García González obtained a bracero contract.[17]

Alberto Magallón Jiménez's oral history reveals the strategies that some migrant men employed to secure steady employment in the United States under the Bracero Program. Magallón Jiménez, like many other migrant men, at times worked as a contract worker and at other times as an undocumented migrant. Once he married his longtime girlfriend in the early 1950s, Magallón Jiménez began working as a bracero and took his wife to the Imperial Valley with him. After living for some time as an undocumented migrant alongside her husband, Magallón Jiménez's wife settled in Mexicali while her husband remained in the Imperial Valley. His constant border crossings, though, spelled trouble for Magallón Jiménez when the Border Patrol detained him aboard a train headed to Indio, California. Afraid he would be deported to the state of Guanajuato in central Mexico, away from his pregnant wife, Magallón Jiménez asked a friend to alert his wife about what was happening and to instruct her to go to the Calexico-Mexicali port of entry to speak with immigration officials. After assuring immigration authorities that the woman who had gone to speak with them was indeed his wife, that she was pregnant, and that they lived in a room they rented in Mexicali, Magallón Jiménez was able to persuade the Border Patrol to deport him to Mexicali instead of sending him on an airplane to central Mexico. Yet as they were about to release him, a Border Patrol officer of Mexican origin warned Magallón Jiménez that if he was again detained, he would be sent to central Mexico because he had already been apprehended too many times.[18]

The threat of deportation to central Mexico prompted Magallón Jiménez to seek employment in Baja California. He worked in the Mexicali Valley picking cotton but returned to the United States as soon as he was able to obtain a bracero contract. He became a "special" bracero in the mid-1950s, making sure to always appear very respectful toward his supervisors in order to keep his privileged position. The special status conferred by employers on braceros like Magallón Jiménez made it easier for them to renew their work contracts and to continue laboring for the same employer.[19] Though other men derided him and other specials for being barberos (suck-ups), he made sure to avoid coming off as a contestón (insolent), malcriado (unmannerly), or huevón (lazy). This approach, however problematic some found it, gave relative job stability and permanency to special braceros and allowed a sizable number of them to form families in Mexicali and settle there. Magallón Jiménez saved enough money from his bracero wages to buy land in Mexicali and to build a two-room adobe house while he waited for his next contract. When he finally obtained another contract to work in the Imperial Valley, he was disappointed to realize that he had been assigned to a large carrot grower. Unsatisfied by the wages he earned bunching carrots, he requested a transfer to an employer who allowed braceros to commute back and forth across the border. Magallón Jiménez recounts in his oral history that his employer also provided him the necessary documents to become a legal resident two or three years after his transfer.

For men like Cirilo Díaz Bojórquez, Alberto Magallón Jiménez, and Severiano G. Villarreal, the special bracero status that they obtained in 1954 made their presence in the U.S.-Mexico borderlands steadier and placed them on a path to later acquire legal permanent residence in the United States. Villarreal began working in the Yuma, Arizona, area as an undocumented migrant in 1951 and worked for the same employer several months at a time during the next few years. He was still undocumented when the Yuma grower requested that Villarreal and a group of other unauthorized migrants enter the United States through San Luis, Arizona, as special braceros in 1954. In his oral history interview, Villarreal recalled crossing the border on July 9, 1954, at eleven in the morning. He explained that the group of men who entered through the San Luis Río Colorado–San Luis port of entry were then taken to the bracero processing center in El Centro, California. Explaining that he worked for this same employer for seven years as a bracero and for another six or eight years as a legal permanent resident, Villarreal affirmed that his experience working for this grower had been pleasant ("a gusto"). Considering that this employer coordinated the entry of a group of undocumented migrants as special braceros in July 1954, he was no doubt one of the many growers who started participating in the Bracero Program when the Border Patrol's Operation Wetback threatened to deport their undocumented labor force.[20]

While Villarreal's employer gained a group of cheap, dependable workers through the Bracero Program, Villarreal obtained increased job security and better working and living conditions as a special bracero.[21] When he and the rest of the specials group reentered the United States as braceros, for instance, his employer provided them trailers equipped with gas stoves. Before this, when they were still undocumented migrants, the workers had lived in a house that only had a wood-burning stove. Though they lived relatively close to the border, Villarreal often had to wait two or three weeks before he was able to find a ride to Mexico for the weekend. Traveling to Mexico became a lot easier when Villarreal and the other braceros he worked with saved enough funds to purchase automobiles. Living only a thirty-minute drive away from the border, he was able to commute every day from San Luis Río Colorado to his job near Yuma. He and other braceros working in the U.S.-Mexico borderlands valued their ability to commute across the border or to regularly visit their families in Mexico for both sentimental and practical reasons. After Villarreal relocated his mother to San Luis Río Colorado and purchased her a house there, for instance, he depended on her social reproductive labor. As a married man, Villarreal later relied on his wife to do his laundry and cook his meals. Interviewed in Blythe, California, in 2006, Villarreal explained that his wife and children obtained legal permanent residence in 1979. His employer had helped him acquire a green card around 1961, approximately eighteen years before the entire family could live together in the United States.

Some of the transborder families who obtained most of their income from wages earned under the Bracero Program were in fact part of a second generation. Esther Garnica's father had labored as a bracero during the program's early years but eventually became a construction worker in Mexicali. With her family's move to Mexicali in 1947, Esther constantly encountered aspirantes (men who aspired to obtain a bracero contract) and braceros who commuted across the border on a constant basis. When Esther met her future husband, Jesús Garnica, he was already a contract worker in the Imperial Valley. Jesús Garnica, who worked approximately sixteen miles north of the border, emphasized in his oral history interview that his family's residence in Mexicali provided him benefits beyond close contact with his wife and children. The former bracero explained that he rarely did his own laundry, as he would usually take it home during weekends. Since Garnica did not have to wash his own clothes, a task many viewed as emasculating, other braceros would remark "how easy he had it" (tú la tienes hecha).[22] By reminding Garnica of the advantages of his arrangement, his peers underscored the emotional pain of separation from their loved ones yet also reinforced patriarchal expectations about the social reproductive labor that women were expected to fulfill.[23]

Josefina Fajardo's family also arrived in Mexicali following her father's footsteps. Josefina's father migrated north when she was a small child but had stopped sending money to his family in Zacatecas. Realizing that her husband might never return to his family in central Mexico, Josefina's mother traveled to the Mexicali Valley in search of him. Unable to find him, Josefina, her mother, and her two siblings went to live with one of her maternal uncles—who had obtained ejido land under Baja California's land redistribution program—in Mexicali. By the time Josefina was a teenager, her family lived three blocks from the school where aspirantes registered for participation in the Bracero Program. There she witnessed the plight of impoverished aspirantes who slept outdoors near the school and begged for money in the neighborhood. So ingrained was the image of destitute aspirantes in her mind that when she met her husband, a bracero, Josefina never suspected that he was a contract worker because he was always well-dressed. Her husband began working in Mexicali after their wedding but soon received an offer to apply for legal residence with support from his previous employer. With legal permanent residence, her husband commuted daily across the border to his job in Holtville (approximately thirty-two miles northeast of Mexicali).[24]

Yet not all bracero families who relocated to the U.S.-Mexico borderlands had access to employer connections that could help them become legal permanent residents in the United States. Herminio and Librada Estrada, for instance, settled in the United States until their youngest daughter became a U.S. citizen and petitioned for her parents to receive permanent residence (likely in the 1980s or 1990s). The Estradas were newlyweds when the Bracero Program began in 1942. Herminio's first bracero contract sent him to Maricopa, Arizona, where he cut lettuce. After this initial contract, Herminio kept working as a bracero under renewed contracts that sent him to El Centro, Salinas, and Yuba City, California. At other times he worked in Avondale, Arizona. Librada and their children moved from Jalisco to San Luis Río Colorado, Sonora, when Herminio was working in Yuma. When the Bracero Program ended, Herminio worked in Sonora's cotton industry. In their oral history interview, Librada remarked that her youngest son took his first steps aboard the bus that she and their four children took to Sonora. She joked that the rest of her children were "Yaquis" because they were born in Sonora—loosely using the word "Yaqui" to describe someone born in Sonora, not its correct definition referring to someone with indigenous Yaqui ancestry. Yet Librada's comment reflects how the family came to see their migration from central Mexico as a transformative process that shaped some of her children's identities and their identification with their new place of residence. Even the food that Librada prepared reflected this transformation. Librada only knew how to make corn tortillas until she moved to Sonora and learned how to make flour tortillas from a friend.[25]

By migrating to Sonora or Baja California, bracero families responded to the life-changing transformations that the Bracero Program caused in their lives. Migrant men like Leonardo Chavira Carrillo, Higinio López, Alberto Magallón Jiménez, and Severiano Villarreal adapted to their new realities by relocating their families to the U.S.-Mexico borderlands, where they had built important social networks with employers and other migrants that afforded them relative job security and permanence. The Bracero Program and the promise of dollar wages were so attractive that even those who belonged to a second generation of migrants to the U.S.-Mexico borderlands, such as Cirilo Díaz Bojórquez, Esther Garnica, and Josefina Fajardo, also became braceros themselves or married braceros who crisscrossed the border. Unable to migrate as whole family units to the United States under the Bracero Program, these Mexican families responded by migrating autonomously and reuniting in Mexicali or San Luis Río Colorado. As more families set up new households in the U.S.-Mexico borderlands, moreover, they made the internal and international migration of others easier. The homes of bracero families became safe landing spaces where migrants could stop on their way to the United States, after completing a work contract, following the disappointment of a deportation, or even as they waited to hear their name called at a contracting center.

If braceros and their families recognized that resettlement was an effective strategy that allowed them to live together or in proximity while the men continued earning higher wages, agribusiness found it convenient as well. As former braceros explained in their oral history interviews, employers were happy to provide them the support letters that they needed to apply for legal permanent residence. Many employers even helped their workers petition for the legal permanent residence of their entire families. While it is certainly possible that these employers were genuinely interested in the well-being of their workers, their actions also demonstrate that agribusiness viewed braceros and border commuters as essential workers whose low wages and dependability were highly attractive.

The autonomous migration of bracero families serves as an important reminder that no family would remain separated by an international border if given a choice. A rich and extensive literature on international migration has demonstrated that parents and their children suffer enormously when parents are forced to leave their children behind and migrate to the United States in search of higher wages.[26] The oral history interviews with former braceros and their families testify to the importance of labor and immigration policies that view migrant workers as more than cheap hands—that view them instead as full human beings who deserve to live alongside their loved ones.

Notes

1. For more on the Bracero Program, see Kitty Calavita, *Inside the State: The Bracero Program, Immigration, and the I.N.S.* (Routledge, 1992); Miroslava Chávez-García, *Migrant Longing: Letter Writing Across the U.S.-Mexico Borderlands* (University of North Carolina Press, 2018); Deborah Cohen, *Braceros: Migrant Citizens and Transnational Subjects in the Postwar United States and Mexico* (University of North Carolina Press, 2011); Lori A. Flores, *Grounds for Dreaming: Mexican Americans, Mexican Immigrants, and the California Farmworker Movement* (Yale University Press, 2016); Erasmo Gamboa, *Mexican Labor and World War II: Braceros in the Pacific Northwest, 1942–1947* (University of Washington Press, 2000); Mireya Loza, *Defiant Braceros: How Migrant Workers Fought for Racial, Sexual, and Political Freedom* (University of North Carolina Press, 2016); Kelly Lytle Hernández, *Migra! A History of the U.S. Border Patrol* (University of California Press, 2010); Don Mitchell, *They Saved the Crops: Labor, Landscape, and the Struggle over Industrial Farming in Bracero-Era California* (University of Georgia Press, 2012); Ana E. Rosas, *Abrazando el Espíritu: Bracero Families Confront the U.S.-Mexico Border* (University of California, 2014); Mario J. Sifuentez, *Of Forests and Fields: Mexican Labor in the Pacific Northwest* (Rutgers University Press, 2016).
2. Luis F. B. Plascencia makes an important argument in observing that the term "guest worker" is a euphemism that "disavow[s] the exploitative history of the World War II contract-labor regime" and frames "arguments about indentured labor through seemingly neutral terminology." Plascencia also contends that the term "bracero" is "dehumanizing in its labeling of human laborers by a body part." I continue to use the term "bracero" throughout this chapter because many former contract workers have expressed their pride and satisfaction at being remembered as braceros despite the indignities and exploitation that they experienced under the program. See Luis F. B. Plascencia, "'Get Us Our Privilege of Bringing in Mexican Labor': Recruitment and Desire for Mexican Labor in Arizona, 1917–2016," in *Mexican Workers and the Making of Arizona*, ed. Luis F. B. Plascencia and Gloria H. Cuádraz (University of Arizona Press, 2018), 127–28.
3. Cirilo Díaz Bojórquez, interview by Annette Shreibati, Blythe, Calif., May 22, 2006, interview no. 1188, Bracero History Archive, Institute of Oral History, University of Texas at El Paso, https://scholarworks.utep.edu/interviews/1188/.
4. In 1927, the Department of Labor and the Bureau of Immigration issued General Order No. 86. This regulation classified non-citizen commuters as immigrants returning from a temporary visit to Canada or Mexico. This formalized a practice that continues today in border regions. See Thomas A. Klug, "Residents by Day, Visitors by Night: The Origins of the Alien Commuter on the U.S.-Canadian Border during the 1920s," *Michigan Historical Review* 34, no. 2 (Fall 2008): 75–98. I thank Luis F. B. Plascencia for pointing out this larger history.

5. Rosas, *Abrazando el Espíritu*, 1, 57.
6. Deborah Cohen, "From Peasant to Worker: Migration, Masculinity, and the Making of Mexican Workers in the U.S.," *International Labor and Working-Class History* 69 (Spring 2006): 83–84.
7. Yet not all migrant men fulfilled their responsibilities as breadwinners, and not all women passively obeyed husbands and fathers. For an excellent analysis of changing gender roles in relation to Mexican migration to the United States, see Pierrette Hondagneu-Sotelo, *Gendered Transitions: Mexican Experiences of Immigration* (University of California Press, 1994).
8. Néstor Rodríguez, "The Battle for the Border: Notes on Autonomous Migration, Transnational Communities, and the State," *Social Justice* 23, no. 3 (1996): 23.
9. For more on the Bracero History Archive, see braceroarchive.org; and Steve Velásquez, "Creating a Bracero Archive: Collaboration, Collections, and Challenges," *Diálogo* 19, no. 2 (Fall 2016): 7–20.
10. Monica Perales, *Smeltertown: Making and Remembering a Southwest Border Community* (University of North Carolina Press, 2010), 10.
11. Henry P. Anderson, *A Harvest of Loneliness: An Inquiry into a Social Problem* (Citizens for Farm Labor, 1964). For more on growers' blacklisting practices, see Mitchell, *They Saved the Crops*, 86.
12. In *Migrant Longing: Letter Writing Across the U.S.-Mexico Borderlands*, Miroslava Chávez-García examines an incredible family archive of correspondence between bracero José Chávez Esparza and his wife, María Concepción Alvarado. Like other bracero families, Chávez and Alvarado relocated to the Imperial Valley–Mexicali borderlands when José obtained a green card that cemented his essential role in the region's labor force. The correspondence between them offers a rare glimpse into the private lives of the men and women separated by the Bracero Program. Unlike the oral history interviews collected from former braceros and their families decades later, this correspondence reflected the feelings, wishes, and desires of the authors at the moment in time when those letters were written. See Chávez-García, *Migrant Longing*.
13. Leonardo Chavira Carrillo, interview by Verónica Cortez, Coachella, Calif., May 20, 2006, interview no. 1215, Bracero History Archive, Institute of Oral History, University of Texas at El Paso, https://scholarworks.utep.edu/interviews/1215/.
14. Margarita López, interview by Rochelle Garza, Perris, Calif., May 26, 2006, interview no. 1081, Bracero History Archive, Institute of Oral History, University of Texas at El Paso, https://scholarworks.utep.edu/interviews/1081/; and Higinio López Silva, interview by Grisel Murillo, Perris, Calif., May 26, 2006, interview no. 1068, Bracero History Archive, Institute of Oral History, University of Texas at El Paso, https://scholarworks.utep.edu/interviews/1068/.
15. I employ the term "translocal" to describe the growing social fields that connected Calvillo, Aguascalientes, with Mexicali, Baja California, in the mid-twentieth century. Decades before migration scholars would employ "trans-

nationalism" to describe migrants' simultaneous social lives in Mexico and the United States, the López family and thousands of other migrant families were building the social networks that would connect Mexican sending towns with their U.S. destinations, eventually making a binational labor program unnecessary for the continuation of circular migration. In this case, the translocal social fields creating "local to local" connections were of course making Mexicali a critical node in the larger migration apparatus. For more on translocality, see Michael P. Smith and Luis E. Guarnizo, *Transnationalism from Below* (Transaction Publishers, 1998); and Clemens Greiner and Patrick Sakdapolrak, "Translocality: Concepts, Applications and Emerging Research Perspectives," *Geography Compass* 7, no. 5 (2013): 373–84.

16. Alejo López Silva, interview by Verónica Cortez, Perris, Calif., May 26, 2006, interview no. 1082, Bracero History Archive, Institute of Oral History, University of Texas at El Paso, https://scholarworks.utep.edu/interviews/1082/.
17. Guadalupe García González, interview by Mireya Loza, Los Angeles, Calif., May 11, 2006, interview no. 1169, Bracero History Archive, Institute of Oral History, University of Texas at El Paso, https://scholarworks.utep.edu/interviews/1169/.
18. Information in this paragraph and the next is from Alberto Magallón Jiménez, interview by Anais Acosta, Salinas, Calif., July 28, 2005, Bracero History Archive, Institute of Oral History, University of Texas at El Paso, https://braceroarchive.org/items/show/153.
19. Calavita, *Inside the State*, 94–103.
20. Information in this paragraph and the next is from Severiano G. Villarreal, interview by Verónica Cortez, Blythe, Calif., May 22, 2006, interview no. 1201, Bracero History Archive, Institute of Oral History, University of Texas at El Paso, https://scholarworks.utep.edu/interviews/1201/. For more on the Special Program and Operation Wetback, see Calavita, *Inside the State*, 73–112; and Lytle Hernández, *Migra!*, 169–95.
21. Like Magallón Jiménez, Cirilo Díaz Bojórquez also explained that braceros were expected to demonstrate to their employers that they could be reliable workers worthy of their legal support. Hard work, Díaz Bojórquez explained, was a requisite of the bracero contract. At the time when he and other braceros applied for legal permanent residence, employers expected to see braceros working hard if they were to grant them the immigration support letters. "And for that reason, we would almost kill ourselves working. We gave it our all to get that letter. Because if you didn't there was no letter," Díaz Bojórquez affirmed. Díaz Bojórquez, interview by Annette Shreibati.
22. Jesús Garnica, interview by Mireya Loza, Blythe, Calif., May 22, 2006, Bracero History Archive, Institute of Oral History, University of Texas at El Paso, https://braceroarchive.org/items/show/291.
23. For more on bracero masculinities, see Cohen, "From Peasant to Worker"; and Loza, *Defiant Braceros*, 63–94.

24. Josefina Fajardo, interview by Verónica Cortez, Heber, Calif., May 24, 2006, interview no. 1294, Bracero History Archive, Institute of Oral History, University of Texas at El Paso, https://scholarworks.utep.edu/interviews/1294/.
25. Herminio Estrada and Librada Estrada, interview by Mónica Pelayo, San Bernardino, Calif., May 26, 2006, interview no. 1149, Bracero History Archive, Institute of Oral History, University of Texas at El Paso, https://scholarworks.utep.edu/interviews/1149/.
26. Some of these works include: Leisy Abrego, *Sacrificing Families: Navigating Laws, Labor, and Love Across Borders* (Stanford University Press, 2014); Joanna Dreby, *Divided by Borders: Mexican Migrants and Their Children* (University of California Press, 2010); Pierrette Hondagneu-Sotelo and Ernestine Avila, "'I'm Here, but I'm There': The Meanings of Latina Transnational Motherhood," *Gender & Society* 11, no. 5 (1997): 548–71; and Rhacel Salazar Parreñas, "Mothering from a Distance: Emotions, Gender, and Intergenerational Relations in Filipino Transnational Families," *Feminist Studies* 27, no. 2 (2001): 361–90.

Bibliography

Abrego, Leisy. *Sacrificing Families: Navigating Laws, Labor, and Love Across Borders.* Stanford University Press, 2014.

Anderson, Henry P. *A Harvest of Loneliness: An Inquiry into a Social Problem.* Citizens for Farm Labor, 1964.

Calavita, Kitty. *Inside the State: The Bracero Program, Immigration, and the I.N.S.* Routledge, 1992.

Chávez-García, Miroslava. *Migrant Longing: Letter Writing Across the U.S.-Mexico Borderlands.* University of North Carolina Press, 2018.

Chavira Carrillo, Leonardo. Interview by Verónica Cortez. Coachella, Calif., May 20, 2006. Interview no. 1215. Bracero History Archive, Institute of Oral History, University of Texas at El Paso. https://scholarworks.utep.edu/interviews/1215/.

Cohen, Deborah. *Braceros: Migrant Citizens and Transnational Subjects in the Postwar United States and Mexico.* University of North Carolina Press, 2011.

Cohen, Deborah. "From Peasant to Worker: Migration, Masculinity, and the Making of Mexican Workers in the U.S." *International Labor and Working-Class History* 69 (Spring 2006): 81–103.

Díaz Bojórquez, Cirilo. Interview by Annette Shreibati. Blythe, Calif., May 22, 2006. Interview no. 1188. Bracero History Archive, Institute of Oral History, University of Texas at El Paso. https://scholarworks.utep.edu/interviews/1188/.

Dreby, Joanna. *Divided by Borders: Mexican Migrants and Their Children.* University of California Press, 2010.

Estrada, Librada, and Herminio Estrada. Interview by Mónica Pelayo. San Bernardino, Calif., May 26, 2006. Interview no. 1149. Bracero History Archive, Institute of Oral History, University of Texas at El Paso. https://scholarworks.utep.edu/interviews/1149/.

Fajardo, Josefina. Interview by Verónica Cortez. Heber, Calif., May 24, 2006. Interview no. 1294. Bracero History Archive, Institute of Oral History, University of Texas at El Paso. https://scholarworks.utep.edu/interviews/1294/.

Flores, Lori A. *Grounds for Dreaming: Mexican Americans, Mexican Immigrants, and the California Farmworker Movement*. Yale University Press, 2016.

Gamboa, Erasmo. *Mexican Labor and World War II: Braceros in the Pacific Northwest, 1942–1947*. University of Washington Press, 2000.

García González, Guadalupe. Interview by Mireya Loza. Los Angeles, Calif., May 11, 2006. Interview no. 1169. Bracero History Archive, Institute of Oral History, University of Texas at El Paso. https://scholarworks.utep.edu/interviews/1169/.

Garnica, Jesús. Interview by Mireya Loza. Blythe, Calif., May 22, 2006. Bracero History Archive, Institute of Oral History, University of Texas at El Paso. https://braceroarchive.org/items/show/291.

Greiner, Clemens, and Patrick Sakdapolrak. "Translocality: Concepts, Applications and Emerging Research Perspectives." *Geography Compass* 7, no. 5 (2013): 373–84.

Hondagneu-Sotelo, Pierrette. *Gendered Transitions: Mexican Experiences of Immigration*. University of California Press, 1994.

Hondagneu-Sotelo, Pierrette, and Ernestine Avila. "'I'm Here, but I'm There': The Meanings of Latina Transnational Motherhood." *Gender & Society* 11, no. 5 (1997): 548–71.

Klug, Thomas A. "Residents by Day, Visitors by Night: The Origins of the Alien Commuter on the U.S.-Canadian Border during the 1920s." *Michigan Historical Review* 34, no. 2 (Fall 2008): 75–98.

López, Margarita. Interview by Rochelle Garza. Perris, Calif., May 26, 2006. Interview no. 1081. Bracero History Archive, Institute of Oral History, University of Texas at El Paso. https://scholarworks.utep.edu/interviews/1081/.

López Silva, Alejo. Interview by Verónica Córtez. Perris, Calif., May 26, 2006. Interview no. 1082. Bracero History Archive, Institute of Oral History, University of Texas at El Paso. https://scholarworks.utep.edu/interviews/1082/.

López Silva, Higinio. Interview by Grisel Murillo. Perris, Calif., May 26, 2006. Interview no. 1068. Bracero History Archive, Institute of Oral History, University of Texas at El Paso. https://scholarworks.utep.edu/interviews/1068/.

Loza, Mireya. *Defiant Braceros: How Migrant Workers Fought for Racial, Sexual, and Political Freedom*. University of North Carolina Press, 2016.

Lytle Hernández, Kelly. *Migra! A History of the U.S. Border Patrol*. University of California Press, 2010.

Magallón Jiménez, Alberto. Interview by Anais Acosta. Salinas, Calif., July 28, 2005. Bracero History Archive, Institute of Oral History, University of Texas at El Paso. https://braceroarchive.org/items/show/153.

Mitchell, Don. *They Saved the Crops: Labor, Landscape, and the Struggle over Industrial Farming in Bracero-Era California*. University of Georgia Press, 2012.

Perales, Monica. *Smeltertown: Making and Remembering a Southwest Border Community*. University of North Carolina Press, 2010.

Plascencia, Luis F. B. "'Get Us Our Privilege of Bringing in Mexican Labor': Recruitment and Desire for Mexican Labor in Arizona, 1917–2016." In *Mexican Workers and the Making of Arizona*, edited by Luis F. B. Plascencia and Gloria H. Cuádraz, 124–78. University of Arizona Press, 2018.

Rodríguez, Néstor. "The Battle for the Border: Notes on Autonomous Migration, Transnational Communities, and the State." *Social Justice* 23, no. 3 (1996): 21–37.

Rosas, Ana E. *Abrazando el Espíritu: Bracero Families Confront the U.S.-Mexico Border*. University of California Press, 2014.

Salazar Parreñas, Rhacel. "Mothering from a Distance: Emotions, Gender, and Intergenerational Relations in Filipino Transnational Families." *Feminist Studies* 27, no. 2 (2001): 361–90.

Sifuentez, Mario J. *Of Forests and Fields: Mexican Labor in the Pacific Northwest*. Rutgers University Press, 2016.

Smith, Michael P., and Luis E. Guarnizo. *Transnationalism from Below*. Transaction Publishers, 1998.

Velásquez, Steve. "Creating a Bracero Archive: Collaboration, Collections, and Challenges." *Diálogo* 19, no. 2 (Fall 2016): 7–20.

Villarreal, Severiano G. Interview by Verónica Cortez. Blythe, Calif., May 22, 2006. Interview no. 1201. Bracero History Archive, Institute of Oral History, University of Texas at El Paso. https://scholarworks.utep.edu/interviews/1201/.

CHAPTER 6

"All of Us Had Our Jobs"

Mexican Women's Work in a Cotton Company Town

GLORIA HOLGUÍN CUÁDRAZ

"We all had our jobs." Such were the words of Sallie Villa Romo, who was born in "los campos" of Litchfield Park in the 1930s and spent most of her childhood working alongside her seven siblings and father—picking cotton, onions, or grapes, or working in the packinghouses of the company town of Litchfield Park, Arizona, located approximately twenty miles west of Phoenix in the southwestern portion of Maricopa County. When Sallie was in fourth grade, the family lost their mother to illness, which crushed them emotionally and altered their lives. For Sallie, it would be the last year she attended school. Instead, all the siblings went to work to ensure the family's survival. "We were very poor, like everybody in the camp. But we always had food. We had our jobs. All of us had our jobs."[1] As Sallie described a typical day in the family, she recalled how all the girls "were supposed to get up very early in the morning and make tortillas and fix the lunches for my dad and my brothers that went out to work very early." In addition, the girls would "have to do their [their brothers' and father's] laundry. I don't even remember a washing machine. It was just the tub and a lavadero . . . a washboard?" When I asked Sallie what she remembered the most about work, she elaborated:

> How hard it was. How you had to come home and, ah, do your own laundry. And we never had enough clothes. That was it. That was real hard.

> And we worked from early [morning] to late afternoon. Come home and there was no mom in the house . . . that's what I remember. It was hard work.[2]

Sallie also describes, however, being surrounded and nurtured by extended family members, tíos and tías, grandparents, and other residents of the camps, who supported the family through their ups and downs. Her oldest sister "kind of took over, held us together—my brother too. And then my dad remarried, soon after."

These passages tell us many things. That Sallie had to work as a child is foremost, a phenomenon that would not change (especially in agriculture) even after child labor laws were passed in the United States to protect children from exploitative and adverse working conditions. That she worked as part of a family unit reveals one way in which labor was organized and arranged within the context of agriculture. The fact that children in the family had to work suggests wages were low, requiring multiple members of the family to work to earn enough for their survival. Indeed, one consistent theme in the Mexican Americans of Litchfield Park Oral History Project was how low the wages were. Moreover, in addition to wage-earning work, we catch a glimpse of a division of labor in the home, such that Sallie's status as a female in the family required her to conduct household tasks that served all the members of her family. The loss of her mother also made apparent how the absence of one parent resulted in the responsibilities of household maintenance falling even more unevenly on the shoulders of the young women in the family.

This chapter focuses on Mexican women who were part of a company town that was central to the development of Arizona's cotton industry and to its economic well-being. These women were among the Mexican families that resided in the labor camps—los campos—built by the company to house workers and their families. The Goodyear Tire and Rubber Company (GYTR) established Litchfield Park, formerly Litchfield Ranch, in 1917 to produce long-staple cotton, essential to its manufacture of pneumatic tires for the burgeoning automobile and truck industry.[3] This chapter delves into the kinds of work Mexican women held in the company town and the various ways in which women worked in paid and unpaid jobs and engaged in formal and informal activities related to the economy of the company town and the maintenance and survival of their households.

In *Mexican Workers and the Making of Arizona*, anthropologist Luis Plascencia and I argued that Mexican workers represent a paradox adequately captured by the concept of an "elastic supply of labor"—that is, a concept that speaks to the availability (or alleged shortage) of workers, and an arrangement that contracts or expands according to the needs of capital.[4] In other words, employers demand access to a flexible labor pool (hence the elasticity)—one that is available when production goals are greatest, and disposable when it is no longer needed. In my own synopsis of the cotton industry's 1917–21 "boom and bust" period in Arizona, I argued that Mexican workers were mobilized and subsequently immobilized by the repressive labor tactics of the Arizona Cotton Growers Association (ACGA) and the cotton industry's intent to control their contracted workforce.[5] We know from archival sources related to the 1917–21 period that Mexican women were recruited to work in the cotton industry and were part of the family units preferred and sought by growers.[6] In my work, I argued there was a gendering of the "elastic supply of labor" based on women's availability to work, to the extent that they were incorporated as part of a preferred labor force in the form of a family unit. In this chapter, I explore the gendering of the elasticity more fully, considering the kinds and range of work Mexican women performed as residents of the camps and workers within the company town, and the extent to which Mexican women were key to the social reproduction of labor and community.

While archival documents establish the presence of Mexican women early in Litchfield Park's history, the kind of information we can glean from them is limited.[7] In this vein, oral histories are valuable for capturing women's memories of their lived experiences as workers and residents of the company town, potentially giving voice to their productive and reproductive roles in the workplace, home, and community. To expound on my findings, I draw from interviews with various narrators, including Armida Vizzerra, whose varied work experiences and participation in the community offer a glimpse into the kinds of jobs held by women who lived in the company town. I do not argue that their lives are representative, but rather that by delving into their lived experiences, we gain a clearer understanding of how women took part in the production process for capital while simultaneously contributing to their families' abilities to subsist, to the social relations within the camp communities, and to the larger company town of Litchfield Park.

The Study

I became involved with the Litchfield Park Historical Society (LPHS) when I was asked by Dr. José Leyba, then an administrator at the Maricopa County Community College District, if I would meet with a group of women committed to documenting the stories of Mexican workers and their families who had worked and lived in the labor camps of Litchfield Park. Dr. Leyba had lived in the camps as a child and recognized how important it was to support these women's efforts. I was an associate professor of sociology in what is now the School of Humanities, Arts, and Cultural Studies at Arizona State University's West Valley campus, with a background in qualitative sociology and a growing interest in the field of oral history. I had just completed an oral history training institute at Columbia University's Center for Oral History and was excited to meet with the women who made up the Oral History Subcommittee of the Litchfield Park Historical Society. We met, and as far as I was concerned, I saw myself as a collaborator in a project that grew out of this community's own desire to document their stories. I was raised in a large working-class family in the agricultural borderlands of California's Imperial Valley.[8] My parents met while working in the fields; my father worked in agriculture his entire life, driving tractors to plow the fields, and my mother devoted her life to raising and attending to eight children. I entered the project feeling familiar with the terrain. Moreover, I was keen to put my sociological interests in race, gender, and social stratification to use, having grown up as a Mexican American woman, now identified as Chicana, in a town dominated by the agricultural industry and the social hierarchies stemming from it.

We formed a partnership and secured funds to start the Mexican Americans of Litchfield Park Oral History Project (MAOH).[9] We decided to conduct videotaped interviews of adults who had worked and/or lived in the camps.[10] As with so many oral history projects, time was of the essence, as many former camp residents were deceased, and many were in their elder years. Our key informant within the committee, Belén Soto Moreno, had grown up in Camp No. 54; her insider status within the Mexican community allowed us to quickly schedule and move forward with the interviews. Over the course of a few years we conducted fifty oral histories, of varied length, from as short as fifteen minutes to as long as two hours. Three-quarters of the oral histories were with women, with additional interviews conducted by LPHS in the years that followed. Most interviews were conducted in English, with a handful in Spanish.

The interviews fell into two separate groups. There were interviews with narrators who had worked directly for the Southwest Cotton Company (SWCC), later renamed Goodyear Farms, and who had a host of stories to share about their lives as workers in the company town. A second group comprised second- or third-generation residents of the camps. Some of these narrators had worked full-time in agriculture, but there were also those who had worked only temporarily or seasonally as children and/or adolescents. These narrators shared stories of their parents' work and social lives and provided vivid memories of growing up in the camps and in a company town, attending Litchfield schools, and witnessing the lives of their parents and/or grandparents.

To capture the history of Mexican women's presence in this company town, I first focus on the cotton industry's early "boom and bust" period from 1917 to 1921. Although Mexican women's participation is not the focal point of analysis in earlier accounts of this period, the preservation of a few archival documents has allowed us to capture their presence and participation in this foundational period.[11] Historian Deena González notes: "It is simply not true that women are absent in the archival record. Rather, we need the historians able and eager to find them."[12] For the second period, I draw from the narrators' stories to capture the variability and nature of their work lives from 1929 to 1986. The select narratives are meant to illustrate the myriad kinds of work undertaken by Mexican women during this period and the value of oral histories for reconstructing Mexican women's history.[13]

Gendering the Elastic Supply of Labor: Goodyear and the Immigration Act of 1917

The entry of Goodyear Tire and Rubber (GYTR) into Arizona in 1917 marks the development of Arizona's large-scale commercial cotton industry. In the twentieth century, the cotton industry became a driving economic engine for the entire Salt River Valley, including central Phoenix, Tempe, Mesa, and Chandler.[14] The emergence of the cotton industry simultaneously shaped the local economy of Maricopa County's West Valley, including Glendale, and the development of neighboring townships such as Avondale, Tolleson, and Goodyear. GYTR established the Southwest Cotton Company (SWCC) in 1917, a subsidiary to oversee management and operations of their investments, and, as part of this investment, the company town of Litchfield Park came into existence.[15]

SWCC moved quickly on several different fronts. It financed loans to growers and banks and arranged to become the biggest buyer of growers' cotton crops. It bought out whatever operations were necessary to guarantee a seamless integration process, from the production of cotton and ginning to milling operations back east. In the East Valley, Goodyear built the first small cotton company town, Ocotillo, Arizona (also known as Cotton City, Egypt, and Goodyear), located in the present-day city of Chandler.[16] In the West Valley, efforts turned to clearing the desert and digging canals, all of which required an extensive amount of arduous manual labor. Workers were needed, and it was soon evident that the local workforce would be insufficient to meet the demands of the thousands of acres expected to be under the plow.

The passage of the Immigration Act of 1917 posed a daunting impediment to GYTR's investments. The act was a restrictionist law supported largely by nativists who desired to curb immigration from eastern and southern Europe. A head tax and literacy requirement were imposed. The act reinforced the 1885 law that prohibited the recruitment of foreign workers for jobs in the United States.[17] The legislation was opposed by cotton and sugar beet growers and by railroads, some of whom had informally, in violation of law, been recruiting workers from Mexico to meet their labor force demands.

But the specter of World War I, the embargo on cotton, and a boll weevil infestation in the South created a demand for the production of long-staple cotton, which the country could ill afford to lose. GYTR's president, Arizona growers and political officials, and growers across the Southwest lobbied the secretary of labor to reinterpret the Immigration Act of 1917 with the pretext that agricultural production during wartime constituted an "emergency."

Under the reinterpretation of the Ninth Proviso of the Immigration Act of 1917, growers throughout the Southwest were granted the authority to directly recruit workers from Mexico for six-month stays, waive the head tax and literacy requirement, and forego the 1885 law. The reinterpreted Ninth Proviso thus led to the first formal state-sanctioned recruitment of workers from Mexico by the United States, which provided the foundation for the Bracero Program yet to come.[18] As part of the agreement, growers were required to provide transportation to and from Mexico, shelter, and wages commensurate with U.S. standards. In return, they were granted permission to withhold a percentage of workers' wages to be delivered upon their return to Mexico.

SWCC established the Arizona Cotton Growers Association (ACGA) to recruit their labor force, organize their labor force needs, and reduce competition between growers for labor and wages. The Arizona Cotton Growers Association specifically focused on recruiting family units as the preferred labor force. From its inception, the gendering of elasticity was inscribed into how employers would organize the labor force. Growers wanted as many hands as possible in the hand-harvesting of cotton; this meant that women's and children's labor was critical to the hand-harvesting of cotton and to the industry's production goals. The latter helps to partially explain the presence of Mexican women as targets of recruitment and their incorporation into the cotton industry's workforce. Rather than recruiting and paying wages to the individual worker, focusing on family units allowed employers to extract labor from every able-bodied person in the family. Children under the age of sixteen or extended family members who accompanied the male head of household could work and earn wages based on the production of household units. Wages were paid to the household, relieving the employer from paying each individual worker.

Meanwhile, with the passage of the Immigration Act of 1917 and the waivers made possible by the reinterpretation of the Ninth Proviso, approximately 72,862 Mexican workers were recruited and brought into the United States during the seven years the reinterpretation was in operation.[19] Of those, 33,460 were brought in by the Arizona Cotton Growers

Association alone.[20] In this respect, the ramifications for the state of Arizona were great. The fact that almost half of the workers were brought in *by one entity for one single-crop industry* speaks volumes about how the reinterpretation of the Ninth Proviso enabled the cotton industry's profit-making and advanced large-scale commercial production in Arizona. Indeed, millions of dollars were made during the boom period, as production went from 33,000 acres to 240,000 acres of long-staple cotton by the 1920–21 season.[21]

Women were very much present among the 33,460 workers recruited and contracted to work for the Arizona Cotton Growers Association, bringing to the forefront the fact that the "elastic supply of labor" was not only racialized but gendered as well. A forty-page report commissioned by the Mexican consul establishes women's participation and presence. The report reveals several important findings. First, women were very much present in the initial boom-and-bust period of the cotton industry's entry into Arizona; of the 160 cases featured in this report, 53 of them consisted of men accompanied by their wives, children, mothers, or other female relatives. Women, whether as wives, daughters, sisters, or extended relatives, were part of the family "units of production" that the cotton industry proclaimed were their ideal basis for recruitment. There were husband/wife partnerships that entered with one or two children, and a handful of others with numbers of children ranging from nine to twelve.[22] Hence, women were a *defining feature of the preferred labor force*, inscribing the gendering of elasticity into the very structure of the cotton industry's approach to production. The implication for women who worked as part of the family unit of production is that, since wages were based on the production of the unit, this contributed to the erasure of women's labor. Moreover, since the ACGA could not officially hire anyone sixteen years of age or younger, one could argue that women were infantilized by being put on equal terms with children, whose production only mattered in relationship to the production of the family unit.

Second, the report also establishes that women were independently part of the recruited workforce: single women, single-parent heads of household, and/or widowed women (some with children) were granted identification numbers and recruited as formal wageworkers. Thus, when it came to wages, women were paid either as part of a larger family unit of production or as independent wage earners (with or without children). Mexican women sought out work. In considering how gender shaped Mexican women's migration during the first half of the twentieth century, Veloz argues that "family-centered motivations" were equally important to the larger economic and political forces shaping the diversity of migration patterns. In her view, "family networks lie at the heart of the broader social networks that have historically sustained migration."[23]

For growers, women's flexibility and their children's availability to work in family units had the desired stabilizing influence that helped create a reliable, compliant workforce. Even though women's reproductive labor in the form of maintaining a household was not in the foreground (since all the workers were considered temporary), their positions as mothers and their reproductive labor as childbearers and caretakers were critical to the overall strategies deployed by the ACGA to ensure its continued access to an "elastic supply of labor."

When cotton market prices collapsed in the 1920–21 season, a crisis unfolded, and the Arizona Cotton Growers Association's response to the economic downturn was inhumane. In short, rather than abide by their contracts, growers quickly abandoned thousands of workers, banished them from the fields, denied them remaining pay, held deposits, and demolished any makeshift shelters and/or housing available to the workers. The following vignettes in the Mexican consul's report provide a glimpse into workers' experiences during the crisis:

> Alejandra Ramírez was brought here by the Arizona Cotton Growers Association, we are informed, something like two or three months ago. She is a widow and has a boy and a girl. She was last employed by the Chandler Improvement Company and on the 2nd day of February, 1921, she was ordered to leave the tent and seek shelter elsewhere. She immediately proceeded to move out her belongings, as well as a great many others who were moving out from other tents nearby, but before she was able to get her belongings out of the tent, the tent was pulled down under the orders and directions of one Mr. Cook, and thereafter the tent was removed from the place and she was left out in the open in company with a great many others.

> Francisco V. Moreno, No. 21459, was imported September 21, 1920, by the Arizona Cotton Growers Association and ordered to work for the West Avondale Ranch. He now has $36.54 due from them, which he is having

> trouble to collect. This man has a wife and six children and is in destitute circumstances. He urges to us to get his pass to the Mexican border.[24]

The vignettes documented in the report establish women's presence in the labor force and the fact that they were among the first formally recruited Mexican workers sanctioned by the United States. Only when the Phoenix Mexican consul stepped in to finance the workers' return did the crisis come to an end.[25]

From the point of view of the growers and agribusiness, women's wage labor had value with respect to their production goals, and women held value to the extent that they were part of a family unit—the unit essential to the productive and reproductive interests of employers and their quest for profits. The pattern for the gendering of the elasticity of labor, I argue, began here, when the very workers growers had sought were disposed of, callously treated, and returned to Mexico, a treatment that would be repeated in the decades to come in the form of the Bracero Program.[26]

The focus on the family unit of production would not be duplicated during the Bracero Program, which in its twenty-six years of existence as a U.S.-Mexico binational agreement focused on contracting individual male wage earners to work in the agricultural industry. In her contribution to this volume, Alina R. Méndez provides evidence, despite Bracero Program policies that undergirded family separation, of braceros who were able to reunify their families in the California/Arizona-Mexico borderlands. The gendering of the elasticity of labor is shaped by the extent to which the very construct of the "preferred labor force" is bound up with the juxtaposition of the individual wage earner against the family unit of production.

The Establishment of a Cotton Company Town in the Salt River Valley

A flurry of activity to build the infrastructure of the company town ensued in 1917. Travel along the twenty miles between Litchfield Park and Phoenix was on dirt roads, using modes of transportation that predated the automobile. By 1921, SWCC had developed 154 miles of roads, an airfield, electricity, wells and concrete canals for the harnessing of water, office headquarters and field offices, cotton gins, and housing for managers, personnel, and laborers. The Arizona Eastern Railroad built a direct railway line to Litchfield Park to facilitate the transport of cotton.[27] In short, GYTR transformed the entire visible landscape of the Salt River Valley.[28]

By 1919, the company town of Litchfield Park could boast a field office, a company store, a six-strand cotton gin, electrical power, and a 325,000-gallon reservoir to provide water to the townsite, as well as a "mess hall and living quarters, a blacksmith shop, machine shop, warehouse and carpenter shop."[29] SWCC also built an "Organization House" in 1918–19, which was used to accommodate executives, employees from Goodyear's Akron headquarters (and later their families), and suppliers; it later became the basis for the Wigwam Resort, which became a top resort in the Southwest. Litchfield Elementary School District was formed almost immediately, with authorization in the form of school bonds for a permanent public school.[30] With personnel composed of engineers, lawyers, and experts in agriculture, SWCC established a crop rotation system that increased the quality and quantity of cotton production.

James B. Allen, in *The Company Town in the American West*, defines a company town in the simplest of terms, as "any community which is owned and controlled by a particular company."[31] Within the social relations of company towns, a defining feature is paternalism, referring to the relationship between "those who govern and the governed, or the employer and the employed," resulting in social control and the employer's unchecked power over its workforce.[32] Allen notes that scholarly literature on company towns in the West fails to adequately examine the presence and participation of racial/ethnic communities.[33] It does an even worse job of delineating the roles of women in these towns. Women tend to be depicted as marginal to the "production process" but central to the culture and the rearing and caretaking of family households. In this respect, their reproductive roles are important, but for the most part, their importance to capital remains invisible.

History of the Camps

The incorporation of the Mexican workforce dates to GYTR's entry into Arizona in 1917. From the onset, Mexican workers were among the two thousand workers who cleared the raw desert land to prepare thousands of acres for planting.[34] Until 1986, when GYTR left Arizona, Mexican workers, both men and women, were integral to its ventures. "Camps," or "campos," defined as "residential enclaves of Mexican laborers and their families," were an integral part of the landscape and operations of the railroad, mining, and agricultural industries, among others.[35] Historian Gilbert G. Gonzalez laments that woefully few historians have studied camps in depth. Yet by 1920, he argues, the notion of a "Mexican camp" was already "common."[36] In corporate agriculture across the Southwest, housing became a key issue, as thousands of workers were required during the various harvest seasons, and the erection of camps, whether makeshift or permanent, became a critical part of the twentieth-century landscape. Arizona was no exception.

Following the collapse of cotton's market price and the financial crisis, conditions began to stabilize in late 1921. Paul Litchfield, who eventually became vice-president and later chairman of the board of GYTR, and for whom the town is named, managed to convince GYTR to maintain its support.[37] GYTR did so, and it diversified the range of its production related to agriculture, expanding into cattle, alfalfa, and hog production, as well as other areas.[38] As full-fledged plans for the company town of Litchfield Park were put into place between 1917 and 1929, workers were housed in centrally located makeshift structures and tents that were later moved and replaced by a row of sixteen adobe houses, approximately three hundred to five hundred square feet in size, alongside the Air Line Canal. This camp was named Algodón—Spanish for "cotton"—or Algodones, as its residents referred to it.[39]

In 1929, SWCC built and moved workers to five camps—numbered 50, 51, 52, 53, and 54—located largely in the periphery of the town, which over the years housed hundreds of permanent workers, both citizens and noncitizens. A typical camp house was approximately three hundred to five hundred square feet. It was a wood-frame house, with a screened window, but built with no insulation, which became challenging for residents during bouts of cold weather. As residents' families grew, and as physical space permitted, workers were allowed to add rooms to their existing homes.

Labor camps in company towns, when compared to camps for seasonal and migratory workers, were of a higher quality with respect to living conditions and the amenities available to their workforces. Historically, living conditions for migratory and seasonal workers are among the bleakest and most desolate.[40] Weber describes the camps that housed migratory cotton workers in California: "The brutal conditions of the camps, from deplorable housing to the lack of beds, ovens, toilets, showers, and running water were a constant source of sickness, accidents, strain, and conflict."[41] In a report on migratory cotton pickers in Arizona made at the end of the Great Depression, Brown and Cassmore had the following to say about the "cotton-pickers' camps":

> [They] conform to the standard rural-slum pattern of Western migratory workers' camps. The usual run of AZ camps consists of a crowded, filthy, makeshift collection of shelters. Although some of the camps house as many as 1,000 people during the picking season, even elementary sanitary provisions are frequently lacking. To visitors, life in the cotton camps gives the impression of being a long round of privation and misery. Among the pickers themselves the living conditions are often resented with intense bitterness.[42]

Across the West, company towns were segregated along racial/ethnic lines and according to national origin.[43] Historian Gilbert G. González stated, "In all company towns the social hierarchy and patterns of segregation mirrored the division of labor."[44] In her overview of the two company towns built by GYTR, Hill argues that segregation was "inscribed" into GYTR's planning details for Litchfield Park. The fact that camps were specifically built to house the year-round or permanently employed members of the Mexican workforce and that they intentionally segregated Mexican workers from the Anglo community reflects the production and reproduction of a social hierarchy along racial/ethnic lines, one that reinforced a class and gendered stratification resonant of the wage differentials in place. The decision to move the camp communities in 1929 to the periphery of town coincides with SWCC's decision to further develop the Wigwam Resort.

In addition to wages, workers were provided housing, utilities, and other amenities while living in and working for the company town. The provision of housing was reconstrued as a benefit, and one that justified the payment of lower wages to a workforce integral to maximizing the production of an industry. What would be considered decent housing then became, as scholars have argued, a means by which paternalism and a form of social control could be exerted upon the workforce.[45]

A "Mexican court" and a "Mexican plaza" were built into a section of town. The arrival of the 1918–19 flu and the deaths of workers led Paul W. Litchfield to commission the building of a cemetery specifically for the company's workers, now designated as the Goodyear Farms Historic Cemetery.[46] In 1923 Litchfield saw to it that a church was built, St. Thomas Aquinas Catholic Mission, which became a cornerstone and central gathering place for camp community residents, used for baptisms, Holy Communion, weddings, funeral rites, and religious ceremonies.[47]

For people of Mexican descent, the concept of a "camp" may hold multiple material and symbolic meanings. It signified an opportunity for steady employment and stability as a place of work, especially if one was among the permanent employees hired by the company. It also provided the possibility of social mobility, depending on what skills and knowledge one brought or learned in the workplace. The camps provided the shelter families needed to raise children and house extended family members in one household. Living in the camps presented the possibility for individuals, families, and extended families to live near each other and to establish roots in the United States. For many families, it meant not having to migrate to work in agriculture. By remaining in one place, they could offer their offspring the benefits and stability that came with steady employment. From a different standpoint, living in the camps also signified separation and segregation along racial/ethnic lines and often meant enduring conditions of poverty, with limited resources to make ends meet.[48]

The decades following the movement of the camps to the periphery of Litchfield Park, beginning with 1930, saw significant economic, social, and technological changes that shaped the agricultural industry, among others. Although it is not possible to delve into particulars of the vast period between 1929 and 1986, general contours are worth noting. In the 1930s, the Great Depression occurred, resulting in the mass deportation of thousands of people of Mexican descent, including those with U.S. citizenship. Historian Eric V. Meeks found that the Anglos who migrated westward from Texas, Arkansas, and Oklahoma "came to make up the largest farm labor force for the first time in the state's [Arizona's] history."[49] The United States' entry into World War II also brought huge changes to the company town, as most men working for the company enlisted to serve in the military. In some aspects of the company town's operations, women were asked to step into the jobs left by the men's absence. The advent of the Bracero Program in 1942 brought in a massive number of workers from Mexico in response to the agricultural industry's proclamation of dire "labor shortages."[50] Workers under this program, which lasted until 1964 (or 1968),[51] did become part of the company's workforce, albeit on a temporary basis, and were housed in the camps. Unlike the recruitment under the Ninth Proviso, employers targeted individual male workers. The World War II era was also marked by the establishment of Goodyear Aircraft, Luke Air Force Base, and other military-based operations that profoundly impacted the local and regional economies of the entire West Valley region of Maricopa County, of which Litchfield Park is a part. As these larger economic changes took hold, women had a broader array of choices for employment, leading many to seek work outside of agriculture and participate in the transformations taking place in the West Valley.

The camps existed until 1986, at which time GYTR shut down its operations in response to a corporate takeover and sold off several properties to remain solvent.[52] These were the camps the families we interviewed would speak of, often with nostalgia and yearnings for their past. A local paper reported on this closing with the headline "70 Years Unfold for Goodyear Farms," describing the end of an era and an end to the camp communities.[53]

The Elasticity of Mexican Women's Labor in Company Towns

To consider the gendering of the elasticity of labor, it is worthwhile to examine how Mexican women and their labor were incorporated into company towns in other twentieth-century industries in the Southwest. In the Southwestern citrus industry, for example, company towns often relied on Mexican labor. Growers preferred to hire family men for the hand-harvesting of citrus. Growers perceived Mexican women largely in the context of their relationship to individual male wageworkers and as part of a family household. Growers presumed that married men were more stable and that their responsibilities toward families would discourage dissent or behaviors that might make their management more difficult. As part of families, women were legitimized and welcomed by the company town; not only would women maintain households, but they would also produce future generations of workers, benefiting the company town, corporate agribusiness, and the state.[54]

In Arizona's mining company towns, Mexican workers and their families were largely segregated and subject to inferior housing; a dual wage system that paid Mexican male workers less necessitated work by Mexican women to supplement incomes.[55] Thus, Mexican women's work in mining towns consisted largely of service-sector work as cooks, maids, and laundresses for the white mining executives and their families. While their work was not directly beneficial to mining production, it was important to the sustenance of their individual households and the executives' households. Historian Christine Marin found in the War Labor Reports of the World War II era that Mexican women were classified as "laborers" in the company town of Miami, Arizona. They dug ditches, filled ore carts with waste materials, made and mixed concrete slabs, sawed wood, and mixed oils for machinery; they sharpened tools and cleaned work tools, equipment, and machines the male miners used in their work.[56] Such evidence verifies the elasticity of Mexican women's labor within mining company towns, one bounded by gender; their labor was both supplemental and peripheral. Yet Mexican women were instrumental and key to the labor struggles for better wages and conditions that ensued in the mining industry.[57]

Other mining historians note the roles of Mexican women in the Southwest industry. In *Smeltertown*, historian Monica Perales carefully documents the ways in which the "smelter counted on women not only to provide wholesome, clean homes for its present workers but also to produce and raise future workers."[58] Although census numbers do not report that many married women worked outside the home, there were jobs in the less formal economy—from preparing lunches for workers to working as parteras (midwives), renting rooms, collecting rent, or operating and teaching in the escuelitas of Smeltertown in El Paso, Texas—that allowed Mexican women to earn income "without directly undermining the position of the man of the house."[59] Work options for Mexican women in the 1920s and 1930s were determined largely along gendered lines; thus, women worked as housekeepers, laundresses, seamstresses, street vendors, and clerks, in positions "that extended private work into the public realm."[60]

Of the one-crop industries that prevailed in the first half of the twentieth century, the sugar beet industry was most like the cotton industry, especially when it came to who was construed as the ideal workforce. The beet industry sought out entire families to work in beet production, encouraging these families to migrate and offering contracts to family units. During the 1917–21 period, the beet industry also benefited from the recruitment of Mexican labor under the temporary admissions program. In one case, the Utah-Idaho Sugar Company argued that it faced a labor shortage and, like the ACGA, actively lobbied the federal government to loosen the restrictions established by the Immigration Act of 1917.[61] Like cotton, the growing and harvesting of sugar beets is a labor-intensive process, requiring workers more seasonally than year-round. In their study of women beet workers in northeastern Colorado and the Great Western Sugar Company, Mary Romero and Eric Margolis describe how beet industry officials contracted entire families:

> Men, women, and children bound themselves over to tend the beets for the whole season, even though there were two periods of full employment in the spring and fall. During those intensive periods workers were expected to work as long as it was light, sometimes 14 or 15 hours a day. Beet workers' wages were among the lowest of any workers in the state, their living conditions appallingly primitive, and their chances of upward mobility truncated at every turn.[62]

Citing a Department of Labor study investigating women's work conditions in the beet industry, the gendering of the elastic supply of labor is evident in: (a) the recruiting and contracting of families as a unit of production, (b) the use of women and children's labor for production, and (c) the reliance on women's reproductive labor to sustain the family and growers' dependence on that labor to ensure a stable workforce.[63]

Women's Labor, Producing "White Gold," and Reproductive Work in a Company Town

Documenting the practices that shaped the work lives of women in the camps entails grasping a very complicated set of conditions that both advantaged and disadvantaged the individuals and families who were a part of these communities.

In some stories about how workers and their families came to work and live in the camps, narrators' accounts would begin with families finding work in Chandler (in the East Valley) or Marinette (in the northwestern part of the valley) first, and then in Litchfield Park. Families with a history of working in the mines were also situated to transition to agricultural work, particularly as cotton became the new "white gold" in Arizona. Like so many of the Mexican families who took part in the massive migration from Mexico during the Mexican Revolution of 1910–20, their migration north during this period was also spurred by the need to leave the violence and economic uncertainty of northern Mexico.[64]

In her landmark study *Dark Sweat, White Gold*, historian Devra Weber observes that "in the United States, Mexican women worked."[65] Yet, despite the fact that cotton workers "became the largest labor force in the agricultural industry," Mexican women's participation is not as widely studied as one might expect.[66] Contrary to the prominent depiction of the single male Mexican immigrant laborer, Mexican women occupied a nebulous position as individual paid laborers on the one hand, and invisible laborers in the context of a "family unit" on the other. Both positions operated simultaneously and were contingent on arrangements specific to time and place. In cotton, growers preferred family units because they guaranteed the availability of more workers to pick cotton and made dissent less likely, as workers with family would be less likely to organize and take risks with their steady income.

Cotton is unique among the single-crop industries in *the extent to which women and children made up part of the ideal workforce in its hand-harvesting.* Unlike mining and smelter work, or the harvesting of citrus, picking cotton was not considered solely men's work. The hand-harvesting of long-staple cotton was labor-intensive, difficult work. Classified as American Egyptian cotton and later labeled Pima cotton, its harvesting is more arduous and painstaking because the cotton plant is shorter and the cotton is removed from a narrower opening in the boll of the plant. The sharp-pointed edges on the boll often led to lacerations on workers' hands. The following description captures the labor process:

> Picking required skill, strength, and endurance. Workers stooped, stood, and often crawled to reach the bolls. . . . Experienced pickers used both hands, quickly picking cotton bolls clean from their casings, avoiding branches and twigs, and working up and down the plant, stuffing cotton in a sack with one hand while picking bolls with the other and pausing only to pack the white bolls tightly into the bag. When the bag was full, the worker hoisted the hundred-pound sack, slid one end back, hefted the other end over one shoulder, and walked to the end of the row, where a contractor's assistant weighed the bag and, deducting for twigs and debris, tallied the weight on a list beside each worker's name. The worker then picked up the bag, climbed a rickety ladder, and emptied the sack of cotton into the wagon.[67]

To produce "white gold" in the Salt River Valley, cultivation and preparation of the land begins almost eight months prior to the picking season. Therefore, a permanent workforce is required, in addition to the thousands required for harvest. Once the ground is evenly distributed, cotton is planted between mid-March and the first week of April. After the plants have germinated and reached a height of two inches, weeding begins. Cotton rows are spaced three to four feet apart and thinned when the plants have reached a height of four to twelve inches. It was formerly common throughout the Southwest for workers to use a short hoe ("el cortito," "mano del diablo") for the thinning process, a practice that was banned in 1984 because bending to use the short hoe resulted in debilitating back injuries for workers. Thinning, which takes place twice during a season, can also be done by uprooting the plant entirely. Meanwhile, assuming the ground has been constantly cultivated and properly irrigated, the crop is ready to be harvested by early September, subject to three pickings during a season that ends in February.[68] The growing season of long-staple cotton requires a steady but smaller workforce from March until August, and a large seasonal workforce once picking begins in September and until it concludes in February.

Within the confines of the company town, it was up to each family unit to decide whether and how women and children would participate in the labor force. This varied from family to family. In some households, a traditional division along gender lines could be found in which only the father worked, with the mother working at home to raise children and attend to the household; in other cases, both parents worked in the fields, and in still other families, the entire household of parents and children would be involved working in the fields. In addition to heterosexual nuclear households there were also households run by single or widowed parents, often because of illnesses or tragedies that befell them. Work was also seasonal, creating situations where children worked during certain periods of the year.[69] Historian Eric V. Meeks aptly notes, "In the early decades of the [twentieth] century, most working-class [Mexican] families could not sustain themselves without taking advantage of all potential wage earners."[70]

Women who worked in the production of cotton often faced an "elasticity to their labor," as they negotiated a gendered division of labor in the realms of production and reproduction to sustain their lives and those of their families.[71] This is evident in Sallie Villa Romo's oral history with which we began, in which she recounted how she picked cotton as a child (as part of a family unit) and then returned home to a gendered division of labor, which left her responsible for attending to the needs of others and contributing to the maintenance of the home. In the following account by her sister, Lucy Villa Moreno, we hear about the reproductive labor performed by her grandmother, her own experiences working in cotton, and, similar to what Sallie describes, how because of her mother's illness, the reproductive labor in their household then fell on the shoulders of the siblings.

Lucy Villa Moreno was born in 1929 in Camp 52 and was the oldest of six siblings. Her grandmother "would do the people's laundry. She was always washing and ironing for the people that lived right there in the city of Litchfield."[72] Lucy attended school until the fifth grade and then had to quit because of her mother's long-term illness. Lucy worked in the fields with her brother. "He would weigh the cotton, and I would pay them, and used to pick them up." She continued:

> When my brother and I worked with the cotton pickers, then it was nice. I always wore this handkerchief around my face so the sun wouldn't burn my skin. But any little breeze and you would cool off real nice. Big hats. The

> toughest was when you would chop cotton [. . .]. We wouldn't even look up until we reached the end of it [the row]. My dad would get the whole field for us, for the family. We worked really hard.

From the two accounts of the Villa sisters, we get a firsthand look at what happened to the work and family lives of the children when the mother was not there to engage in the reproductive labor necessary to attend to the needs of the family and the maintenance of the household. The indispensability and elasticity of women's reproductive labor becomes blatantly clear. The responsibilities that women carried and the work they did to maintain their homes and raise their families, to cook, clothe, do laundry, clean, nurse, and grow food in the gardens, all made their family's lives and opportunities possible. Without women to sustain and nurture these households, the social fabric of the households and the community at large suffered. Scholars have consistently found that women's familial and social networks were the lifeline for sustaining and building secure and meaningful communities.[73] The ability to live near one's extended family loomed large in the benefits articulated by the women we interviewed. This provided an infrastructure of support for the various kinds of labor they were involved in, but especially for the reproductive labor in the home. While maintaining the sustainability of a company town requires an intensive investment in resources to manage a large resident workforce, the work that women did on a day-to-day basis mattered.[74] It fortified their husbands' and children's ability to work (facilitating the income stream), and it fortified the company's ability to rely on its workforce and generate the desired profits.

In some narrators' accounts of their work histories, there was little separation in their descriptions between the work their father or mother did and their own. Amelia Cabrera's family moved to Camp 52 when she was seven years old. Her entire family picked cotton. The seasonal nature of cotton production often sent families looking to migrate to other areas to pursue this line of work. Amelia's family would migrate during the summers to California and do similar work there.

> Remember those gusanos [worms] going all over your body? Oh my God. [You] would carry your sack of cotton, all those gusanos would crush on your shirt. We used to put handkerchiefs around our faces and wear those

> big hats, because it was really . . . it was bad, but it was fun. I enjoyed it, working in the fields. I always tried to put at least one hundred pounds in there. That would be what? Three dollars probably, one hundred pounds at that time.[75]

Born during the Great Depression, Connie Mesquita grew up in Camp 52, with her parents and a large family of thirteen children.[76] The second-oldest child, Connie grew up in a household where her father worked in the fields full-time. He would leave to start his workday at four o'clock in the morning, while her mother did the housework, managed the home, and performed jobs to supplement the family income. Connie's mother would fix the children breakfast and get all of them ready to go to school. There were days when her mother would do "the washing and ironing for the nurses at the doctor's offices, and the teachers at the school." Her mother also augmented the family income by making snow cones for the men who played on the baseball team. She recalled how her mother "would take a nap and she would get up when the guys would come at about ten o'clock at night. And we used to make snow cones and sell it to them. And they were all sitting out in the front waiting for the snow cones." All thirteen children, however, grew up working. Connie recalled, "We all picked cotton. My dad used to take us to pick cotton on the weekends and then sometimes after school. He used to take us to pick cotton. He used to come home from work and take us." When I asked Connie how old she was when she first began picking cotton, she said, "Eight years old, about eight years old. He started us all young and [taught] us how to work. And I thank God all the time for that, 'cause we all learned how to work." We can see here how the elasticity of labor extended to the entire family unit, even as certain parameters circumscribed the mother's labor, as an independent wage earner generating income for the household by providing domestic services for others in the company town, all while continuing to do the reproductive labor of nurturing and tending to the family.

Angelita Parilla Moreno was born in 1928, the sixth of seven siblings. Her father worked approximately forty years for SWCC / Goodyear Farms as a blacksmith and a foreman in the fields. "Well, he left early in the morning because it was so hot in the summers. And then he was gone all day. We wouldn't see him 'til we were home from school. All I know is that he worked in the fields, and I worked for him too. When I got out of school, we just went right from the eighth grade to the fields to help out." Angelita worked picking cotton and in the alfalfa fields, trying to eliminate the weeds. She said, "It was very hot. We were all covered up, all you could see was our eyes. It was bonnets and then the bandannas across our face and long sleeves; it was very, very hot."[77]

Lucy López Goss was born in 1952 and was part of the second generation born at Camp 50. Her father worked at the cotton gin and as a foreman, and when she was in high school the family moved to Camp 53. Her father worked the night shift at the cotton gin. She recalled her mother's typical day:

> My mom was home all the time. So, I mean to me, it was nice coming home to tortillas—the smell of tortillas and beans, and she was always there for us and pretty much, she worked hard. She washed for us, and of course, back then, they didn't have dishwashers, and the laundry, also outside, hanging up the clothes outside on the lines.[78]

Lucy recalled working in the fields while she was in high school, primarily to earn money for school clothes. "It was a good experience because I said I was never, never going back to working in the fields. It taught me, go to school, finish school and have a better life. I mean, and it wasn't bad, it wasn't a bad life, it's just . . . why are these people suffering, working out in the fields?"

Amid the stories about the hand-harvesting of cotton was the finding that working in the fields was but one of many jobs. Whether it was work in agriculture or work within the confines of the company town, women reported an array of jobs as part of the work experiences that occupied their lives.

As the company town of Litchfield Park developed, so did the kinds of work available, creating a range of ways in which men, women, and children could be employed in the company town. Women often found employment in the gendered service jobs in the company town, which were often the only paid work available to immigrant women.[79] Obtaining jobs in domestic and/or childcare work in the private homes of the Anglo families of the company town thus became one of the avenues for Mexican women to earn income outside of the home. The development and expansion of the Wigwam Resort required service workers including cooks, laundresses, and housekeepers. Former mayor of Avondale Marie López Rogers, who grew up in Camp 50, spoke about how her maternal and paternal grandmothers worked doing laundry at the Wigwam Resort. Both of her grandmothers were widowed early in their marriages, and they earned livings for their families by cleaning the sheets and linens for the resort. She recalls, "I remember they would have a big bonfire out there and a tub; our job was to mix the water and the sheets to make sure they were clean."[80]

To better capture the variety of jobs performed by women, I delve into the narratives of Armida Vizzerra, whose work experiences encompass what women conveyed in the oral histories, and Nicky Salazar, whose work as the housekeeper for the P. W. Litchfield family provides a glimpse into the kind of service work Mexican women did and how she viewed her work in that context.

Armida Vizzerra: "I Built This House, Adobe by Adobe"

Armida Vizzerra was born in 1917 in Las Prietas, Sonora, Mexico.[81] Her life story offers a glimpse into the array of changes in work, family, and social and cultural life experienced by those whose lives traversed the twentieth century. Throughout the interview, Armida would recount a story and then quickly interject another memory or observation, often on the lighter side of things, that revealed a life composed of hard work interspersed with good times; hard work and humorous moments; hard work and fiestas, música y baile. Equally interjected was a steadfast sense of pride about the full range of her life. When I asked her what she remembered about those years, Armida's response was clearly emotional, containing a kind of quiet stoicism combined with a nostalgic remembrance of moments of her life.

Armida's parents, Antonio Figueroa Moreno and Cesaria Olivas Moreno, migrated to the United States in 1917 at the behest of her father's boss, Mr. Hendrickson. Her father had been working in the gold mines of Minas Prietas, but when the mine closed, his employer took him to Cananea, one of the largest copper mines in Sonora, Mexico, and the site of numerous labor conflicts from the time it opened in 1899. His employer then took the family to Don Luis, Arizona, a mining town on the outskirts of Bisbee, in Cochise County. The family lived there for fourteen years. When Armida was but six years old, in 1923, her father died suddenly, leaving her mother to raise their family of five children. Her oldest brother quit school and went to work in the mines in Aravaipa Canyon, Arizona, to help support the family. The family went back and forth to Don Luis, depending on the availability of work. When the mining work ran out, the family then sought work picking cotton. Armida remembered that during the Depression the family would make five dollars a week chopping cotton at ten cents an acre. She recalled getting groceries and still having money left because "everything was so cheap."

Eventually, the family migrated to Coolidge to pick short-staple cotton. While they were there, her uncle and his wife came to Coolidge to move the family to the camps in Litchfield Park. Within a week her uncle and then his wife both died suddenly, leaving four children in need of a home. Armida's mom took them in and raised them as her own, bringing their family size to nine children. Armida remembered gratefully how the Grijalva family showed her and her siblings how to do the work involved in picking and chopping cotton, and other crops as well:

> And then over here [Marionette, Arizona] they had Pima cotton, and my sister and I, we went to pick, and we didn't know how to do it. So, this family, they went with us and showed us how to do it. The thing that I remember most was that when we came out after we picked the cotton, we just sat down on the end and both of us just sat down and started crying. Because when we were picking in Coolidge, the ball, you know, was bigger. So we would fill the sack, and over here we just got about that much. But then this cotton was, when you weighed it, it was heavier, and we didn't know that, so we just sat down there and cried.

Armida lived in Camp 54 from 1933 until 1947. For Armida, on a typical day when she was living in the camps, she would wake up early, join her brother, and work in the fields all day. Her sister would help take care of her two younger brothers, of whom the youngest was disabled. "We would get up early and go work and come back and just, we didn't have any TV or anything, not too many people had radios either, but we didn't care because we would play games and whatever."

Armida remembered working in the field when the braceros were brought to Goodyear Farms:

> Porque también trabajé en el fil cuando vinieron los braceros [I also worked in the fields when the braceros came]. I worked then too. We were, that's when we were planting cabbage. They gave us a pan full of the little plants, you know, that started. And then we'd walk every twelve, every foot we'd drop one; we'd walk back and forth in the fields, and there was one of the men from Mexico. There was some from the camp too and they were behind, and they had a little stick and would put dirt in it, so then you had to go back and forth in all the field, working there.

Over the course of the interview, I learned that Armida had worked in several different capacities, in some cases paid work, in others unpaid. She worked picking and chopping cotton; with family members she would travel to pick grapes, cabbage, lettuce, and onions. Because she arrived at the camps with a knowledge of English, she was often asked to volunteer and translate, whether within her community to conduct transactions, or by employers, doctors, and the like around the company town. The company relied on her to communicate to monolingual Spanish speakers. As a young woman, she assisted Dr. Hilton with translating and assisting women in the camps during childbirth. Her translating skills were also needed in a Red Cross clinic, where the wives of the company's managers volunteered and where medical assistance was provided to workers and families from the camps. During World War II, Armida worked at the post office, and she recalled writing letters to the men from the camps and the town who were serving in the war. Armida also assisted her husband driving the trucks that carried water from the irrigation pumps. Her husband was asked to remain in the camps and not enlist because the company needed him to drive the service trucks. Remembering this jogged her memory about the quality of the water at the camps. She stopped the flow of the interview and asked my co-interviewer, Belén:

> Did you ever taste it? The water from the camp? It was salty, so bad, and we couldn't wash our hair with it 'cause if you put the shampoo on it would look like you were putting lard, or something . . . So, we used to, sometimes

> we even would, ahh, when we were coming back from work. When we were working chopping cotton [laughs] we'd stop by one of the pumps and jump in [laughs]. So, we would wash our hair there, but we had a lot of fun.

Armida was called upon to interpret, first by Dr. Pen, and later by Dr. Hilton. When I asked her if she was paid for this, she said, "No, I just did it. It wasn't my job."

> And when someone was going to have a baby, he would always call me too. And sometimes I didn't want to be in the room, you know, because I thought maybe they would be, since they weren't related to me or anything, they were just my friends, so I'd tell him, I'll just stand out in the door, leave the door a little bit open. And he would just laugh. And I remember the first time, Cruzita was the first baby that they gave me. And the first time that Dr. Pen and my sister was having the baby and they called me, and as soon as she was born Dr. Pen handed her to me . . . "My God, what am I supposed to do?" and he said, "You bathe her." I said, "Oh my goodness." But I went ahead and did it.

Armida also worked in the private homes of the Anglo women in town, which continued after she and her husband moved from the camps and relocated to Avondale.

> And then I worked for Mrs. Zieske and Mrs. Abraham, the ones that owned the store, and Mrs. Sweeney, she was a teacher. I used to work for them too. For Mrs. Sweeney I would take care of Billy, and for Mrs. Zieske I would work at the house and iron for her. And then I worked for Mrs. Smith, Mr. Batch. They told me that his first wife was Mr. Litchfield's sister, and then I guess she died, and he married this other lady, and I took care of her. They used to send me to La Loma. Have you heard about that? Mr. Batch used to send me there to get some roses. 'Cause they had lots of roses there. Mr. and Mrs. Salazar lived there, and I would, and Mr. and Mrs. Pablos, and he would send me to go get roses for his wife. And I worked for him 'til she died.

As the years proceeded, Armida's family decided to move out of the camps, as was the case for many of the families, especially after World

War II. Avondale became the home for many of the families from the camps. Armida was extremely proud of the fact that she built her own home. She exclaimed, "I built this house, adobe by adobe—and that one, and that one, and two across there and one where they're building a new one there now." When family members attempted to persuade her to leave her home and move to one of the new developments, Palm Valley, she said, "No. I'm going to die in this house I built. I'm going to die here." Her grandson tried again: "But Nana." To which Armida responded, "Uh uh. Don't 'but Nana' me. If you don't like it, you can go with your mom. I'm staying here."

Nicky Salazar: "I Thought La Loma Was Mine"

Other Mexican women in the company occupied different roles in the wage-earning continuum. In 1919, Paul Litchfield personally purchased acreage to build a private retreat and home on what became known as Rancho La Loma in Litchfield Park. The family built a main residence in 1925, and four cottages were added on to the eighty-acre property by 1932.[82] As one of the elite families of the company town, if not the most important of them all, they relied on the labor of Mexican women to perform the management, laundering, housekeeping, childcare, and seamstress duties necessary to maintain a household. In rural and growing cities across the Southwest, such gendered tasks had already been marked as work to be done primarily by Mexican women.[83] The growth of corporate agribusiness across the region and the establishment of families that occupied privileged positions in these communities spawned a new demand for service-sector jobs related to household management and family rearing and maintenance. Nicky Salazar was ninety-three years old when she was interviewed in the original house on the grounds of La Loma.[84] She had become the housekeeper for the Litchfield family when her husband was asked to take over the groundkeeping duties at La Loma. Nicky Salazar, her husband, and her children lived in one of the cottages on the property, and Nicky worked as a housekeeper while her husband took care of the grounds. Her story provides insights into what historian Monica Perales depicts as women's "emotional ownership" over their work.[85] Throughout the interview, Nicky was extremely proud of the work she had done for the Litchfield family. She remembered how Mr. Litchfield insisted that she be the one to launder his shirts, since she was the only one who could do it so finely. She shared, "Mr. Litchfield did not want his shirts to be done by the laundry. He would give them to me and say, 'You wash very beautifully, and you iron them better than any laundry. Take them.' I would iron his shirts—shirts that were very big—shirts that were big, white, and beautiful. Yes. I worked for them for many years."[86] Nicky had nothing but fond memories to share about the years she worked and lived at La Loma. Her children had free rein of the property, and when Mrs. Litchfield gave Nicky permission to grow her own garden, she quickly had her children clear the ground. "I thought La Loma was mine," she exclaimed, to express her love for the place and the fondness she felt for the Litchfields.

> I thought La Loma was mine, because I planted and grew tomatoes, chiles, I had chickens, I had a little goat, I made butter, cheese, cottage cheese, and I felt very happy there. When I left I missed it so much. Because where I went, I had to pay for water, lights, the house—I had to pay for everything. And here I didn't have to pay. Mrs. Litchfield would tell me to grow what I wanted; I had roses; I would take her flowers every weekend—beautiful flowers that I had. And she liked my flowers very much. All this to tell you that all that makes me feel happy to remember the part of my life that I spent there.[87]

We glean from Armida Vizzerra's and Nicky Salazar's oral histories how their work lives illustrate the gendered elasticity of their labor. In Armida's account we hear the variety and flexibility of the jobs she performed. From manually laboring in the fields as a child and later as an adult (in a variety of crops), to assisting the local doctor with childbirth, to caregiving, translating, and childcare, the elasticity of her labor power—her ability to work and the range of places where she worked—is evident throughout her life. We gather from her story that her mother took on an additional five children (when tragedy stuck a relative's household), which deeply embroiled her mother in the reproductive labor required to take care of a family double the size of her own. When Armida married and had her own children, she continued to work to support her family, attending to her own family's needs while working in other people's homes and taking care of their familial needs. Throughout her life she negotiated a flexibility of her labor within the confines of both her own household and that of her employers. Public historian Jean Reynolds concluded in her research on Mexican women's work in mid-twentieth-century Phoenix, "Women negotiated the maze of intersecting social advantages and disadvantages to provide for and sustain their families . . . and they contributed along with all others to Phoenix's mid-twentieth-century economic growth."[88] In Nicky Salazar's memories of her life working in the Litchfield household, the domestic work itself reflects a gendered division of labor performed for the household, while the elasticity of her labor went beyond traditional duties and encompassed choices around gardening and raising farm animals that contributed to and enhanced her family's life and that of her employers. Both women articulated a deep sense of pride in their work lives, a theme common throughout most of the oral histories. Women understood that life was about more than work; it was about forming human bonds, relationships, and social gatherings and spaces that nurtured a sense of belonging and community. Historian Vicky Ruiz notes, "Whether living in a labor camp, a boxcar settlement, mining town, or urban barrio, Mexican women nurtured families, worked for wages, built fictive kin networks, and participated in formal and informal community associations."[89]

Conclusion

In sum, Mexican women's work in the company town of Litchfield Park was central. Women's work in production, as wageworkers, especially as hand-harvesters of cotton, played an important role in the success of the cotton industry in Arizona. This fact is not to be understated, as women were key to the cotton industry's elastic supply of labor as independent wage earners and/or as members of a family unit of production. In either case, women worked, and in the agricultural fields of Arizona they worked under material and climatic conditions that were harsh, grueling, and adverse. In so doing, Mexican women contributed immensely to Arizona's economic well-being and the significant profits made by Goodyear Tire and Rubber and other corporate interests. As residents of a company town, women were part of the formal and informal labor force (paid and unpaid), providing evidence of my contention that they constituted an elastic supply of labor that was both racialized and gendered. In my previous work with Luis Plascencia, we presented the elastic supply of labor as "the concept [that] names a strategy within capital accumulation."[90] This is evident in the ACGA's strategy to recruit workers in the thousands, control their "mobility and immobility" while under the growers' charge,[91] and create a system (through the formation of the ACGA and the capping of wages) whereby workers would be paid the least amount possible—all to maximize profits—after which growers abandoned their accountability to the workforce they so "desired."[92] Plascencia and I further argued that "the notion of an elastic supply of labor both reveals and obscures important power relations and the role of the state in aiding the position of corporations vis-à-vis labor in producing wealth."[93] By sanctioning the reinterpreted Ninth Proviso, the U.S. government set in motion a practice and a relationship with agribusiness and corporations that served as a blueprint for twentieth-century policies to maintain access to an elastic supply of labor. In so doing, the state sanctioned the gendering of that labor for agribusiness, configuring how individual women's and families' work lives would be organized and exploited, and whose profits would be built on their backs.

The gendering of elasticity in the labor force required women to strategically negotiate their position in production and reproduction. Although a woman's decision whether or not to work outside of her home can be viewed as a personal one, such a decision is often mediated by the kinds of wages workers are paid and whether they are sufficient to sustain the needs of a family. Hence women's choices were constrained by the larger forces shaping those decisions and whether employers would pay a fair wage. In this respect, the burden weighed more heavily on some women than others; some women's typical days began with managing an entire family that was going to work, continued with manual work all day in the harsh conditions of the fields, and then included returning home and beginning the reproductive work involved in managing a family and all the tasks involved to prepare for yet another workday. Other women in the company town did not work in the fields and focused instead on managing their households and raising and attending to their children. In some cases, women supplemented their income streams by engaging in paid and part-time work as laundresses, seamstresses, housekeepers, childcare providers, and caregivers. In other cases, such work was full-time work. The wage work that Mexican women did outside the home to generate income—cleaning for the predominantly Anglo families of the company town, helping to raise their children, taking care of their elderly—supported and enhanced the lives of the company's leaders and their families. Women also worked in the public sectors of the company town, in local businesses and stores. As bearers of and caretakers of children, women's roles in reproduction were important. From the perspective of social reproduction, women's reproductive roles resulted in future generations of the workforce; in several cases, these families had a multigenerational presence in the company town, verifying the extent to which a gendered and racialized division of labor was reproduced. To reiterate Weber's observation, "In the United States, Mexican women worked."[94]

The oral histories reveal the complexity of women's lives, allowing us to hear their experiences and the ways in which women defined their lives as meaningful. Their memories of work are not merely about the exploitative, harsh conditions; they are also about the ways in which women formed relationships in these spaces and how they created the full range of human experiences, even in adverse conditions. Their stories reveal how resilience was undergirded by camaraderie, friendships, loyalties to families, and a collective will to survive.

Women claimed a strong sense of belonging and relationship to place in their remembrances of the camps and the communities they formed in the company town. They articulated a deep sense of pride about their work lives and their contributions to the history of the town. In this respect, their memories and shared histories are an integral part of Arizona's history.

Acknowledgments

I want to thank the anonymous reviewers, the editors of this anthology, and my colleagues in the Synergy Writing Group at ASU, whose insightful suggestions improved the final manuscript. I am especially grateful to my dear friend and colleague Dr. Luis F. B. Plascencia for his tireless consultation and review of my work. His expertise on the Ninth Proviso, labor legislation, and policy without a doubt enhances my work in this area.

Notes

1. Sallie Villa Romo, interview by Gloria Cuádraz, 2006, Mexican Americans of Litchfield Park Oral History Project, Litchfield Park Historical Society / Arizona State University (this repository is hereafter cited as MAOH, LPHS/ASU). All quotes and information attributed to Sallie Villa Romo in this section come from this interview. The LPHS was renamed the P. W. Litchfield Heritage Center. In keeping with the original agreement, references from here on out refer to Litchfield Park Historical Society; videotaped interviews may be found at the P. W. Litchfield Heritage Center and the Chicano Research Collection at Arizona State University.
2. In quotes from oral history interviews in this chapter, ellipses set within brackets indicate omission, while unbracketed ellipses represent pauses or similar features of the speaker's discourse itself.
3. "Goodyear Cotton Plantation," *Arizona* 7 (1917): 3.
4. An Arizona cotton grower is infamously noted for the notion of an "elastic supply of labor," saying about the 1919–20 cotton season, "Thus, in the face of the greatest demand for labor the world has ever seen, with the country at the highest point of prosperity it has ever known, the cotton growers of the Salt River Valley maintained as perfectly an elastic supply of labor as the world has ever seen and maintained an even low level of prices for wages throughout its territory. Outsiders looked, studied, and went away amazed at the accomplishment of such an organization." Cited in Malcolm Brown and Orin Cassmore, *Migratory Cotton Pickers in Arizona* (Government Printing Office, 1939); also cited in Luis F. B. Plascencia and Gloria H. Cuádraz, eds., *Mexican Workers and the Making of Arizona* (University of Arizona Press, 2018), 3.
5. Gloria H. Cuádraz, "The Mobilization and Immobilization of 'Legally Imported Aliens': Cotton in the Salt River Valley, 1917–1921," in Plascencia and Cuádraz, *Mexican Workers*, 90–123.
6. Thomas E. Campbell Papers, Arizona State Library, Archives, and Public Records, Phoenix, Ariz.
7. See Servicio Consular Mexicano (Mexican consulate), letter and report, February 5, 1921, Thomas E. Campbell Papers, M61, Arizona State Library, Archives, and Public Records, Phoenix, Ariz. The collection includes a number of letters and documents for the period in question.
8. For works on the Imperial Valley's agricultural history, see Benny J. Andrés, *Power and Control in the Imperial Valley: Nature, Agribusiness, and Workers on the California Borderland, 1900–1940* (Texas A&M University, 2016); and Alina R. Méndez, "Cheap for Whom? Migration, Farm Labor, and Social Reproduction in the Imperial Valley / Mexicali Borderlands, 1942–1969" (PhD diss., University of California, San Diego, 2017).
9. This project was initially made possible by two grants from the Arizona Humanities Council. Internal grants from ASU and matching funds from private-

sector sources also contributed to the project's success. We are grateful for all their support.

10. The working interview team typically consisted of myself as the interviewer or a student interviewer, a student videographer, and, depending on availability, one or two members of the LPHS Oral History Subcommittee. We conducted interviews in narrators' preferred locations, either in their homes, in family or friends' homes, or at ASU for those willing to come to campus. I am grateful to Sarah Homan, Belén Soto Moreno, and Sonja Hendricks from the LPHS Oral History Subcommittee, ASU student videographers Tino Martínez and Ed Burleson, and ASU student Elizabeth Martínez, who assisted me in conducting interviews.
11. Mark Reisler, *By the Sweat of Their Brow: Mexican Immigrant Labor in the United States, 1900–1940* (Greenwood Press, 1976), 1–47; Herbert B. Peterson, "Twentieth-Century Search for Cíbola: Post–World War I Mexican Labor Exploitation in Arizona," in *An Awakening Minority: The Mexican Americans*, 2nd ed., ed. Manuel Servín (Glencoe Press, 1974), 113–32.
12. Deena González, "Gender on the Borderlands: Re-textualizing the Classics," in *Gender on the Borderlands: The Frontiers Reader*, ed. Antonia Castañeda et al. (University of Nebraska Press, 2007), 21.
13. Devra Anne Weber, "Oral History and Mexican Farmworkers," *Oral History Review* 17 (Autumn 1989): 47–62.
14. For histories of GYTR and its impact on Arizona's economy, see Reisler, *Sweat of Their Brow*; Peterson, "Twentieth-Century Search for Cíbola"; Nancy Hill, "The Imprint of Cotton Production on Arizona Landscapes" (PhD diss., Arizona State University, 2007), 133–69; Cuádraz, "Mobilization and Immobilization"; Clyde E. Schetter, *Story of a Town: Litchfield Park* (Litchfield Park Library Association, 1976); Scott Walker, "Making the Desert Bloom: Mexicans and Whites in the Agricultural Development of the Salt River Valley, 1867–1930" (PhD diss., Arizona State University, 2012).
15. James B. Allen, *The Company Town in the American West* (University of Oklahoma Press, 1966), 146–49. Allen identifies Litchfield Park as one of sixteen company towns in Arizona. Marinette, although depicted as a "cotton plantation," does not meet the criteria of a company town, leaving Litchfield Park as the only company town in Arizona not dedicated to copper mining, milling, smelting, or other metals.
16. Hill, "Imprint of Cotton Production," 95–131, 135–46.
17. Samuel P. Orth, "The Alien Contract Labor Law," *Political Science Quarterly* 22, no. 1 (1907): 49–60. For discussions pertaining to the Immigration Act of 1917, the Ninth Proviso, and its impact on Mexican labor in Arizona, see Reisler, *Sweat of Their Brow*, 3–48; Peterson, "Twentieth-Century Search for Cíbola"; Luis F. B. Plascencia, "'Get Us Our Privilege of Bringing in Mexican Labor': Recruitment and Desire for Mexican Labor in Arizona, 1917–2016," in Plascencia and Cuádraz, *Mexican Workers*, 124–78; Eric V. Meeks, *Border Citizens: The Making of Indians, Mexicans, and Anglos in Arizona* (University of Texas Press,

2007), 78–80, 109–13; Cuádraz, "Mobilization and Immobilization"; Edwin Charles Pendleton, "History of Labor in Arizona Irrigated Agriculture" (PhD diss., University of California, Berkeley, 1950), 105–59. For the act's impact in Texas, see Neil Foley, *The White Scourge: Mexicans, Blacks, and Poor Whites in Texas Cotton Culture* (University of California Press, 1997), 45–63.

18. Luis F. B. Plascencia, "State-Sanctioned Coercion and Agricultural Contract Labor: Jamaican and Mexican Workers in Canada and the United States, 1909–2014," in *On Coerced Labor: Work and Compulsion After Chattel Slavery*, ed. Marcel van der Linden and Magaly Rodríguez García (Brill, 2016), 236–37.
19. The data is cited in Reisler, *Sweat of Their Brow*, 38, and taken from a report, U.S. Department of Labor, *Annual Report of the Commissioner-General of Immigration* (1921), 7. Plascencia, in "State-Sanctioned Coercion," 240–41, argues that the data is an estimate at best, since numerous questions can be posed about how these numbers were achieved and the criteria for exclusion. He also argues that the recruitment of workers from Mexico continued until fiscal year 1922–23 under extensions granted for "certain especially meritorious cases." With respect to women, unless they were officially provided an identification and number, it is unlikely they were counted among the official numbers.
20. Pendleton, "History of Labor."
21. Walker, "Making the Desert Bloom," 180–81.
22. Walker, 180–81.
23. Larisa L. Veloz, "'Even the Women are Leaving': Gendered Migrations Between Mexico and the United States; Revolutionary Diasporas, Depression-Era Depatriations, and Wartime Bracero Controls, 1900–1950" (PhD diss., Georgetown University, 2015), 7–8.
24. Servicio Consular Mexicano (Mexican consulate), letter and report, February 5, 1921, Thomas E. Campbell Papers, M61, Arizona State Library, Archives, and Public Records, Phoenix, Ariz.
25. Peterson, "Twentieth-Century Search for Cíbola"; Reisler, *Sweat of Their Brow*; Cuádraz, "Mobilization and Immobilization"; Hill, "Imprint of Cotton Production"; Pendleton, "History of Labor"; Walker, "Making the Desert Bloom."
26. Plascencia, "State-Sanctioned Coercion" and "Get Us Our Privilege"; Meeks, *Border Citizens*, 99, 126, 156, 163–64, 166–68, 246.
27. Hugh Allen, *The House of Goodyear* (Corday and Gross Company, 1949), 5–7; Hill, "Imprint of Cotton Production," 33–168.
28. Walter V. Woehlke, "What Cotton Did to Arizona," *Sunset* 47 (1921): 21–23; "Goodyear's Cotton Project Near Phoenix, Arizona," *The Earth*, August 1917, 10–11; "Goodyear Cotton Plantation," 3 (see note 2).
29. Schetter, *Story of a Town*, 5.
30. Schetter, 4.
31. J. Allen, *Company Town*, 6.
32. J. Allen, in *Company Town*, 122–27, argues that most company towns were "fully paternalistic, although the degree of company control varied widely." For

a discussion of paternalism in company towns where a Mexican labor force was central, see José M. Alamillo, *Making Lemonade out of Lemons: Mexican American Labor and Leisure in a California Town, 1880–1960* (University of Illinois Press, 2006), 25–30; Monica Perales, *Smeltertown: Making and Remembering a Southwest Border Community* (University of North Carolina Press, 2010), 105–6; Devra Weber, *Dark Sweat, White Gold: California Farm Workers, Cotton, and the New Deal* (University of California Press, 1994), 45–46; Gilbert G. Gonzalez, *Labor and Community: Mexican Citrus Worker Villages in a Southern California County, 1900–1950* (University of Illinois Press, 1994), 36–39, 41; Gilbert G. González, "Women, Work, and Community in the Mexican Colonias of the Southern California Citrus Belt," *California History* 74 (1995): 58–67; Foley, *White Scourge*, 118–19, 122, 128; Katherine Benton-Cohen, *Borderline Americans: Racial Divisions and Labor War in the Arizona Borderlands* (Harvard University Press, 2009), 104–7, 146.

33. Indeed, Gilbert G. Gonzalez criticizes Allen for "scarcely mention[ing] Mexican labor." G. Gonzalez, *Labor and Community*, 8–9.
34. Paul W. Litchfield, *Industrial Voyage: My Life as an Industrial Lieutenant* (Doubleday, 1954).
35. G. Gonzalez, *Labor and Community*, 8.
36. G. Gonzalez, 7–9.
37. Schetter, *Story of a Town*; Susan Smith, "Litchfield Park and Vicinity" (MA thesis, University of Arizona, 1948); "The Story of Goodyear Farms," Litchfield Park Archives, P. W. Litchfield Heritage Center, Litchfield Park, Ariz.
38. Schetter, *Story of a Town*; "Story of Goodyear Farms" (see previous note). For a history of GYTR, see H. Allen, *House of Goodyear*.
39. Hill, "Imprint of Cotton Production," 156; Schetter, *Story of a Town*, 6.
40. G. Gonzalez emphasizes the vast differences between the living conditions of citrus communities in the company towns of Southern California and those of migratory communities: *Labor and Community*, 10–11. Weber contends that the deplorable conditions in the camps led workers to participate in the "largest agricultural strike to date in the history of the United States: the cotton strike of 1933": *Dark Sweat*, 78. See also Kim Frontz, "From Homesteads to Cotton Camps: Albert C. Stewart—Missionary with a Camera; A Photo Essay," *Journal of Arizona History* 52, no. 4 (2011): 373–90; Christopher Holden, "Bitter Harvest: Housing Conditions of Migrant and Seasonal Farmworkers," in *Farmworkers' Lives, Labor, and Advocacy*, ed. Charles D. Thompson and Melinda F. Wiggins (University of Texas Press, 2002), 169–93; Susan Zamudio-Gurrola, "Housing Farm Workers: Assessing the Significance of Bracero Labor Camps in Ventura County" (master's thesis, University of Southern California, 2009).
41. Weber, *Dark Sweat*, 72–73.
42. Brown and Cassmore, *Migratory Cotton Pickers*, 5.
43. J. Allen, *Company Town*, 102.

44. G. Gonzalez, *Labor and Community*, 9. In *Smeltertown*, Perales describes the vast differences in the quality of the company town's housing for the managerial class versus the Mexican workforce (pp. 61–80).
45. Alamillo, *Making Lemonade*; Foley, *White Scourge*; G. González, *Labor and Community*; Perales, *Smeltertown*; Zaragosa Vargas, *Proletarians of the North: A History of Mexican Industrial Workers in Detroit and the Midwest, 1917–1933* (University of California Press, 1993).
46. Bradford Luckingham, *Epidemic in the Southwest, 1918–1919*, Southwestern Studies 72 (Texas Western Press, 1984).
47. Frances Serrano Martin, interview by the author, 2007, MAOH, LPHS/ASU; Celeste Crouch, "History of St. Thomas Aquinas Church, Litchfield Park, Arizona," Litchfield Park Archives, P. W. Litchfield Heritage Center, Litchfield Park, Ariz.
48. Meeks, in *Border Citizens*, argues that in Arizona, ethnic Mexicans and Indigenous tribes "became 'border citizens'—people whose rights of belonging were in question, leaving them on the margins of the national territory and of American society and culture" (18).
49. Meeks, *Border Citizens*, 118. For a discussion of "the questionable whiteness of Okies," see pp. 117–26.
50. In a scathing critique, Plascencia questions the integrity of employers' "labor shortage" claims, arguing it "is salient to producing an elastic supply of labor that is tractable, can be coerced to work at lower wages, accepts poor and dangerous working conditions, meets high productivity standards, and allows employers to achieve desired profit margins." Plascencia, "Get Us Our Privilege," 124–25. See also Meeks, *Border Citizens*, 163, 166–68.
51. In 1964, Congress ended the large-scale recruitment, but the Department of Labor allowed the recruitment to continue until 1968. Plascencia, "Get Us Our Privilege," 135–37.
52. For the few remaining families that lived in the camps, GY arranged to house them in mobile homes in Perryville, Arizona. See Cruz Pariga Dominguez and Belen Soto Moreno, *Los Campos: The Camps of Litchfield Park, 1929–1986* (D&L Press, 2017); see also the video produced by Gloria Cuádraz and directed by student Edward Burleson, *Voices from the Camps of Litchfield Park*, 2006, DVD.
53. Jean A. Reynolds, "Farm Labor Camps Turn to Dust, Employees Move On," *The Westsider*, May 20, 1986.
54. G. Gonzalez, "Women, Work, and Community," 58–67; G. Gonzalez, *Labor and Community*; Alamillo, *Making Lemonade*; Matt García, *A World of Its Own: Race, Labor, and Citrus in the Making of Greater Los Angeles, 1900–1970* (University of North Carolina Press, 2001); Margo McBane, "The Role of Gender in Citrus Employment: A Case Study of Recruitment, Labor, and Housing Patterns at the Limoneira Company, 1893 to 1940," *California History* 74 (1995): 68–81. As scholars have noted, women's labor was key when it came to working in the packinghouses for the citrus industry. Mexican women cannery workers were also key in efforts to organize and unionize. See Vicki L. Ruiz, *Cannery*

Women, Cannery Lives: Mexican Women, Unionization, and the California Food Processing Industry, 1930–1950 (University of New Mexico Press, 1987); Patricia Zavella, *Women's Work and Chicano Families: Cannery Workers of the Santa Clara Valley* (Cornell University Press, 1987).

55. Christine Marin, "Always a Struggle: Mexican Americans in Miami, Arizona, 1909–1951" (PhD diss., Arizona State University, 2005).
56. Christine Marin and Luis F. B. Plascencia, "*Mexicano* Miners, Dual Wage, and the Pursuit of Wage Equality in Miami, Arizona," in Plascencia and Cuádraz, *Mexican Workers*, 220.
57. Benton-Cohen, *Borderline Americans*; Linda Gordon, *The Great Arizona Orphan Abduction*, rev. ed. (Harvard University Press, 2001); Anna O'Leary, "The Morenci Miners Women's Auxiliary During the Great Arizona Copper Strike, 1983–1986," in Plascencia and Cuádraz, *Mexican Workers*, 248–69.
58. Perales, *Smeltertown*, 142.
59. Perales, 144.
60. Perales, *Smeltertown*, 144–45; Sarah Deutsch, *No Separate Refuge: Culture, Class, and Gender on an Anglo-Hispanic Frontier in the American Southwest, 1880–1940* (Oxford University Press, 1987), 15–16, 38–39.
61. Matthew C. Godfrey, "'Much Suffering Among Mexicans': Migrant Workers in Idaho and the Utah-Idaho Sugar Company, 1917–1921," *Agricultural History* 94, no. 4 (2020): 600–628.
62. Mary Romero and Eric Margolis, "Tending the Beets: *Campesinas* and the Great Western Sugar Company," *Revista Mujeres* 2 (1985): 17.
63. Romero and Margolis, "Tending the Beets," 21.
64. Meeks, *Border Citizens*, 71–97; Veloz, "Even the Women," 21–67.
65. Weber, *Dark Sweat*, 58.
66. Weber, *Dark Sweat*; another landmark study is Foley, *White Scourge*.
67. Weber, *Dark Sweat*, 62.
68. Waldo B. Christy, "American Egyptian Staple Cotton in Arizona" (PhD diss., University of Chicago, 1920), 21–27; Joseph C. McGowan, "History of Extra-Long Staple Cotton" (MA thesis, University of Arizona, 1961); Erik-Anders Shapiro, "Cotton in Arizona: A Historical Geography" (MA thesis, University of Arizona, 1989); Brown and Cassmore, *Migratory Cotton Pickers*, 63–66; Marsha L. Weisiger, *Land of Plenty: Oklahomans in the Cotton Fields of Arizona, 1933–1942* (University of Oklahoma Press, 1995), 40–44; Meeks, *Border Citizens*, 78–80, 109–113; Pendleton, "History of Labor," 105–59.
69. Meeks, *Border Citizens*, 88–93; Vicki L. Ruiz, *From Out of the Shadows: Mexican Women in Twentieth-Century America* (Oxford University Press, 1998), 18–47.
70. Meeks, *Border Citizens*, 89.
71. Similarities can be found in the sugar beet industry, where women were also central to production, and subject to discriminatory and exploitative practices like those found in the cotton industry. For comparisons to the beet industry,

see Vargas, *Proletarians*; Jim Norris, *North for the Harvest: Mexican Workers, Growers, and the Sugar Beet Industry* (Minnesota Historical Society Press, 2009); Romero and Margolis, "Tending the Beets," 17–28; Godfrey, "Much Suffering," 600–628; Deutsch, *No Separate Refuge*, 129–30, 202–3; Megan L. Bilotte, "Becoming Native: Family Labor and Belonging in the Sugar Beet Fields of Northern Colorado, 1900–1969" (PhD diss., University of Wisconsin–Madison, 2020); Dennis Nodín Valdés, "*Betabeleros*: The Formation of an Agricultural Proletariat in the Midwest," *Labor History* 30, no. 4 (1989): 536–62. For an understanding of repressive measures with respect to contract labor, see Plascencia, "State-Sanctioned Coercion," 236–37.

72. Lucy Villa Moreno, interview by Gloria Cuádraz, 2006, MAOH, LPHS/ASU. All information and quotes attributed to Lucy in this section come from this interview.
73. Alamillo, *Making Lemonade*; Deutsch, *No Separate Refuge*; García, *World of Its Own*; G. Gonzalez, *Labor and Community*; G. Gonzalez, "Women, Work, and Community"; Perales, *Smeltertown*; Weber, *Dark Sweat*; Ruiz, *From Out of the Shadows*; Zavella, *Women's Work*.
74. J. Allen, *Company Town*, 108–27.
75. Amelia Cabrera, interview by Elizabeth Martínez, 2008, MAOH, LPHS/ASU
76. Connie Mesquita, interview by Gloria Cuádraz, 2006, MAOH, LPHS/ASU. All information and quotes attributed to Connie in this paragraph come from this interview.
77. Angelita Parilla Moreno, interview by Gloria Cuádraz, 2006, MAOH, LPHS/ASU.
78. Lucy López Goss, interview by Elizabeth Martínez, 2006, MAOH, LPHS/ASU. All information and quotes attributed to Lucy in this paragraph come from this interview.
79. Ruiz, *From Out of the Shadows*, 9–10; Alamillo, *Making Lemonade*, 42–43; Perales, *Smeltertown*, 98–99, 142–46; Weber, *Dark Sweat*, 59–61, 63–69, 77–78.
80. Marie López Rogers served on the city council of Avondale from 1996 to 2014; her term as mayor began as an appointment in 2006; she was elected in 2007 and served until 2014, when she resigned to run for County Board of Supervisors. Marie López Rogers, interview by Elizabeth Martínez, April 17, 2007, MAOH, LPHS/ASU.
81. Armida Vizzerra, interview by Gloria Cuádraz, 2006, MAOH, LPHS/ASU. All quotes and information attributed to Vizzerra in this section come from this interview.
82. *Litchfield Legends Newsletter*, Litchfield Park Historical Society, 2009.
83. Perales, *Smeltertown*, 195–96; Ruiz, *From Out of the Shadows*, 8–9. For a discussion of women's unpaid and paid labor in domestic work, see Mary Romero, *Maid in the U.S.A.* (Routledge, 1992), 20–31.
84. Nicky Salazar, interview by Elizabeth Martínez, 2008, MAOH, LPHS/ASU. All quotes and information attributed to Salazar in this section come from this interview.

85. Perales, *Smeltertown*, 142–48.
86. "El señor Litchfield no quería las camisas lavadas de la laundry. Me las daba y me decía, 'Tu lavas más bonito y planchas más bonito que la laundry,' me decía. 'Tú llévate.' Yo le planchaba las camisas—unas camisas grandes, blancas, bonitas. Sí. De manera que trabajé por unos años con ellos." Translations from Spanish to English in this chapter are by the author, unless otherwise noted.
87. "Yo creía que La Loma era mía, porque yo sembraba tomates, sembraba chiles, tenía gallinas, tenía una vaquita, hacía mantequilla, queso, cottage cheese, yo me sentía muy feliz aquí. Cuando yo me fui yo extrañaba mucho. Porque donde yo me fui tenía que pagar la agua, la luz, la casa, tenía que pagar por todo. Y aquí no pagaba. Me decía la señora Litchfield, 'Siembra la que tú quieras.' Tenía rosales, le llevaba flores cada fin de semana . . . unas bonitas flores tenía yo. Y a ella le gustaron mucho mis flores. De manera que todo eso me hace sentirme feliz de acordarme de la vida que pasé aquí."
88. Jean Reynolds, "Mexican American Women Workers in Mid-Twentieth-Century Phoenix," in Plascencia and Cuádraz, *Mexican Workers*, 247.
89. Ruiz, *From Out of the Shadows*, 7.
90. Plascencia and Cuádraz, *Mexican Workers*, 26–27.
91. Cuádraz, "Mobilization and Immobilization," 90 123.
92. Plascencia, "Get Us Our Privilege," 124–78.
93. Plascencia and Cuádraz, *Mexican Workers*, 26.
94. Weber, *Dark Sweat*, 58.

Bibliography

Alamillo, José M. *Making Lemonade out of Lemons: Mexican American Labor and Leisure in a California Town, 1880–1960*. University of Illinois Press, 2006.

Allen, Hugh. *The House of Goodyear*. Corday and Gross Company, 1949.

Allen, James B. *The Company Town in the American West*. University of Oklahoma Press, 1966.

Andrés, Benny J. *Power and Control in the Imperial Valley: Nature, Agribusiness, and Workers on the California Borderland, 1900–1940*. Texas A&M University, 2016.

Benton-Cohen, Katherine. *Borderline Americans: Racial Divisions and Labor War in the Arizona Borderlands*. Harvard University Press, 2009.

Bilotte, Megan L. "Becoming Native: Family Labor and Belonging in the Sugar Beet Fields of Northern Colorado, 1900–1969." PhD dissertation, University of Wisconsin–Madison, 2020.

Brown, Malcolm, and Orin Cassmore. *Migratory Cotton Pickers in Arizona*. Government Printing Office, 1939.

Cabrera, Amelia. Interview by Elizabeth Martínez. 2008. Mexican Americans of Litchfield Park Oral History Project, Litchfield Park Historical Society / Arizona State University.

Campbell, Thomas E. Papers. Arizona State Library, Archives, and Public Records, Phoenix, Ariz.

Christy, Waldo B. "American Egyptian Staple Cotton in Arizona." PhD dissertation, University of Chicago, 1920.

Cuádraz, Gloria H. "The Mobilization and Immobilization of 'Legally Imported Aliens': Cotton in the Salt River Valley, 1917–1921." In Plascencia and Cuádraz, *Mexican Workers*, 90–123.

Cuádraz, Gloria H., producer. *Voices from the Camps of Litchfield Park*. Directed by Edward Burleson. 2006. DVD.

Deutsch, Sarah. *No Separate Refuge: Culture, Class, and Gender on an Anglo-Hispanic Frontier in the American Southwest, 1880–1940*. Oxford University Press, 1987.

Dominguez, Cruz Pariga, and Belen Soto Moreno. *Los Campos: The Camps of Litchfield Park, 1929–1986*. D&L Press, 2017.

Foley, Neil. *The White Scourge: Mexicans, Blacks, and Poor Whites in Texas Cotton Culture*. University of California Press, 1997.

Frontz, Kim. "From Homesteads to Cotton Camps: Albert C. Stewart—Missionary with a Camera; A Photo Essay." *Journal of Arizona History* 52, no. 4 (2011): 373–90.

García, Matt. *A World of Its Own: Race, Labor, and Citrus in the Making of Greater Los Angeles, 1900–1970*. University of North Carolina Press, 2001.

Godfrey, Matthew C. "'Much Suffering Among Mexicans': Migrant Workers in Idaho and the Utah-Idaho Sugar Company, 1917–1921." *Agricultural History* 94, no. 4 (2020): 600–628.

González, Deena. "Gender on the Borderlands: Re-textualizing the Classics." In *Gender on the Borderlands: The Frontiers Reader*, edited by Antonia Castañeda, Susan H. Armitage, Patricia Hart, and Karen Weathermon, 15–29. University of Nebraska Press, 2007.

Gonzalez, Gilbert G. *Labor and Community: Mexican Citrus Worker Villages in a Southern California County, 1900–1950*. University of Illinois Press, 1994.

Gonzalez, Gilbert G. "Women, Work, and Community in the Mexican Colonias of the Southern California Citrus Belt." *California History* 74 (1995): 58–67.

"Goodyear Cotton Plantation." *Arizona* 7 (1917): 3.

Gordon, Linda. *The Great Arizona Orphan Abduction*. Revised ed. Harvard University Press, 2001.

Hill, Nancy. "The Imprint of Cotton Production on Arizona Landscapes." PhD dissertation, Arizona State University, 2007.

Holden, Christopher. "Bitter Harvest: Housing Conditions of Migrant and Seasonal Farmworkers." In *Farmworkers' Lives, Labor, and Advocacy*, edited by Charles D. Thompson and Melinda F. Wiggins, 169–93. University of Texas Press, 2002.

Litchfield, Paul W. *Industrial Voyage: My Life as an Industrial Lieutenant*. Doubleday, 1954.

Litchfield Park Historical Society. Archives. P. W. Litchfield Heritage Center, Litchfield Park, Ariz.

López Goss, Lucy. Interview by Elizabeth Martínez. 2006. Mexican Americans of Litchfield Park Oral History Project, Litchfield Park Historical Society / Arizona State University.

López Rogers, Marie. Interview by Elizabeth Martínez. April 17, 2007. Mexican Americans of Litchfield Park Oral History Project, Litchfield Park Historical Society / Arizona State University.

Luckingham, Bradford. *Epidemic in the Southwest, 1918–1919*. Southwestern Studies 72. Texas Western Press, 1984.

Marin, Christine. "Always a Struggle: Mexican Americans in Miami, Arizona, 1909–1951." PhD dissertation, Arizona State University, 2005.

Marin, Christine, and Luis F. B. Plascencia. "*Mexicano* Miners, Dual Wage, and the Pursuit of Wage Equality in Miami, Arizona." In Plascencia and Cuádraz, *Mexican Workers*, 203–26.

McBane, Margo. "The Role of Gender in Citrus Employment: A Case Study of Recruitment, Labor, and Housing Patterns at the Limoneira Company, 1893 to 1940." *California History* 74 (1995): 68–81.

McGowan, Joseph C. "History of Extra-Long Staple Cotton." MA thesis, University of Arizona, 1961.

Meeks, Eric V. *Border Citizens: The Making of Indians, Mexicans, and Anglos in Arizona*. University of Texas Press, 2007.

Méndez, Alina R. "Cheap for Whom? Migration, Farm Labor, and Social Reproduction in the Imperial Valley / Mexicali Borderlands, 1941–1969." PhD dissertation, University of California, San Diego, 2017.

Mesquita, Connie. Interview by Gloria Cuádraz. 2006. Mexican Americans of Litchfield Park Oral History Project, Litchfield Park Historical Society / Arizona State University.

Moreno, Angelita Parilla. Interview by Gloria Cuádraz. 2006. Mexican Americans of Litchfield Park Oral History Project, Litchfield Park Historical Society / Arizona State University.

Norris, Jim. *North for the Harvest: Mexican Workers, Growers, and the Sugar Beet Industry*. Minnesota Historical Society Press, 2009.

O'Leary, Anna. "The Morenci Miners Women's Auxiliary During the Great Arizona Copper Strike, 1983–1986." In Plascencia and Cuádraz, *Mexican Workers*, 248–69.

Orth, Samuel P. "The Alien Contract Labor Law." *Political Science Quarterly* 22, no. 1 (1907): 49–60.

Pendleton, Edwin Charles. "History of Labor in Arizona Irrigated Agriculture." PhD dissertation, University of California, Berkeley, 1950.

Perales, Monica. *Smeltertown: Making and Remembering a Southwest Border Community*. University of North Carolina Press, 2010.

Peterson, Herbert B. "Twentieth-Century Search for Cíbola: Post–World War I Mexican Labor Exploitation in Arizona." In *An Awakening Minority: The Mexican Americans*, 2nd ed., edited by Manuel Servín, 113–32. Glencoe Press, 1974.

Plascencia, Luis F. B. "'Get Us Our Privilege of Bringing in Mexican Labor': Recruitment and Desire for Mexican Labor in Arizona, 1917–2016." In Plascencia and Cuádraz, *Mexican Workers*, 124–78.

Plascencia, Luis F. B. "State-Sanctioned Coercion and Agricultural Contract Labor: Jamaican and Mexican Workers in Canada and the United States, 1909–2014." In *On Coerced Labor: Work and Compulsion After Chattel Slavery*, edited by Marcel van der Linden and Magaly Rodríguez García, 225–66. Brill, 2016.

Plascencia, Luis F. B., and Gloria H. Cuádraz, eds. *Mexican Workers and the Making of Arizona*. University of Arizona Press, 2018.

Reisler, Mark. *By the Sweat of Their Brow: Mexican Immigrant Labor in the United States, 1900–1940*. Greenwood Press, 1976.

Reynolds, Jean. "Mexican American Women Workers in Mid-Twentieth-Century Phoenix." In Plascencia and Cuádraz, *Mexican Workers*, 227–47.

Romero, Mary. *Maid in the U.S.A.* Routledge, 1992.

Romero, Mary, and Eric Margolis. "Tending the Beets: *Campesinas* and the Great Western Sugar Company." *Revista Mujeres* 2 (1985): 17–28.

Ruiz, Vicki L. *Cannery Women, Cannery Lives: Mexican Women, Unionization, and the California Food Processing Industry, 1930–1950*. University of New Mexico Press, 1987.

Ruiz, Vicki L. *From Out of the Shadows: Mexican Women in Twentieth-Century America*. Oxford University Press, 1998.

Salazar, Nicky. Interview by Elizabeth Martínez. 2008. Mexican Americans of Litchfield Park Oral History Project, Litchfield Park Historical Society / Arizona State University.

Schetter, Clyde E. *Story of a Town: Litchfield Park*. Litchfield Park Library Association, 1976.

Serrano Martin, Frances. Interview by Gloria Cuádraz. 2007. Mexican Americans of Litchfield Park Oral History Project, Litchfield Park Historical Society / Arizona State University.

Shapiro, Erik-Anders. "Cotton in Arizona: A Historical Geography." MA thesis, University of Arizona, 1989.

Smith, Susan. "Litchfield Park and Vicinity." MA thesis, University of Arizona, 1948.

Valdés, Dennis Nodín. "*Betabeleros*: The Formation of an Agricultural Proletariat in the Midwest." *Labor History* 30, no. 4 (1989): 536–62.

Vargas, Zaragosa. *Proletarians of the North: A History of Mexican Industrial Workers in Detroit and the Midwest, 1917–1933*. University of California Press, 1993.

Veloz, Larisa L. "'Even the Women are Leaving': Gendered Migrations Between Mexico and the United States; Revolutionary Diasporas, Depression-Era Depatriations, and Wartime Bracero Controls, 1900–1950." PhD dissertation, Georgetown University, 2015.

Villa Moreno, Lucy. Interview by Gloria Cuádraz. 2006. Mexican Americans of Litchfield Park Oral History Project, Litchfield Park Historical Society / Arizona State University.

Villa Romo, Sallie. Interview by Gloria Cuádraz. 2006. Mexican Americans of Litchfield Park Oral History Project, Litchfield Park Historical Society / Arizona State University.

Vizzerra, Armida. Interview by Gloria Cuádraz. 2006. Mexican Americans of Litchfield Park Oral History Project, Litchfield Park Historical Society / Arizona State University.

Walker, Scott. "Making the Desert Bloom: Mexicans and Whites in the Agricultural Development of the Salt River Valley, 1867–1930." PhD dissertation, Arizona State University, 2012.

Weber, Devra. *Dark Sweat, White Gold: California Farm Workers, Cotton, and the New Deal.* University of California Press, 1994.

Weber, Devra Anne. "Oral History and Mexican Farmworkers." *Oral History Review* 17 (Autumn 1989): 47–62.

Weisiger, Marsha L. *Land of Plenty: Oklahomans in the Cotton Fields of Arizona, 1933–1942.* University of Oklahoma Press, 1995.

Woehlke, Walter V. "What Cotton Did to Arizona." *Sunset* 47 (1921): 21–23.

Zamudio-Gurrola, Susan. "Housing Farm Workers: Assessing the Significance of Bracero Labor Camps in Ventura County." Master's thesis, University of Southern California, 2009.

Zavella, Patricia. *Women's Work and Chicano Families: Cannery Workers of the Santa Clara Valley.* Cornell University Press, 1987.

PART IV

Sounds and Silences

CHAPTER 7

Turning On the Journey

Silences, Music, and the Politics of Listening in the Bracero Program

LILIANA TOLEDO-GUZMÁN

—¿Y cantaban?
—Sí, sí cantaban, se oía la cantadera de ellos allá donde estaba la casa.

—LAURENTINA RAMOS JUÁREZ

Between 1942 and 1964, four million Mexicans, primarily men, moved to the United States to work temporarily in the fields as part of the Bracero Program, causing the separation of their families. Migrating as temporary workers in the agricultural industry was a complex process involving the intertwining of internal politics in both Mexico and the United States. This included the long-lasting exclusion of farm laborers from the Mexican modernization project and the instrumentalization of this abandonment by the U.S. government during and after World War II. One of the hallmarks of President Manuel Ávila Camacho's term in Mexico (1940–46) was the strengthening of relations with the United States, which translated into economic and political projects, from the addition of Mexico to the Allied powers during World War II to the signing of bilateral programs such as the Bracero Program.[1] Such a shift was part of the reassessment of internal and external politics and the deradicalization of the formerly revolutionary political discourses in Mexico, which in the 1930s included oil expropriation, the claiming of socialist education, and an extensive land distribution program during Lázaro Cárdenas's presidency.[2]

There is extensive literature on the Bracero Program and how it was configured and changed over time. In general terms, the Bracero Program was not the first bilateral negotiation between the Mexican and U.S. governments to provide temporary workers to the United States. One of the Bracero Program's precedents was the temporary workers' action enacted in 1917 in the context of the First World War and the Mexican Revolution.[3] A detailed analysis of the Bracero Program was made by Ronald Mize and Alicia Swords. The authors saw temporary labor as a manifestation of capitalism, which reached a critical point with the NAFTA agreement, and which created the "illegal problem" that has been an issue throughout the twentieth century.[4] Following Mize and Swords, in this chapter I examine how oral histories and musical repertoire depict the continuities of temporary labor exploitation, the reliance on utilizing rural Mexicans as temporary workers in the United States, and the neglectful treatment braceros received from the U.S. and Mexican governments.

Modernity became a leitmotiv of the period known as "el milagro mexicano" due to Mexico's economic growth after World War II.[5] While the Mexican cities grew and the United States was positioned as a world power after World War II, radio, films, cartoons, and magazines portrayed the imaginary of modern life and progress in urban areas.[6] A dual mythical space was created for current and prospective braceros and their families. Those who stayed in Mexico evoked their relatives' lives on the other side of the border from what they heard, read, and watched in the media about the agreement signed between the U.S. and Mexican governments. Braceros experienced a similar process in the United States, imagining the place they left behind. The music repertoire created and consumed by braceros and their families emerged in the space opened by the imagination when they separated.

The radio played an important role in creating such evocations before, during, and after braceros' journeys. Evangelina Basúa, a former bracero's wife, gives testimony about the extent to which this period was remarkably aural. Basúa said she learned about the Bracero Program through the radio: "They announced it a lot."[7] Originally from Sinaloa and eventually established in Glendale, Arizona, Basúa and her husband, after listening to advertisements on the radio, were convinced to move to Empalme, Sonora, so that he could become a bracero. The objective was the same for them as for others: to have a better quality of life. Radio advertisements targeted a specific audience: Mexicans who lived in such hardship that they were willing to get a job in another country and separate from their families. Basúa's comment about the radio is not isolated. References to the radio are frequent in the archives related to the Bracero Program, and during this period, new themes in music that reported the experiences of temporary workers gained relevancy.

As Leah Bassel suggests, the politics of listening are characterized by the interdependence of speaking and listening.[8] A radio advertisement in Mexico claimed that men could earn fifty cents per hour if they became braceros in the United States. Given the sixty-five cents the target audience earned for a full day's work in Mexico for similar jobs, becoming a bracero seemed attractive.[9] The interplay between global and local events and the development of new industries occurred in parallel and influenced diplomatic as well as familial and interpersonal relationships. All these events fostered a bracero musical repertoire that contradicted and contested the positive and triumphalist discourses about the Bracero Program that came from official sources from Mexico and the United States, and that are found in some oral histories compiled in the Bracero History Archive.

In this chapter, I explore how listening, as a category of analysis, can contribute to investigating the Bracero Program. Listening can be understood in different ways. I focus overall on listening to lyrics and, to a lesser extent, to the music that accompanies the lyrics. Moreover, I examine how braceros may have labeled other braceros based on how they spoke. In analyzing some of the Bracero Program's auditory components, I aim to expand its sonic narratives. I connect these topics with Leah Bassel's concept of *the politics of listening*, which aims to balance "unequal concentrations of narrative resources and distributions of symbolic power (e.g., in media resources, popular culture as well as formal political spaces)."[10] I do not use Bassel's category in all its dimensions, which are more applicable to contemporary social justice and migration issues in the European context. Instead, I explore the *politics of listening* from a historiographical perspective, aiming to better understand and complement braceros' oral histories by examining braceros' voices in corridos and songs.[11]

As testimonies in the Bracero Archive demonstrate, singing and listening to the radio were among braceros' most important entertainments. The pieces I explore in this chapter are "Canto del bracero," recorded by

Pedro Infante in 1953; "Corrido del bracero," by Jesús "Chuy" Negrete, recorded in 1975 by activists Los Alacranes Mojados and Los Mascarones; and "La quema de los braceros," an anonymous corrido published in 1959 in Phoenix, Arizona, in the Spanish-language newspaper *El Sol*.[12] This repertoire is linked to different domains of production, including mass media, activism, and the press, and it pertains to different periods that bring different perspectives on the Bracero Program. Another dimension of listening I explore, using the Bracero History Archive interviews, is braceros' perceptions of other braceros based on how they spoke. This is not an exhaustive exploration of the bracero repertoire but an attempt to build on existing investigations utilizing sources that point to the act of listening to music, lyrics, and narrations.

Radio was one of Mexico's most important means of entertainment and communication before and during the Bracero Program, and music occupied most of the programming on the principal stations from 1930 to 1950. XEW devoted 92 percent of its programming to music, and XEB dedicated 60 to 80 percent to Mexican orchestras' repertoire, between 1938 and 1948.[13] These percentages give an idea of the kind of content the Mexican population in general, and braceros and their relatives in particular, accessed. The radio was positioned as a massive form of mediation of meanings through advertisements, music, and news.

Owning a radio was not only an aural means of communication but a hallmark of modernity.[14] One of the men who went to the United States near the end of the Bracero Program was Antonio V. Pérez Herrera, born on December 27, 1942, in Michoacán. Herrera was living in Scottsdale, Arizona, when he was interviewed as part of the Bracero Oral History Project. One of the moments that made an impression on Antonio was when he saw his brother, a bracero, arrive in Mexico with new clothes and carrying a radio. Antonio was fascinated; in his eyes, his brother looked modern.[15]

The Bracero History Archive stories swing between episodes of mistreatment and celebratory narrations of the Bracero Program, from making economic progress to being neglected by the U.S. and Mexican authorities. Some oral interviews with Mexican immigrant workers reflect the lingering positive effects of the Bracero Program: "We were happy," recalled Ramona Acosta, born in 1918 in Phoenix, Arizona. Such emotions and positive effects shaped her reaction to César Chávez's movement:

"By that time, there was no evil, no discrimination."[16] Acosta stated that individuals who participated in the marches alongside César Chávez were predominantly youth who were not employed in agricultural labor. In her testimony, Acosta characterized braceros as being "all happy," suggesting a contrast in the perceptions of these two groups, braceros and strikers, during the labor movement. She compared the strike movement led by Chávez to contemporary migration issues, noting that, in her view, it would not be appropriate for her to participate in marches advocating for undocumented migrants: "Why am I going to march if I'm not illegal? Why am I going to march if I haven't suffered in the U.S.?" Acosta's response raises questions about how migrant communities develop varying perspectives on new waves of migrants and how solidarity is interpreted differently at the group level. From her viewpoint, only those who are involved as temporary workers have the authority to advocate for the rights of that group.

Acosta's views can shed light on the internal conflicts within the bracero community in relation to the labor movement. Why did Antonio V. Pérez Herrera and Ramona Acosta not mention the adverse aspects of the Bracero Program in their interviews? The silences (i.e., lack of critique of the Bracero Program) in oral histories may correlate to trauma, fear of retaliation, or selective memory. Tuning in to other aural evidence, such as songs and references to braceros' voices, provides a richer context with which to grasp the Bracero Program. The radio carried back home by Pérez Herrera's brother offers a clue to a critical source: songs, advertisements, and news broadcasting shared via radio.

Music, Feelings, and Braceros' Stories

Musical repertoire was a means of transmitting emotions and news among braceros that would have been difficult to share by other means, like direct oral communication. Historian Ana Elizabeth Rosas argues that popular songs, including "El bracero mexicano," corridos, and love songs, offered Mexican immigrant men, women, and children the "lyrics, spirit, and tone . . . to convey their feelings."[17] Music that addressed braceros' negative experiences functioned as an effective means of communication in a surveilled environment and a transnational space. For example, the U.S. government censored the letters braceros sent to their relatives in Mexico, especially when they narrated histories of abuses. Letters often failed to reach their recipients across the border. Additionally, braceros lacked basic legal representation when it was necessary.

Musical repertoire serves as a valuable historical source by narrating tragedies, such as workplace accidents due to negligence, more openly than oral testimonies do. Particularly, corridos' anonymity enabled braceros to share the conditions and psychological effects of living as temporary workers. Finally, the vocabulary in the musical repertoire and what the news reported about braceros' working conditions show that braceros and some sectors of the population were aware of the inhumane conditions under which they worked. Braceros' recognition of their condition of exploitation, as expressed in music, challenges the romanticized and dehumanizing assumption that braceros were hard-working machines who could endure the most difficult tasks without noticing their hardships.

"Canto del bracero," "Corrido del bracero," and "La quema de los braceros" focus on narrating the hardships of being a bracero without necessarily exposing one's specific bracero identity. One of the main differences between oral histories in the Bracero History Archive and sources like music is that the latter can be anonymous. Braceros interviewed face-to-face might have self-censored in testimonies like those compiled in the Bracero History Archive. Many of these interviews took place in the United States, and both the interviewers and the sponsor institutions were from the United States, which means that most of the interviewees might have acquired U.S. citizenship by the time the interview occurred. These matters may have influenced the ways in which braceros recalled their experiences and reconstructed the past.

Songs about braceros became pedagogical devices capable of crossing borders and transcending censorship, as letters and people did not. It was common for songs in the braceros' repertoire to include a warning verse for those who wanted to work temporarily in the United States. For example, the last stanza of "Canto del bracero" states: "If you plan to go, stop, or if you are there, come back."[18] Verónica Calvillo claims that overall the bracero music repertoire expresses the "emotional exhaustion" of braceros.[19] She has identified work and morality as the two main themes in fourteen recordings of bracero-related music, which she found at the Strachwitz Frontera Collection, UCLA.[20]

"Canto del Bracero" and "Corrido del Bracero"

Pedro Infante, the well-known Mexican singer of the Golden Age of Mexican Cinema, recorded "Canto del bracero," a piece by Rubén Méndez del Castillo, in 1953 for the Peerless Records label, which distributed Mexican music in Mexico, Latin America, and the U.S. Southwest.[21] I analyze this song in two ways. First, I examine how the music and lyrics addressed the Bracero Program and what ideas they replicate, confirm, or negate. Second, I explore the politics surrounding this song, considering the popularity of Pedro Infante in Mexico and the United States, the political connections of the song's composer Rubén Méndez, and the song's insertion into the Mexican system of media stars. By exploring the lyrics and the context in which the song was produced, I aim to hypothesize different levels on which it may have been understood at the time of its release.

The first point to notice in Infante's song is the semantics of the word *bracero*. The first stanza alludes to a bracero "with no passport," indicating that *bracero* became a generic word to name field workers in the United States, regardless of their legal status. The practice of crossing to the United States and eluding migratory authorities in the post–World War II period is reinforced in the song by the expression "me colé" (I sneaked in):

> Cuando yo me fui pa'l norte
> Me colé por California
> Yo no tenía cartilla ni pasaporte
> Ni amigos ni palancas en migración
> Pero me colé con resolución.
>
> (When I traveled north
> I sneaked in through California
> Without a card or passport

Friends, or connections in migration
But I entered with determination.)[22]

The song refers to a bracero as a temporary worker in the United States, using a more expansive popular understanding of the term beyond the official meaning of a worker enrolled in the Bracero Program. Further, it draws from a meaning of the word that dated to many decades earlier. The term *bracero* appeared in the Mexican press in the late nineteenth century, designating the workers who arrived in Mexico City, usually from rural areas. *La Voz de México*, concerned about braceros' alcohol consumption, asked in 1899: "How will healthy food be provided to braceros, who possess nothing more than a poor blanket and a few pawnbroker tickets tied to their pants?"[23] A bracero, since the nineteenth century, was the rural "other" in a modern place. *La Voz de México* blames employers for braceros' conditions of deprivation, foreshadowing the denunciation of braceros' treatment forty years later.

The continuity with the terminology used in Mexico to designate certain kinds of workers indicates that the Bracero Program relied on a preexisting context of poverty and social inequality in Mexico. As a result, the Bracero Program perpetuated the idea of the bracero as a premodern, underpaid laborer on a transnational scale. Importantly, during the Bracero Program, laborers developed their own sense of identity and possibly established hierarchies and varied experiences among themselves based on their ethnicity. Testimonials suggest that there was an internal subdivision among braceros, and some considered those from southern Mexico to be different and less self-sufficient—specifically, braceros who came from Indigenous populations. When the interviewer asked Socorro Flores Pando, a former bracero from Delicias, Chihuahua, about the differences among braceros, he replied:

> Yes, of course . . . just by seeing them, just by talking, you get to know the people from here in the state of Chihuahua. Other states already have different tones of speech and different ways of expressing themselves and everything. And those from the south, and then from Oaxaca, all that, well, many times I had to go with them here, guiding them. . . . And I served as a guide, because they hardly knew Spanish. . . . What they wore, they even

wore white underwear or something like that. And they were, well, it was another way of being for them.[24]

How braceros articulated speech was crucial for Socorro Flores to determine the condition of the otherness of his bracero fellows: they did not speak Spanish well, and their tone when speaking was as different as their clothes. Producers, singers, and composers were aware of how voice tone may indicate ethnicity. Pedro Infante used this resource to represent a bracero in his song by mispronouncing the word *discriminación*, which he pronounces as "descreminación." The mispronunciation is intended to indicate that the central character is a rural man, probably from an Indigenous ethnic background. Mexican cinema used such stereotypical ways of speaking to indicate ethnic membership and, probably, to create empathy with viewers from rural Mexico and make movies more profitable. A similar example in the film industry was *Tizoc* (1957), starring Pedro Infante himself, who exploited vocal stereotypification to personify an Indigenous man from the mountains of Oaxaca.[25]

"Canto del bracero" has the structure of a fable narrated in the first person, which is also a feature of some kinds of corridos. The singer narrates the story of a past experience in order to warn others not to go to the United States to work. The character in this song claims to be a bracero. However, he has no documents supporting his legal presence in the United States. Why does the singer associate his legal status with his lack of friends and lovers? "Canto del bracero" speaks about unofficial ways of crossing the U.S.-Mexico border as a temporary worker. The first stanza replicates what many scholars have discussed about the bracero program. First, the program did not discourage migrants from crossing illegally to the United States; it did just the opposite. The promise of higher wages in the United States compared to Mexico pushed many men to look for temporary work there, whether through official or unofficial channels. Secondly, it has been amply documented that even if those who aspired to become braceros wanted to follow the legal procedure, they had to pay bribes to be included on the list of workers who would be sent to the United States. This was the case with Antonio V. Pérez Herrera, who had to pay a two-hundred-peso bribe to be included on the list to become a bracero. Herrera stated that the list for the contracting center in Empalme, Sonora, was not created by government personnel, confirming what other braceros have said about having to pay bribes to be considered for work.[26] This indicates that braceros may not have been fully aware of the various parties involved in the process, as well as the corrupt mechanisms or practices related to recruiting temporary workers at border locations like Empalme, Sonora. In conclusion, being a bracero was a fluid concept that may or may not have referred to a specific legal status in the United States.[27]

Interviewee Ramona Acosta, as mentioned above, claimed that there was no discrimination during the Bracero Program or in the fields, whereas songs like "Canto del bracero" assert the opposite. The debate over whether there was discrimination against Mexicans and Mexican Americans in the 1960s occupied an essential place in political discussions in Arizona. In 1962, Phoenix mayor Samuel Mardian Jr. claimed that people of ethnic minorities did not experience discrimination thanks to the "Anglo community's generosity and civil stewardship."[28] In response, Herbert Ely, the president of the Phoenix Council of Civil Unity, pointed out that discrimination did exist in Phoenix. Moreover, Ely claimed that any social gains obtained were due to the efforts of ethnic minorities to change the legal framework that impeded them from fully enjoying citizenship.[29] The musical repertoire about the Bracero Program generally resonates with Ely's political position, as shown in "Canto del bracero," but it also demonstrates braceros' awareness of their precarious working conditions.

Recorrí varios estados
De la Unión Americana
En Arizona y Texas y por Louisiana
Siempre sentí la falta de estimación
Que's que dicen que's descreminación.

(I toured various states
Of the United States
In Arizona and Texas and Louisiana
I always felt underestimated
Some say it is discrimination.)

Oral testimony included in the documentary *Harvest of Loneliness: The Bracero Program* confirms discriminatory practices and poor working conditions. One bracero recounted that, when they were being transported to their places of work, after going the bathroom, they had to wipe themselves with newspapers, and to urinate, they had to open the door of the train. These testimonies show that, in addition to the exhausting journeys, the conditions inside the trains did not meet minimum standards.[30] Pedro Gómez, another bracero, reported that braceros were transported in a boxcar for cattle where they had to travel standing because the floorboards were wet.[31] Returning to the song, the moral of its fable, as its ending articulates, is to encourage agricultural workers in Mexico to stop pursuing the American Dream:

> Si tú piensas ir, detente
> O si estás allá, regresa
> Donde está tu terruño y está tu gente
> Y el rinconcito aquel que te vio nacer
> Donde está el amor que puedes perder.
>
> (If you're thinking about going, reconsider
> Or if you are already there, return.
> Go back to your homeland, where your people reside
> And to the little corner where you were born
> Where the love you can lose is.)

This song allows us to explore the politics of listening, not just in terms of the music and the lyrics, but also by analyzing the context in which songs were produced, performed, and distributed. Pedro Infante was among Mexico's most popular singers by the 1950s and was widely known among Mexican, Mexican American, and Latin American audiences.[32] Infante was not an activist but an artist who became part of the media industry. Beyond fostering empathy for the workers, the industry he was part of must have seen a marketing opportunity in exploiting and commodifying bracero experiences. Moreover, it is plausible to consider this song as a cultural diplomacy product meant to discourage Mexican migration to the United States, considering the political networks that surrounded Infante's music and film productions, starting with the composer of this theme.

"Canto del bracero" was not of anonymous authorship, as are corridos in general. It was composed by Rubén Méndez, an established composer who by the 1950s had already built strong connections with the Mexican elites. For example, the Mexican president Miguel Alemán Valdés invited him to join a 1951 working tour in Guanajuato, the composer's home state. Alemán's invitation to Méndez was a strategic move to attract local audiences there. From the composer's perspective, accompanying the Mexican president might have been convenient in terms of networking and public image. Méndez was one of the best-known composers of the time, and over the next decade Mexico's most important record labels asked to record Méndez's songs, which were played in Mexico and among Spanish-speaking audiences in the United States.

It is impossible to claim that Méndez's popularity directly resulted from the Guanajuato tour with President Miguel Alemán. Nevertheless, these events are evidence of a feature of Mexican politics from 1950 onward: the bonds between the mass media and the political elites.[33] Later, in 1970, the Mexican candidate of the Partido Revolucionario Institucional (Institutional Revolutionary Party, or PRI), Luis Echeverría Álvarez, invited Rubén Méndez to be part of his campaign for the presidency of Mexico, which Echeverría won as expected.[34]

Such alliances between the state and Mexican mass media did not weaken but rather strengthened throughout the years. They also expanded across the U.S.-Mexico border. Rubén Méndez was famous both in Mexico and among Mexican Americans, as evidenced by the interview Armando del Moral conducted with him and Tito Guízar on Radio KALI's *De visita con las estrellas*, produced in Los Angeles.[35] Radio stations in Mexico, such as XEW, also fostered international artists, including Pedro Infante, who sustained a transborder career, as his successful concerts in the Million Dollar Theater in Los Angeles prove. In the 1940s, XEW, owned by Emilio Azcárraga Vidaurreta, was the most powerful radio station in Mexico, and during World War II, XEW became the most important means of propaganda for the United States.[36]

Given Méndez's political connections, the polarized political climate after World War II, and his outreach to Mexican American audiences, it is likely that when he composed "Canto del bracero," he was aware of its monetary implications and interested in its monetary benefits. This song may reflect how an accomplished composer like Méndez could have sought financial gain by tackling social issues associated with the Bracero Program on both sides of the border, like discrimination, mistreatment, and loneliness. The abandonment of rural areas in Mexico and migration from those areas to the United States and Mexican cities after World War II under difficult conditions was an issue a great portion of the population was aware of and had experienced first- or secondhand. The chorus of "Canto del bracero" leaves no room for doubt: being a bracero was viewed as an emotionally damaging experience.[37] Regardless of the political or monetary intent of "Canto del bracero," emotional dread was a recurrent theme of the bracero repertoire:

> Ay, qué triste es la vida
> Qué triste vida es la del bracero
> Ay, cuánta decepción
> Cuánta desolación.
>
> (Oh, how sad life is
> What a sorrowful life the bracero leads
> Oh, so much disappointment
> So much desolation.)

The musical aspects of this song evoke a sense of sadness. It is written in 3/4 time, typical in many corridos, but the tempo is languid, which gives it a nostalgic atmosphere. Two musical layers representing Mexico and the United States strengthen the contemplative emotion. In the introduction and stanzas, the instrumental accompaniment unequivocally reflects Mexico. The traditional rhythm of a corrido is used, starting with the guitarrón's bass and then two strums with the vihuela and guitar that complete the 3/4 cycle. Simultaneously, a slide guitar, typical of U.S. country music, plays the melody. In the chorus, in which Infante imagines life in Mexico, a mariachi accompanies him, and the slide guitar disappears. The overlaying of two soundscapes reminiscent of Mexico and the United States likely formed part of a marketing strategy that aimed to capitalize on a socially relevant theme. Although Infante's song mentions discrimination, it seeks to discourage migration rather than denounce braceros' mistreatment. Such denunciation, however, was part of other repertoires that did not belong to the music industry but were born from social movements. This was the case with "Corrido del bracero."

"Corrido del bracero," by Los Mascarones and Los Alacranes Mojados, is another example in the musical repertoire that expresses the emotional and negative experiences of braceros, but its inception was directly political and attached to the Chicano Movement. The composer of this piece was Jesús "Chuy" Negrete, from Chicago, who was one of the most influential musicians in the Chicano Movement music scene. This corrido appeared on the album *¡Levántate campesino!* (1975), along with other songs that formed part of the protest song movement.[38] It begins:

De México vine buscando dinero
Llegué de bracero por el mes de abril
Dejé mi ranchito triste, abandonado
Allá por los cerros donde yo nací.

Allá en Matamoros crucé la frontera
Por falta de modos crucé de ilegal.
Señores les cuento cómo ando sufriendo
Que me han dado ganas de volver pa' atrás.

(I came from Mexico looking for money
I arrived as a bracero in the month of April
I left my little ranch sad, abandoned
There in the hills where I was born.

There in Matamoros, I crossed the border
Due to a lack of options, I crossed illegally.
Gentlemen, let me tell you about my suffering
It has made me want to go back.)[39]

"Corrido del bracero" begins by anthropomorphizing the ranchito as a subject suffering from abandonment by the bracero. In Mexican Spanish, *ranchito* may refer to a ranch itself, but informally it might be a synonym for home, state, or even country. Thus, the word *ranchito* in the bracero repertoire carries a sense of belonging at different scales. Scholar Alex E. Chávez examines the intertwining of the film industry, in which Pedro Infante was a significant figure, and music in the portrayal of the rancho in the movie *Allá en el rancho grande,* released in 1939, and in the song of the same title. Chávez argues that the concept of the rancho in films was connected to haciendas, which were the hierarchical spaces where masculinity and class were configured in the late nineteenth and early twentieth centuries.[40]

The singer in "Corrido del bracero" shares the sorrow he has experienced in the United States and expresses longing for his homeland. The song laments an unstable life of moving physically between different places in the Sunbelt region:

Piscando algodón allá por Laredo
Lavando platillos allá en San Antonio
Anduve en las milpas allá en California
Piscando cebolla, me puse a llorar

Crecieron mis hijos, después de diez años
Por mi mala suerte allá en la labor
Señores les cuento cómo ando sufriendo
Que me han dado ganas de volver pa' atrás.

(Picking cotton in Laredo
Washing dishes in San Antonio
I walked in the cornfields in California
Picking onions, I started crying

My children grew up after ten years
Because of my bad luck at work.
Gentlemen, I tell you how I am suffering
How it has made me want to go back.)

This musical piece is an excellent source for exploring gender issues related to bracero families. A character representing the bracero's wife appears at the end of the corrido. She complains about her husband's habit of drinking and wasting money:

Tengo tres años casada, y nomás sufriendo errores
Tú gastando puro dólar, yo sufriendo los dolores
Los hombres ser muy gallos, los hombres ser muy machos
Pero son desobligados además de ser borrachos.

(I have been married for three years, and suffer from mistakes
You've been spending money, and I'm suffering from the pain
Men are very cocky, men are very macho
But they are irresponsible besides being drunk.)

The conclusion of "Corrido del bracero" hints at disappointment and despair over the bracero's wage and the lack of opportunities for braceros and their entire families. In a different stanza, the bracero sings, "They tell me that here you can clean up, making money, but that has not happened to this poor bracero," referring to the American Dream and the propagation of the idea that the United States was a land of opportunities.[41] According to historian Camille Guérin-Gonzales, the American Dream was a decisive factor in Mexican immigrants' decision to become braceros. However, they were unaware of the financial and social limitations they and their families would face once they arrived in the United States.[42]

Although the themes that the corrido addresses are tragedies, the narration is written in a comic and satirical way. For Jesús "Chuy" Negrete, laughing was a strategy to convey a political message, aligned with his collaboration with the Mexican theater troupe Los Mascarones. In an interview, Negrete stated: "If you can make people laugh and educate them at the same time, that's what I try to strive for. To laugh and to be politicized, to make them cry and be politicized."[43] The corrido is in F major and alternates sections in 2/4 and 3/4 time at a fast pace, which suggests that it is music to dance to, giving it sonically a more festive than tragic tone. Drawing from theater, Negrete mixed sung and spoken parts to represent a dialogue with his character's wife, which he addresses humorously despite the female character's discourse being a complaint.

Beyond the comic and festive tone of this corrido, it is worth noting that examining the situation through the lens of gender expands the meaning of listening. This expanded meaning includes listening to others and being attentive to silence. According to historian Ana Elizabeth

Rosas, braceros were usually reluctant to speak up about their feelings and traumatic experiences as braceros. On the other hand, braceros' daughters and wives experienced emotional exhaustion because of the lack of intimate conversations with their bracero relatives. Rosas's work explores the ways in which braceros' silence was a coping mechanism for trauma and shows that the psychological effects of exploitative working conditions extended to braceros' families in Mexico. Women's emotional exhaustion was alleviated by gathering in groups with other women who had experienced similar situations. The act of listening to other women was a way to heal the suffering of being separated from their families. The possibility of resonating with other women's voices helped them cope with the emotional and physical burden of overseeing the family alone. In the context of the Bracero Program, listening involved more than just the musical content aired on the radio; it entailed actively listening to individuals who had shared similar experiences.[44]

Oral Testimonies and Their Silences

"Canto del bracero" and "Corrido del bracero" depict the bracero's life as full of suffering. The voices in these songs align with testimonials in recent documentaries like *Harvest of Loneliness*, in which an ex-bracero says that health officials treated them "like animals" during examinations, stressing feelings of fear and tiredness: "There were doctors that with these two fingers, stick them in your testicles. It was not gentle. . . . A lot of people would faint."[45] The documentary contrasts with some testimonials in the Bracero History Archive. While it is undeniable that some braceros may have had positive experiences, it is equally true that certain favorable perspectives on the Bracero Program can overshadow its negative aspects. What factors contributed to the varied narratives about the Bracero Program as expressed by different braceros?

One question in analyzing oral histories relates to trauma and the interviewees' positionality. Memories of the past may change over time according to the historical moment the subject is living. Whereas the assessment in the braceros' narratives is positive overall, scholars such as Verónica Calvillo argue that braceros experienced "humiliating inspections and illegal hiring practices."[46] Working with oral histories represents a challenge in terms of discussing the information provided by the interviewees and how the data was collected.[47] This is not to say that one narrative or another of the Bracero Program represents *the truth,* but rather that different sources may complicate how history is written. Moreover, the absence of detailed testimonies of mistreatment of braceros in oral histories might be evidence of their traumatic experiences.

The testimony of bracero Domingo López, collected by historian Ana Elizabeth Rosas, illustrates that braceros might have preferred to keep silent and avoid communicating what they lived as a defense mechanism. According to Rosas, "He [Domingo] explained that the exhaustion of laboring in the fields of Fresno, California, was not as devastating as the emotional shocks that the program had inflicted on him. . . . He admitted to Azucena [his daughter] that it was difficult for him to transition out of the mood occasioned by his mistreatment when he reunited with her and her siblings."[48] Domingo's silence adds another layer of complexity yet to be explored; specifically, the bracero's silence should not be viewed as a lack of evidence of mistreatment but rather as evidence of a psychological burden. One interviewee in *Harvest of Loneliness* claimed: "One of the things that my grandma said [about my grandfather] is that he was ashamed of a lot of the things that happened, and that's why he doesn't want to talk about it."[49] Silence may also denote power dynamics and the absence of mechanisms enabling braceros to improve their labor conditions.

Music that depicted the hardships faced by temporary workers served to defy the censorship that was used to silence braceros. The U.S. government censored letters that contained information about tragic events. This practice was something that U.S. consulate official Churchill Murray warned against. For example, the government withheld a letter from a bracero who anonymously informed the family of another bracero named Antonio Torres Vigil about Vigil's death.[50] Censorship also took a psychological toll on braceros and their extended families—parents, wives, fiancées, and children who remained in Mexico.

Oral histories tend to focus on the positive. Bracero Ángel Moreno reported that becoming a temporary worker "changed his life for the better,"[51] and Héctor Ponce, a bracero from Chihuahua, recalled that he "was employed by a group of brothers who treated him extremely well; they often invited him into their home, and they offered to help arrange for his residency in the hopes that he would stay to work there permanently."[52] These examples shed light on the agency of the different actors involved in the Bracero Program, such as ranchers. According to the bracero agreement, the U.S. government was the official employer of braceros from 1948 to 1951. During this period, the U.S. government issued executive orders stating that braceros had to work directly with growers.

Although some braceros may have worked with good employers, as some oral histories recount, historian Deborah Cohen claims that it was precisely in this period that braceros complained the most.[53] Cohen, citing Henry P. Anderson, writes: "While braceros were legally afforded 'a certain freedom of choice,' many involved in the program concluded that braceros deserved no more freedom or respect 'than any other commodity shipped in international trade.'"[54] Carlos Corella, a former soldier and later an employee of the U.S. Department of Labor in charge of escorting braceros from one side of the border to the other, refers to that process as "importation of braceros."[55] If braceros were regarded overall as merchandise to be imported, what notions about humanity did the bracero musical repertoire express that may help to complicate oral testimonies?

In some oral histories, braceros regarded their job positively, but when braceros were directly asked about medical examinations, many of them mentioned that they were required to undergo blood tests, delousing, and fumigation with DDT. In his testimony, ex-bracero Ángel Moreno narrates that the first time he arrived in the United States, all the workers gathered in a stadium. There were so many of them, he said, that they had to remain standing while traveling by train. In the stadium, the workers were given a small lunch.[56] On the other hand, the aforementioned Carlos Corella said that at Rio Vista Bracero Reception Center, in Socorro, Texas, representatives of the U.S. departments of labor, immigration, and public health inspected newly arrived braceros, and disinfected and deloused them.[57] Such procedures raise questions about the contract conditions for braceros. These policies had their immediate precedents in the 1920s.

Since the early twentieth century, it had been common for Mexican workers to cross the border to work as temporary laborers and then return to Mexico.[58] Nevertheless, as Kelly Lytle Hernández explains, "Congress established the Border Patrol's law-enforcement authority with the passage of the Act of February 27, 1925."[59] Statements that depicted Mexicans as nonhumans emerged from debates about migratory regulations, like the 1920 declaration in the U.S. Senate: "There never was a more docile animal in the world than the Mexican."[60] In *Harvest of Loneliness,* one testimony describes how a manager at a reception center revealed his recruitment method, which focused on evaluating the men's character. According to this manager, "A good bracero had to be timid, docile, unlettered, and impoverished; anyone who was well-dressed or well-spoken would be rejected."[61] These criteria indicate that the hiring process aimed to select men who were more susceptible to abuse, which may explain why braceros were often reluctant to speak out about mistreatment or to recount their experiences. In controlling Mexican immigration, the U.S. Congress faced the paradox of limiting the entrance of immigrants when they needed cheap laborers to satisfy the country's internal market and expansionist capitalist project; historian Natalia Molina refers to this balance of priorities as "the immigration regime."[62] The paradox was addressed during World War II when the Bracero Program was launched to satisfy these demands.

The claim that Mexican workers were "docile animals" naturalizes and obscures the social conditions that led braceros to endure inhumane labor conditions, and conceals braceros' awareness of such conditions. The claim made in the U.S. Senate in 1920 disregards the extreme conditions under which many Mexicans lived at that time after ten years of revolutionary conflict, the internal and external political and economic forces that fostered people's migration under unfavorable conditions, and the ways in which certain political actors in Mexico and the United States benefited from the need created by a context of violence and precariousness. Music humanized braceros by contesting naturalistic explanations of inequality, like "docility," and it became a means for transmitting awareness.

The radio and newspapers were key media for transmitting migratory issues, news, and diplomatic resolutions from both sides of the border. For example, as part of postrevolutionary Mexican propaganda, in the 1920s, the Mexican government sponsored radio broadcasts in the United States advertising that the Mexican government was aware of Mexican citizens working there and sought their safe return to Mexico. Besides propaganda, the Mexican government was testing its abilities to reach audiences beyond the border with broadcasts. The Mexican and U.S. governments had dealt with temporary worker issues at least twenty years before the Bracero Program was launched.[63] The bracero musical repertoire offers a different viewpoint on the Bracero Program apart from the triumphalist discourses of both the U.S. and Mexican governments.

The Corrido "La Quema de los Braceros"

Although the Bracero Program must have fulfilled temporary workers' basic needs while they worked in the United States, evidence suggests that braceros had inadequate living and working conditions, faced discrimination in housing and transportation, and suffered mental and physical health issues. In the first year of the Bracero Program, the Spanish-language newspaper *El Sol* in Phoenix, Arizona, published an article titled "Horrible Death of Another Bracero."[64] The news tells the story of a bracero from Michoacán who was sleeping in a furrow when he was run over by a tractor, causing him fatal injuries. This accident happened four days before he was to start working at the Izabell Hartner Ranch. The bracero who passed away left six children in Mexico. The word "another" in the headline suggests this was not an isolated event.

Another news article reported in June 1943 on a bracero diagnosed with insanity. Along with this diagnosis, the physician acknowledged that the bracero suffered from malnutrition and heatstroke.[65] *El Sol* attributed this event to the weather and warned that June was not yet the hottest month in Arizona. In fact, two months later the same newspaper reported that Salvador S. Ramírez, Antonio Osorno Amaro, Vázquez Guante (no first name provided), and Francisco Soto López had died due to a heatwave.[66] On the same date, *El Sol* reported from Los Angeles and Mexico City that 110 braceros were protesting in the Mexican embassy because they had received only 47.5 cents per hour, less than the amount the U.S. government had promised.

Stories of braceros who died because of inhumane labor conditions were not uncommon and are consistently found in music. The lyrics of "La quema de los braceros," a corrido published on *El Sol*'s front page in 1959, narrate the events that happened on June 8 of that year.[67] Twenty-year-old Nato Manuel Gloria fell asleep while driving a truck that was transporting braceros from Mesa to Tolleson to work in the onion fields.

The "death truck," as they call it in the corrido, exploded in the crash due to a gasoline container located underneath it. The truck's door got stuck while braceros tried to get out unsuccessfully. Tony Guerrero, the main driver, who was inside the truck sleeping on the floor, died along with seventeen Mexican braceros who could not escape. Thirty-nine were hospitalized for burns.

El Sol reported on June 12 that the truck belonged to the Garin Produce Company from Salinas, California. According to the news, Arizona did not have regulations regarding the maximum number of people a truck of this type could carry.[68] The tragedy depicted in "La quema de los braceros" was a small part of the deplorable conditions in which Arizona food-industry workers labored. Not just braceros but also drivers endured such conditions. Val Cordova, the attorney who defended the twenty-year-old driver Nato Manuel Gloria, said to the jury: "Gloria is the pawn, the sacrificial lamb of the Garin Co. and Agricultural Commodities. . . . There was only 16 inches of room for each of the 48 persons sitting on four rows of wooden seats."[69] Despite the defense's efforts, on March 25, 1960, the Garin Company of California and Nato Manuel Gloria were found guilty of negligence.[70] *El Sol* ended one of the various chronicles devoted to the crash with a crucial question: "What caught our attention is, what time do those poor men sleep?"[71] The car accident opened a discussion about new regulations for braceros in Arizona. Secretary of Labor James P. Mitchell announced that employers were responsible for providing safe transportation to workers, including certified drivers.

Historian Lori A. Flores documents a similar episode that occurred in 1963 in which more than thirty braceros died on their way to work in California's Salinas Valley. Braceros were transported in a truck like the one described in the corrido "La quema de los braceros." The truck driver crossed an unmarked railroad crossing and failed to notice an approaching train. The train collided with the truck, causing the compartment carrying the braceros to detach and leading to the instant death of many.[72] Car accidents also occurred on the way to the U.S.-Mexico border. In 1953, a truck carrying braceros originally from Durango crashed in Mazatlán. Three men died and ten were injured on their way to Nogales.[73]

The *El Sol* corrido, as is common in this genre, ends with a moral aiming to warn men who pursued the idea of becoming a bracero:

Aquí cortamos señores
este corrido primero
de lo que puede pasarle
al que anda de bracero.

Seguiremos relatando
cuanto haya en este caso
para que vean lo que cuesta
servir de soldado raso.

(Gentlemen, here we conclude
the first corrido
about what can happen
to the one who becomes a bracero.

We will continue sharing
more when we can
so that you can see the costs
of serving as a foot soldier.)[74]

"La quema de los braceros" resembles the oral testimony of bracero José Guadalupe Hernández, who described living in train cars: "There are times when we go to bed to sleep and wake up in other parts where work is most needed, we work on the railway." Later Hernández said that he did not buy the health insurance he was offered because he did not want to spend money, since his wage was very low: "But we will strive to assist these individuals and create a better future for my children, who have endured pure poverty in Mexico. With so much sacrifice and pain in my heart, I will continue to persevere."[75]

An interesting feature of "La quema de los braceros" is that it portrays agricultural labor as a voluntary act with the phrase "andar de bracero," indicating that the burden fell on the braceros and suggesting that temporary workers had numerous options, which was not the case in a situation of economic instability. The corrido serves to recuperate the marginalized voices of deceased braceros while simultaneously interrogating and contesting the prevailing narratives perpetuated by both the U.S. and Mexican governments. These dominant discourses have historically overlooked the braceros' calls for improved labor conditions and enhanced living standards. The word *bracero* came from the Spanish word *brazos*. In this corrido, the word *braceros* refers to individuals who work manually, depicting braceros as laborers engaged in vegetable harvesting, akin to soldier-machines. The corrido portrays braceros as soldiers of the fields who would die for the homeland, but what homeland did braceros serve?

Conclusion

Extensive scholarship has addressed the Bracero Program from different perspectives and has considered legal, environmental, and migratory issues. In this chapter, I have built on the literature regarding music of the Bracero Program by focusing on the aural repertoire's usefulness as a set of historical documents that served as a means of communication that challenged the discourses of the U.S. and Mexican governments about the program. Corridos have dominated the scholarship on music and the Bracero Program, for good reason. Although Mexican temporary workers may be addressed through different musical genres, corridos provide crucial information, from workers' emotional states to specific names, dates, and sites of tragic events like the crash that occurred in Arizona. More broadly, corridos and other forms of aural transmission contribute to a deeper understanding of the Bracero Program and address some of the issues in oral histories collected by institutions. Other sources, like music, can contribute to exploring such oral history sources against the grain.

The repertoire and oral testimonies addressed major political debates at the time, like discrimination or the inhumane conditions in which braceros worked, in different ways. In some instances, such as in the interview with Ramona Acosta, the interviewee denies the prevalence of discrimination, as Phoenix's mayor did in 1962. Acosta's attitude reflects how power dynamics worked at the time in Arizona (i.e., the dominated accepted the methods, discourses, and ideas of the dominator as a mechanism to cope with domination). The musical repertoire of the Bracero Program consistently denounced the exploitation and discrimination faced by braceros, emphasizing emotions in their narratives and challenging the silence imposed on braceros as a control mechanism. Music about the Bracero Program was composed to be listened to. Also, music humanized braceros by letting them express suffering, hopes, and awareness.[76] Finally, each piece was placed within a distinct political framework and role: from commercialization, as seen in "Canto del bracero," to being a part of a broader political movement, as in "Corrido del bracero," to being integrated into the everyday and immediate time frames of the newspaper, as in "La quema de los braceros." My analysis in this chapter of the music repertoire from the mid-twentieth century has aimed to show how music can illuminate oral histories. As such, music constitutes a critical historical source for studying the Bracero Program.

Notes

1. Soledad Loaeza, "La reforma política de Manuel Ávila Camacho," *Historia Mexicana* 63, no. 1 (2013): 300.
2. Ryan M. Alexander, *Sons of the Mexican Revolution: Miguel Alemán and His Generation*, Diálogos Series (University of New Mexico Press, 2016); Ricardo Pérez Montfort, *Lázaro Cárdenas del Río: Un mexicano del siglo XX*, vol. 2, Debate Historia (Debate, 2019).
3. Fernando Saúl Alanís Enciso, *El primer programa bracero y el gobierno de México, 1917–1918* (El Colegio de San Luis, 1999).
4. Ronald L. Mize and Alicia C. S. Swords, *Consuming Mexican Labor: From the Bracero Program to NAFTA* (University of Toronto Press, 2011).
5. Aurora Gómez-Galvarriato Freer, "La construcción del milagro mexicano: El Instituto Mexicano de Investigaciones Tecnológicas, el Banco de México y la Armour Research Foundation," *Historia Mexicana* 69, no. 3 (2020): 1247–1309, https://doi.org/10.24201/hm.v69i3.4022.
6. Gustavo Garza Villarreal, "'Milagro económico,' modernización y urbanización, 1940–1980," chapter 3 in *La urbanización de México en el Siglo XX* (El Colegio de México, 2005), 40–68, https://muse.jhu.edu/pub/320/oa_monograph/chapter/2587745.
7. Evangelina Basua, interview by Alejandra Díaz, Glendale, Ariz., January 11, 2008, Bracero History Archive, https://braceroarchive.org/items/show/667, at 10:16.
8. Leah Bassel, *The Politics of Listening: Possibilities and Challenges for Democratic Life* (Palgrave Macmillan, 2017), 3.
9. Mae Ngai, *Impossible Subjects: Illegal Aliens and the Making of Modern America*, updated ed. (Princeton University Press, 2014), 163.
10. Bassel, *Politics of Listening*, 6.
11. Corrido is a genre whose popularity in Mexico can be tracked from the nineteenth century. Although corridos encompass many themes, including love,

some of the most popular are narrative corridos, which tell stories about current political moments. There are different hypotheses regarding the origin of corrido. For Vicente T. Mendoza, corridos came from the Spanish *romance*. See Vicente T. Mendoza, *El corrido mexicano* (Fondo de Cultura Económica, 1976). Others, like Celedonio Serrano Martínez, challenged Mendoza. Serrano Martínez claimed that corridos come fundamentally from Nahua musical traditions. See Celedonio Serrano Martínez, *El corrido mexicano no deriva del romance español* (Centro Cultural Guerrerense, 1963). Regardless of their origin, due to their narrative character, corridos have been a constitutive sonorous element in Mexican and Mexican American social movements in the twentieth and twenty-first centuries, from the Mexican Revolution to student protests in the 1960s. Celestino Fernández described corrido as one of the two most popular music genres among the Mexican working classes—i.e., el pueblo—along with canción ranchera. It is the connection with the people from below that makes corridos crucial for expanding the narratives of the Bracero Program and makes them an essential source of historical information.

12. "Corrido del bracero" appeared on a compilation from 2005: Estevan César Azcona and Russel Rodriguez, compilers, *Rolas de Aztlán: Songs of the Chicano Movement*, Smithsonian Folkways Recordings SFW CD 40516, 2005.
13. Joy Elizabeth Hayes, *Radio Nation: Communication, Popular Culture, and Nationalism in Mexico, 1920–1950* (University of Arizona Press, 2000), 71, 72.
14. The term "aural" pertains to the auditory sense. Over the past decade, there has been a significant emergence of scholarly research focused on this concept within the field of sound studies. Some of the most relevant examples are Ana María Ochoa, *Aurality: Listening and Knowledge in Nineteenth-Century Colombia* (Duke University Press, 2014); and Alex E. Chávez, *Sounds of Crossing: Music, Migration, and the Aural Poetics of Huapango Arribeño*, Refiguring American Music (Duke University Press, 2017). In this volume, Yvette J. Saavedra analyzes how Mexicans were portrayed on the radio utilizing strong and exaggerated accents; see chapter 8.
15. Antonio V. Pérez Herrera, interview by Marina Kalashnikova, Scottsdale, Ariz., January 11, 2008, Bracero History Archive, http://braceroarchive.org/items/show/747.
16. Ramona Acosta, interview by Alejandra Díaz, Phoenix, Ariz., January 9, 2008, Bracero History Archive, http://braceroarchive.org/items/show/654.
17. Ana Elizabeth Rosas, *Abrazando el Espíritu: Bracero Families Confront the US-Mexico Border* (University of California Press, 2014), 149.
18. "Si tú piensas ir, détente, o si estás allá, regresa." See Pedro Infante, "Canto del bracero," video, 3:01, posted May 16, 2008, by miradormex, YouTube, https://www.youtube.com/watch?v=BJ6AewsZONk.
19. Verónica Calvillo, "Mexican Immigrants' Perceptions and Attitudes: Evidence from Popular Songs of the Bracero Program Era," *Diálogo* 19, no. 2 (2016): 54.
20. Calvillo, "Mexican Immigrants' Perceptions," 50.

21. Pedro Infante was one of the most important figures of the Golden Age of Mexican Cinema, which ran roughly from 1936, when *Allá en el rancho grande* premiered, to the 1950s. Infante was an actor and singer with whom working-class Mexicans and Mexican Americans identified. As Sal Acosta claims, Infante represented the Mexican working class on both sides of the border and was regarded as an ídolo del pueblo. Infante was featured in Spanish-speaking newspapers in Arizona before and after his death in 1957, which is telling of how relevant he was among Mexican Americans in the period that coincided with the Bracero Program. See Sal Acosta, "Pedro Infante and the Mexican Imagination," in *Oxford Research Encyclopedia of Latin American History*, March 28, 2018, https://doi.org/10.1093/acrefore/9780199366439.013.383.
22. All quotes from the lyrics to "Canto del bracero" come from Pedro Infante, "Canto del bracero," video, 3:01, posted May 16, 2008, by miradormex, YouTube, https://www.youtube.com/watch?v=BJ6AewsZONk. All English translations throughout the chapter are mine, unless otherwise noted.
23. "La embriaguez," *La Voz de México*, September 22, 1899, p. 3, https://hndm.iib.unam.mx/consulta/publicacion/visualizar/558075bf7d1e63c9fea1a489.
24. Socorro Flores Pando, interview by Myrna Parra-Mantilla, Cuauhtémoc, Chihuahua, June 13, 2003, Bracero History Archive, https://braceroarchive.org/items/show/31. In quotes from oral interviews in this chapter, all ellipses indicate omission.
25. Federico Navarrete Linares, *México racista: Una denuncia* (Grijalbo, 2016).
26. Pérez Herrera, interview.
27. It is important to note that legal status did not necessarily mean improvement in working conditions. See Calvillo, "Mexican Immigrants' Perceptions," 58.
28. Eric V. Meeks, *Border Citizens: The Making of Indians, Mexicans, and Anglos in Arizona*, 2nd ed. (University of Texas Press, 2020), 155.
29. Meeks, *Border Citizens*, 156.
30. Gilbert G. Gonzalez, Vivian Price, and Adrian Salinas, dirs., *Harvest of Loneliness: The Bracero Program*, documentary, 57:49, Films for the Humanities & Sciences and Films Media Group, 2010, at 15:20. The film is available on YouTube: posted May 25, 2014, by Becca Manwiller-Thompson, https://www.youtube.com/watch?v=PcV2EOo-Xdc.
31. Gonzalez, Price, and Salinas, *Harvest of Loneliness*, at 15:00.
32. S. Acosta, "Pedro Infante."
33. The alliances among Mexican businessmen and the political class have been widely studied by many scholars in Mexico; see, for example, Ricardo Pérez Montfort, *Estampas de nacionalismo popular mexicano: Diez ensayos sobre la cultura popular y nacionalismo*, 2nd ed. (CIESAS, 1994).
34. The PRI ruled Mexico from its foundation in 1929 as the Party of the Mexican Revolution to 2000. Many scholars have characterized this party as authoritarian: see Joy Langston, *Democratization and Authoritarian Party Survival* (Oxford University Press, 2017).

35. "Graciosa entrevista a Tito Guízar y Rubén Méndez por Armando del Moral," video, 6:08, posted February 26, 2010, by cervantescenter, YouTube, https://www.youtube.com/watch?v=-Oj0mtQ-6Cc.
36. Hayes, *Radio Nation*, xv.
37. Amaia Ibarraran-Bigalondo, "African-American and Mexican-American Protest Songs in the 20th Century: Some Examples," *Journal of Popular Music Studies* 29, no. 2 (2017): e12211, https://doi.org/10.1111/jpms.12211.
38. Stevan Cesar Azcona, "Movements in Chicano Music: Performing Culture, Performing Politics, 1965–1979" (PhD diss., University of Texas at Austin, 2008).
39. Los Mascarones and Los Alacranes Mojados, "Corrido del bracero," on *Rolas de Aztlán: Songs of the Chicano Movement*, comp. Estevan César Azcona and Russel Rodriguez, Smithsonian Folkways Recordings SFW CD 40516, 2005, compact disc. The song can be found on YouTube: posted November 6, 2014, by Release—Topic, https://www.youtube.com/watch?v=jDFDUJlFns0. For all quotes from the song in this chapter, see this recording.
40. Chávez, *Sounds of Crossing*.
41. Original Spanish: "Me dicen que aquí se barre el dinero, pero no le toca a este pobre bracero." Translation based on the liner notes from Azcona and Rodriguez, *Rolas de Aztlán*, with some adjustments.
42. Camille Guérin-Gonzales, *Mexican Workers, American Dreams: Immigration, Repatriation, and California Farm Labor, 1900–1939* (Rutgers University Press, 1994); Mayra Lizette Avila, "La Pena Negra: Mexican Women, Gender, and Labor During the Bracero Program, 1942–1964" (PhD diss., University of Texas at El Paso, 2018), 9.
43. Rubén Martinez, "In Memoriam: Jesus 'Chuy' Negrete," Julian Samora Research Institute, Michigan State University, accessed September 2, 2024, https://jsri.msu.edu/publications/nexo/vol-xxv/no-1-fall-2021/in-memoriam-jesus-chuy-negrete.
44. See Rosas, *Abrazando el Espíritu*, especially part 2 of the book, "Love and Longing." More research is needed, including a gender approach, to examine how the Bracero Program was a project that involved families and not isolated individuals. Gloria Holguín Cuádraz points out how the agriculture industry in the cotton town Litchfield Park, the case she analyzed, relied on whole families. Each member had a function in the labor organization. For Cuádraz, the family was the unit of production since the program preferred to hire married men. See chapter 6, by Cuádraz, in this volume.
45. Gonzalez, Price, and Salinas, *Harvest of Loneliness*, at 17:35. Quotes from this film use the original translations into English from the film's own subtitles.
46. Calvillo, "Mexican Immigrants' Perceptions," 49.
47. For more information about the complexities of conducting anthropological-historical research with oral histories designed by a third party, see Schensul, Schensul, and LeCompte, "In Depth Open Ended Interviewing; Semistructured Interviewing," ch. 6 in *Essential Ethnographic Methods: A Mixed Methods Ap-*

proach (AltaMira Press, 2012); and Sarah Flicker, "'Ask Me No Secrets, I'll Tell You No Lies': What Happens When a Respondent's Story Makes No Sense," *Qualitative Report* 9, no. 3 (September 2004): 528–37.

48. Rosas, *Abrazando el Espíritu*, 222.
49. Gonzalez, Price, and Salinas, *Harvest of Loneliness*, at 53:00.
50. Rosas, *Abrazando el Espíritu*, 137.
51. Ángel M. Moreno, interview by Manuel Sanmiguel, Phoenix, Ariz., January 12, 2008, Bracero History Archive, http://braceroarchive.org/items/show/734.
52. Héctor Ponce, interview by Karim Ley-Alarcón, El Paso, Tex., November 12, 2005, Bracero History Archive, http://braceroarchive.org/items/show/233.
53. Deborah Cohen, *Braceros: Migrant Citizens and Transnational Subjects in the Postwar United States and Mexico* (University of North Carolina Press, 2011), 23.
54. Cohen, *Braceros*, 23.
55. Carlos Corella, interview by Rebecca Craver, February 5, 2003, Bracero History Archive, http://braceroarchive.org/items/show/37, at 3:52.
56. Moreno, interview.
57. Corella, interview.
58. Natalia Molina, *How Race Is Made in America: Immigration, Citizenship, and the Historical Power of Racial Scripts* (University of California Press, 2014), 32–33, 38.
59. Kelly Lytle Hernández, *Migra! A History of the U.S. Border Patrol* (University of California Press, 2010), 35.
60. Calvillo, "Mexican Immigrants' Perceptions," 59.
61. Gonzalez, Price, and Salinas, *Harvest of Loneliness*, at 19:00.
62. Molina, "How Race Is Made," 35.
63. Sonia Robles, *Mexican Waves: Radio Broadcasting Along Mexico's Northern Border, 1930–1950* (University of Arizona Press, 2019), 23.
64. "Horrible muerte de otro bracero," *El Sol* (Phoenix, Ariz.), July 2, 1943, p. 8, https://chroniclingamerica.loc.gov/lccn/sn86090862/1943-07-02/ed-1/seq-8/.
65. "Enloquece un bracero," *El Sol*, June 4, 1943, p. 1, https://chroniclingamerica.loc.gov/lccn/sn86090862/1943-06-04/ed-1/seq-1/.
66. "El calor mata cuatro braceros," *El Sol*, August 6, 1943, p. 1, https://chroniclingamerica.loc.gov/lccn/sn86090862/1943-08-06/ed-1/seq-1/.
67. "La quema de los braceros," *El Sol*, July 10, 1959, p. 1, https://chroniclingamerica.loc.gov/lccn/sn86090862/1959-07-10/ed-1/seq-1/. Corrido, a lyrical musical genre, has historically been shared through various ephemeral means due to its popular nature. In twentieth-century Mexico, one of the most common methods of disseminating corridos was via leaflets, which are linked to "folios de cordel" (string folios), a type of poetic literature that dates back to the sixteenth century. The transient nature of the corrido often makes it challenging to associate specific corrido lyrics with particular melodies, except in instances where the corridos were recorded. See Grecia Monroy Sánchez, "Lírica y política en las hojas volantes de la imprenta de Antonio Vanegas Arroyo," *Boletín de Lite-*

ratura Oral 2 (2019): 195–201, https://revistaselectronicas.ujaen.es/index.php/blo/article/view/4732. In the case of "Corrido del bracero," it remains unclear what melodies and harmonies, if any, accompanied these lyrics and who performed it. However, the aim of this chapter is not to identify the music but to acknowledge the political significance of the corrido in relation to the Bracero Program. This significance is evident through its presence in newspaper publications, such as the Spanish-speaking newspaper *El Sol*.

68. "Mueren incinerados 16 pobres braceros," *El Sol*, June 12, 1959, p. 1, https://chroniclingamerica.loc.gov/lccn/sn86090862/1959-06-12/ed-1/seq-1/.
69. Wayne Blanchard, "1959—June 8, Farm Labor Truck/Bus Crash, Fuel Explosion/Fire, Near Phoenix, AZ," Deadliest American Disasters and Large-Loss-of-Life Events (website), February 16, 2020, https://www.usdeadlyevents.com/1959-june-8-farm-labor-truck-bus-crash-fuel-explosion-fire-near-phoenix-az-17/.
70. Blanchard, "Farm Labor Truck/Bus Crash."
71. "Mueren incinerados 16 pobres braceros."
72. Lori A. Flores, "A Town Full of Dead Mexicans: The Salinas Valley Bracero Tragedy of 1963, the End of the Bracero Program, and the Evolution of California's Chicano Movement," *Western Historical Quarterly* 44, no. 2 (Summer 2013): 127, https://doi.org/10.2307/westhistquar.44.2.0124.
73. "Three Braceros Killed in Crash," *The Americas Daily* (Miami, Fla.), April 10, 1957, https://chroniclingamerica.loc.gov/lccn/sn82001257/1957-04-10/ed-1/seq-10/.
74. "La quema de los braceros."
75. Rosalva Casillas, "José Guadalupe Hernández," item no. 3175, Bracero History Archive, http://braceroarchive.org/items/show/3175.
76. Bassel, *Politics of Listening*, 3.

Bibliography

Acosta, Ramona. Interview by Alejandra Díaz. Phoenix, Ariz., January 9, 2008. Bracero History Archive. http://braceroarchive.org/items/show/654.

Acosta, Sal. "Pedro Infante and the Mexican Imagination." In *Oxford Research Encyclopedia of Latin American History*, March 28, 2018. https://doi.org/10.1093/acrefore/9780199366439.013.383.

Alanís Enciso, Fernando Saúl. *El primer programa bracero y el gobierno de México, 1917–1918*. El Colegio de San Luis, 1999.

Alexander, Ryan M. *Sons of the Mexican Revolution: Miguel Alemán and His Generation*. Diálogos Series. University of New Mexico Press, 2016.

Avila, Mayra Lizette. "La Pena Negra: Mexican Women, Gender, and Labor During the Bracero Program, 1942–1964." PhD dissertation, University of Texas at El Paso, 2018.

Azcona, Stevan Cesar. "Movements in Chicano Music: Performing Culture, Performing Politics, 1965–1979." PhD dissertation, University of Texas at Austin, 2008.

Bassel, Leah. *The Politics of Listening: Possibilities and Challenges for Democratic Life*. Palgrave Macmillan, 2017.

Basua, Evangelina. Interview by Alejandra Díaz. Glendale, Ariz., January 11, 2008. Bracero History Archive. https://braceroarchive.org/items/show/667.

Calvillo, Verónica. "Mexican Immigrants' Perceptions and Attitudes: Evidence from Popular Songs of the Bracero Program Era." *Diálogo* 19, no. 2 (2016): 49–62.

Chávez, Alex E. *Sounds of Crossing: Music, Migration, and the Aural Poetics of Huapango Arribeño*. Refiguring American Music. Duke University Press, 2017.

Cohen, Deborah. *Braceros: Migrant Citizens and Transnational Subjects in the Postwar United States and Mexico*. University of North Carolina Press, 2011.

Corella, Carlos. Interview by Rebecca Craver. February 5, 2003. Bracero History Archive. http://braceroarchive.org/items/show/37.

El Sol. "La quema de los braceros." July 10, 1959, p. 1. https://chroniclingamerica.loc.gov/lccn/sn86090862/1959-07-10/ed-1/seq-1/.

Flicker, Sarah. "'Ask Me No Secrets, I'll Tell You No Lies': What Happens When a Respondent's Story Makes No Sense." *Qualitative Report* 9, no. 3 (September 2004): 528–37.

Flores, Lori A. "A Town Full of Dead Mexicans: The Salinas Valley Bracero Tragedy of 1963, the End of the Bracero Program, and the Evolution of California's Chicano Movement." *Western Historical Quarterly* 44, no. 2 (Summer 2013): 125–43. https://doi.org/10.2307/westhistquar.44.2.0124.

Flores Pando, Socorro. Interview by Myrna Parra-Mantilla. Cuauhtémoc, Chihuahua, June 13, 2003. Bracero History Archive. https://braceroarchive.org/items/show/31.

Garza Villarreal, Gustavo. "'Milagro económico', modernización y urbanización, 1940–1980." Chapter 3 in *La urbanización de México en el Siglo XX*, 40–68. El Colegio de México, 2005. https://muse.jhu.edu/pub/320/oa_monograph/chapter/2587745.

Gómez-Galvarriato Freer, Aurora. "La construcción del milagro mexicano: El Instituto Mexicano de Investigaciones Tecnológicas, el Banco de México y la Armour Research Foundation." *Historia Mexicana* 69, no. 3 (2020): 1247–1309. https://doi.org/10.24201/hm.v69i3.4022.

Gonzalez, Gilbert G., Vivian Price, and Adrian Salinas, dirs. *Harvest of Loneliness: The Bracero Program*. Films for the Humanities & Sciences; Films Media Group, 2010.

Guérin-Gonzales, Camille. *Mexican Workers, American Dreams: Immigration, Repatriation, and California Farm Labor, 1900–1939*. Rutgers University Press, 1994.

Hayes, Joy Elizabeth. *Radio Nation: Communication, Popular Culture, and Nationalism in Mexico, 1920–1950*. University of Arizona Press, 2000.

Hernández, Kelly Lytle. *Migra! A History of the U.S. Border Patrol*. University of California Press, 2010.

Ibarraran-Bigalondo, Amaia. "African-American and Mexican-American Protest Songs in the 20th Century: Some Examples." *Journal of Popular Music Studies* 29, no. 2 (2017): e12211. https://doi.org/10.1111/jpms.12211.

Infante, Pedro. "Canto del bracero." Video, 3:01, posted May 16, 2008, by miradormex, YouTube. https://www.youtube.com/watch?v=BJ6AewsZONk.

Langston, Joy. *Democratization and Authoritarian Party Survival*. Oxford University Press, 2017.

Loaeza, Soledad. "La reforma política de Manuel Ávila Camacho." *Historia Mexicana* 63, no. 1 (2013): 251–358.

Los Mascarones and Los Alacranes Mojados. "Corrido del bracero." On *Rolas de Aztlán: Songs of the Chicano Movement*, compiled by Estevan César Azcona and Russel Rodriguez. Smithsonian Folkways Recordings SFW CD 40516, 2005. Compact Disc.

Meeks, Eric V. *Border Citizens: The Making of Indians, Mexicans, and Anglos in Arizona*. 2nd ed. University of Texas Press, 2020.

Mendoza, Vicente T. *El corrido mexicano*. Fondo de Cultura Económica, 1976.

Mize, Ronald L., and Alicia C. S. Swords. *Consuming Mexican Labor: From the Bracero Program to NAFTA*. University of Toronto Press, 2011.

Molina, Natalia. *How Race Is Made in America: Immigration, Citizenship, and the Historical Power of Racial Scripts*. University of California Press, 2014.

Monroy Sánchez, Grecia. "Lírica y política en las hojas volantes de la imprenta de Antonio Vanegas Arroyo." *Boletín de Literatura Oral* 2 (2019): 195–201. https://revistaselectronicas.ujaen.es/index.php/blo/article/view/4732.

Moreno, Ángel M. Interview by Manuel Sanmiguel. Phoenix, Ariz., January 12, 2008. Bracero History Archive. http://braceroarchive.org/items/show/734.

Navarrete Linares, Federico. *México racista: Una denuncia*. Grijalbo, 2016.

Ngai, Mae. *Impossible Subjects: Illegal Aliens and the Making of Modern America*. Updated ed. Princeton University Press, 2014.

Ochoa, Ana María. *Aurality: Listening and Knowledge in Nineteenth-Century Colombia*. Duke University Press, 2014.

Pérez Herrera, Antonio V. Interview by Marina Kalashnikova. Scottsdale, Ariz., January 11, 2008. Bracero History Archive. http://braceroarchive.org/items/show/747.

Pérez Montfort, Ricardo. *Estampas de nacionalismo popular mexicano: Diez ensayos sobre la cultura popular y nacionalismo*. 2nd ed. CIESAS, 1994.

Pérez Montfort, Ricardo. *Lázaro Cárdenas del Río: Un mexicano del siglo XX*. Vol. 2. Debate Historia. Debate, 2019.

Ponce, Héctor. Interview by Karim Ley-Alarcón. El Paso, Tex., November 12, 2005. Bracero History Archive. http://braceroarchive.org/items/show/233.

Robles, Sonia. *Mexican Waves: Radio Broadcasting Along Mexico's Northern Border, 1930–1950*. University of Arizona Press, 2019.

Rosas, Ana Elizabeth. *Abrazando el Espíritu: Bracero Families Confront the US-Mexico Border*. University of California Press, 2014.

Schensul, Jean, Stephen Schensul, and Margaret LeCompte. "In Depth Open Ended Interviewing; Semistructured Interviewing." Chapter 6 in *Essential Ethnographic Methods: A Mixed Methods Approach*. AltaMira Press, 2012.

Serrano Martínez, Celedonio. *El corrido mexicano no deriva del romance español*. Centro Cultural Guerrerense, 1963.

CHAPTER 8

Remembering the Rancho

Nineteenth-Century Discourses and Creating Stories of Mexican California, 1920–1945

YVETTE J. SAAVEDRA

> *Americans flocked to the New Paradise of the Pacific, crowding out the old families of the Californians and the fast-dying Indians. . . . The march of progress engulfed even the outlying ranchos of San Francisco. The growing metropolis of Los Angeles quickly became an American City of industry and commerce where once had stood the sleepy Spanish village.*
>
> —*THE ROMANCE OF THE RANCHOS*, EPISODE 12, "NEWHALL REGION, RANCHO DEL VALLE AND SAN FRANCISCO," NOVEMBER 26, 1941

> *Mexicans were to be assigned a place in the mythic past of Los Angeles—one that could be relegated to a quaint section of a city designed to delight tourists and antiquarians. Real Mexicans were out of sight and increasingly out of mind.*
>
> —GEORGE SÁNCHEZ, ANALYSIS OF THE CREATION OF LA PLACITA OLVERA IN *BECOMING MEXICAN AMERICAN*, 1993

Between September 1941 and May 1942, the Title Insurance and Trust Company of Los Angeles sponsored *The Romance of the Ranchos*, a weekly radio program dramatizing the history of Southern California's ranchos from the late eighteenth-century Spanish period through the early twentieth century. Week after week "the wandering vaquero" narrated stories of "romance and adventure connected with the growth" of Southern California.[1] Each episode featured a Southern California rancho and provided dramatized stories following a formulaic, chronological structure that began by briefly detailing Spanish land grants, transitioned into Californio/Mexican rancho ownership, and culminated in American settlement and development. Airing on CBS radio station KNX during its prime evening hours on Wednesdays and Sundays, the half-hour program sought to transport listeners to California's "vividly colorful yesterdays" of "the [Mexican] dons."[2]

When *The Romance of the Ranchos* debuted in September 1941, its historical drama format distinguished it from other radio programs that featured Latin American music and culture. During the 1930s and 1940s U.S. media centered Latin American countries, people, and cultures to support Good Neighbor relations. Radio programs and Hollywood feature films brought an exoticized Latin America and its people to U.S. audiences through aural sounds and visual representations of location and culture.[3] *Romance* differed because instead of speaking about and describing Latin American people, it included representations of Mexican/Californio people in its historical narratives of Southern California.[4] Despite the often problematic nature of these representations, its inclusion of Mexican/Californio peoples in regional history provides a crucial ethno-cultural dimension of California's history that was frequently absent. Meant to entertain and educate, *Romance*'s episodes related the region's history through dramatizations of events described in the extensive land records held by the show's sponsor, the Title Insurance and Trust Company of Los Angeles (TI), the region's largest title company.[5] For many, these documents provided the program a historical credibility that helped it be named an "excellent nonfiction radio show" and a "powerful force in intellectual engagement."[6] Promising "romance," "adventure," and narratives "dealing with characters bigger than life," the show was a hit, and when its first run ended in 1942, CBS Pacific continued to run repeats until 1948. The show garnered several awards, including being named "most effective institutional series" by City College of New York and winning third place in *Billboard*'s "best drama" category in 1946 and 1948.[7]

Broadcast during World War II, *Romance* aired when wartime mobilization called for broader reconceptualizing of race through racial liberalism and ethnic pluralism.[8] Governmental efforts to educate the populace about race and ethnicity included the production of radio programming reflecting the country's pluralist history and at the same time encouraging Americanism through assimilation. Although *The Romance of the Ranchos* was not a government-sponsored show, its themes coincide with these broader efforts. Its popularity as a historical drama during the 1940s invites an analysis of the program's function as a cultural production whose narrations created and disseminated knowledge about place and people. Like the nineteenth-century travelogues and diaries that vividly described the Southwest and its people to eager Euro-American readers, *Romance* provided non-Mexican audiences an avenue through which to familiarize themselves with and racialize Los Angeles's Mexican population and history.

Unfortunately, like those travelogues, whose authors' descriptions of Mexicans/Californios reflected colonialist and white supremacist beliefs, *Romance*'s episodes, because they were based on TI's land records, conveyed racialized (hi)stories.[9] Although TI was a privately owned nonstate entity, its records detailing land ownership, transfer, and loss constitute a colonial archive detailing the consequences of territorial conquest. As historian Ann Laura Stoler contends in her work on colonial power and archival production, the colonial archive is an ethnographic space that simultaneously relies on and constructs a racial/ethnic common sense about the people and places described in the records as well as "the cultural semantics of a political moment."[10] Although not explicitly racist, TI's records are imbued with racial meaning because they detail the judicial proceedings and judgments resulting from the enactment of the racialized land policies of U.S. expansion.[11] Because they constitute a rich colonial archive of land loss, by using these records as the basis for its (hi)stories, *Romance* conveyed the racialized common sense about Mexican declension and the triumph of American Manifest Destiny.

Interested in how nineteenth-century colonialist discourses influence twentieth-century representations and lived experiences of Mexicans, I approached this project following two paths. The first was to examine the function of the historical narratives in *The Romance of the Ranchos* as a discursive technique that enabled the extension of nineteenth-century racialization of Mexicans into the twentieth century.[12] In reviewing the show's thirty-five half-hour-long episodes detailing the history of

Southern California, I identified a recurring pattern pertaining to the use of racialized and gendered rhetoric that contrasted representations of Euro-American and Californio/Mexican masculinities.[13] Specifically, I found that the show often (re)presented Mexicans/Californios as racially and morally deficient, defeated people, and women as beautiful, passive señoritas waiting to be saved by white men. I argue that by representing Mexican masculinity as subordinate to white masculinity, the series functioned as a project of settler-colonial emplotment that carried nineteenth-century racialized and gendered (mis)representations of Mexicans into the twentieth century, while simultaneously uplifting and reinscribing the supremacy of white hegemonic masculinity.

The second path was to briefly survey the period's Spanish-language radio broadcasts to explore how Los Angeles's Mexican community situated itself in relation to white supremacist renderings of Mexican identity. Consisting of limited, often early-morning time slots purchased by Mexican radio brokers, these programs spoke to the Mexican community and its racialized, classed, and political realities. Utilizing Dolores Casillas's analytical concept of the "counterpublic," I read these broadcasts as examples of "a parallel space to circulate oppositional interpretations of identity and desires."[14] Building on Casillas's contention that Spanish-language programming allowed Mexicans to "affirm their distinct class and ethnic identities,"[15] I see these Spanish-language broadcasts as a way in which Mexican communities defined their own cultural identities and repositioned themselves against racialized caricatures and cultural misrepresentations. By analyzing *Romance*'s racialized representations of Mexicans alongside Spanish-language radio programming, I show how these broadcasts reflect a larger social dialectic involved in redefining American identity and belonging within the shifting sociocultural dynamics of the early twentieth century. At a time when the uncertainties of war called for the delimiting of American identity and citizenship, *Romance*'s centering of American exceptionalism and the supremacy of American white hegemonic masculinity was significant. Efforts to assert this superiority contributed to a racial nexus informing Euro-Americans' popular perceptions about Mexicans and influenced Mexicans' societal positioning within 1940s Los Angeles's changing racial/ethnic landscape.

Nineteenth-Century Discourses and the (Re)making of Mexicans in 1940s Los Angeles

In this chapter I make the conceptual link between the 1940s representations of Mexicans in *The Romance of the Ranchos* and nineteenth-century racial discourses by tracing Euro-Americans' long history of physical and discursive violence against Mexicans in the Southwest. Expressed through racialized rhetoric, Euro-American racial imaginings of Mexicans were framed through and supported by assertions of white supremacy. During the 1850s, finding themselves outnumbered by Mexican and Indigenous populations who actively resisted colonization, Euro-Americans worried about "the darker races" and their supposed "plan of violence, rape, and destruction," and they asserted control through white vigilante violence.[16] As historian William Deverell contends in his study on the building of Los Angeles, by the 1870s, as the demographics changed in favor of Euro-Americans, methods of dominance shifted from physical violence to discursive control.[17] This discursive racial reframing of the past—what Deverell terms *whitewashing*—became even more important when Mexican migration to the Southwest rose between 1880 and 1920. He contends that for "city-building whites," Los Angeles's status as the "City of the Future" depended on a racial/ethnic order that "restrain[ed] its ethnic history" and allowed Euro-Americans to deploy racial discourses that characterized Mexicans as a passive, docile, unskilled laboring group who followed the racial scripts afforded them.[18]

In Anglos' early twentieth-century historical reframing, Mexican/Californio history was retold using nineteenth-century racialized discourses. The (hi)story was one of a romantic yet failed Mexican Past vanquished by the racialized linear progression from savagery to civilization. Deverell found that whites imagined Mexicans as simple, carefree people lost to the triumph of Manifest Destiny, white supremacy, and progress.[19] Building on this contention, I show how *The Romance of the Ranchos* (re)established and redeployed nineteenth-century racial and gendered discourses and stereotypes that positioned Mexicans as a conquered people. More specifically, I assert that its narrations of the Mexican Past reflected a discursive reframing that helped assuage increasing racial anxieties caused by the city's changing demographics during the 1940s.

U.S. mobilization for World War II dramatically increased Los Angeles's minority populations, leaving an indelible mark on its racial composition.[20] A labor shortage grudgingly shifted sexist and racially discriminatory hiring practices by creating job openings for women and racial minorities.[21] These increased job opportunities prompted large-scale African American migration. After the bombing of Pearl Harbor, Executive Order 9066 federally sanctioned an already virulent anti-Asian racism by imposing Japanese internment. Forced internment further changed the city's racial dynamics and landscape by opening vacated neighborhoods up to resettlement by African Americans.[22] Additionally, because Los Angeles's ethnic Japanese community was integral to local agricultural production, internment caused a farm labor shortage that increased support for the Bracero Program and expanded Los Angeles's Mexican population.[23]

Amid these changes, calls for American patriotism were wedded to federal efforts toward racial liberalism aimed at demarcating an American identity that transcended racial/ethnic difference and prioritized assimilation into white, middle-class culture.[24] In 1940s Los Angeles, Mexican American youth emboldened by wartime shifts challenged the racial status quo and became the focus of racialized violence premised on perceptions of them as un-American and unpatriotic.[25] Rooted in white supremacist ideas of Mexican criminality, racial and moral inferiority, and inability to assimilate, Mexican Americans were targeted by the Los Angeles city government, the criminal justice system, and news outlets that portrayed them as threats to American stability. Within this context, as a popular cultural production of the time, the racialized representations of Mexicans in *The Romance of the Ranchos* cannot be separated from the larger racial nexus that long defined Euro-American superiority by reiterating Mexican deficiencies in the American imagination.

"Welcome to the Romance of the Ranchos": (Re)presenting the Past

Each week audiences tuned into KNX Los Angeles for *The Romance of the Ranchos'* newest episode. Inspired by a 1929 brochure of the same title, the episodical drama series detailed the region's land grants and centered the life stories of prominent historical figures.[26] Of the show's thirty-five episodes, eighteen were about ranchos and thirteen were biographical stories that classified the historical figures presented as "founding fathers, interlopers, speculators, and finally the movers and shakers or the people who brought progress."[27] Each episode began with announcer Bob LeMond proclaiming an important accomplishment or providing a timeline of events related to a particular location. After a brief prelude describing the show's purpose and sponsor and detailing TI's important role in maintaining land records, LeMond introduced narrator Frank Graham. Accompanied by the rhythmic sounds of Mexican folkloric guitar, Graham, who styled himself the "wandering vaquero," greeted the audience with the pleasant phrase "Buenos días, señoras y señores" (Good day, ladies and gentlemen). Throughout the introduction Graham used Spanish phrases and spoke English with an exaggerated Spanish accent.[28] After the introductory segment, Graham set the historical scene and excitedly invited the audience to "relive the romance of the ranchos."

As early as the 1880s, Americans' imaginations had been regaled with stories of Southern California's Spanish fantasy heritage. Steeped in the fiction of peaceful Spanish colonization, the stories describe grandiose Spanish dons overseeing lush rancho lands and kindly mission priests bringing *civilization* to the region's Indigenous populations.[29] This imagined past was rooted in a white-supremacist racial fiction that distanced the region from the Indigenous and Afro-Mexican roots of Mexican settler colonialism.[30] American audiences imagined California as a place of captivating landscapes and a romantic rancho past, exemplified by Helen Hunt Jackson's famous 1884 novel *Ramona*.[31] By 1915, Los Angeles boosters interested in Spanish/Mexican historical romanticism fostered a revival highlighting and marketing this idyllic and colorful past. In the 1920s this materialized through Spanish-style architecture, a designated Camino Real complete with mission tours, and the establishment of Olvera Street, a Mexican-themed marketplace located at the original site of El Pueblo de Los Ángeles.[32] Reflective of what Renato Rosaldo termed imperial nostalgia—the practice of colonial agents mourning for the very forms of life that they altered or destroyed—these sites represent the materialization of colonial discourses through symbols, performance, and ritual.[33] These representations allowed Euro-Americans to witness animated romantic imaginings of the Spanish/Mexican past and immerse themselves in the colorful, tranquil environs of the dons, without engaging with the violence of Spanish or American colonization. Because these physical sites were limited to those who could travel to them, by 1940 radio was key to expanding access to this fantasy past.

As listeners tuned into *Romance*'s weekly episodes, they heard teleological stories centered on American exceptionalism and the "inevitable march toward [American] progress."[34] Colonial violence was reframed as tales of Spanish missionaries' "benevolent efforts" to "convert and teach" the "docile" "Indians who stayed behind to become neophytes," and stories of "Spanish dons" speaking wistfully about their visions to develop their "great ranchos."[35] The narratives added adventure while supporting American discourses about Mexican and Indigenous peoples' presumed inferiority and inability to establish order for themselves by portraying the region as unstable and violent. Throughout the series, Californios dealt with a "bungling" Mexican government,[36] rebelled against despotic governors,[37] lost land due to inadequate/inaccurate recordkeeping,[38] reveled in economic recklessness due to Californios' "lavish extravagance,"[39] and endured endemic violence by "heathen Indians on the warpath."[40]

As an aural medium, radio programs used vocal and audible features to signal race for listeners. Creating what Casillas, Ferrada, and Hinojos term *vocal bodies*, the show "translate[d] the voice into a textured indication of race through cadence, pitch, and volume" and allowed listeners to "associate sound with racialized understandings about 'different'-sounding voices."[41] On *Romance*, Mexican and Indigenous men's vocal bodies spoke with exaggerated accents, varying intonation, and a slower cadence. Specifically, Mexican characters spoke English with heavy Spanish accents that varied in pitch. Class distinctions between Californios and poorer groups were made through the speed, pitch, and volume of their voices. Additionally, the Californio dons' reminiscences were usually accompanied by folkloric guitar to convey a nostalgic and sad framing of their aspirations, dispossession, and death.

Similarly, Indigenous men's vocal bodies spoke slow, broken, grammatically incorrect English. For example, in an episode detailing Benjamin Wilson's travel in New Mexico and his exchange with a nameless Apache leader, the Indigenous character responds to Wilson's plea for mercy with, "Me know, me sorry, me try tell them, they no listen . . . they want kill white men . . . my braves not be without scalp, no can stop."

Wilson replies, "You must know, your whole tribe is doomed, you can't make war on the white man and win."[42] The Apache leader grunts and helps him escape.[43] His improper English and grunting convey racialized perceptions of Indigenous men as violent and ignorant, and as having an overall lack of reason and civilization.[44] Euro-Americans are portrayed as victims, and the violence against them is not presented as a response to conquest, but rather as an unprovoked attack on friendly Americans. Wilson's admonition against fighting "the white man" restores Manifest Destiny's racial order and reestablishes American superiority. In these examples, the accents, the words, and the ways in which these words are said aurally differentiate Mexican and Indigenous men's vocal bodies from those of white Americans, who speak clearly and at a moderate pace.

Comparatively, Mexican women's vocal bodies were racialized, gendered, and classed differently. In the show's thirty-five episodes, women were only marginally included as Californios' wives and daughters, or as Americans' love interests.[45] Portrayed as beautiful señoritas seeking strong, industrious men to protect them, their characters were voiced in a sensual, soft, and gentle manner. For example, in narrations of courtships between Californio women and American men, women "welcomed [these men] into [their] homes," and they "eyed" the "handsome Americano[s]" and "pined [their] hearts away" hoping for them to declare their love and propose marriage.[46] Represented as romantic courtships, these pairings do not represent the complex gendered dynamics of conquest.[47] For instance, in the episode about Arcadia Bandini and Abel Stearns's courtship, the dynamics of coerced marriage are only implicitly displayed. When Stearns visits the wealthy patriarch Juan Bandini after a long absence, Bandini informs the forty-year-old Stearns of his young daughter Arcadia's romantic interest, only allowing her to passively agree with him.[48] Although Arcadia's age is not stated, the listener is clued into an age difference when she is presented to Stearns.[49] Taken by Arcadia's beauty, Stearns fumbles for the gift he's brought her, and embarrassingly produces a doll and hands it to her, uttering, "I, I didn't realize . . . how long it had been since. . . ." as she disappointedly, yet graciously, accepts the gift. Seeing her reaction, Stearns gives her a silk shawl that he had intended to sell, before declaring that the shawl "now shall crown one of the loveliest heads in Alta California."[50] Next, the program presents an unsubstantiated, likely fictionalized conversation between Arcadia and Stearns. During a moonlight stroll, when discussing their age difference, Stearns awkwardly states, "I am an old man . . . over forty years old," to which Arcadia replies, "To me you are young." Reassured, Stearns presents a string of pearls and proposes marriage, to which she replies, "Yes, this is what I have desired."[51] Juan Bandini grants his approval, the wedding "happen[s] immediately," and the rest of the episode focuses on Stearns's success as a landowner.[52]

Using phrases such as "found love in California," "settled down," or "married the beautiful daughter of a Spanish don," these stories erase the ways in which the intimate dynamics of colonialism affected Californio women's lives, bodies, and decisions. By centering on men's romantic conquest and by limiting women's voices, the show emphasized "Americano charm" and presented American men as selective suitors for California's eager, "bright-eyed Spanish beauties."[53] Through representations of chaotic conditions, the presumed inferiority of Californio and Mexican men, and Americans' *romantic conquest* of women longing for strong, industrious men, the program framed pre-U.S. California as a primitive space in need of American intervention and masculinity to bring civilization and progress to the region.

With Americans' arrival in the region, the narratives recounted *positive* stories about industrious businessmen, the welcoming of an American occupation, and the assertion of control over Mexican bandits. Episodes detailed developments in transportation and commerce,[54] land booms and tourism,[55] the discovery of oil and the building of the aqueduct system,[56] and the establishment of American government and legal systems,[57] each framed through a white savior trope that presented the (hi)stories "as straightforward, impartial narratives of heroic characters, intercultural friendships, and the humanistic struggle to overcome daunting odds."[58] Reiterating the social, political, and economic ideals of Manifest Destiny, American men were presented as benevolent saviors who used their economic savvy and commitment to American democratic institutions and ideals to become bearers of progress. For example, Benjamin D. Wilson, whose experiences spanned both the Mexican and U.S. periods, is described as "a man who stands out as one of the greatest of the early American pioneers who helped to make California a part of the United States and is typical of many other men like him."[59] For these *typical* men, progress meant financial freedom and individualism.

For instance, *Romance*'s portrayal of Wilson's desire to conduct business in Mexican territory centered the governor's dislike of Americans. Asserting economic freedom, Wilson's character emphatically states that he "stand[s] on [his] rights as an American to carry on [his] business" while in Mexican territory.[60] In contrast, in his memoir Wilson wrote that "the governor would not give permission to Americans to trade" and acknowledged that Americans were "there as interlopers and smugglers."[61] This example illustrates *Romance*'s creative license when writing its historical narratives. The show's emphasis on the *inherent American* right to do business and to challenge an unfair government conveyed the core ideals of freedom, individualism, and the desire to be self-made men to its audience. By depicting American actions in this way, the program marked Euro-American men as the "new, progressive, hard-hitting, fast-moving element that characterized the American spirit" and who "lead the March of Progress."[62]

Supporting the narrative of American progress and the white savior trope, the American conquest was represented as a welcome intervention. Statements that "Californians as well as Americanos would welcome" American occupation and that "together they could make something of this country" and "live prosperously" frame the takeover as a "happy ending" leading to regional growth.[63] When Californio Pío Pico returns from asking for help against the American encroachment, his character states, "I found only indifference . . . they were willing the Americanos should have it . . . and that is for the best . . . the Americanos will build up this country, I for one will give them . . . my support."[64] When Pico is described as "a loyal and distinguished American" who added to his "enormous land holdings," listeners can infer that Californios were easily integrated after the war; however, this inference is quickly dismissed when the narrator provides an ominous foreshadowing by stating that "as the new era was about to dawn, slowly the noose of debt tightened around the necks of the old Californios."[65] This description reiterates the stereotypes of Mexican cultural deficiency, defined through the Californios' fiscal extravagance. Additionally, the allusion to lynching places the responsibility for any loss and/or punishment on Mexicans, not on the white supremacist policies of American colonization.[66]

In contrast to the positive portrayals of American men, Californio/Mexican men's stories were often framed through a lens of defeat and deficiency. Of the series' thirty-five episodes, only four centered on Mexicans. Two were about wealthy Californios, Antonio María Lugo and José Antonio Carrillo, while the other two detailed the "tales" of "bandits" Tiburcio Vásquez and Joaquín Murrieta.[67] Lugo's and Carrillo's stories defined their success through "their ownership of the greatest haciendas" and "their eminence as patriarch[s]."[68] Their "colorful" stories ended "when California saw itself in the coveted glances of . . . the United States . . . and before many of the sleepy inhabitants were aware . . . the American occupation was underway . . . and the sleepy pueblo began to undergo a gradual change."[69] By describing Mexicans' reaction to conquest as "sleepy," the show used racial stereotypes of laziness and obtuseness to implicitly justify the American takeover. By portraying Californios' colonial dispossession as a gradual yet inevitable change, it discursively rendered Lugo and Carrillo great men but relegated them to the past.

In a story that illustrates American control over California's bad Mexican element, the show featured Joaquín Murrieta, "a man with a deep hatred for Americanos," who "stood against the march of progress."[70] Murrieta was a Sonoran who migrated to California as part of the Gold Rush. Racist injustice and violence, including the murder of his wife, led him to fight against Euro-American oppression.[71] In *Romance*'s version, Murrieta is described as "the most famous and most feared bandit who ever roamed the hills and valleys of our California. Often painted as the Robin Hood of the west, he was in reality a young man blinded by revenge, who became one of the most bloodthirsty highwaymen of history."[72] Illustrative of early twentieth-century media's racial stereotyping of Mexicans as a morally deficient people given to "dishonesty, excessive violence, inherent cruelty, and theft,"[73] Murrieta is referred to as a Mexican bandit or bandido, a popular representation of presumed Mexican criminality.[74]

Although the show describes Murrieta as a "bloodthirsty villain," it deploys the trope of a good man driven to violence by bad circumstance. Graham relates that Murrieta "was upset about the Mexican War, but he took the defeat philosophically, he forgave the Americans," and in "1849 [he] rode to the gold fields" from Sonora with his wife.[75] In Northern California Murrieta was attacked by white miners, who also raped and killed his wife, Carmen. Downplaying the racist attack and erasing the rape, the program described them as the acts of "rough characters . . .

who resented anyone but Americans" and who complained they were "sick and tired of Mexicans taking gold that belongs to us good American citizens."[76] These *rough characters* accost Joaquín and harass his wife, saying, "For a Mexican you're a pretty piece of calico, me and you could get along just fine." While Murrieta is beaten, another man attacks Carmen—indicated by his grunting as he speaks. When she defends herself, he kills her, and he justifies the murder saying, "She made me do it, I didn't want to." Later, "finding the lifeless body of his lovely young wife, [Murrieta] wildly vowed vengeance on the rowdies who had killed her."[77] Calmed by his friends, Joaquín agrees that "not all Americanos are bad" and leaves the camp.

Building up to Murrieta's transition into a bandido, we see another act of racist violence. Shortly after Joaquín arrives in San Francisco an American accuses him, shouting, "That dirty Mexican stole my mule," although in fact he purchased it a day earlier. Soon a "drunken bloodthirsty mob" attacks Joaquín and prepares for "a necktie party" or lynching.[78] Dissuaded from the lynching by Joaquín's American friend Bill Burns, the group severely whips Joaquín, a spectacle aurally represented by the sound of a whip hitting flesh, which fades out after several lashes. After he regains consciousness, Joaquín thanks Burns for his kindness and tells him that "Americanos shall pay for this . . . with each lash I swore revenge against all Americanos, I will show them no more mercy than they have shown me. I vow death and destruction to all Americanos!"[79] After this, he is portrayed as an indiscriminate murderer whose violence ends at the hands of a posse.

The retelling of Murrieta's story provides insights about how the show directed the portrayals of and audience perceptions about American and Mexican masculinity and racial violence. Interestingly, although clearly presenting the bandido stereotype and centering Mexican criminality, the show's title, "Robin Hood of the West," indicates a recognition, albeit brief, of Mexican cultural perceptions of Murrieta as a social bandit, a person "without revolutionary ideology nor plans of social reform . . . who corrects injustices committed against the poor and helpless."[80] Careful not to legitimate this perception, the narration quickly refocuses attention on his "bloodthirsty acts."[81] In a second example, the show's writers described those enacting racist violence as "drunken," "roughnecks," and "rowdies," motivated by "resentment" and alcohol. In comparison to these *bad* Americans, Burns represents the *good* American who is helpful, compassionate, and levelheaded, until Joaquín's indiscriminate acts of violence compel him to join the posse sent to capture him. These distinctions are significant because they allow the audience to temporarily sympathize with Murrieta—and to an extent be critical of the racist physical violence of *bad* Americans. The distinction between good Americans such as Burns and racist bad Americans such as the "drunken mob" is important because it reorients the listener back toward the established racial order that legitimized and normalized *reasonable, justified* violence and the quotidian racism that Mexicans encountered.[82]

Broadcasting Mexican Lives

While early twentieth-century historical romanticism and *The Romance of the Ranchos* perpetuated racialized perceptions of Mexicans in the Euro-American imagination, Spanish-language broadcasts in Los Angeles and other areas of the Southwest were directed at the Mexican community.[83] This programming was integral in shaping Mexicans' social, cultural, and political citizenship in the United States during the first half of the twentieth century.[84] By centering culture, news, products, and opportunities relevant to their communities, these shows constituted an aural space through which Mexicans contested the one-dimensional, romantic nostalgia of the American imagination and spoke to their lived realities.

During the 1920s and 1930s Spanish-language radio brokers purchased airtime on English-language radio stations throughout the Southwest. Following a "brokerage system" that consisted of "block programming," airtime ranged from thirty minutes to two hours of Spanish-language programming at a time.[85] Relegated to early-morning time slots, broadcasts aired from 4 to 6 a.m. and provided programming for Mexican laborers as they prepared for work.[86] Although this time slot was defined as an undesirable one by English-language radio stations seeking a white, middle-class listenership with buying power,[87] Spanish-language radio announcers familiar with Mexicans' lived realities as immigrant and/or low-wage workers saw it as a prime time to reach the quickly growing Mexican community.

Successful Spanish-language programs such as Los Angeles–based *Los Madrugadores* (The Early Risers) provided radio announcers like Pedro González the opportunity to engage local audiences, create a shared identity, and establish a platform for community advocacy and activism.[88] First airing in the mid-1920s, *Los Madrugadores* gained popularity in a context marked by economic instability and heightened racial anxiety.[89] In contrast to racialized representations of Mexicans in popular culture, Spanish-language programs positively centered Mexican identity and featured live musical performances, important news, advertisements, and community announcements.[90] As people tuned in to listen to music and topics that interested them, the shows and announcers grew in popularity. Increased awareness of the Mexican community's consumer potential led radio stations to allocate more time slots for foreign-language programming.[91] By 1931 González had expanded his early morning slot to include an afternoon block from one to seven in the evening.[92] This popularity allowed him to use his airtime to speak out against "social injustices and discrimination he witnessed on a daily basis."[93]

During the early 1930s, amid nativist calls for Mexican repatriation and worsening racial tensions, González's on-air advocacy for Mexican rights and his critique of blatant racism was deemed threatening and he was labeled a "rabble rouser."[94] During the 1930s González was often falsely accused and arrested on minor charges, in efforts to silence him.[95] In 1939, he lost his radio show after being falsely accused and convicted of rape. After serving six years of a fifty-year term, he was deported to Mexico. Decades later, his accuser admitted that the police had coerced her accusation by threating to send her to reform school.[96] Authorities' forceful response to González's on-air advocacy and challenging of racial injustice indicates that they believed in, and worried about, these programs' potential to elicit ethnic pride and help raise a collective identity and consciousness against racism. It shows that these programs created a space for Mexican identity to exist in opposition to dominant perceptions.[97] This space challenged the efforts at discursive and physical erasure through repatriation, Americanization, and narratives of a Spanish fantasy past.

As the United States began to teeter on the edge of World War II, the federal government turned to radio to disseminate ideas advocating for U.S. intervention abroad.[98] When the country entered the war in

December 1941, radio programming was used to create a cohesive home front. Because wartime propaganda juxtaposed Nazi totalitarianism and military rule against Americans' "natural love for freedom and democracy," the United States had to reckon with its "extreme discrimination" and racism.[99] Seeking to reconceptualize race and ethnicity through an Americanism and a patriotism that prioritized nation over racial and ethnic difference, the government launched the Americans All campaign.[100] Rooted in the dual discourses of racial liberalism and pluralism, these campaigns sought a unified front based on Americanism.[101] Radio networks supported Americanism through a "renewed English-only American patriotism" based on assimilation.[102] These efforts included radio programs geared at teaching about and fitting racial/ethnic minorities into an inclusive American narrative.[103] These narratives fell short because they utilized racial/ethnic and immigrant tropes and stereotypes that did not reflect groups' specific realities.

The goal of wartime unity influenced Spanish-language programming and marked Mexican immigrants as its intended audience. During the 1930s, fears of subversive foreign-language programming led to increased restrictions, and these worsened during wartime.[104] Aware of these increased restrictions, when Raúl Cortez applied for a broadcasting license with the Federal Communications Commission (FCC) he appealed to patriotism. Cortez, a World War II veteran, posited "that securing a Spanish-language signal would lend support for the war on behalf of Chicanos," promote American unity, and help "socialize Latino immigrants into the American way of life."[105] Granted the license in 1946, Cortez became the first Chicano to own and operate a full-time Spanish-language radio station. The extension of the AM band during the late 1940s allowed for continued growth of Spanish-language radio.[106]

Spanish-language programs of the 1940s, like those of the 1920s and 1930s, represented the social and economic realities of the Mexican community. As Robles found in her study on Spanish-language broadcasting in the Southwest, Mexican listeners, both immigrants and American-born, would "get up at about three o'clock in the morning and make some coffee, smoke cigarettes, and listen to . . . the radio," and "the early morning hours [were] when the *pocho* or Chicano can listen while his wife is preparing breakfast and putting up his lunch."[107] These recollections reflect working-class Mexican people's realities and counter stereotypical representations of them as carefree and lazy. Broadcasters understood that Mexicans saw themselves as hard workers laboring to build a life for their families, and they provided programming relevant to their experiences. Recognizing Mexicans' working-class status and limited means for leisure, sponsors advertised products and services instead of entertainment and travel.[108] Centering on ethnic unity, advertisements deliberately mentioned Spanish-speaking customer service, spoke about getting a "better value from another Mexican," and mentioned specific businesses that welcomed Spanish speakers.[109] Although these efforts indicated Mexicans' integration into American consumer society,[110] the promises of "Americans All" remained largely unfulfilled for Mexicans.

Nineteenth-Century Discourses and the 1940s Home Front: The Romance of Ranchos

The Romance of the Ranchos sought to incorporate California's Mexican past into the region's history; however, by relying on the racialized discourses of a romantic "Spanish" past, Manifest Destiny, Westward Expansion, and Mexican banditry, its narratives represented Mexicans in a one-dimensional way. Its use of stereotyped language and behavior, and even its use of romance, did little to effect change in perceptions of Mexicans; rather, this served to reinscribe perceptions of Mexicans as racially and morally deficient. For example, in representing Murrieta as a bandit who "terrorized the countryside" and threatened American stability, the program reinscribed Mexicans' alleged criminality at a time when news outlets wrote of Mexican "gangs" and "marauders, [who,] prowling the streets at night, brought a wave of assaults, [and] finally murders."[111] Describing Murrieta as "drunken," "bloodthirsty," and lacking control, the show reiterated 1940s police officials' perceptions about "the Mexican elements' . . . desire to kill, or at least let blood," and warnings that "when there is added to this inborn characteristic that has come down through the ages—the use of liquor, then we certainly have crimes of violence [*sic*]."[112] Not unlike the racialized representations of Mexicans in *The Romance of the Ranchos,* 1940s print media representations illustrate how the discursive links to nineteenth-century conceptualizations of Mexican criminality—as presented in *Romance*—materialized in routine harassment, culminating in the racially motivated violence of the so-called Zoot Suit Riots in June 1943.

Comparatively, *Romance*'s positive representation of Euro-American men, masculinity, and freedom supported ideals central to defining American superiority both in the nineteenth century and on the 1940s home front. In this context *The Romance of the Ranchos*' portrayals of American superiority and the benefits of American *democratic* intervention indirectly spoke to and supported U.S. motivations and perceptions of itself as the arsenal of democracy during the Second World War, and, one could argue, even into the Cold War.

Airing at a time when radio programming was meant to center U.S. pluralistic history, *The Romance of the Ranchos* sought to educate its listenership about California's Mexican history and people. Unfortunately, its reliance on nineteenth-century colonialist discourses in framing its narratives resulted in the use of racialized aural cues and stereotypes that reiterated the racial tropes that racial liberalism was supposed to counter. The series portrayed Euro-American men as the bearers of progress, while simultaneously defining Mexicans as deficient in every regard, rendering them ghosts of the past who fought a losing battle against American colonization's juggernauts of modernity and progress.

Notes

1. *The Romance of the Ranchos*, episode 1, "Rancho San Rafael," aired September 7, 1941, on KNX, Los Angeles, Calif. For this chapter, I listened to all thirty-five half-hour-long episodes of *The Romance of the Ranchos*. They were collected by the Old Time Radio Researchers Group (OTRR). This and other programs from the "Golden Age of Radio (1930–1960)" are available on its website: see https://www.otrr.org/. All episodes of *Romance of the Ranchos* are available on Internet Archive: see https://archive.org/details/OTRR_Romance_Ranchos_Singles. The program originally ran from September 17, 1941, through May 10, 1942, and repeated through 1948, on the CBS Western flagship station KNX, Los Angeles. For more information about the program, see Stan Claussen, "The Romance of the Ranchos," in *Radio Rides the Range: A Reference Guide to Western Drama on the Air, 1929–1967*, ed. Jack French and David S. Siegel (McFarland & Company, 2014), 147–53. In quotes of spoken dialogue and narration from the radio show throughout this chapter, all ellipses indicate omission.
2. *The Romance of the Ranchos*, episode 6, "Rancho San Pedro and Rancho Palos Verdes," aired October 15, 1941.
3. Discussion of Good Neighbor Policy and media: for films, see Dale Adams, "Saludos Amigos: Hollywood and FDR's Good Neighbor Policy," *Quarterly Re-*

view of Film and Video 24, no. 3 (2007): 289–95; for radio, see Darlene Sadlier, *Americans All: Good Neighbor Cultural Diplomacy in World War II* (University of Texas Press, 2012), 84–118.

4. Although *The Romance of the Ranchos* was not about Latin America, I read its representations of Mexicans within the context of media representations of Latin Americans because the racialized perception of U.S. Mexicans as a recalcitrant population was juxtaposed against images of happy, singing, colorful "neighbors to the south." For these representations, see Ana M. López, "Are All Latins from Manhattan? Hollywood, Ethnography and Cultural Colonialism," in *Film and Nationalism*, ed. Alan Williams (Rutgers University Press, 2002), 195–214.
5. Incorporated in 1893 but existing in various iterations as early as the 1880s land boom, the Title Insurance and Trust Company (TI), now TICOR Title, held hundreds of thousands of documents related to land in Southern California; these dated to the Spanish colonial period but largely comprised documents from the Mexican and U.S. periods. For a detailed history of TI, see Judson A. Greiner, "Growing Together for a Century: Southern California and the Title Insurance Company," *Southern California Quarterly* 75, no. 3/4 (Fall/Winter 1993): 351–439, https://www.jstor.org/stable/41171685.
6. John V. Pavlik, *Masterful Stories: Lessons from Golden Age Radio* (Routledge, 2017), 120.
7. Claussen, "Romance of the Ranchos," 151.
8. For a detailed discussion and critique of these efforts, see Barbara Savage, "Americans All, Immigrants All: Cultural Pluralism and Americanness," in *Broadcasting Freedom: Radio, War, and the Politics of Race, 1938–1948* (University of North Carolina Press, 1999), 21–62.
9. For racial representations in travel accounts, see Richard Henry Dana, *Two Years Before the Mast: A Personal Narrative of a Sailor's Life at Sea* (Harper and Brothers, 1840); and Charles Nordoff, *California: For Health, Pleasure, and Residence; A Book for Travelers and Settlers* (Harper and Brothers, 1873). For the consequences of these racial representations, see Stephen Pitti, *The Devil in Silicon Valley: Northern California, Race, and Mexican Americans* (University of California Press, 2003); and Hal Rothman, *The Devil's Bargain: Tourism in the Twentieth-Century American West* (University Press of Kansas, 1998).
10. Ann Laura Stoler, *Along the Archival Grain: Epistemic Anxieties and Colonial Common Sense* (Princeton University Press, 2009), 24, 34.
11. The Federal Land Act of 1851 required a judicial process to determine the validity of Mexican land grants. Claimants were required to provide extensive documentation for their claim. For the land process in Southern California, see Yvette Saavedra, *Pasadena Before the Roses: Race, Identity, and Land Use in Southern California, 1771–1890* (University of Arizona Press, 2018), 123–54.
12. All episodes of *The Romance of the Ranchos* are available on Internet Archive: see https://archive.org/details/OTRR_Romance_Ranchos_Singles.

13. I use the combined term *Mexican/Californio* because although the show used the term *Mexican* in its narratives, it was specifically referring to Californios, or the elite landed class. This is an important distinction because the terms illustrate popular perceptions regarding race, citizenship, and social position. By the end of the 1850s, the racially coded *Californian* referred to white Americans and indicated the decline of Californios' sociocultural power. However, the discursive *replacement* of the Californio was accompanied by the white supremacist land dispossession, denial of citizenship rights, and social marginalization of Californios, and by their definition as *not* American. The decline of the Californio elite resulted in their integration into the general, landless Mexican population, and the term *Mexican* came to represent a racialized and class designation, defining them as a racial other.
14. My analysis is informed by Nancy Fraser's conceptualization of the subaltern counterpublic in her analysis of discourse and the public sphere. Specifically, my use of this analytical framework stems from the work of Chicana scholar Dolores Inés Casillas, who applied the concept to her groundbreaking study of U.S. Spanish-language radio and public advocacy. See Nancy Fraser, "Rethinking the Public Sphere: A Contribution to the Critique of Actually Existing Democracy," *Social Text*, no. 25/26 (1990): 61; Dolores Inés Casillas, *Sounds of Belonging: U.S. Spanish-Language Radio and Public Advocacy* (New York University Press, 2014), 8–9.
15. Casillas, *Sounds of Belonging*, 9.
16. William Deverell, *Whitewashed Adobe: The Rise of Los Angeles and the Remaking of Its Mexican Past* (University of California Press, 2004), 21.
17. Deverell, *Whitewashed Adobe*, 7.
18. Deverell, 84, 37–40.
19. Deverell examines the annual La Fiesta parade in Los Angeles and the racial/ethnic tensions around its representations of Mexicans and regional history. See Deverell, *Whitewashed Adobe*, 41–90.
20. For a discussion of the changing racial/ethnic composition engendered by WWII, see Laura Pulido, *Black, Brown, Yellow, and Left: Radical Activism in Los Angeles* (University of California Press, 2006), 34–41.
21. For a discussion of Black workers in defense factories, see Josh Sides, *L.A. City Limits: African American Los Angeles from the Great Depression to the Present* (University of California Press, 2004), 57–94; for Mexican American women defense workers, see Elizabeth Escobedo, *From Coverall to Zoot Suits: The Lives of Mexican American Women on the WWII Home Front* (University of North Carolina Press, 2013), 73–101. For sexual segmentation, see Ruth Milkman, "Redefining 'Women's Work': The Sexual Division of Labor in the Auto Industry During World War II," *Feminist Studies* 8, no. 2 (1982): 337–72.
22. Japanese internment vacated the enclave of Little Tokyo. This became an important hub for the recently arrived Black migrant community and was renamed "Bronzeville." For a discussion of Black migration to Los Angeles, see

Sides, *L.A. City Limits*, 45–48; for a discussion of the relationship between Japanese Americans and African Americans in Los Angeles, see Scott Kurashige, *The Shifting Grounds of Race: Black and Japanese Americans in the Making of Multiethnic Los Angeles* (Princeton University Press, 2007).

23. By 1940 about 90 percent of Los Angeles's ethnic Japanese population were tenant farmers integral to perishable crop production. For a discussion of Japanese and Mexican communities in Los Angeles, see Yu Tokunaga, *Transborder Los Angeles: An Unknown Transpacific History of Japanese-Mexican Relations* (University of California Press, 2022), 21.
24. Escobedo, *From Coveralls to Zoot Suits*, 5–11.
25. See Catherine S. Ramírez, *The Woman in the Zoot Suit: Gender, Nationalism, and the Cultural Politics of Memory* (Duke University Press, 2009); Eduardo Pagan, "Los Angeles Geopolitics and the Zoot Suit Riot, 1943," *Social Science History* 24, no. 1 (2000): 223–56; Edward Escobar, *Race, Police, and the Making of a Political Identity: Mexican Americans and the Los Angeles Police Department, 1900–1945* (University of California Press, 1999).
26. E. Palmer Conner, *The Romance of the Ranchos* (Title Insurance and Trust Company, 1929).
27. A two-part episode on Benjamin Davis Wilson, a Christmas program about the San Gabriel Mission, and an episode about the development of transportation in the region are included in this episode count. Those episodes, respectively, are episodes 14 and 15, "The Life Story of Benjamin D. Wilson," December 10 and 17, 1941; episode 16, "Christmas at Mission San Gabriel," December 24, 1941; and episode 34, "Transportation: From Oxcart to Airliner," May 3, 1942. For a general breakdown of the program, see Claussen, "Romance of the Ranchos."
28. Before his death from suicide in 1950s, Graham was a well-established voice actor whose credits included Disney's 1942 live-action/animated film *Saludos Amigos*. Set in Brazil, this was one of six Disney projects connected to the Good Neighbor Policy. See Adams, "Saludos Amigos"; and Julianne Burton, "Don (Juanito) Duck and the Imperial-Patriarch Unconscious: Disney Studios, the Good Neighbor Policy and the Packaging of Latin America," in *Nationalisms and Sexualities*, ed. Andrew Parker et al. (Routledge, 1992), 21–41. For Graham's career and death, see "Radio Star Frank Graham Commits Suicide," *Los Angeles Times*, September 4, 1950.
29. Carey McWilliams, *North from Mexico: The Spanish-Speaking People of the United States* (J. B. Lippincott Co., 1949), 35.
30. As settler colonialists, Californios also emphasized a Spanish identity to create and sustain an ethnic/cultural hierarchy in relation to Indigenous groups. They linked this identity and status to land ownership. After American colonization, the distinction was framed through an Anglo-American white supremacist racial model. For the links between race, identity, and land, see Saavedra, *Pasadena Before the Roses*.

31. Jackson's intention in *Ramona* was to bring attention to the injustice and inhumane treatment of Indigenous communities. Unfortunately, audiences instead focused on her description of the landscapes and the romantic elements. For a discussion of Jackson's California imagery, see Dydia DeLyser, *Ramona Memories: Tourism and the Shaping of Southern California* (University of Minnesota Press, 2005).
32. For historical romanticism in Southern California, see Deverell, *Whitewashed Adobe*; and Phoebe S. Kropp, *California Vieja: Culture and Memory in a Modern American Place* (University of California Press, 2006).
33. Renato Rosaldo, "Imperial Nostalgia," in "Memory and Counter-memory," special issue, *Representations* 26 (Spring 1989): 107–22.
34. *The Romance of the Ranchos*, episode 3, "Rancho San Jose," aired September 21, 1941.
35. *Ranchos*, episode 6; *The Romance of the Ranchos*, episode 8, "Rancho Ex-Mission de San Fernando," aired October 29, 1941.
36. *The Romance of the Ranchos*, episode 7, "Rancho Paso de Bartolo Viejo," aired October 22, 1941.
37. *Ranchos*, episode 8.
38. *The Romance of the Ranchos*, episode 4, "Rancho Agua de la Centinela," aired October 1, 1941; *The Romance of the Ranchos*, episode 5, "Rancho Rodeo de las Aguas," aired October 8, 1941.
39. *Ranchos*, episode 7.
40. *Ranchos*, episode 3; *Ranchos*, episode 6.
41. Dolores Casillas, Juan Ferrada, and Sara Hinojos, "The Accent on Modern Family: Listening to Representations of the Latina Vocal Body," *Aztlán* 43, no. 1 (2018): 63.
42. *Ranchos*, episode 14. These episodes were based on Benjamin Wilson's 1877 memoir. See David Wilson and Arthur Wood, "Observations on the Early Days of California and New Mexico," *Annual Publication of the Historical Society of Southern California* 16 (1934): 74–150.
43. Wilson narrates the complex relationships between Apache, Mexicans, and Americans in his memoir. He describes the Mexican government's violence against the Apache—an element that the broadcast dismissed by stating that the Apache had used "signal fires" to indicate a "war dance," because they "were out for trouble." *Ranchos*, episode 14.
44. Arlene Hirschfelder and Paulette E. Molin, "I Is for Ignoble: Stereotyping Native Americans," Jim Crow Museum, February 22, 2018, https://www.ferris.edu/HTMLS/news/jimcrow/native/homepage.htm.
45. The program included no Indigenous women and only a few white women.
46. *Ranchos*, episode 2; *The Romance of the Ranchos*, episode 31, "Don Juan Temple," aired April 12, 1942; *The Romance of the Ranchos*, episode 9, "Rancho Los Cerritos and Los Alamitos," aired November 5, 1941.

47. My critique does not question Californio women's desire for or interest in American men, but rather how the portrayal of these pairings exclusively in romantic terms neglects the reality that many Californios trafficked their daughters to American men. For a discussion of these dynamics, see Miroslava Chávez-García, *Negotiating Conquest* (University of Arizona Press, 2004); M. Raquél Casas, *Married to a Daughter of the Land* (University of Nevada Press, 2007); Erika Pérez, *Intimate Colonialisms: Interethnic Kinship, Sexuality, and Marriage in Southern California, 1769–1885* (University of Oklahoma Press, 2018).
48. *Ranchos*, episode 9.
49. When the couple married in 1841, Stearns was forty-three and Bandini was fourteen. See Ronald C. Woolsey, "A Capitalist in a Foreign Land: Abel Stearns in Southern California Before the Conquest," *Southern California Quarterly* 75, no. 2 (1993): 107.
50. *Ranchos*, episode 9.
51. *Ranchos*, episode 9.
52. *Ranchos*, episode 9.
53. *Ranchos*, episode 31; *Ranchos*, episode 14; *Ranchos*, episode 9.
54. *The Romance of the Ranchos*, episode 11, "Ranchos San Vicente and Santa Monica," aired November 19, 1941; *Ranchos*, episode 6; *Ranchos*, episode 34.
55. *Ranchos*, episode 11; *Ranchos*, episode 31; *The Romance of the Ranchos*, episode 24, "Rancho La Ballona," aired February 18, 1942.
56. *Ranchos*, episode 2; *Ranchos*, episode 9; *The Romance of the Ranchos*, episode 28, "William Mulholland and the Southland Water System," aired March 22, 1942.
57. *The Romance of the Ranchos*, episode 13, "Rancho San Antonio and Don Antonio Maria Lugo," aired December 3, 1941.
58. Matthew W. Hughey, *The White Savior Film: Content, Critics, and Consumption* (Temple University Press, 2014), 8.
59. *Ranchos*, episode 14.
60. *Ranchos*, episode 14.
61. Wilson and Wood, "Observations," 79.
62. *Ranchos*, episode 3.
63. *Ranchos*, episode 8; *Ranchos*, episode 15.
64. *Ranchos*, episode 7.
65. *Ranchos*, episode 7.
66. For a discussion of Anti-Mexican lynching, see William Carrigan and Clive Webb, *Forgotten Dead: Mob Violence Against Mexicans in the United States, 1848–1928* (Oxford University Press, 2013); and Monica Muñoz Martinez, *The Injustice Never Leaves You: Anti-Mexican Violence in Texas* (Harvard University Press, 2018).
67. Tiburcio Vásquez and Joaquín Murrieta were well-known social bandits between 1850 and 1880. Euro-Americans considered them violent outlaws. Among Cali-

fornia's Mexican population the two were regarded as heroes who fought against American rule.

68. *Ranchos*, episode 13; *The Romance of the Ranchos*, episode 35, "The Story of the Carrillo Family," aired May 10, 1942.
69. *Ranchos*, episode 13.
70. *The Romance of the Ranchos*, episode 29, "Joaquín Murrieta, Infamous Robin Hood of the West," aired March 29, 1942.
71. Luis Leal, "Introduction," in *Life and Adventures of the Celebrated Bandit Joaquín Murrieta*, by Ireneo Paz, trans. Frances P. Belle (Arte Público Press, 1999), xvii–xxii.
72. *Ranchos*, episode 29.
73. Mark C. Anderson, "'What's to Be Done with 'Em?': Images of Mexican Cultural Backwardness, Racial Limitations, and Moral Decrepitude in the United States Press, 1913–1915," *Mexican Studies* 14, no. 1 (1998): 26.
74. Lindsay Pérez Huber and Daniel G. Solorzano, "Visualizing Everyday Racism: Critical Race Theory, Visual Microaggressions, and the Historical Image of Mexican Banditry," *Qualitative Inquiry* 21, no. 3 (2015): 226.
75. *Ranchos*, episode 29.
76. *Ranchos*, episode 29.
77. *Ranchos*, episode 29.
78. *Ranchos*, episode 29.
79. *Ranchos*, episode 29.
80. *Ranchos*, episode 29. The concept of the social bandit was presented by Eric Hobsbawm; see Eric Hobsbawm, *Bandits* (Delacorte Press, 1969), 13; and Leal, "Introduction," xi. For a discussion of the multiple tellings and retellings of Murrieta's story, see Susan Johnson, *Roaring Camp: The Social World of the California Gold Rush* (W. W. Norton, 2000).
81. *Ranchos*, episode 29.
82. My analysis applies Sara Ahmed's concept of orientation and perception toward an object. Ahmed contends that because "consciousness is intentional" and influences our perception of the world, this perception then orients us toward or away from an object. Above, Murrieta is the object: the Mexican bandit. The temporary sympathy the audience feels for him humanizes him, contradicting the established racial consciousness of white supremacy. The distinction between the good and bad American helps reorient the audiences' perception away from Murrieta as victim of racist violence, by showing that the violence was due to rowdy individuals, not a result of a racist social system. For Ahmed's orientation toward objects, see *Queer Phenomenology: Orientations, Objects, Others* (Duke University Press, 2006), 23–27.
83. This refers to Spanish-language programming originating in the United States. For Mexican radio broadcasting, see Sonia Robles, *Mexican Airwaves: Radio Broadcasting Along Mexico's Northern Border, 1930–1950* (University of Arizona Press, 2019).

84. Mari Castañeda, "The Significance of U.S. Spanish-Language Radio," in *Latinos and American Popular Culture*, ed. Patricia M. Montilla (Praeger Press, 2013), 71.
85. Casillas, *Sounds of Belonging*, 36; Robles, *Mexican Airwaves*, 40.
86. Castañeda, "Significance of U.S. Spanish-Language Radio," 71; George Sánchez, *Becoming Mexican American: Ethnicity, Culture, and Identity in Chicano Los Angeles, 1900–1940* (Oxford University Press, 1993), 183.
87. Casillas, *Sounds of Belonging*, 36.
88. Casillas, 39.
89. Casillas, 36.
90. Robles, *Mexican Airwaves*, 41; Sánchez, *Becoming Mexican American*, 183; Casillas, *Sounds of Belonging*, 37, 40.
91. Castañeda, "Significance of U.S. Spanish-Language Radio," 71.
92. Casillas, *Sounds of Belonging*, 41.
93. Robles, *Mexican Airwaves*, 42. For an additional discussion of González's case, see Casillas, *Sounds of Belonging*, 41.
94. Casillas, *Sounds of Belonging*, 42; Castañeda, "Significance of U.S. Spanish-Language Radio," 72.
95. Casillas, *Sounds of Belonging*, 42.
96. The plaintiff recanted her testimony decades later, admitting that her accusation was a result of police coercion. See Casillas, *Sounds of Belonging*, 42.
97. Casillas, *Sounds of Belonging*, 8.
98. Michele Hilmes, *Radio Voices: American Broadcasting, 1922–1952* (University of Minnesota Press, 1997), 230.
99. Hilmes, *Radio Voices*, 235.
100. Hilmes, 250–51.
101. Escobedo, *From Coveralls to Zoot Suits*, 6.
102. Casillas, *Sounds of Belonging*, 42.
103. Savage, "Americans All, Immigrants All," 21–62.
104. Casillas, *Sounds of Belonging*, 43.
105. Casillas, *Sounds of Belonging*, 43; Castañeda, "Significance of U.S. Spanish-Language Radio," 74.
106. Charles Tatum, *Chicano Popular Culture: Que Hable el Pueblo* (University of Arizona Press, 2017), 145.
107. Nellie Foster, "The Corrido: A Mexican Culture Trait Persisting in Southern California" (MA thesis, University of Southern California, 1939), 22; quoted in Robles, *Mexican Waves*, 40. The etymology of the term *pocho* is rooted in post-revolutionary Mexico's effort to define lo mexicano or Mexicanness. Mexican writer José Vasconcelos used "pocho" as a pejorative term for Americanized Mexicans in the United States, whom he perceived as having abandoned Mexico and its culture. In her study on the cultural persistence of Mexican corridos among Southern California's Mexican population, Nellie Foster uses "pocho" as synonymous with "Chicano." Although the reason for this is unclear, it could

indicate how Spanish-language music serves as a form of cultural purveyance. I, like Robles, find that this is possible through Spanish-language radio programming as well. For a detailed discussion of the etymology of the term *pocho*, see Paloma Martínez-Cruz, "The Intimate Life of the Pocha: A Genealogy of the Self-Ironic Turn in Chicano Culture," in *The Routledge History of Latin American Culture*, ed. Carlos Salomon (Routledge, 2018), 338–49.

108. Casillas, *Sounds of Belonging*, 47.
109. Casillas, 47–48.
110. Casillas, 48.
111. Gene Sherman, "Youth Gangs Leading Cause of Delinquency," *Los Angeles Times*, June 2, 1942.
112. These statements were part of a report by E. Duran Ayres of the Los Angeles sheriff's Foreign Relation Bureau to the 1942 Los Angeles grand jury. See E. Duran Ayres, "Statistics: The Nature of the Mexican American Criminal, 1942," Sleepy Lagoon Defense Committee Records (Collection 107), UCLA Special Collections, Charles E. Young Research Library, https://oac.cdlib.org/view?docId=hb6m3nb79m&query=&brand=oac4.

Bibliography

Adams, Dale. "Saludos Amigos: Hollywood and FDR's Good Neighbor Policy." *Quarterly Review of Film and Video* 24, no. 3 (2007): 289–95.

Ahmed, Sarah. *Queer Phenomenology: Orientations, Objects, Others*. Duke University Press, 2006.

Anderson, Mark C. "'What's to Be Done with 'Em?': Images of Mexican Cultural Backwardness, Racial Limitations, and Moral Decrepitude in the United States Press, 1913–1915." *Mexican Studies* 14, no. 1 (1998): 23–70.

Ayres, Ed. Duran. "Statistics: The Nature of the Mexican American Criminal, 1942." Sleepy Lagoon Defense Committee Records (Collection 107). UCLA Special Collections, Charles E. Young Research Library. https://oac.cdlib.org/view?docId=hb6m3nb79m&query=&brand=oac4.

Burton, Julianne. "Don (Juanito) Duck and the Imperial-Patriarch Unconscious: Disney Studios, the Good Neighbor Policy and the Packaging of Latin America." In *Nationalisms and Sexualities*, edited by Andrew Parker et al., 21–41. Routledge, 1992.

Carrigan, William, and Clive Webb. *Forgotten Dead: Mob Violence Against Mexicans in the United States, 1848–1928*. Oxford University Press, 2013.

Casas, María Raquél. *Married to a Daughter of the Land*. University of Nevada Press, 2007.

Casillas, Dolores Inés. *Sounds of Belonging: U.S. Spanish-Language Radio and Public Advocacy*. New York University Press, 2014.

Casillas, Dolores Inés, Juan Ferrada, and Sara Hinojos. "The Accent on Modern Family: Listening to Representations of the Latina Vocal Body." *Aztlán* 43, no. 1 (2018): 61–88.

Castañeda, Mari. "The Significance of U.S. Spanish-Language Radio." In *Latinos and American Popular Culture*, edited by Patricia M. Montilla, 69–85. Praeger Press, 2013.

Chávez-García, Miroslava. *Negotiating Conquest*. University of Arizona Press, 2004.

Claussen, Stan. "The Romance of the Ranchos." In *Radio Rides the Range: A Reference Guide to Western Drama on the Air, 1929–1967*, edited by Jack French and David S. Siegel, 147–53. McFarland & Company, 2014.

Conner, E. Palmer. *The Romance of the Ranchos*. Title Insurance and Trust Company, 1929.

Dana, Richard Henry. *Two Years Before the Mast: A Personal Narrative of a Sailor's Life at Sea*. Harper and Brothers, 1840.

DeLyser, Dydia. *Ramona Memories: Tourism and the Shaping of Southern California*. University of Minnesota Press, 2005.

Deverell, William. *Whitewashed Adobe: The Rise of Los Angeles and the Remaking of Its Mexican Past*. University of California Press, 2004.

Escobar, Edward. *Race, Police, and the Making of a Political Identity: Mexican Americans and the Los Angeles Police Department, 1900–1945*. University of California Press, 1999.

Escobedo, Elizabeth. *From Coverall to Zoot Suits: The Lives of Mexican American Women on the WWII Home Front*. University of North Carolina Press, 2013.

Fraser, Nancy. "Rethinking the Public Sphere: A Contribution to the Critique of Actually Existing Democracy." *Social Text*, no. 25/26 (1990): 56–80.

Greiner, Judson A. "Growing Together for a Century: Southern California and the Title Insurance Company." *Southern California Quarterly* 75, no. 3/4 (Fall/Winter 1993): 351–439. https://www.jstor.org/stable/41171685.

Hilmes, Michele. *Radio Voices: American Broadcasting, 1922–1952*. University of Minnesota Press, 1997.

Hobsbawm, Eric. *Bandits*. Delacorte Press, 1969.

Hughey, Matthew W. *The White Savior Film: Content, Critics, and Consumption*. Temple University Press, 2014.

Johnson, Susan. *Roaring Camp: The Social World of the California Gold Rush*. W. W. Norton, 2000.

Kropp, Phoebe S. *California Vieja: Culture and Memory in a Modern American Place*. University of California Press, 2006.

Kurashige, Scott. *The Shifting Grounds of Race: Black and Japanese Americans in the Making of Multiethnic Los Angeles*. Princeton University Press, 2007.

Leal, Luis. "Introduction." In *Life and Adventures of the Celebrated Bandit Joaquín Murrieta*, by Ireneo Paz, translated by Frances P. Belle. Arte Público Press, 1999.

López, Ana M. "Are All Latins from Manhattan? Hollywood, Ethnography and Cultural Colonialism." In *Film and Nationalism*, edited by Alan Williams, 195–205. Rutgers University Press, 2002.

Martinez, Monica. *The Injustice Never Leaves You: Anti-Mexican Violence in Texas.* Harvard University Press, 2018.

Martínez-Cruz, Paloma. "The Intimate Life of the Pocha: A Genealogy of the Self-Ironic Turn in Chicano Culture." In *The Routledge History of Latin American Culture,* edited by Carlos Salomon, 338–49. Routledge, 2018.

McWilliams, Carey. *North from Mexico: The Spanish-Speaking People of the United States.* J. B. Lippincott Co., 1949.

Milkman, Ruth. "Redefining 'Women's Work': The Sexual Division of Labor in the Auto Industry During World War II." *Feminist Studies* 8, no. 2 (1982): 337–72.

Nordoff, Charles. *California: For Health, Pleasure, and Residence; A Book for Travelers and Settlers.* Harper and Brothers, 1873.

Pagán, Eduardo Obregón. "Los Angeles Geopolitics and the Zoot Suit Riot, 1943." *Social Science History* 24, no. 1 (2000): 223–56.

Pavlik, John V. *Masterful Stories: Lessons from Golden Age Radio.* Routledge, 2017.

Pérez, Erika. *Intimate Colonialisms: Interethnic Kinship, Sexuality, and Marriage in Southern California, 1769–1885.* University of Oklahoma Press, 2018.

Pérez Huber, Lindsay, and Daniel G. Solorzano. "Visualizing Everyday Racism: Critical Race Theory, Visual Microaggressions, and the Historical Image of Mexican Banditry." *Qualitative Inquiry* 21, no. 3 (2015): 223–38.

Pitti, Stephen. *The Devil in Silicon Valley: Northern California, Race, and Mexican Americans.* University of California Press, 2003.

Pulido, Laura. *Black, Brown, Yellow, and Left: Radical Activism in Los Angeles.* University of California Press, 2006.

Ramírez, Catherine S. *The Woman in the Zoot Suit: Gender, Nationalism, and the Cultural Politics of Memory.* Duke University Press, 2009.

Robles, Sonia. *Mexican Airwaves: Radio Broadcasting Along Mexico's Northern Border, 1930–1950.* University of Arizona Press, 2019.

The Romance of the Ranchos. 35 episodes. Aired September 17, 1941–May 10, 1942, on KNX, Los Angeles, Calif. https://archive.org/details/OTRR_Romance_Ranchos_Singles.

Rosaldo, Renato. "Imperial Nostalgia." In "Memory and Counter-memory," special issue, *Representations* 26 (Spring 1989): 107–22.

Rothman, Hal. *The Devil's Bargain: Tourism in the Twentieth-Century American West.* University Press of Kansas, 1998.

Saavedra, Yvette J. *Pasadena Before the Roses: Race, Identity, and Land Use in Southern California, 1771–1890.* University of Arizona Press, 2018.

Sadlier, Darlene. *Americans All: Good Neighbor Cultural Diplomacy in World War II.* University of Texas Press, 2012.

Sánchez, George. *Becoming Mexican American: Ethnicity, Culture, and Identity in Chicano Los Angeles, 1900–1940.* Oxford University Press, 1993.

Savage, Barbara. *Broadcasting Freedom: Radio, War, and the Politics of Race, 1938–1948.* University of North Carolina Press, 1999.

Sides, Josh. *L.A. City Limits: African American Los Angeles from the Great Depression to the Present.* University of California Press, 2004.

Stoler, Ann Laura. *Along the Archival Grain: Epistemic Anxieties and Colonial Common Sense.* Princeton University Press, 2009.

Tatum, Charles. *Chicano Popular Culture: Que Hable el Pueblo.* University of Arizona Press, 2017.

Tokunaga, Yu. *Transborder Los Angeles: An Unknown Transpacific History of Japanese-Mexican Relations.* University of California Press, 2022.

Wilson, David, and Arthur Wood. "Observations on the Early Days of California and New Mexico." *Annual Publication of the Historical Society of Southern California* 16 (1934): 74–150.

Woolsey, Ronald C. "A Capitalist in a Foreign Land: Abel Stearns in Southern California Before the Conquest." *Southern California Quarterly* 75, no. 2 (1993): 101–18.

PART V

Representation and Belonging

CHAPTER 9

The Benito Juárez Squadron

The Recruitment of Tejana Servicewomen and Their Reclamation of Cultural Citizenship During World War II

VALERIE A. MARTÍNEZ

On March 26, 1944, in a "mass demonstration of international goodwill," the unprecedented induction of twenty women of "Latin American" descent into the United States Women's Army Corps attracted a crowd of thousands to the San Antonio Municipal Auditorium.[1] For two invigorating hours, an audience that included several American and Mexican government and military dignitaries watched a pageantry of various artists twirling and stomping to traditional Mexican dances across the seventy-five-foot stage as the music of the Randolph Field Band filled the air. Behind this picturesque scene were two sizable American and Mexican national seals fitted along the sides of the forty-four-foot backdrop. In the center of the large stage hung a picture of the Indigenous hero and former Mexican president Benito Juárez.[2] The military's strategic utilization of the first Indigenous leader of the nascent nation presented an opportunity for the Mexican American population to see themselves physically reflected in him. They too could be heroic figures fighting for their country.

Through the collaborative efforts of the San Antonio district recruiting office, the Brooks Field Air WAC recruiting team, and leading Latin American citizens and organizations, the Women's Army Corps solicited two hundred women of Latin American descent within the San Antonio

FIGURE 9.1 March 26, 1944, San Antonio Municipal Auditorium induction ceremony. Courtesy of the Archivo Histórico de la Genaro Estrada de la Secretaría de Relaciones Exteriores, México City.

recruiting district for el Escuadrón Benito Juárez, or the Benito Juárez Squadron. These women would train together as a squadron under the "Bee-Jays" insignia and then be assigned to work in various positions in airfields across the state and nation. The recruitment campaign of predominantly Tejana Mexican American women during the wartime period underscored the importance of the United States' Good Neighbor Policy to the hemispheric goal of pan-American unity. Sensitive to the political atmosphere, head recruitment captain John V. Deuel proclaimed in an article: "Currently, Mexican soldiers and aviators are valiantly fighting in all fronts of the war. We know that Mexican women are also anxious to complete their duty and the Benito Juárez Squadron offers them the opportunity to be known from the Pampas of Argentina all the way to Canada."[3] This rousing statement attests that Latin American servicewomen were not only patriotic military participants for a national cause but also transnational political actors who influenced and were used to influence international relations. This squadron of women, known as "Bee-Jays," was created as the embodiment of peaceable democratic ideals and, in the political sphere, of unification and pan-Americanism.

The events in San Antonio and the creation of the Benito Juárez Squadron highlight the broader engagement of Mexican American women in the war effort. In Arizona, as in Texas and other Southwestern states with well-established Mexican and Mexican-heritage populations, wartime efforts increasingly militarized multiple facets of daily life. As is argued throughout this volume, wartime exigencies in the U.S. Southwest shaped not only families' spiritual and religious practices, as seen in Andrea Tovar's chapter, "Digital Reminiscing," but also the labor, racial composition, and dynamics of the workforce, as demonstrated in Gloria Holguín Cuádraz's chapter, "All of Us Had Our Jobs," and Yvette J. Saavedra's chapter, "Remembering the Rancho." For Mexican American women in Texas and throughout the U.S. Southwest, military participation during World War II also afforded them an opportunity to assert their patriotism and bodily autonomy during this moment of increased economic independence while military, political, and civil-rights leaders recognized their importance on an international scale.[4] Thus, in this chapter I argue that while male leaders utilized the women's bodies and military participation to further their diplomatic goals, Latina servicewomen defined a feminist civil-rights project that claimed the legal rights afforded to all U.S. citizens as well as full ownership of their highly policed lives, bodies, and sexuality.

Latin American resistance to the early twentieth-century military interventions by the United States prompted President Franklin D. Roosevelt to create an initiative that would forestall further alienation of potential allies.[5] In essence, the 1933 Good Neighbor Policy would "replace a militaristic, imperial approach to U.S.-Latin America diplomacy with a more 'cooperative' strategy," wherein Latin American countries would have the potential to "redefine relations on more favorable terms."[6] By the Second World War, American fears of Axis influence in Latin American countries fueled an increase of activity in international relations including tourism, investment, and infrastructural changes such as the construction of the Pan-American Highway stretching from Alaska to Argentina.[7]

In Mexico, President Manuel Ávila Camacho embraced the opportunity to strengthen inter-Americanism. According to historian Emilio

Zamora, before the bombing of Pearl Harbor in 1941, Camacho's foreign affairs secretary, Ezequiel Padilla, encouraged other Latin American countries to join the U.S. effort to create pan-American unity as a way to fight against racial discrimination and "to prepare the ground for the new relations that Mexico and other Latin American countries expected with the United States."[8] Ávila Camacho and his staff fervently worked to sign agreements with the United States in order to present a united front against the Axis powers, including stabilizing the Mexican peso / American dollar ratio and enacting the Mexican contracted labor agreement known as the Bracero Program, which ran from 1942 to 1964.[9] However, owing to severe racial discrimination against Mexican-origin people, the Mexican government placed a ban on Texas that prevented the state from receiving contract laborers until 1947. The creation of the Bracero Program and the subsequent efforts by Texas to assuage relations between it and its neighboring country highlighted the oscillating negotiating power of Mexico in the international and national context of pan-Americanism and, as I argue, set the stage for the recruitment of Latin American women for the Benito Juárez Squadron.

"¡Sea Una de las Primeras!!": The Recruitment of "Las Bee-Jays"

The initial military recruitment campaign officially began on February 28, 1944, with the goal of recruiting women of Latin American descent between the ages of twenty and fifty from sixty-nine counties within the San Antonio recruiting district.[10] The Air WAC recruiting staff of twenty-six Army Air Force officers and enlisted personnel ran a successful publicity drive for the squadron. They employed five different radio stations to run twelve programs per week, they purchased 250 inches of advertising and 500 inches of news release, and on three days each week a team performed patriotic skits in three local theaters.[11] Captain John V. Deuel, head of the recruitment effort, reported that their "most concerted and forceful drive" ultimately resulted in 125 applicants.[12] In Texas, nine newspapers ran recruitment ads and publicity stories beginning February 20 and 21, which provided a description of key political figures and organizations that were involved in the recruitment process in the

1940s. These consisted of the president of the Mexican Chamber of Commerce, the president of the Pan-American Optimist Club, the assistant consul general of Mexico, the consul of Mexico, the consul general of Nicaragua, the consul of Honduras, and the principal of Sidney Lanier High School.[13] While newspapers in Arizona did not report the recruitment efforts, select news sources in Missouri and Utah reported the recruitment campaign and the subsequent enlistment of the women.

The location of the news stories also affected the presentation of the advertisements for the squadron. While other English-language newspapers across the city and state ran stories on the squadron, in San Antonio the Spanish-language newspaper *La Prensa* strategically invoked the image of Benito Juárez to appeal to the predominantly Mexican American population. Created in 1913 by Mexican-born Ignacio E. Lozano, *La Prensa* originated as a means of communication for those living outside the motherland (Mexico) to maintain cultural ties with la matria through printed news from Mexico.[14] During World War II, Lozano continued publishing Mexico's news for Mexican Americans in Texas as well as publicizing the organizational activities of Mexican-origin people residing in the United States. Specifically, the newspaper exalted the creation of the squadron and its connection to Mexican nationalist hero Benito Juárez. Indeed, mentions of hemispheric cooperation were pervasive throughout media outlets in the U.S. Southwest, especially in Arizona. For example, on February 10, approximately two weeks before the first recruitment ads ran in San Antonio, the bilingual Phoenix-based newspaper *El Mensajero* discussed the Committee for Americanism and Inter-American Solidarity's upcoming "PanAmerican Week" planned for April 14–16, 1944. The committee boasted of how they worked on "bringing in from Mexico City the highest class talent obtainable in the

FIGURE 9.2 *La Prensa*, February 27, 1944.

musical and artistic fields"[15] These performative acts of unity typically included celebrations of music and pageantry similar to the ceremony for the squadron's debut in San Antonio.[16] The urgency of cooperation was also underscored, as Lozano ran at least twenty articles and advertisements in *La Prensa* from February to March that emphasized the importance of U.S.-Mexico pan-American unity.

On February 27, 1944, for example, an advertisement beckoned Latin American women to "be one of the first" to join the squadron. Placed near the text is a photo of Benito Juárez along with another announcement that reads, "Do it now—today!" The newspaper then pictured noble-looking members of the Women's Army Corps in the center of the advertisement. The photo of Benito Juárez is most striking in this instance, however. In his analysis of the recruitment campaign, Captain Deuel stated, "A name was chosen which is held in high esteem by the Latin American people, as well as being representative of democratic traditions."[17] The symbolism of Juárez was not lost on the newspaper, which stated,

> A music band will play Mexican music, there will be many acts in the interesting program that will all be in Spanish in honor of the women in the "Benito Juárez" Squadron, called this in honor of the great hero of Mexico who fought for liberty and rights against a foreign aggressor in the last century, and who is recognized along with Lincoln of America and Simón Bolívar of South America, in the annals of history.[18]

The conflation of Abraham Lincoln and Benito Juárez is common, as both national leaders "emancipated" their public subjects, one from enslavement and the other from despotism. Accordingly, Lincoln financially and politically supported Juárez in his fight against the French, to which Juárez reciprocated by arresting Confederate officials during the Civil War when they attempted to coax the Mexican president into supporting their cause.[19] *La Prensa* strategically positioned the trinity of liberators of the Americas together: Juárez, who united Mexico to fight against a foreign power; Bolívar, Latin America's liberator from Spanish colonialism; and Lincoln, the U.S. president who emancipated African and African American enslaved people. This compilation of heroes/liberators personified hemispheric democracy.

The newspaper depicts another iconic Mexican figure, Fr. Miguel Hidalgo y Costilla, father of the war for Mexican independence from Spain, to make a binational appeal to the Mexican American population. In the March 12 article, two of the first recruited women for the squadron, Francisca Fierros and Dora Salas, stand with WAC representative Mildred Beaudet, "contemplating" a statue of Hidalgo.[20] The suggestively staged photo is intriguing, as the women were intentionally placed in front of the statue, which had been given to the city of San Antonio as a gift from Mexico. An inscription at the base of the statue reads, "In behalf of his Excellency Manuel Ávila Camacho, President of the Republic of Mexico, Colonel Gonzalo N. Santos presents this statue of the Father of Mexican Independence to the city of San Antonio, Texas, September 16, 1941."[21] This gift to the city was an expression of cooperation between Mexico and the United States while the Good Neighbor Policy was in effect. Its chosen location in San Antonio emphasized the city as the "home of Pan Americanism," as the director of the Pan American Round Tables of San Antonio presciently proclaimed in 1937.[22]

While larger forces in the U.S. military shaped the recruitment policies that inserted these predominantly Mexican American women into international politics, the servicewomen had their own gendered reasons for enlistment, including the desire for bodily and sexual autonomy. Notions of cultural citizenship first proposed by anthropologists in the 1980s provide a model for understanding gendered narratives of enlistment. In my work, I consider those frameworks as part of my critical feminist lens.[23] According to Renato Rosaldo, Rina Benmayor, and William V. Flores, cultural citizenship embodies the everyday social activities that include the claiming of rights in society.[24] Cultural citizenship is a claim of empowerment, meaning the process of asserting the "human, social, and cultural rights" that Mexicans, as a racialized and ethnicized group, sought during the 1940s as they combated their "second-class citizenship" status, as described by Gloria Holguín Cuádraz in her chapter in this book.[25] The theoretical model of cultural citizenship viewed through a feminist perspective allows me to broaden the meaning of predominant definitions of citizenship to include not only the legal rights of those born in the United States, but also Latina servicewomen's expressions of sociocultural rights during World War II. Indeed, as military scholar Cynthia Enloe states, "to be a skeptically critical, feminist-informed military analyst requires not just that one explores the multi-layered politics of masculinities. It calls upon us to become energetically curious about women's varied and dynamic roles vis-à-vis the constructions and reconstructions of masculinity."[26] During a period of increased surveillance of Latina bodies and lives, women who enlisted in the U.S. military wanted equal access and opportunity in education and employment, and claimed this through their practice of cultural citizenship.

"Sipping Margaritas!": Latina Servicewomen Redefining the Contours of Citizenship

Throughout the early twentieth century, the Mexican community faced inadequate housing conditions, discrimination in worksites, and financial insecurity.[27] Similar to the conclusion of World War I, many Mexican Americans in the period immediately following World War II believed military participation was one of the best ways to claim the basic civil liberties and rights afforded to U.S. citizens and to fight against second-class citizenship. Studies on Latino military participation in World War II explain that Latinos served during the war to cement their citizenship status, gain equal treatment and ready access to public services, and assert their masculinity.[28] This analysis is invaluable and demonstrates the process wherein Latinos (that is, men) chose to demand full citizenship status in society. Nevertheless, a critical feminist analysis of Latinas' military participation unveils their personal claims to citizenship, which included not only the limited legal rights afforded to all U.S. citizens but also full ownership of their highly policed lives, bodies, and sexuality.[29]

This was not an easy task for women during a period of societal anxieties over their increased economic and social independence and decreased supervision of them. With the extension of wartime opportunities in the defense industries and the military to women, critics of their military and workforce participation believed that the strict sexual and social boundaries placed upon women would disintegrate as their economic autonomy and social freedom increased. People who supported traditional gender roles for women questioned the single woman who ventured out into the workforce or overseas, as she was a threat "to stable family life and to the moral fiber of the nation"—her sexual freedom could potentially be "on the loose."[30] In the 1940s, Mexican families feared the sexual potency of their young female family members, as family reputations rested on their daughters' purity. A strict chaperonage system was in place that guided, supervised, and directed young women's interactions with their male counterparts.[31] Thus, as the military, society, and their own community and family members policed the most intimate areas of women's lives, the Mexican American servicewomen asserted their cultural citizenship by claiming not only full equitable treatment in the public realm but also autonomy in their private lives.

For women, the difficulty of asserting such claims was a result of institutional domination in the family and in the military; females serving in the predominantly masculine institution that was the military encountered strict regulations that their male counterparts did not face.[32] For example, the U.S. Army imposed limits on the highest rank a woman could receive. Women also could not enlist if they had "children under fourteen or dependent children between eighteen and twenty-one."[33] Other regulations specifically aimed at controlling women's bodies, sexual reproduction, and intimate contact with enlisted men and officers. While the army did encounter some approval, a vast sense of disapproval of women's participation in the military in positions other than the traditional "feminine" status as a nurse proliferated across the nation, as societal anxieties over the "woman soldier" increased. The army therefore attempted to uphold "proper and respectable" gender roles for women during their time in the military. For example, "with a permission slip from her superior officer, [a] WAC officer could socialize off duty with an enlisted husband or relative, and likewise, an enlisted woman could socialize with an officer husband or relative."[34] Notions of respectability dominated the wartime discourse around female enlistment. The servicewomen of the Benito Juárez Squadron and other Latina servicewomen used their own bodies, through their prewar actions and wartime enlistment, or through their assertions of cultural citizenship, to regain the control that had been stripped from them.[35]

During the early 1940s, as the servicewomen reached their late teens and early twenties, the young, impressionable women immersed themselves in the urban employment landscape. In San Antonio, prewar employment afforded at least eight of the Benito Juárez Squadron members purchasing power and a sense of economic autonomy that allowed them to assert their cultural citizenship; however, it is not known how much of their wages they contributed to the family economy.[36] According to the 1940 census, all the women in the squadron who worked outside of their homes, with the exception of one, lived with their nuclear families, including their mother and/or father and their siblings.[37] For example, while Benito Juárez Squadron member (BJ Wac) Francisca Fierros worked as a maid, her father Noé Fierros owned his own barbershop, her sister worked in a beauty parlor, and her brother was a laborer. Her youngest two siblings did not work. Fierros's mother passed away in 1933. The family had an annual income of approximately $600, which would place the Fierros family within the average family income of people living in West San Antonio.[38] In 1944, the Fierros family lived approximately eight blocks east of the Alazán and Apache Courts housing projects. It can be deduced that while Francisca did have purchasing power, most of her wages may have gone to the family income, affording her less money to purchase leisure items. Nevertheless, her ability to contribute to the family economy may have provided Fierros with a sense of pride and promoted an independence that eventually led her to choose to enlist in the military.

Even though the young future servicewomen recognized their economic independence, some women seemed to struggle between a desire for personal autonomy and a desire for their family's approval of their actions. The young women had to negotiate between the boundaries of cultural respectability and their desire for social freedom. According to historian Vicki L. Ruiz, women wishing to circumvent traditional familial supervision had three choices: to openly rebel, to clandestinely rebel, or to acquiesce.[39] Heterosexual encounters with men were arguably the most strident expressions of generational conflict. In her studies on chaperonage and dating practices of young Mexican American women during the 1920s and 1930s, Ruiz explores the importance of a woman's purity to family status and reputation. In an interview, when asked if she was allowed to date boys during her teenage years, BJ Wac Mercedes Vallejo (Ledesma) Flores responded, "No, God! We had to go home and do our chores!"[40] Because the family's values relied upon the daughter's chastity, a strict model of chaperonage evolved, which usually involved older siblings or relatives, with the ever-present dueña (mother or woman of the house) taking on most of the responsibility.[41] Young women during the 1940s were under constant supervision during the few sanctioned social events, such as parties or dances held at church, at schools, or in the neighborhood in a backyard or community center. In fact, Flores recalled, dances were a family affair: "You know my daddy loaded us all on the wagon. [. . .] My daddy would take us all because he was the MC [master of ceremonies] or whatever. He was always the boss and everything."[42] She continued describing the dance scene:

> The mothers went in and sat down. If she didn't see you, she'd get up and go look for you to see where you were. And we'd get up and talk with the other girls that were there. The guys had to stand outside. When the music started, they came in. All the mothers were at the door, uh. All the mothers here . . . all the mothers there. All the guys outside. And there were the mothers. The guys didn't even want to come and dance because they were right by us. We had fun anyways.[43]

Nevertheless, Flores recalled several instances that demonstrated her free will and her strong and somewhat rebellious nature in the face of constant supervision. She stood up for herself in grade school when someone pushed her off the swings "because they were white and I was Mexican," and she played Halloween tricks on her neighbors by knocking down mailboxes and throwing pages of Sears Roebuck catalogs at their homes.

Mobility for service and employment also offered freedom from parental supervision for Latinas across the U.S. Southwest and in Puerto Rico.[44] In Arizona, Beatrice Kissinger, a retired navy nurse, remembered that she had an independent spirit during her youth in the prewar and early war years. The daughter of a homemaker and a New Deal Civilian Conservation Corps laborer, Kissinger graduated from Tucson High School in 1940. After high school, Kissinger traveled to the border town of Nogales, approximately seventy miles south of Tucson, where she worked briefly selling hats to men at J. C. Penney before management fired her for not knowing how to compute the sales correctly. Though jobless, Kissinger did not have trouble passing the time. She stated that she and her girlfriends would party with mariachis and sip margaritas all night.[45] Although Kissinger claimed ownership over her own life by moving away from home, obtaining a job, and spending her time in a leisurely

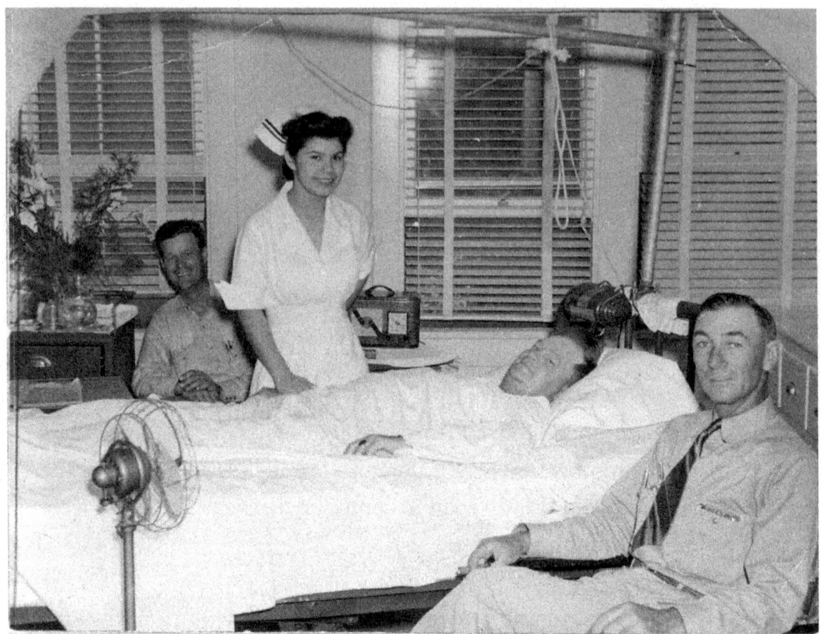

FIGURE 9.3 Beatrice Amado Kissinger. Photo courtesy of the University of Texas at Austin Voces Oral History Center, Austin, Texas.

way, she was still under the supervision of a patriarchal figure. Noticing her behavior, a doctor in Nogales whom her parents knew told her, "Bea, you are just wasting your time, you're going to end up to no good." He then gave her the physical examination required for nursing school and sent her to St. Mary's Hospital in Tucson, even though Kissinger was "having a ball and didn't want to go to nursing school."[46] While Kissinger claimed cultural citizenship, this assertion lasted briefly, as her life was still under the control of outside forces wishing to restrict her behavior.

Complete defiance was another method to assert ownership of one's life, as expressed by María Sally Salazar, WAC veteran. At the age of nineteen, living at home in Laredo, Texas, Salazar told her parents that she was going to visit her older sister, who was living in San Antonio. Once there, she used her sister's birth certificate to enlist in the war in 1942. She did this because women needed to be twenty-one years of age to enlist, which she was not. She went back home and did not say a word. Her parents only learned about her enlistment when the mail carrier delivered a package to her father stating that the Women's Army Corps had accepted Salazar, albeit under her sister's name Amelia. "What is this?" her father exclaimed, to which Salazar remained silent. Outraged, Salazar's father threatened to report his daughter to prevent her departure. Salazar recalled that her mother fearfully replied, "Look, she went with Amelia's birth certificate and she might get in trouble; don't report her."[47] Therefore, for fear of reprisal by the federal government, the family chose not to report their daughter. Salazar's disobedience and the claim she asserted over her own life would ultimately gain her passage into the war.

This was not the only instance when Salazar claimed ownership over her life. As she recounted during the interview, when Salazar was a "young and stupid" freshman in high school, she became pregnant. Salazar's father would not let her marry the baby's father, and after the baby died at six months, he wanted her to go back to school. Nonetheless, Salazar dropped out of school and instead chose to enlist in the army. Salazar defied societal norms of respectable adolescent behavior by becoming pregnant at a young age and out of wedlock as well as by enlisting in a predominantly male institution while underage. Even during her adolescence, although Salazar did not economically contribute to society through employment, she had a sense of belonging to a community, an essential aspect of cultural citizenship. Therefore, Salazar openly claimed a right to her own body and life, which she did by engaging in premarital sex and through her enlistment, both acts done without her parents' approval and presumably despite the disapproval of the larger community.

In a similar story, in 1932, around the age of fifteen, BJ Wac Linda L. Martínez asserted her cultural citizenship and took control of her life and sexuality despite her family's disapproval. Linda married Agustín Martínez in Dawson, Texas, according to an oral history I conducted with her niece.[48] Together, the couple had a son whom they named Agustín Jr. around 1935. However, tragedy struck the little family when Agustín Sr. passed away at some point before 1940.[49] Martínez and her young son moved in with her mother and her older sister, who was also a widow. The government employed Martínez as a seamstress, and she was able to earn $322 in 1939. Tragedy once again struck Martínez when her son Agustín suddenly passed away at the age of seven from diphtheria. The deaths of her husband and son and the disapproval of her family left

Martínez with little enticement to stay at her home in San Antonio. Bereft, she remained strong in the face of adversity and decided not to let heartache or her family's ostracism affect her future. She joined the army.

Women found other ways to reclaim their cultural citizenship through individual and collective expressions of social freedom, including interaction with enlisted men and officers. Most of the women remembered attending dances sponsored by the military in the camps at which the women could congregate with the men freely. San Antonio native and WAC veteran Concepción Alvarado Escobedo recalled meeting her husband at one of the dances. In her interview, Escobedo exclaimed that he took one glance at her and decided she would be his wife.[50] BJ Wac Manuela Martínez also met her husband at a dance hosted at Kelly Air Force Base in San Antonio.[51] Nevertheless, the military also controlled the physical locations where the socialization took place.

Women could express themselves more liberally in unrestricted locations, especially if they had weekend furloughs. Puertorriqueña WAC veteran Carmen Contreras Bozak, for example, asserted her cultural citizenship through her multiple relationships with servicemen both overseas and on the home front. It is unclear whether Bozak was sexually active with the men; however, the military did not deter her ownership of her life and dating practices. While stationed in Caserta, Italy, in June

FIGURE 9.4 Carmen Contreras Bozak. Photo courtesy of the University of Texas at Austin Voces Oral History Center, Austin, Texas.

1944, Lieutenant Robert R. Germain expressed the intimacy between the two military participants in a letter he sent to Bozak. Germain, or "Bob," wrote:

> I must always think about you, my sweet, and it's been two days that sleep hasn't been able to catch me. I pass my time at work, thinking about you.—I return to the house and I spend the day thinking about what happened between us these last two months and about what we thought about during this time—our desires, our plans for the future, our little house in California, our four children—our life full of happiness and love. Every night I pray that all these things will happen and that soon we'll be able to return to America in order to truly start living.[52]

The military attempted to assert full control over the women's bodies, but through intimate relationships the women could still claim power over their lives. The servicemen acted as extensions of the military's institutional power, as they also attempted to control the women's sexual behavior, albeit unsuccessfully. For example, correspondence between Bozak and Lieutenant Brandt McIntyre demonstrates this power struggle. In April of 1943 McIntyre, or "Mac," wrote to Carmen exclaiming his concern over her previous letter, which mentioned interactions with other soldiers. Mac wrote: "Dearest, why must you torture me so, telling me of other soldiers? Think of the sleepless nights and the anxiety you are causing me. Why, I know a man whose old girl told him something like that, and he died."[53] The hyperbolic statement was an attempt by Mac to regulate Bozak's social freedom in a way that did not seem like a strict patriarchal demand. However, on Christmas day of that same year, Mac wrote to Carmen explaining his own encounter with a female native of Cairo. Mac wrote: "I have a record of having kissed one girl since we landed in the Middle-East. . . . I kissed her innocently, supposing that it was accepted in the same spirit in which it was meant. But she shook my faith in mankind, when she charged me ten piasters for the deed done (Don't let your imagination get started; I wouldn't have told it if there were more to the story than that)."[54]

Whereas Mac purported he might die at the prospect of Bozak interacting with other soldiers, he, on the other hand, could kiss another woman "innocently." The final sentence quoted above suggests the sexual promiscuity of servicemen with native women while overseas. Although sexual liaisons may have been a common act by enlisted men, and sometimes an act to gloat over among men, they were still "hidden" or kept secret from the women, presumably out of respect for their virtue as women or to prevent arguments. Nevertheless, Bozak asserted her claims to full citizenship by maintaining multiple relationships with men regardless of American societal norms. Her friendships and/or relationships with servicemen continued until the military honorably discharged her in 1945.

Not all young women openly defied their parents or combated social beliefs about the importance of a woman's sexual containment. BJ Wac Flores recalled of her upbringing: "We were not raised just Mexican. We were raised Polish, German, and Mexican, and we'd behave how we were supposed to behave as young ladies. You could never see us just running around or anything like that. You know when I got out of my mother's and my father's wings, was when I signed up to go into the Air Force." Flores's parents supported her decision to enlist in the military. She states that her family was very patriotic and proud to have sons in the military serving from World War II to Vietnam. Teary-eyed, Flores recalled that the primary reason she enlisted in the service was to help her mother feed her brothers. Flores chose to send her allotment pay home to help with the family's finances.[55]

Young women in the United States, including those of Mexican heritage, made a concerted effort to balance their desires for economic independence and social autonomy with restrictive familial ideals of respectability and responsibility during the prewar and war years. When the women volunteered for the military, they made claims to their own bodies even if they could potentially be putting themselves in danger. However, the larger society was still extremely hesitant about the idea of a "woman soldier" and the freedom associated with enlistment. Such freedom became the basis of a slanderous rumor campaign that peaked in 1943 as the public became aware of the unsupervised behavior of the servicemen and servicewomen. Their concern centered on the sexual morality of the enlisted. Slanderous rumors about the WACs' sexual promiscuity, multiple pregnancies, prostitution, and immoral character ran rampant across the nation. News columnists claimed that the government issued condoms to WACs while others claimed that army doctors were rejecting virgin women.[56] The spread of such incriminating rumors further compelled parents to object to their daughters' enlistment and forced the families of servicewomen to defend the honor of their daughters and ensure their good character. However, WACs had a nearly nonexistent venereal disease rate and a low pregnancy rate. The military also did not issue any forms of contraceptive or information on preventative measures to the women. On the other hand, military installations provided condoms to servicemen, who sometimes even enjoyed the pleasure of "comfort women" and prostitutes while stationed in various bases in the United States and overseas.[57]

Unfortunately, slander greeted the women upon their return. Flores was particularly angered by accusations of immoral behavior. However, the source of the accusations seemed to anger Flores more than the attacks themselves. Flores recalled:

> I know the Mexican people talk because they were the ones that would tear their people. "Oh, we were taken because we were going to be for the soldiers," when we weren't even allowed on their base. We were at Kelly Air Force Base. Kelly is on this side and we were on this side. And with a ten-foot fence with barbed wire on top and security on the bottom, but the Mexican people, because we were in the service to serve the soldiers, in other words like prostitutes. [. . .] The Mexican old ladies would say things about us. But you know what? I had something to tell them too. And I would say just because you are a whore doesn't mean we are.[58]

Nevertheless, despite their protests, many WAC enlistees continued to face public accusations of "sexual deviancy." The army even had to adjust its recruitment policies to combat the slander campaign. According to critics in the public, either the army attracted sexually loose women or "the experience of military life would make them that way."[59] Hence, asserting cultural citizenship in a wartime nation that restricted and dictated women's social value was a difficult task for Latina military participants. Nevertheless, the women made claims to the full citizenship status they deserved through their voluntary military enlistment and their previous prewar employment, which provided a sense of economic independence and pride at helping or providing for their families as daughters. By expressing their social value in both the private and public spheres, the women established control over their bodies, lives, and sexuality, despite the disapproval and hypersurveillance of the military, their community, and their families.

Conclusion

Latina servicewomen in all military branches, including as members of the Benito Juárez Squadron, promoted an atmosphere of "cooperation" across the U.S. Southwest in the context of discriminatory policies and practices targeting Mexican nationals and Mexican American people in the United States. However, in an atmosphere of fear of Axis infiltration in Latin American countries, Mexico wielded an unprecedented amount of power. The recruitment initiative for the Benito Juárez Squadron should be understood within the context of wartime policy discussions. The United States and Mexico were negotiating not only contract laborers, antidiscrimination laws, and the military intervention of an all-Mexican male unit in the Pacific, but also the creation of an all–"Latin American" squadron of women. While these women were (un)consciously shaping international politics during World War II, military participation also influenced the most intimate areas of their lives. A critical feminist lens unveils a gendered argument for enlistment, whereby women could assert their cultural citizenship. When asked why she chose to join the military, Manuela Martínez Portillo answered, "I wanted to go because I wanted to go."[60] No one had told her to join, and no one stopped her, or could have if they tried. In their nineties, BJ Wacs Flores and Portillo said that if their nation called them to serve again, they would proudly do so. For squadron member Elvira (Vera) Muñoz and navy nurse Beatrice Amado Kissinger, military participation was an opportunity to escape their low-wage jobs. For squadron members such as Linda Ledesma Martínez and Beatrice Hernández, perhaps the military also served as an escape from a life in which their young children had died far too soon. For WAC veteran Carmen Contreras Bozak, the possibilities of love and adventure were endless. The oral histories of Latina servicewomen demonstrate that military participation fostered a space, albeit a restrictive one, for Latinas to assert their cultural citizenship in the form of patriotism, escapism, social and economic independence, or sexual freedom. Through their military participation, Latinas across the U.S. Southwest defended their right to bodily autonomy during a wartime period that restricted their lives, bodies, and sexual behaviors.

Notes

1. "First Latin-American WAC Squadron Activated Here," *San Antonio Express* (San Antonio, Tex.), March 27, 1944, p. 5. I use "Latin American" here to be consistent with the use of the term at the time and because this was a popular form of self-identification for people of Mexican descent as they attempted to differentiate themselves from Mexican nationals during a period when the term *Mexican* was associated with inferiority and undocumented status. Richard García, "The Mexican American Mind: A Product of the 1930s," in *History, Culture, and Society: Chicano Studies in the 1980s*, ed. Mario T. García and Bert N. Corona (Bilingual Press, 1983), 89. When discussing both Mexican nationals and Mexican Americans, I will utilize the all-encompassing term "Mexican." Persons of Mexican descent born in the United States are called "Mexican American." The term "Mexican national" is used to refer to persons born in Mexico. The term "Tejana" refers to a woman of Mexican heritage born in Texas. "Latina" will be used to describe U.S.-born women of Latin American descent from Central and South America (excluding Brazil) and the Caribbean.
2. "Mexican Girls Join Air WACs—Outtakes," film, March 26, 1944, Fox Movietone News Story 51–492, Fox Movietone News Collection, Moving Image Research Collections, University of South Carolina, Columbia, S.C., https://digital.tcl.sc.edu/digital/collection/MVTN/id/908.
3. "Benito Juárez será el nombre que llevará un escuadrón de WACS que está organizándose," *La Prensa* (San Antonio, Tex.), February 20, 1944, p. 2. "En los actuales momentos soldados mexicanos y aviadores, existen peleando valientemente en todos los frentes de la guerra. Sabemos que las mujeres mexicanas, también están ansiosas por cumplir con su deber y el 'Escuadrón Benito Juárez,' les ofrece la oportunidad de que sean conocidas, desde las pampas de la Argentina, hasta el Canadá." All English translations provided in this chapter are my own.
4. For more works that explore the larger World War II and military experiences of Mexican American women, see: Sherna Berger Gluck, *Rosie the Riveter Revisited: Women, the War, and Social Change* (Twayne Publishers, 1987); Richard Santillán, "Rosita the Riveter: Midwest Mexican American Women During World War II, 1941–1945," *Perspectives in Mexican American Studies* 2 (1989): 115–47; Christine Marin, "Mexican Americans on the Home Front: Community Organizations in Arizona During World War II," *Perspectives in Mexican American Studies* 4 (1993): 75–92; Maggie Rivas-Rodríguez, ed., *Mexican Americans and World War II* (University of Texas Press, 2005); Maggie Rivas-Rodríguez and Emilio Zamora, eds., *Beyond the World War II Latino Hero: The Social and Political Legacy of a Generation* (University of Texas Press, 2009); Catherine S. Ramírez, *The Woman in the Zoot Suit: Gender, Nationalism, and*

the Cultural Politics of Memory (Duke University Press, 2009); Marianne M. Bueno, "Military Formations: Mexican American Civil Rights and Community Belonging During the World War II Era" (PhD diss., University of California Santa Cruz, 2012); Patricia Portales, "Women, Bombs, and War: Remapping Mexican American Women's Home Front Agency in World War II Literature, Theater, and Film" (PhD diss., University of Texas at San Antonio, 2012); Elizabeth Escobedo, *From Coveralls to Zoot Suits: The Lives of Mexican American Women on the World War II Home Front* (University of North Carolina Press, 2013); Maggie Rivas-Rodríguez and Ben Olguín, eds., *Latina/os and World War II: Mobility, Agency, and Ideology* (University of Texas Press, 2014); Lora Key, "We're All Americans Now: How Mexican American Identity, Culture, and Gender Forged Civil Rights in World War II and Beyond" (PhD diss., University of Arizona, 2020); Laura Lee Oviedo, "Forsaken Bodies, for Sake of Nation: The Labor and Militarization of Tejanas y Puertorriqueñas in the Hemispheric Borderlands During WWII" (PhD diss., Texas A&M University, 2023). For a firsthand perspective on the Puerto Rican woman's experience, see Carmen García Rosado, *Las Wacs: Participación de la mujer boricua en la Segunda Guerra Mundial* (Río Piedras, P.R.: Impresora Oriental Inc., 2006).

5. Cynthia Enloe, *Bananas, Beaches, and Bases: Making Feminist Sense of International Politics* (University of California Press, 2000), 124.
6. Enloe, *Bananas, Beaches, and Bases,* 125; Emilio Zamora, *Claiming Rights and Righting Wrongs in Texas: Mexican Workers and Job Politics During World War II* (Texas A&M University Press, 2009), 65.
7. Enloe, *Bananas, Beaches, and Bases,* 125.
8. Zamora, *Claiming Rights,* 66.
9. Two foundational works on the Bracero Program are: Richard B. Craig, *The Bracero Program: Interest Groups and Foreign Policy* (University of Texas Press, 1971); and Kitty Calavita, *Inside the State: The Bracero Program, Immigration, and the I.N.S.* (Routledge, 1992). Additional literature exploring the more intimate areas of the bracero experience such as family dynamics and expressions of sentiment through corridos includes Ana Elizabeth Rosas, *Abrazando el Espíritu: Bracero Families Confront the US-Mexico Border* (University of California Press, 2014); and the chapters by Alina R. Méndez and Liliana Toledo-Guzmán in this volume.
10. Captain John V. Deuel to Commanding General, Army Air Force Central Flying Training Command, March 29, 1944, file 324.5 #10, W.A.A.C's from April 1944 to–, box 694, series 324.5, Women's Army Corps Oct. 21, 1943–Nov. 1944, Records of the Army Air Forces, Record Group 18 (RG 18), National Archives at College Park (NACP), College Park, Md.
11. Deuel to Commanding General, March 29, 1944.
12. Deuel to Commanding General, March 29, 1944.
13. "Air-WAC Recruiters Establish 'Benito Juarez' Squadron Here," *San Antonio Light* (San Antonio, Tex.), February 21, 1944, p. 12. Newspapers in Texas in-

cluded the *San Antonio Express*, the *San Antonio Light*, *La Prensa*, the *Brownsville Herald*, the *Valley Morning Star*, the *Laredo Times*, the *Port Arthur News*, the *Wichita Daily Times*, and the *Corsicana Daily Sun*.

14. Emilio Zamora, "Las Escuelas del Centenario in Dolores Hidalgo, Guanajuato: Internationalizing Mexican History," in *Recovering the Hispanic History of Texas*, ed. Monica Perales and Raúl A. Ramos (Arte Público Press, 2010), 39.
15. "April 14, 15 and 16 Committee Pick Phoenix," *El Mensajero* (Phoenix, Ariz.), February 10, 1944.
16. In my manuscript "Embajadoras: Latina Servicewomen and Hemispheric Politics During World War II," I further interrogate the performance of hemispheric unity and the broken promises of the pan-American ideal.
17. Deuel to Commanding General, March 29, 1944 (see note 10).
18. "Nuevo Escuadrón de WAC," *La Prensa* (San Antonio, Tex.), February 27, 1944, p. 2. "Una banda de música, tocará aires mexicanos, habrá muchos actos, en el interesante programa, que será todo en español, en honor de estas mujeres del Escuadrón 'Benito Juárez,' llamado así en honor del gran héroe de México, que luchó por la libertad y el derecho, contra una agresión del exterior, en la última centuria, y quien se destaca, con el Lincoln de América y Simón Bolívar de la América del Sur, en los anales de la historia."
19. Jim Tuck, "Mexico's Lincoln: The Ecstasy and Agony of Benito Juárez," *MexConnect*, April 1, 1999, http://www.mexconnect.com/articles/274-mexico-s-lincoln-the-ecstasy-and-agony-of-benito-Juárez; William S. Kiser, *Illusions of Empire: The Civil War and Reconstruction in the U.S.-Mexico Borderlands* (University of Pennsylvania Press, 2022).
20. "Saludo al Escuadrón 'Benito Juárez,'" *La Prensa* (San Antonio, Tex.), March 12, 1944, p. 5.
21. "Don Miguel Hidalgo y Costilla Statue—San Antonio, TX, USA," Waymarking.com, Groundspeak Inc., posted October 11, 2008, http://www.waymarking.com/waymarks/WM4XV1_Don_Miguel_Hidalgo_y_Costilla_Statue_San_Antonio_TX_USA.
22. Mrs. John Case Griswold, San Antonio, Tex., to Mrs. John Maltsberger, Cotulla, Tex., April 9, 1937, box 2, folder 11, record group 03, Pan American Round Table of San Antonio Records, 1909–2017, University of Texas at San Antonio Archives and Special Collections, San Antonio, Tex.
23. Select works by scholars who have used a critical feminist approach to war and gender studies from World War II to the present include Cynthia Enloe, *Does Khaki Become You? The Militarization of Women's Lives* (Pandora Press, 1988); Leisa D. Meyer, *Creating GI Jane: Sexuality and Power in the Women's Army Corps During World War II* (Columbia University Press, 1996); Douglas Walter Bristol Jr. and Heather Marie Stur, *Integrating the US Military: Race, Gender, and Sexual Orientation Since World War II* (Johns Hopkins University Press, 2017); Beth Bailey, Alesha E. Doan, Shannon Portillo, and Kara Dixon Vuic, eds., *Managing Sex in the U.S. Military: Gender, Identity, and Behavior* (University

of Nebraska Press, 2022). Select BIPOC feminist scholars who have influenced this work and author include Chela Sandoval, Patricia Hill Collins, Antonia I. Castañeda, Emma Pérez, Gloria Anzaldúa, Norma Cantú, Laura Rendón, Chandra Talpade Mohanty, and Katherine McKittrick. Chela Sandoval, *Methodology of the Oppressed* (University of Minnesota Press, 2000); Patricia Hill Collins, *Black Sexual Politics: African Americans, Gender, and the New Racism* (Routledge, 2004); Antonia I. Castañeda, *Three Decades of Engendering History: Selected Works of Antonia I. Castañeda*, ed. Linda Heidenreich and Antonia I. Castañeda (University of North Texas Press, 2014); Emma Pérez, "The Imaginary as Will to Feel: Beyond the Decolonial Turn in Chicanx/Latinx Feminism," *Aztlán: A Journal of Chicano Studies* 45, no. 1 (2020): 243–56; Emma Pérez, *The Decolonial Imaginary: Writing Chicanas into History* (Indiana University Press, 1999); Gloria Anzaldúa, *Borderlands / La Frontera: The New Mestiza; The Critical Edition*, ed. Norma Cantú (Aunt Lute Books, 2021); Laura Rendón, *Sentipensante (Sensing/Thinking) Pedagogy: Educating for Wholeness, Social Justice, and Liberation*, 2nd ed. (Routledge, 2023); Chandra Talpade Mohanty and Linda E. Carty, eds., *Feminist Freedom Warriors: Genealogies, Justice, Politics, and Hope* (Haymarket Books, 2018); Katherine McKittrick, *Demonic Grounds: Black Women and the Cartographies of Struggle* (University of Minnesota Press, 2006).

24. Renato Rosaldo, "Cultural Citizenship and Educational Democracy," *Cultural Anthropology* 9, no. 3 (August 1994): 402; William V. Flores and Rina Benmayor, "Constructing Cultural Citizenship," in *Latino Cultural Citizenship: Claiming Identity, Space, and Rights*, ed. William V. Flores and Rina Benmayor (Beacon Press, 1997), 1.
25. W. Flores and Benmayor, "Constructing Cultural Citizenship," 12. In her dissertation, "Military Formations," Marianne Bueno also utilizes the framework of cultural citizenship to understand how Mexican American women in defense industries and the military claimed their rights as American citizens. Bueno, "Military Formations," 65, 75, 130–31, 142–43. In Cuádraz's chapter in this volume, "All of Us Had Our Jobs," the author describes second-class citizenship as a process through which one's lower socioeconomic status was a result of discriminatory labor and wage practices and policies.
26. Cynthia Enloe, "The Recruiter and the Sceptic: A Critical Feminist Approach to Military Studies," *Critical Military Studies* 1, no. 1 (2015): 7.
27. Zaragosa Vargas, *Labor Rights Are Civil Rights: Mexican American Workers in Twentieth-Century America* (Princeton University Press, 2005), 203–4.
28. Lorena Oropeza, *Raza Sí Guerra No: Chicano Protest and Patriotism During the Viet Nam War Era* (University of California Press, 2005), 20.
29. Approximately 350,000 women participated in all branches of the military during World War II. By 1943 over 60,000 women were Women's Army Corps participants, or WACs. The number of Women's Air Force Service Pilots, WASPs, amounted to 1,074. Navy nurses totaled more than 11,000, and army nurses were present all around the world, numbering approximately 57,000.

Mary T. Sarnecky, "Women, Medicine, and War," in *A Woman's War Too: U.S. Women in the Military in World War II*, ed. Paula Nassen Poulos (National Archives and Records Administration, 1996), 75, 79.

30. Elaine Tyler May, *Homeward Bound: American Families in the Cold War Era* (Basic Books, 1988), 68–69.
31. Vicki L. Ruiz, *From Out of the Shadows: Mexican Women in Twentieth-Century America* (Oxford University Press, 1998), 65.
32. Meyer, *Creating GI Jane*, 2.
33. Bettie J. Morden, *The Women's Army Corps, 1945–1978* (Center of Military History, United States Army, 1990), 15.
34. Morden, *Women's Army Corps*. 15.
35. When referring to women who were members of the Benito Juárez Squadron, I will refer to them as either "squadron members" or "BJ Wacs." Since the availability of women from the squadron was severely limited, I used oral histories of other Latina Wacs housed in the Voces Oral History Project at the University of Texas LILAS/Benson Library. Women who did not participate in the squadron will be referred to as "Latina Wacs" or "WAC veterans."
36. According to the 1940 census record, the following BJ Wacs were employed before the war: Francisca Fierros (maid); Doris V. Gillis (beauty operator); Beatrice Hernández (sales representative at Woolworth's); María I. Lafarge (laundress); Linda L. Martínez (seamstress); Elvira (Vera) Muñoz (maid); María T. Segura (researcher for the WPA); Otilia Vela (housekeeper). BJ Wacs who did not work: Faustina Hernández, Mercedes Vallejo (Ledesma) Flores, Natalia P. Pérez, Concepción Pompa, Dora J. Salas, Mary A. Spelman, Minnie Villarreal. BJ Wacs who engaged in home or house work: Leonor Martínez, Manuela Martínez. I could not find the 1940 census record for Nellie Esensee. All records were located through Ancestry.com, *1940 United States Federal Census* (online database), Ancestry.com Operations Inc., 2012. Original data from U.S. Bureau of the Census, *Sixteenth Census of the United States, 1940* (National Archives and Records Administration, 1940), T627.
37. Elvira (Vera) Muñoz was a live-in maid for a Swedish family in San Antonio.
38. The 1940 census states that Francisca made $150, her sister Angelina made $300, and her brother Anito made $150. Her father did not report his income. To determine the socioeconomic location of the family in San Antonio in terms of annual income, a 1940 housing report is useful. The Housing Authority of the City of San Antonio conducted a study beginning in 1937 and provided a description of the city during the period. It stated, "The rapid transition of San Antonio from an outpost of the West to a modern city, with a metropolitan population of 300,000 people, has left dislocations in its physical make-up; a maladjusted economy, together with local characteristics of its people, have made this a city of many low-income families. Result: The problem of safe and sanitary housing for low-income families at rents which these families can afford to pay." City of San Antonio, *1940 Annual Report of*

the Housing Authority of the City of San Antonio, Texas (Housing Authority of the City of San Antonio, Texas, 1940), 1. As the report laid out a proposed plan to develop city housing projects in the lowest-income areas of the city, including the predominantly Mexican American West Side, it included the varying income brackets of the families that lived in the future housing sites. Out of the 1,263 citizens the tenant relocation staff interviewed, the majority had annual incomes between $300 and $799. Seventy-one families made less than $300, and twenty-five families made "$1200 and over." City of San Antonio, *1940 Annual Report*, 12.

39. Ruiz, *From Out of the Shadows*, 61.
40. Mercedes Vallejo (Ledesma) Flores, interview by Valerie A. Martínez, Houston, Tex., December 13, 2014.
41. Ruiz, *From Out of the Shadows*, 65.
42. M. Flores, interview. In quotes from oral interviews in this chapter, ellipses set within brackets indicate omission, while unbracketed ellipses indicate pauses or similar features of the speaker's discourse itself.
43. M. Flores, interview.
44. For an in-depth examination of Puertorriqueñas, see Oviedo, "Forsaken Bodies"; and Rosado, *Las Wacs*, 2006.
45. Beatrice Amado Kissinger, interview by Ernesto Portillo, Tucson, Ariz., March 26, 2005, no. 270, Voces Oral History Project Archive, Nettie Lee Benson Latin American Collection, University of Texas at Austin.
46. Kissinger, interview.
47. María Sally Salazar, interview by Nicole Cruz, Laredo, Tex., September 28, 2002, no. 411, Voces Oral History Project Archive, Nettie Lee Benson Latin American Collection, University of Texas at Austin. All quotes and information attributed to Salazar in this paragraph and the next come from this interview.
48. Cristela D. Stewart (niece of Linda L. Martínez), phone interview by Valerie A. Martínez, June 9, 2016.
49. The 1940 census lists Martínez as a widow.
50. Concepción Alvarado Escobedo, interview by Sandra Freyberg, Brownsville, Tex., September 13, 2003, no. 356, Voces Oral History Project Archive, Nettie Lee Benson Latin American Collection, University of Texas at Austin.
51. Manuela (Martínez) Portillo, Pedro Portillo, Jesusita Martínez Durán, and Gabriella Martínez, group interview with family members by Valerie A. Martínez, San Antonio, Tex., July 20, 2016.
52. Robert "Bob" Germain to Carmen Contreras, June 1, 1944, included in Carmen Contreras Bozak, interview by Vivian Torre, Miami, Fla., September 14, 2002, no. 237, Voces Oral History Project Archive, Nettie Lee Benson Latin American Collection, the University of Texas at Austin.
53. Brandt McIntyre to Carmen Contreras, April 28, 1943, included in Bozak, interview.
54. Bozak, interview.

55. M. Flores, interview.
56. Emily Yellin, *Our Mothers' War: American Women at Home and at the Front During World War II* (Free Press, 2004), 130.
57. Yellin, *Our Mothers' War*, 131.
58. M. Flores, interview.
59. Leisa D. Meyer, "Creating G.I. Jane: The Regulation of Sexuality and Sexual Behavior in the Women's Army Corps During World War II," in "The Lesbian Issue," special issue, *Feminist Studies* 18, no. 3 (Autumn 1992): 584.
60. Portillo et al., group interview with family members.

Bibliography

Anzaldúa, Gloria. *Borderlands / La Frontera: The New Mestiza; The Critical Edition*. Edited by Norma E. Cantú. Aunt Lute Books, 2021.

Army Air Forces. Records. Record Group 18. National Archives at College Park (NACP), College Park, Md.

Bailey, Beth, Alesha E. Doan, Shannon Portillo, and Kara Dixon Vuic, eds. *Managing Sex in the U.S. Military: Gender, Identity, and Behavior*. University of Nebraska Press, 2022.

Bozak, Carmen Contreras. Interview by Vivian Torre. Miami, Fla., September 14, 2002. No. 237. Voces Oral History Project Archive, Nettie Lee Benson Latin American Collection, University of Texas at Austin.

Bristol Jr., Douglas Walter, and Heather Marie Stur. *Integrating the US Military: Race, Gender, and Sexual Orientation Since World War II*. Johns Hopkins University Press, 2017.

Bueno, Marianne M. "Military Formations: Mexican American Civil Rights and Community Belonging During the World War II Era." PhD dissertation, University of California Santa Cruz, 2012.

Calavita, Kitty. *Inside the State: The Bracero Program, Immigration, and the I.N.S.* Routledge, 1992.

Castañeda, Antonia I. *Three Decades of Engendering History: Selected Works of Antonia I. Castañeda*. Edited by Linda Heidenreich and Antonia I. Castañeda. University of North Texas Press, 2014.

City of San Antonio. *1940 Annual Report of the Housing Authority of the City of San Antonio, Texas*. Housing Authority of the City of San Antonio, Texas, 1940.

Collins, Patricia Hill. *Black Sexual Politics: African Americans, Gender, and the New Racism*. Routledge, 2004.

Craig, Richard B. *The Bracero Program: Interest Groups and Foreign Policy*. University of Texas Press, 1971.

Enloe, Cynthia. *Bananas, Beaches, and Bases: Making Feminist Sense of International Politics*. University of California Press, 2000.

Enloe, Cynthia. *Does Khaki Become You? The Militarization of Women's Lives*. South End Press, 1983.

Enloe, Cynthia. "The Recruiter and the Sceptic: A Critical Feminist Approach to Military Studies." *Critical Military Studies* 1, no. 1 (2015): 3–10.

Escobedo, Concepción Alvarado. Interview by Sandra Freyberg. Brownsville, Tex., September 13, 2003. No. 356. Voces Oral History Project Archive, Nettie Lee Benson Latin American Collection, University of Texas at Austin.

Escobedo, Elizabeth R. *From Coverall to Zoot Suits: The Lives of Mexican American Women on the World War II Home Front.* University of North Carolina Press, 2013.

Flores, Mercedes (Ledesma). Interview by Valerie A. Martínez. Houston, Tex., December 13, 2014.

Flores, William V., and Rina Benmayor, eds. *Latino Cultural Citizenship: Claiming Identity, Space, and Rights.* Beacon Press, 1997.

Fox Movietone News Collection. Moving Image Research Collections, University of South Carolina, Columbia, S.C.

García, Richard A. "The Mexican American Mind: A Product of the 1930s." In *History, Culture, and Society: Chicano Studies in the 1980s,* edited by Mario T. García and Bert N. Corona, 67–93. Bilingual Press, 1983.

Gluck, Sherna Berger. *Rosie the Riveter Revisited: Women, the War and Social Change.* Twayne Publishers, 1987.

Key, Lora. "We're All Americans Now: How Mexican American Identity, Culture, and Gender Forged Civil Rights in World War II and Beyond." PhD dissertation, University of Arizona, 2020.

Kiser, William S. *Illusions of Empire: The Civil War and Reconstruction in the U.S.-Mexico Borderlands.* University of Pennsylvania Press, 2022.

Kissinger, Beatrice Amado. Interview by Ernesto Portillo. Tucson, Ariz., March 26, 2005. No. 270. Voces Oral History Project Archive, Nettie Lee Benson Latin American Collection, University of Texas at Austin.

Marin, Christine. "Mexican Americans on the Home Front: Community Organizations in Arizona During World War II." *Perspectives in Mexican American Studies* 4 (1993): 75–92.

May, Elaine Tyler. *Homeward Bound: American Families in the Cold War Era.* Basic Books, 1988.

McKittrick, Katherine. *Demonic Grounds: Black Women and the Cartographies of Struggle.* University of Minnesota Press, 2006.

Meyer, Leisa D. "Creating G.I. Jane: The Regulation of Sexuality and Sexual Behavior in the Women's Army Corps During World War II." In "The Lesbian Issue," special issue, *Feminist Studies* 18, no. 3 (Autumn 1992): 581–601.

Meyer, Leisa D. *Creating GI Jane: Sexuality and Power in the Women's Army Corps During World War II.* Columbia University Press, 1996.

Mohanty, Chandra Talpade, and Linda E. Carty, eds. *Feminist Freedom Warriors: Genealogies, Justice, Politics, and Hope.* Haymarket Books, 2018.

Morden, Bettie J. *The Women's Army Corps, 1945–1978.* Center of Military History, United States Army, 1990.

Oropeza, Lorena. *Raza Sí Guerra No: Chicano Protest and Patriotism During the Viet Nam War Era*. University of California Press, 2005.

Oviedo, Laura Lee. "Forsaken Bodies, for Sake of Nation: The Labor and Militarization of Tejanas y Puertorriqueñas in the Hemispheric Borderlands During WWII." PhD dissertation, Texas A&M University, 2023.

Pan American Round Table of San Antonio Records, 1909–2017. University of Texas at San Antonio Archives and Special Collections, San Antonio, Tex.

Pérez, Emma. *The Decolonial Imaginary: Writing Chicanas into History*. Indiana University Press, 1999.

Pérez, Emma. "The Imaginary as Will to Feel: Beyond the Decolonial Turn in Chicanx/Latinx Feminism." *Aztlán: A Journal of Chicano Studies* 45, no. 1 (2020): 243–56.

Portales, Patricia. "Women, Bombs, and War: Remapping Mexican American Women's Home Front Agency in World War II Literature, Theater, and Film." PhD dissertation, University of Texas at San Antonio, 2012.

Portillo, Manuela (Martínez), Pedro Portillo, Jesusita Martínez Durán, and Gabriella Martínez. Group interview with family members by Valerie A. Martínez. San Antonio, Tex., July 20, 2016.

Ramírez, Catherine S. *The Woman in the Zoot Suit: Gender, Nationalism, and the Cultural Politics of Memory*. Duke University Press, 2009.

Rendón, Laura. *Sentipensante (Sensing/Thinking) Pedagogy: Educating for Wholeness, Social Justice, and Liberation*. 2nd ed. Routledge, 2023.

Rivas-Rodríguez, Maggie, ed. *Mexican Americans and World War II*. University of Texas Press, 2005.

Rivas-Rodríguez, Maggie, and Ben Olguín, eds. *Latina/os and World War II: Mobility, Agency, and Ideology*. University of Texas Press, 2014.

Rivas-Rodríguez, Maggie, and Emilio Zamora, eds. *Beyond the Latino World War II Hero: The Social and Political Legacy of a Generation*. University of Texas Press, 2009.

Rosado, Carmen García. *Las Wacs: Participación de la mujer boricua en la Segunda Guerra Mundial*. Río Piedras, P.R.: Impresora Oriental Inc., 2006.

Rosaldo, Renato. "Cultural Citizenship and Educational Democracy." *Cultural Anthropology* 9, no. 3 (August 1994): 402–11.

Rosas, Ana Elizabeth. *Abrazando el Espíritu: Bracero Families Confront the US-Mexico Border*. University of California Press, 2014.

Ruiz, Vicki L. *From Out of the Shadows: Mexican Women in Twentieth Century America*. Oxford University Press, 1998.

Salazar, María Sally. Interview by Nicole Cruz. Laredo, Tex., September 28, 2002. No. 411. Voces Oral History Project Archive, Nettie Lee Benson Latin American Collection, University of Texas at Austin.

Sandoval, Chela. *Methodology of the Oppressed*. University of Minnesota Press, 2000.

Santillán, Richard. "Rosita the Riveter: Midwest Mexican American Women During World War II, 1941–1945." *Perspectives in Mexican American Studies* 2 (1989): 115–47.

Sarnecky, Mary T. "Women, Medicine, and War." In *A Woman's War Too: U.S. Women in the Military in World War II*, edited by Paula Nassen Poulos, 71–81. National Archives and Records Administration, 1996.

Stewart, Cristela D. Phone interview by Valerie A. Martínez. June 9, 2016.

Vargas, Zaragosa. *Labor Rights Are Civil Rights: Mexican American Workers in Twentieth-Century America*. Princeton University Press, 2005.

Yellin, Emily. *Our Mothers' War: American Women at Home and at the Front During World War II*. Free Press, 2004.

Zamora, Emilio. *Claiming Rights and Righting Wrongs in Texas: Mexican Workers and Job Politics During World War II*. Texas A&M University Press, 2009.

Zamora, Emilio. "Las Escuelas del Centenario in Dolores Hidalgo, Guanajuato: Internationalizing Mexican History." In *Recovering the Hispanic History of Texas*, edited by Monica Perales and Raúl A. Ramos, 38–66. Arte Público Press, 2010.

CHAPTER 10

Between Place and Plot

Reimagining the Story of Arizona

ANITA HUÍZAR-HERNÁNDEZ

I was not always interested in Arizona.[1] Growing up in the sprawling suburbs of the Phoenix metro area, I never gave the state or its history much thought. Like all fourth graders in Arizona, I learned the five C's (copper, cotton, cattle, citrus, and climate), memorized the state flower (the saguaro cactus blossom), and even won a contest to include my hand-drawn decorative border (of cacti and cowboy boots) on the front page of the program for our class concert. That version of Arizona, however, seemed so distant from my own. Where were the endlessly repeating master-planned houses, all the same 1980s HOA-mandated cream color? Where were the shopping malls, the Harkins theaters, the chain restaurants? Our fourth-grade unit on Arizona was as foreign to me as the previous year's focus on dinosaurs. Both seemed like they belonged to a world that had gone extinct.

To my surprise, when my family moved to the Boston area a few years later, I discovered that the Arizona I had encountered in the fourth grade was very much alive and well, at least in the imaginations of our new neighbors. There I was, shivering in the New England cold, clutching the straps of my JanSport backpack, when the questions began: "You're from ARIZONA?" "Wow!" "Do you own a horse?" "Did you ride it to school?" "Do you know what an ATM is?" Everywhere we went, people seemed to think we had stepped directly out of a John Wayne movie, as if Arizona existed not only in a different place but also a different time, one dominated by rugged rural landscapes and (almost certainly white) cowboys struggling against them.

Complicating matters further, I was one of few children, if not the only child, of Mexican heritage at my new school. Though I had grown up in a majority-white neighborhood in Arizona, Mexican culture was nevertheless a pervasive presence in our food, our language, and our built environment. In the small Massachusetts town I moved to, Mexican culture was suddenly foreign, and as a result, so was I. My new friends nicknamed me "Anita fajita" (rhyme taking precedence over geographic specificity, fajitas being a Tex-Mex food), though in their Boston accents it sounded more like "Aniter fajiter." It was unclear to me how exactly my new friends conceptualized the relationship between my geographic and ethnic identities. What *was* clear was that they understood me to be very, very different from them.

I was surprised and a little disoriented by the culture clash I experienced, but as a middle schooler my mind was much more preoccupied with navigating my new social surroundings than with critically assessing them. When my family returned to Arizona just as I was about to begin high school, I left any questions I may have had about my Massachusetts experience behind. I settled back into life in my home state without giving that home state so much as a second thought.

It wasn't until graduate school that I began to question how certain narratives had become associated with Arizona and the impact those narratives had both inside and outside the state. I had begun my studies with an interest in the relationship between story and place, but my intended focus was nineteenth- and twentieth-century postindependence Latin American literature. Then, in 2010 two key bills passed through the Arizona legislature that drew my attention back to the state. The first was Senate Bill 1070, which among other things empowered local law enforcement to use controversial racial profiling tactics to police unauthorized immigration within the state. The second was House Bill 2281, which banned the teaching of ethnic studies in the state's K–12 public and charter schools. The two laws were mutually reinforcing, forbidding the study of difference to sanction the control of difference. That is to say, they were both tied up in advancing a racially circumscribed image of Arizona. As I closely followed the news coverage and the cultural firestorm that ensued, I was reminded of my earlier moments of disorientation when I had been confronted with an image of Arizona that simply did not match the reality I had experienced. For the first time, I started to wonder what was causing the disconnect.

I wanted to study Arizona.

I come to the study of Arizona not as a historian, but rather as a scholar trained in Chicanx/Latinx literary and cultural studies who brings historical intent to the questions about placemaking and belonging that are at the center of this volume. In my work I investigate the ways in which literature, film, and other forms of expressive culture have consolidated or challenged certain myths about Arizona, the U.S. (South)west, and the U.S.-Mexico borderlands. It was only as I began to probe the genealogy of stories told about Arizona that I began to understand the bewilderment I had repeatedly experienced as a child. Those stories pointed to a wide chasm that separated the way people imagined Arizona from the complex realities the state contained.

As I soon discovered, the serious investigation of that complexity has been the subject of substantial academic attention. The Autumn/Winter 2020 *Journal of Arizona History* special double issue "Exploring Arizona's Diverse Past," edited by Katherine G. Morrissey, provides a compelling view of the current state of the dynamic inquiry into Arizona's history. In what follows, I want to respond to the invitation Katherine Benton-Cohen gives in her contribution to that special issue to join a growing conversation about how we might understand Arizona and its relationship to the nation and the world.[2] As a nonhistorian, I take up her call with a specific stake in narrative, building on that special issue's focus on the *history* of Arizona to here consider the *story* of Arizona, as well as the often significant problems that arise from the disconnect between the two. In particular, I turn my attention to three central narrative threads within Arizona's contemporary landscape: its metropolises, its border(s), and its politics.

A Metropolitan Story

As I found when my family relocated to the Boston area, the story of metropolitan Arizona in many ways remains unknown. In the case of the state's suburbs, this is partly by design, as the built environment of endlessly repeating, nearly identical master-planned communities and strip malls often feels as if it has no story to tell. Anonymous and impersonal, this sea of sameness obscures the complexities inherent within the story of the state's metropolitan development in the recent, as well as the more distant, past. In the postwar period, Arizona has grown substantially, transforming the state's landscape from one dominated by small, largely rural communities to one with an ever-growing urban and suburban population. As historian Andrew Needham notes, "Between the 1940 and 2010 censuses, Arizona rose from the forty-third most populous state to the sixteenth. In those years, the state's population rose from just over five hundred thousand to more than six million people."[3] Much of that growth happened in the suburbs, part of a national postwar phenomenon supported by federal investment in the expansion of infrastructure like highways and electrical grids.[4] In Arizona, as Needham explains, "the 1950 and 1960 censuses showed metropolitan portions" of the state "adding population at rates of 84 percent and 133 percent respectively. Rural parts of the state showed a population increase of only 8 percent in the 1950 census and actually lost 2.6 percent of their population in the 1960 census."[5] And yet, the story the census was telling about Arizona by the mid-twentieth century is in many ways not a familiar one even sixty years later.

The intricacies of Arizona's story of postwar metropolitan growth are largely invisible in the forms that shape many people's encounters with the state: popular culture and tourism. In the realm of popular culture, there are few representations of Arizona that do not tell a rural story, whether the focus is a desolate Western past or a dangerous border present.[6] Some notable exceptions bear mentioning. As early as the 1950s, Mario Suárez wrote about the Chicano community that called El Hoyo, a barrio in Tucson, its home. Refugio Savala's *The Autobiography of a Yaqui Poet* (1980) also depicts the city of Tucson through the eyes of the author, a Yaqui refugee fleeing the forced displacement of his people at the hands of the Mexican government. The main characters in Barbara Kingsolver's early novels *The Bean Trees* (1988) and its sequel *Pigs in Heaven* (1993) likewise come in and out of Tucson as part of their cross-country travails. Moving farther north, Stella Pope Duarte's collection of short stories *Women Who Live in Coffee Shops and Other Stories* (2010) offers a vivid window into the multiethnic communities that make their home in urban

Phoenix. Oscar Mancinas's *To Live and Die in El Valle* (2020), though not specifically naming Arizona, is deeply grounded in the greater Phoenix metropolitan area known as "the Valley." Finally, in *Sinking Bell: Stories* (2022), Diné author Bojan Louis depicts the area in and around Flagstaff, exploring the complex relationships that are all too often invisible within the tourist-driven narratives that celebrate the natural beauty of northern Arizona. The preceding chapters in this volume likewise tell a more complex metropolitan story, from Gloria Holguín Cuádraz's analysis of Litchfield Park's history as a cotton company town to Lillian Gorman's recovery of Tucson's significant impact on the trajectory of bilingual education in the United States. These exceptions, however, have received far less attention than the many films, television shows, and literary accounts that portray Arizona as a physical and cultural desert.

The state's tourism industry is heavily invested in promoting an ahistorical image of the state as a playground for enjoying nature and nightlife. Popular natural attractions such as Sedona and the Grand Canyon draw tourists from around the world to marvel at the beauty of their unique landscapes. Physically removed from the state's most populous metropolitan centers and culturally removed from the Indigenous communities on whose land these natural attractions reside, many tourist experiences in these scenic locations offer visitors an Arizona experience that has little to do with most Arizonans.[7] In a similar fashion, the upscale resorts, shopping, and entertainment in the popular destination city of Scottsdale offer an encounter with Arizona that is hardly indicative of the state's regional, racial, and economic complexities.

The dismissal of metropolitan Arizona has created a narrative vacuum around the largest share of the state's population, contributing to the persistent idea that Arizona is devoid of its own unique culture or past. Lured by economic growth, affordability, and a milder (at least in the winter) climate, many of the people who rushed to fill Arizona's cities and suburbs in the mid-twentieth century came from other parts of the United States. As Needham writes, in 1960 in "northeastern Phoenix, the fastest growing area of the metropolis," 86 percent of newcomers had relocated from the Northeastern and Midwestern United States.[8] This continual influx of newcomers from elsewhere saw Arizona as a blank canvas on which to imprint their own cultural traditions. This attitude persists, as Arizona sports fans will lament when they say that attending a professional sporting event in Arizona is like being at a home game for the visiting team.

The idea that Arizona is a blank canvas, however, is not a new one, nor is it unique to its metropolises. Quite the opposite, the elision or outright erasure of Arizona's past connects the story of its modern cities to the longer genealogy of narratives that underpinned the expansionist doctrine of Manifest Destiny, which infamously portrayed the western United States as a "virgin land." Those nineteenth- and early twentieth-century stories, like the stories of Arizona today, are full of contradictions.[9] In the past, stories of the West claimed simultaneously that the land was free for the taking and also needed to be wrested from the hands of Indigenous and Latinx communities; in the present, the story of Arizona's cultural identity portrays it as both (anachronistically) solely rural and (inaccurately) wholly transplanted from other areas of the country. Both narratives are rooted in a radical decontextualization and dehistoricization of the state's story, presenting their own kinds of erasure that exist in tension with one another under the persistent misconception that Arizona remains terra nullius.

It is beyond the scope of this essay to delve into the details of modern urban and suburban culture in Arizona, which is itself far from monolithic, though several scholars have begun to probe metropolitan Arizona's complex past.[10] Whether the recovery of that past will begin to complicate dominant perceptions (or dismissals) of Arizona's urban and suburban landscape remains to be seen. What is certain, however, is that Arizona's metropolitan landscape is continually changing. Now, seventy years on from the beginning of Arizona's explosive population growth in urban and suburban areas, significant numbers of residents have multigenerational ties to the region, undermining the perceived truism that everyone is a transplant from somewhere else. The racial identity of metropolitan Arizona is also changing rapidly, as the state's suburbs have become more diverse, and notably more Latinx.[11] As these changes indicate, the assumption that metropolitan Arizona does not have its own story to tell is as dangerous a mischaracterization of the state as its Manifest Destiny–era virgin land mythology. Both are indicative of a long-standing gap separating the state's actual story from its perceived reality, as well as the persistent allure of narratives that portray Arizona as a place without a past.

A Border Story

In contrast to the narrative vacuum surrounding Arizona's metropolitan story, Arizona's border story has received an inordinate amount of attention inside and outside the state. Arizona is a state of many borders, including those of twenty-three Native Nations. Nevertheless, it is almost always the U.S.-Mexico border that dominates, if not wholly consumes, the conversation. Increased consideration, however, has not led to heightened clarity. When it comes to Arizona's border story, erasure and distortion have been at the center.

Especially in recent decades, certain politicians—both inside and outside Arizona—have heralded the securing of the border that divides Arizona, USA, from Sonora, Mexico, as a cornerstone of their agenda. In order to legitimize their calls for increased militarization, they have depended on a border story steeped in criminality and danger. This story, however, is based more in fiction than fact. In the wake of the passage of SB 1070, in the summer of 2010 former Arizona governor Jan Brewer falsely claimed that "law enforcement agencies" in the state "found bodies in the desert either buried or just lying out there that have been beheaded."[12] Seven years later, on April 11, 2017, former U.S. attorney general Jeff Sessions reiterated those false claims in a speech in Nogales, Arizona, claiming that "along this border . . . transnational gangs like MS-13 and international cartels flood our country with drugs and leave death and violence in their wake. . . . Depravity and violence are their calling cards, including brutal machete attacks and beheadings."[13] Chicana feminist theorist Adela C. Licona has termed Brewer's and Sessions's remarks "non/images," false claims that circulate in a "regime of distortion."[14] These non/images are buttressed by the all-too-familiar images of politicians posing for photo ops at the Arizona-Sonora border wall. The 2024 election season is no exception, as endless commercials debate who is or is not tough on border issues. Anti-immigrant sentiment pervades the airwaves, and polling indicates that a new version of SB 1070, Proposition 314, enjoys widespread support.[15]

It is not just politicians, however, who write and rewrite Arizona's border story. A recent film depicting the Arizona-Sonora borderlands, *The Marksman* (2021), portrays a reality that is not so distant from that described by Brewer and Sessions. In the film, a cowboy-hat-wearing Liam

Neeson plays a former Marine turned minuteman-type vigilante who unofficially patrols the border in order to report unauthorized crossers to the U.S. Border Patrol. After discovering and then reporting a woman and her son crossing, Neeson's character suddenly finds himself protecting them in a shootout with cartel members who are pursuing them. Through a series of events, he ends up becoming the boy's guardian, agreeing to take him to Chicago to reunite with family, all while eluding the cartel. Though the film attempts to flip the script, the same cast of characters—the white rancher, the undocumented child, the ruthless cartel member—are notably present.

The Mexican actor and filmmaker Mario Fortino Alfonso Moreno Reyes—who was better known by his stage name, Cantinflas—brilliantly satirizes this border story in his 1968 film *Por mis pistolas.* The infamous Mexican comedian employs his characteristic wordplay to code-switch his way across the Arizona-Sonora border, dancing linguistic circles around a clueless U.S. border agent. There is no fence, and the only indication that this is a border between two nations is a candy-cane-striped porta-potty-type structure with a sign that reads "U.S. Customs and Immigration Services" and a solitary locked gate that exists absurdly without being attached to anything on either side. The scene culminates with the border agent, having granted Cantinflas and his horse a tourist visa, scrambling to locate the misplaced gate key. Cantinflas offers to simply walk around the gate, which the border agent incredulously rebukes as strictly (though ridiculously) prohibited. With the border agent unable to find the key, Cantinflas successfully unlocks the gate with his own key and passes through the border as the agent declares, "Welcome to Arizona!"

Though the porousness of the border is purposefully exaggerated in *Por mis pistolas* for comedic effect, it also gestures toward a different border story characterized not by restriction and danger but by movement and exchange. That is the border story that many of Arizona's Chicanx and Latinx authors have told. In *Images and Conversations* (1983), *Songs My Mother Sang to Me* (1992), and *Beloved Land* (2004), Patricia Preciado Martin compiles the oral histories of Mexican Americans in Arizona whose border stories are much broader than the geopolitical dividing line itself. In many cases, they have ties to the land that predate the creation of the contemporary border. Its impact, however, does not go unfelt. Family ranches become expensive guest ranches that court tourists from other parts of the United States. Once-pervasive ways of earning a living become obsolete as U.S. expansion brings with it increased urbanization and Americanization. This is also the history that informs Andrea Tovar's contribution to this volume, which discusses her own family's experience with ranching in the Arizona borderlands. In Preciado Martin's and Tovar's accounts, the people who share their stories bear witness to a linguistic and cultural resilience that defies characterizations of the Arizona-Sonora border as an impenetrable line of separation.

Probing the nature of the cultural hybridity that is fundamental to the Arizona-Sonora borderlands is at the center of Alberto Ríos's work. Ríos has built his career writing about the state, particularly its border region, where he spent his childhood in the Ambos Nogales area. Ríos's poetry and prose charts a very particular kind of cross-border cartography of Arizona that is grounded in the quiet quotidian reality of people who make their lives in these borderlands. It is this life and the everydayness of it that takes center stage in Ríos's writing, which includes novels, short stories, essays, and poetry. This is especially true of Ríos's autobiographical *Capirotada: A Nogales Memoir* (1999), a cross-border story that demonstrates how the line between countries was a reality to be negotiated, not an impermeable boundary. This permeability is also evident in Alina R. Méndez's contribution to this book, in which she shows how bracero workers and their families maintained their ties despite the borderline that often separated them.

The Arizona-Sonora border today is, of course, very different from what it was for the people in Ríos's writings and the bracero workers in Méndez's chapter. Authorized and unauthorized crossing has become more difficult, as the United States has invested billions in policing the people and goods that pass across the line.[16] Border-policing changes in neighboring California and Texas have purposefully funneled border crossers through the more dangerous Arizona-Sonora corridor, a deadly dynamic powerfully portrayed by Tijuanense / Southern Californian author Luis Alberto Urrea in *The Devil's Highway* (2004) and Salvadoran American author Javier Zamora in *Solito* (2022). As Urrea's and Zamora's texts demonstrate, the number of migrant deaths in the Arizona-Sonora border region has risen dramatically because of these policy changes, adding another layer of complexity to Arizona's border story.[17]

Indigenous authors have pushed this complexity further, challenging the singular focus of Arizona's border story and rejecting the false binaries that have defined its characterization. In *Ocean Power: Poems from the Desert* (1995), Tohono O'odham poet and linguist Ofelia Zepeda centers how her community resists the logic of U.S. and Mexican geopolitical divisions that do not define the "land that we know."[18] As Zepeda explains in the afterword of *Ocean Power*, the creation of the current U.S.-Mexico border in 1854 bifurcated the Tohono O'odham territory, which lies both north and south of the dividing line. As a result, the Tohono O'odham must navigate around an externally imposed border regime that neither reflects nor respects their own geography.

Imagining beyond the current border regime is at the center of Mojave poet, essayist, and linguist Natalie Diaz's work. An enrolled member of the Gila River Indian Tribe, Diaz explores in her writing a multiplicity of border stories, from the borders that surround reservations to those that divide past from present. Her investment in a capacious understanding of borders and their stories is also evident in her founding directorship of Arizona State University's Center for Imagination in the Borderlands, which centers "an Indigenous perspective" on the borderlands and approaches Arizona as "a crucible for the many questions we find ourselves asking regionally, nationally and throughout the world—the futurities of water, land, language, borders, migration, race, extraction, art, surveillance technology, incarceration, abolition, the body, etc."[19]

Despite the best efforts of politicians who depend on caricatures of borders to justify their platforms, as the authors mentioned here have demonstrated, Arizona's border story is not and has never been static. As Chicana feminist and borderlands theorist Gloria Anzaldúa writes in her seminal text *Borderlands / La Frontera: The New Mestiza* (1987):

> Borders are set up to define the places that are safe and unsafe, to distinguish *us* from *them*. A border is a dividing line, a narrow strip along a steep edge. A borderland is a vague and undetermined place created by the emotional residue of an unnatural boundary. It is in a constant state of transition.[20]

In August 2021, that constant state of transition was powerfully captured in images of Arizona's monsoon rains washing away sections of then-president Donald Trump's new border wall near Douglas, Arizona.[21] Pictures of floodgates torn off their hinges and water flowing freely from one side to the other gesture toward an altogether different border story, one in which a wall is never the final word.

A Political Story

In recent decades, Arizona has been closely associated with U.S. conservatism.[22] Though Arizona has been home to notable Democratic politicians and progressive political movements throughout its history, its relationship to U.S. conservative politics has come to overshadow this other legacy. From Barry Goldwater to John McCain, some of Arizona's most recognizable politicians have for many years symbolized the state's solidly red profile. Until very recently, Arizona's electoral history largely backed up this reputation. Between 1952 and 2016, the Republican candidate for president carried the state's largest county, Maricopa, in every election. At the state level, the Democrats have not held a majority in the Arizona House of Representatives since the passage of the 1965 Voting Rights Act.

Arizona's location along the nation's southern border with Mexico has provided a convenient backdrop against which to elaborate a story of a state on the front lines of a war to keep America American. By 2010, Arizona governor Jan Brewer made SB 1070 and resistance to the corresponding national boycott it provoked a centerpiece of her successful campaign to remain the state's top executive. The narrative Brewer and other like-minded Arizona politicians latched on to was one of the federal government, specifically the Obama administration, abandoning an Arizona that was supposedly under siege. Their response to that abandonment was filling the federal gap with their own state solution in the form of SB 1070. The defiance inherent within SB 1070's rebuke of not only unauthorized immigrants but also the federal government is illustrated in what became an iconic image of Governor Brewer wagging her finger at President Obama on the tarmac at the airport in Mesa, Arizona, in the wake of SB 1070's passage.[23] Her rebuke of President Obama became symbolic of the narrative of Arizona as a conservative bulwark on the border.

In a somewhat ironic twist, however, the dominance of this popular narrative also spurred the consolidation of a formidable progressive infrastructure that has since challenged the state's conservative reputation. As Lisa Magaña and César S. Silva argue in their book *Empowered!*

¡Empoderados! Latinos Transforming Arizona Politics (2021), SB 1070 galvanized Arizona's Latinx population, particularly its immigrant activists, who have built upon their grassroots advocacy to both consolidate long-term progressive political power and see their communities represented in elected and appointed political leadership.

Though this shift has been evident within Arizona for some time, it was not until the 2020 U.S. presidential election that most of the rest of the nation took notice. Together with Georgia, Arizona became a central protagonist in the prolonged determination of the outcome of that election. The state did, eventually, cast its electoral votes for President Joe Biden, who became the first Democratic candidate for president to carry Maricopa County since Harry S. Truman in 1948. Since Biden's historic win, pundits from across the political spectrum have scrambled to write the story of when and how Arizona turned purple, or even blue, and how long it will remain that way.[24]

The waters have become even more muddied as Arizona again occupies the national spotlight, this time for the role it stands to play in tightly contested races for both U.S. president and Arizona's second U.S. Senate seat. At the time of this writing, the future direction of the narrative of Arizona's political identity remains to be determined. Will some segments of Arizona's Latinx community veer right, as certain polls have indicated? If so, what role will they play in shaping the future of U.S. politics? One reality that has emerged when looking at Arizona post-2020 is that it is no longer the stronghold for a certain brand of conservatism whose future remains uncertain. No matter the results of the next election, Arizona will be part of the reshaping of U.S. political parties. The once-dominant Goldwater-McCain brand of conservatism has been supplanted with Charlie Kirk and a Turning Point USA–style politics.[25] Where that leaves former McCain Republicans in the long term remains to be seen. What is clear is that the story many people thought they knew about Arizona politics needs revision.

Conclusion

There is an urgent need to consider the ways in which Arizona is both a real and constructed space. Though the stories that circulate about Arizona are not necessarily all true, they nonetheless do produce very real consequences. From portrayals of Arizona's metropolises as devoid of their own history, to depictions of the U.S.-Mexico border as a war zone that must be controlled, to a narrative about Arizona politics as reliably conservative in the Goldwater-McCain tradition, the accepted stories of Arizona—true or not—have shaped the state's political and cultural development and have mediated its relationship to the rest of the nation and even the world.

What is at stake here is a question of not only real but also perceived authenticity. In many cases, what masquerades as the "authentic" Arizona story is one defined by a white, rural society struggling for survival along a literal and metaphorical frontier. While elements of this narrative are undoubtedly reflective of the lived experiences of some Arizonans, it is incomplete. Historians have already made significant strides in filling in some of those gaps, yet, as Benton-Cohen argues, "Arizona history deserves more attention than ever from historians and academic presses."[26] To that, I would add that the genealogy of stories about Arizona, be they true or false, similarly demands increased analysis in order to fully attend to the way the state has been imagined within and beyond its own borders.

It has been many years since my childhood encounter with Arizona, not as a place but as a plot. The story of Arizona that my New England friends introduced me to was one in which I did not see myself, or anyone I knew, reflected. I have now come to appreciate how these mismatched expectations also form part of the state's narrative landscape and shape the work that remains to be done to tell a different Arizona story.

Notes

1. This chapter is an updated version of a previously published essay, reprinted here with permission. For the previous version, see Anita Huízar-Hernández, "Between Place and Plot: Reimagining the Story of Arizona," *Journal of Arizona History* 63, no. 3 (2022): 263–79.
2. See Katherine Benton-Cohen, "Lead, Follow, or Get Out of the Way? Arizona History and the Nation," *Journal of Arizona History* 61 (Autumn/Winter 2020): 667–92.
3. Andrew Needham, "Change and Continuity in the Time of the Blob: Growth Politics in Postwar Arizona History," *Journal of Arizona History* 61 (Autumn/Winter 2020): 536.
4. Needham, "Change and Continuity," 540.
5. Needham, "Change and Continuity," 542.

6. See, for example, the predominantly rural-focused titles that come up in an IMDB search for the subject "Arizona": https://www.imdb.com/find?q=Arizona&s=tt&ttype=ft&ref_=fn_ft (accessed April 8, 2022).
7. For more on the fraught relationship between Indigenous communities and the state's natural attractions, see Sarana Riggs, "Commemorating Our Indigenous Presence," Grand Canyon Trust, February 20, 2019, https://www.grandcanyontrust.org/blog/commemorating-our-indigenous-presence.
8. Needham, "Change and Continuity," 543.
9. For a detailed account of how the ideology of Manifest Destiny impacted the development of late nineteenth- and early twentieth-century Arizona, see Anita Huízar-Hernández, *Forging Arizona: A History of the Peralta Land Grant and Racial Identity in the West* (Rutgers University Press, 2019).
10. A far from exhaustive list of those studies includes: Elizabeth Tandy Shermer, *Sunbelt Capitalism: Phoenix and the Transformation of American Politics* (University of Pennsylvania Press, 2013); Geraldo Cadava, *Standing on Common Ground: The Making of a Sunbelt Borderland* (Harvard University Press, 2013); Andrew Needham, *Power Lines: Phoenix and the Making of the Modern Southwest* (Princeton University Press, 2014); Janine Schipper, *Disappearing Desert: The Growth of Phoenix and the Culture of Sprawl* (University of Oklahoma Press, 2008); Patricia Gober, *Metropolitan Phoenix: Place Making and Community Building in the Desert* (University of Pennsylvania Press, 2006); Lydia Otero, *La Calle: Spatial Conflicts and Urban Renewal in a Southwest City* (University of Arizona Press, 2010); Luis F. B. Plascencia and Gloria H. Cuádraz, eds., *Mexican Workers and the Making of Arizona* (University of Arizona Press, 2018); Andrew Ross, *Bird On Fire: Lessons from the World's Least Sustainable City* (Oxford University Press, 2011); and Michael F. Logan, *Desert Cities: The Environmental History of Phoenix and Tucson* (University of Pittsburgh Press, 2006).
11. Needham, "Change and Continuity," 564.
12. Brian Montopoli, "Where Did Jan Brewer's Beheading Claim Come From?," *CBS News*, July 9, 2010, https://www.cbsnews.com/news/where-did-jan-brewers-beheading-claim-come-from/.
13. "Attorney General Jeff Sessions Delivers Remarks Announcing the Department of Justice's Renewed Commitment to Criminal Immigration Enforcement," Office of Public Affairs, The United States Department of Justice, April 11, 2017, https://www.justice.gov/opa/speech/attorney-general-jeff-sessions-delivers-remarks-announcing-department-justice-s-renewed.
14. Adela C. Licona, "The Non/Image of the Regime of Distortion," in *Precarious Rhetorics*, ed. Wendy S. Hesford, Adela C. Licona, and Christa Teston (Ohio State University Press, 2018), 169.
15. Rafael Carranza, "Border Security Measure Proposition 314 Getting Lost on a Long Ballot," *Arizona Republic*, October 3, 2024, https://www.azcentral.com/story/news/politics/elections/2024/10/03/what-to-know-about-proposition-314-the-border-security-ballot-measure/75463410007/.

16. "The Cost of Immigration Enforcement and Security," American Immigration Council, August 14, 2024, https://www.americanimmigrationcouncil.org/research/the-cost-of-immigration-enforcement-and-border-security.
17. Daniel E. Martínez, Robin C. Reineke, Raquel Rubio-Goldsmith, and Bruce O. Parks, "Structural Violence and Migrant Deaths in Southern Arizona: Data from the Pima County Office of the Medical Examiner, 1990–2013," *Journal on Migration and Human Security* 2 (2014): 257–86.
18. Ofelia Zepeda, *Ocean Power: Poems from the Desert* (University of Arizona Press, 1995), 83.
19. "Home," Center for Imagination in the Borderlands, Arizona State University, accessed October 22, 2024, https://imaginationborderlands.asu.edu/.
20. Gloria Anzaldúa, *Borderlands / La Frontera: The New Mestiza*, 3rd ed. (Aunt Lute Books, 2007).
21. Brian Kahn, "Trump's Border Wall Torn Apart by Arizona Monsoon Rains," *Gizmodo*, August 22, 2021, https://gizmodo.com/trumps-border-wall-torn-apart-by-arizona-monsoon-rains-1847535174.
22. See Geraldo Cadava, "Barry and Beyond: Conservatism in Arizona Before, During, and After Its Most Famous Representative," *Journal of Arizona History* 61 (Autumn/Winter 2020): 569–88.
23. "Jan Brewer Gets an Earful from Obama in Ariz.," *CBS News*, January 26, 2012, https://www.cbsnews.com/news/jan-brewer-gets-an-earful-from-obama-in-ariz/.
24. Examples of this spectrum of political punditry include: Greg Moore, "Why Is Arizona Turning Blue? Here Are the Best Reasons, Starting with Latinos," *Arizona Republic*, November 4, 2020, https://www.azcentral.com/story/opinion/op-ed/greg-moore/2020/11/04/why-arizona-turning-blue-answers-start-latino-voters/6163875002/; D. Hunter Schwarz, "Arizona Still Feels Red as Voters Embrace a Conservative Shade of Blue," *Deseret News*, May 13, 2021, https://www.deseret.com/2021/5/13/22432531/arizona-voters-embrace-a-conservative-shade-of-blue-2020-election-phoenix-sinema-kelly-trump; Jennifer Medina, "In Arizona, a Swing State Swings to the Far Right," *New York Times*, May 5, 2022, https://www.nytimes.com/2022/05/05/us/politics/arizona-mid terms-swing.html.
25. Michelle Goldberg, "America Is on the Brink of a Great Political Realignment: It's Already Visible in Arizona," *New York Times*, October 14, 2024, https://www.nytimes.com/2024/10/14/opinion/trump-arizona-republican-party.html.
26. Benton-Cohen, "Lead, Follow," 669.

Bibliography

Anzaldúa, Gloria. *Borderlands / La Frontera: The New Mestiza*. 3rd ed. Aunt Lute Books, 2007.

Benton-Cohen, Katherine. "Lead, Follow, or Get Out of the Way? Arizona History and the Nation." *Journal of Arizona History* 61 (Autumn/Winter 2020): 667–92.

Cadava, Geraldo. "Barry and Beyond: Conservatism in Arizona Before, During, and After Its Most Famous Representative." *Journal of Arizona History* 61 (Autumn/Winter 2020): 569–88.

Cadava, Geraldo. *Standing on Common Ground: The Making of a Sunbelt Borderland.* Harvard University Press, 2013.

Gober, Patricia. *Metropolitan Phoenix: Place Making and Community Building in the Desert.* University of Pennsylvania Press, 2006.

Huízar-Hernández, Anita. *Forging Arizona: A History of the Peralta Land Grant and Racial Identity in the West.* Rutgers University Press, 2019.

Licona, Adela C. "The Non/Image of the Regime of Distortion." In *Precarious Rhetorics,* edited by Wendy S. Hesford, Adela C. Licona, and Christa Teston, 168–87. Ohio State University Press, 2018.

Logan, Michael F. *Desert Cities: The Environmental History of Phoenix and Tucson.* University of Pittsburgh Press, 2006.

Martínez, Daniel E., Robin C. Reineke, Raquel Rubio-Goldsmith, and Bruce O. Parks. "Structural Violence and Migrant Deaths in Southern Arizona: Data from the Pima County Office of the Medical Examiner, 1990–2013." *Journal on Migration and Human Security* 2 (2014): 257–86.

Needham, Andrew. "Change and Continuity in the Time of the Blob: Growth Politics in Postwar Arizona History." *Journal of Arizona History* 61 (Autumn/Winter 2020): 535–67.

Needham, Andrew. *Power Lines: Phoenix and the Making of the Modern Southwest.* Princeton University Press, 2014.

Otero, Lydia. *La Calle: Spatial Conflicts and Urban Renewal in a Southwest City.* University of Arizona Press, 2010.

Plascencia, Luis F. B., and Gloria H. Cuádraz, eds. *Mexican Workers and the Making of Arizona.* University of Arizona Press, 2018.

Ross, Andrew. *Bird On Fire: Lessons from the World's Least Sustainable City.* Oxford University Press, 2011.

Schipper, Janine. *Disappearing Desert: The Growth of Phoenix and the Culture of Sprawl.* University of Oklahoma Press, 2008.

Tandy Shermer, Elizabeth. *Sunbelt Capitalism: Phoenix and the Transformation of American Politics.* University of Pennsylvania Press, 2013.

Zepeda, Ofelia. *Ocean Power: Poems from the Desert.* University of Arizona Press, 1995.

Contributors

Vanessa Fonseca-Chávez is an associate professor of English and assistant vice provost at Arizona State University. She received her MA in Hispanic Southwest studies at the University of New Mexico and her PhD in Spanish cultural studies at Arizona State University. Fonseca-Chávez's research focuses on the ways rural communities reflect their understanding of place through storytelling and the contestation of dominant narratives. She is the author of *Colonial Legacies in Chicana/o Literature: Looking Through the Kaleidoscope* (2020), from the University of Arizona Press, and the co-editor of three books, including *La Plonqui: The Literary Life and Work of Margarita Cota-Cárdenas* (2023), also from the University of Arizona Press. She is the co-director, with Levi Romero, of the Following the Manito Trail project, which looks at historic economic migration patterns by Hispanic New Mexicans, or Manitos, to other parts of the United States and how these communities carry their culture, traditions, and language with them. With Yvette J. Saavedra, Fonseca-Chávez is the co-founder and co-editor of the BorderVisions book series with the University of Arizona Press.

Lillian Gorman is a proud Chicana with deep roots in New Mexico. She is an associate professor in the Department of Spanish and Portuguese and director of the Spanish as a Heritage Language Program at the University of Arizona. She graduated with a BA in Spanish and an

MA in Hispanic Southwest studies from the University of New Mexico. She received her PhD from the University of Illinois at Chicago. Her research interests focus on issues of language and identity within U.S. Latina/o/x communities and U.S. Latina/o/x popular culture. Her book *Zones of Encuentro: Language and Identities in Northern New Mexico* was recently published as part of the Global Latin/o Américas Series by the Ohio State University Press. Her essays have appeared in edited volumes including *Explorations in Ethnography, Language and Communication: Capturing Linguistic and Cultural Diversities*, and *Querencia: Reflections on the New Mexico Homeland.* She served as a University of Arizona HSI Fellow and as the scholar-in-residence at the Center for Regional Studies at the University of New Mexico in 2020. She is the recipient of the 2023 University of Arizona "Mentoring Future Scholars Award" from the Office of the Provost.

Gloria Holguín Cuádraz is an associate professor of sociology in the School of Humanities, Arts, and Cultural Studies at Arizona State University. She earned her doctorate in sociology from the University of California, Berkeley. She publishes in the areas of higher education, oral history, Arizona labor history, feminist methods, and testimonio. She is co-editor of two anthologies: *Mexican Workers and the Making of Arizona* (University of Arizona Press, 2018) and *Claiming Home, Shaping Community: Testimonios de los Valles* (University of Arizona Press, 2017). She is a member of the Latina Feminist Group, authors of *Telling to Live: Latina Feminist Testimonios* (Duke University Press, 2001). Her book in progress, "*Los Campos*: Cotton, Power, and the Mexican Community in Arizona," is based on oral histories and archival research in one of the few cotton company towns in the Southwest. From 2014 to 2017, she was co–lead editor of *Chicana/Latina Studies: The Journal of Mujeres Activas en Letras y Cambio Social.* She is a proud recipient of the MALCS Tortuga Award and the Arizona Humanities Council's Dan Shilling Public Humanities Scholar of the Year Award.

Anita Huízar-Hernández is an associate professor in the School of International Letters and Cultures and associate director of the Hispanic Research Center at Arizona State University. Born and raised in Arizona, Huízar-Hernández's teaching and research focus on the ways literature,

film, and other forms of expressive culture have consolidated or challenged myths about Arizona, the West, and the U.S.-Mexico borderlands. Her first book, *Forging Arizona: A History of the Peralta Land Grant and Racial Identity in the West*, was published by Rutgers University Press in 2019. Huízar-Hernández's current book project examines writing produced by the Cristero diaspora in the United States, a group of Catholic Mexican exiles who fled across the border because of the Mexican Revolution's secularization project. Huízar-Hernández is also engaged in multiple collaborative digital public-facing projects.

Christine Marin is Professor Emerita and an archivist-historian at Arizona State University. Dr. Marin is the founder of the prestigious archival repository the Chicano/a Research Collection and Archives at the Hayden Library in Tempe, Arizona. At ASU, she taught courses on Mexican American history and Chicana/Latina history across academic units. Arizona Humanities awarded her the 2021 Juliana Yoder Friend of the Humanities Award for her work to support and promote the humanities. Dr. María E. Montoya, president of the Western History Association, selected Dr. Marin in 2021 as the historian to be awarded the association's Honorary Lifetime Membership Award, in recognition of her scholarship as a historian of the American West. Her recent publications include "Amazing Grace Keeps the Platters Spinning: A Photo Essay on Radio and Television Trailblazer Graciela Gil Olivarez," with Monica de la Torre, in *Feminist Media Histories: An International Journal* (2021); and "Mexicano Miners, 'Dual Wage,' and the Pursuit of Wage Equality in Miami, Arizona," with Luis F. B. Plascencia, in *Mexican Workers and the Making of Arizona* (2018), edited by Gloria Holguín Cuádraz and Luis F. B. Plascencia.

Valerie A. Martínez is an associate professor of history at Our Lady of the Lake University in San Antonio, Texas. She specializes in twentieth-century Mexican American history, U.S. military and labor history, and women's and gender studies. Her National Endowment for the Humanities–funded project, *Embajadoras: Latina Servicewomen and Hemispheric Politics During World War II*, reconceptualizes traditional notions of diplomacy and international actors by investigating how the recruitment and service of Latina women in the Benito Juárez Squadron

during World War II embodied the pan-American ideal of an imagined hemispheric system of unity and reciprocity in the Americas. Her transnational research in both Mexico and the United States has been funded by several entities. She is also the co-recipient of an NEH grant to create an oral history project dedicated to women veterans, a core member of the Ethnic Studies Network of Texas, and the chair of the National Association for Chicana and Chicano Studies Tejas-Foco Pre-K–12 Committee.

Alina R. Méndez is an assistant professor in the Chicano and Latin American Studies Department at California State University, Fresno. She received her PhD in United States history from the University of California, San Diego, and a BA in Latin American history from the University of California, Berkeley. Her article "More Than Victims or Villains: Representations of Mexican Migrant Men in the Imperial Valley–Mexicali Borderlands, 1942–1954" was published in *California History.* She also contributed a primary source project titled "Gendered Invisibility: Ethnic Mexican Women and the Bracero Program" to the online journal and database *Women and Social Movements in the United States, 1600–2000.* Méndez is currently revising her award-winning dissertation into a book manuscript tentatively titled "Border Braceros: Migration, Farm Labor, and Social Reproduction in the Imperial Valley–Mexicali Borderlands, 1942–1968." Her research has received support from the Ford Foundation, the Andrew W. Mellon Foundation / School for Advanced Research, the Center for U.S.-Mexican Studies, the Fulbright Program, the University of California Institute for Mexico and the United States, and the Archie Green Fund for Labor Culture and History.

Karen R. Roybal is an associate professor of Southwest studies at Colorado College. She is an interdisciplinary scholar whose research and teaching focus on Southwest studies, archival studies, Chicanx and Latinx literature and history, and cultural studies. Roybal is the author of *Archives of Dispossession: Recovering the Testimonios of Mexican American Herederas, 1848–1960* (University of North Carolina Press, 2017) and co-editor of the book *New Transnational Chicanx Perspectives on Ana Castillo* (University of Pittsburgh Press, 2021). She has published numerous book chapters and peer-reviewed articles on Chicanx litera-

ture, borderlands history, archival studies, Native/Indigenous art, Chicana feminism, and Southwest studies. Her current book project extends her research on nineteenth-century practices of dispossession enabled through settler-colonial structures to address continued cycles of spatial/physical displacement of marginalized communities. Roybal specifically examines aesthetic forms of resistance to this displacement represented in visual culture, literature, musical compositions, and embodied stories.

Yvette J. Saavedra is an associate professor in the Department of Women's, Gender, and Sexuality Studies at the University of Oregon. Saavedra is an interdisciplinary, intersectional sociocultural historian and Chicana studies scholar whose research focuses on nineteenth- and twentieth-century U.S. history, U.S.-Mexico borderlands history, the U.S. West, Chicana/o history, Chicana feminism, and the history of gender and sexuality. She is the author of *Pasadena Before the Roses: Race, Identity, and Land Use in Southern California, 1771–1890*, published by the University of Arizona Press in 2018. Other publications include "Of Chicana Lesbian Terrorists and Lesberadas: Recuperating the Lesbian/Queer Roots of Chicana Feminism, 1970–2000," in *Feminist Formations* (2021), and "Speaking for Themselves: Rancheras and Respectability in Mexican California, 1800–1850," in *California History* (2023).

Liliana Toledo-Guzmán is an adjunct faculty member at the University of Arizona, where she earned her PhD in history, and lead archivist at the Pimeria Alta Historical Society and Museum in Nogales, Arizona. She obtained her bachelor's degree in music and her master's in history in Mexico. Her areas of interest include the history of rural education, gender studies, borderlands, and music. Her work has been published in *The Oxford Research Encyclopedia of Latin American History* and by Penguin Random House Mondadori. She was a graduate fellow in The Border Hub, a digital project initiative of the University of Arizona Libraries, funded by the Andrew W. Mellon Foundation. Her research examines the impact of local and global events on the professionalization of women musicians in twentieth-century Mexico. In addition to her role as a historian, Toledo-Guzmán has participated in various musical ensembles, ranging from traditional Mexican music to symphonic and chamber music. She is currently a member of Colectiva Tsunami, a network of Mexican women musicians dedicated to exploring and performing the works of contemporary Latin American women composers.

Andrea Tovar earned her EdD at Arizona State University in 2009 and is a previous clinical assistant professor at ASU, where she taught undergraduate- and graduate-level courses in the MAC, InMAC (Teach for America and Arizona Teachers Academy), and iTeachAZ programs across the curriculum in inclusive instructional planning and methodologies, language and literacy, bilingual education, and special education. Her more than twenty-five years of teaching and supervision experience range from serving as a Head Start teacher and site director, teaching and programming in summer outreach for gifted and at-risk students, to teaching community college courses to support adult English learners (ELs). She was an elementary school teacher, a reading interventionist, and a reading specialist. She has presented research on RTI/MTSS principles and practices at national and international conferences in content ranging from reading instruction and assessment to socio-tech infusion to peer collaboration for enhancing school and community action planning for ELs. Tovar authored one of Arizona's first Southwestern-multicultural children's fairy tales.

Index